New Perspectives
on Environmental Justice

New Perspectives on Environmental Justice

Gender, Sexuality, and Activism

EDITED BY RACHEL STEIN

RUTGERS UNIVERSITY PRESS

NEW BRUNSWICK, NEW JERSEY, AND LONDON

F.W. Olin College Library

LIBRARY OF CONGRESS CATALOGING-IN-PUBLICATION DATA

New perspectives on environmental justice : gender, sexuality, and activism / edited by Rachel Stein.

    p.   cm.

Includes bibliographical references and index.

ISBN 0–8135-3426-7 (hardcover : alk. paper) — ISBN 0-8135-3427-5 (pbk : alk. paper)

    1. Environmental justice.   2. Women environmentalists.   3. Women in politics. I. Stein, Rachel.

GE220.N48   2004

363.7—dc22   2003020114

A British Cataloging-in-Publication record for this book is available from the British Library

Manufactured in the United States of America

To the honest human body, and the body's world

CONTENTS

ACKNOWLEDGMENTS

First, to all those working in the field—activists, artists, scholars, students—this book is a tribute in your honor, and royalties will be donated to environmental justice groups furthering such efforts. Thank you for your intrepid involvement, your courage, and your commitment to creating a more just world. I also thank all of the contributors to this volume, who have so generously shared their work and energy in these pages.

I wish to thank Audra Wolfe, our acquiring editor at Rutgers University Press, for her enthusiastic support and her attentive guidance in completing this project, and Adi Hovav, for her gracious assistance with preparing the manuscript. Thank you also to Ann Youmans, our meticulous copy editor.

Siena College has generously supported this project in many ways. I thank the School of Liberal Arts and in particular Dean Richard Ognibene for the reassigned time that allowed me to complete this book. I thank Matt Lindstrom and the Siena Program for Sustainable Land Use and Just Communities for awarding me subvention funds to lower publication expenses and make the book affordable to a wider audience. Thank you to the students in the Environmental Justice Seminar for your honest outrage and concern about these issues, which kept them burning in my mind. My many supportive friends and colleagues at Siena sustained my spirits through a hard winter: particular thanks to Jerry Dollar for shared interests from afar, to Lisa Nevarez for shared space and mordant humor, and to Jenny McErlean for her fighting spirit.

Untold thanks to Katie Hogan for reassurance and reading. To T. V. Reed for suggestions for the title. To Greta Gaard, for having said that there should be a first book. To Priscilla Ybarra, for saying that there should be another book. Many thanks to Joni Adamson and Mei Mei Evans, for telling me that I could do it again, alone.

Thanks to my parents and sister, Shirley, Larry, and Susan Stein, for love, appreciation, and continuity. Thanks to my children, Josh and Anna Stein, for asking repeatedly, "You are writing about *what?*" Thanks to Stephanie Andersen for her enthusiasm. And many, many thanks to my partner, Stephen Andersen, for technical and life support, love, and laughter.

FOREWORD

Our bodies are a mirror of our mother, and of Mother Earth. And so we walk, healthy, beautiful, vibrant, voluptuous through the minefield of industrialism! It is a minefield of toxic chemicals and of toxic sexual images that poison and entrap our bodies. It is a minefield of laws that justify taking and destroying all that is beautiful, pristine, all that is the integrity of life. It is a minefield of laws that take control even of our own bodies themselves.

The stories on these pages chronicle the link between struggles for environmental justice and struggles for human dignity. In the faces and struggles of these activists, we find the stories of the sacred mother, our Zuni sacred site (recently saved from a coal strip mine), Celilo Falls (falls of a woman's hair), the White Buffalo Calf Woman (who must watch the demise of the Buffalo Nation, and subsequently the Buffalo people), and we see and feel the story of Water; the most sacred of our medicines, our women's medicines. And we know that as each natural element is challenged, transformed, or contaminated, our bodies too will be impacted, our breast milk contaminated, and our children's future darkened.

So it is that we become Ogitchidaakwewag: women who defend the people, women who stand for the Earth. It is because we as women understand our bodies are this mirror, and our lives are intertwined, and depend on the greatest mother of all, Mother Earth.

WINONA LADUKE

New Perspectives
on Environmental Justice

Introduction

RACHEL STEIN

"The fact is that women are the first environment," says Katsi. "We accumulate toxic chemicals. . . . They are stored in our body fat and are excreted primarily through our breast milk. What that means is that through (this) . . . sacred natural link to our babies, they stand the chance of getting concentrated dosages. . . . How are we going to recreate a society where the women are going to be healthy?"

—Winona LaDuke, *All Our Relations: Native Struggles for Land and Life*

The body as home, but only if it is understood that bodies can be stolen, fed lies and poison, torn away from us. They rise up around me—bodies stolen by hunger, war, breast cancer, AIDS, rape; the daily grind of factory, sweatshop, cannery, sawmill; the lynching rope; the freezing streets; the nursing home and prison.

—Eli Clare, *Exile and Pride: Disability, Queerness, and Liberation*

Land remains the common ground for all radical action. But land is more than rocks and trees. . . . For immigrants and native alike, land is also the factories where we work, the water our children drink, and the housing project where we live. For women, lesbians, and gay men, land is that physical mass called our bodies.

—Cherríe Moraga, The Last Generation: Prose and Poetry

Why Gender? Why Sexuality?

While traditional, mainstream environmental organizations have generally defined the environment in terms of uninhabited wilderness areas and plants and animals that need to be conserved and protected from human depredations, the environmental justice movement has instead defined the environment as "where we live, work, play, and worship." This more inclusive view of human/natural interaction brings environmental issues *home*, so to speak, and makes it clear that environmental injustice includes a range of urban and rural issues that expose poor communities and communities of color to unfair risks and burdens. Environmental injustices encompass diverse issues such as land claims, clear-cutting of forests, radiation exposure from uranium mining and nuclear wastes, dumping of industrial toxic wastes, struggles over water rights and water quality, hazardous work sites and underemployment, substandard housing, toxic schools, transportation, economic disinvestment, deteriorating infrastructures, as well as numerous other physical/social ills. When, as in the opening quotations from LaDuke, Clare, and Moraga, we view our bodies as "homes," "lands," or "environments" that have been placed at risk, stolen from us, and even killed due to social or physical harms that may be exacerbated due to our gender and sexuality—we may understand the need for new perspectives on environmental justice that encompass such factors within our analysis.

Environmental justice activists and scholars have clearly established the connections between race, class, and environmental ills, amassing strong evidence that communities of color and communities of the poor suffer far more from such problems than do whiter and wealthier communities, and so, in contrast to the mainstream environmental movement, environmental justice organizations are composed of poor people and people of color, working to protect their communities. But another aspect of grassroots environmental justice movements that has received far too little attention is that women, primarily women of color and working-class women, compose approximately 90 percent of the active membership of many organizations (Di Chiro 1992, 109). Because environmental ills strike *home* for vulnerable communities, and because women have often been responsible for that domain, women engage in these movements in order to protect and restore the well-being of families and communities threatened by environmental hazards or deprived of natural resources needed to sustain life and culture. While most environmental justice organizations are not gender restricted, women also account for up to 60 percent of the leadership of people-of-color environmental justice organizations, notes environmental sociologist Dorcetta Taylor. She explains that this predominance of women activists is a marked contrast to mainstream organizations: "In no other sector of the environmental movement . . . can one find such high percentages of women of color occupying positions as founders and leaders of organizations, workshop and conference organizers, researchers, strategists, lawyers, academics, policymakers, community organizers, and environmental educators" (Taylor 1997, 58). Cynthia Hamilton and Celene Krauss, sociologists who write about women's leadership and involvement in environmental justice movements, note that working-class women and women of color often become involved out of the need to protect loved ones from environmental and social ills that threaten home, neighborhoods, and work sites. Krauss states that:

working-class women of diverse racial and ethnic backgrounds identify
the toxic waste movement as a women's movement, composed primarily
of mothers. . . . By and large it is women, in their traditional role as mothers, who make the link between toxic wastes and their children's ill
health. . . . This is not surprising, as the gender-based division of labor in a
capitalistic society gives working-class women the responsibility for the
health of their children. . . . Ideologies of motherhood, traditionally relegated to the private sphere, become political sources that working-class
women use to initiate and justify their resistance. (Krauss 1994, 260–61)

Hamilton, writing about Concerned Citizens of South Central Los Angeles—a
group founded by women of color fighting the location of an incinerator in
their neighborhood—similarly notes that "women with no political experience,
who had no history of organizing, responded first as protectors of their children" (Hamilton 1994, 211). However, the well-being of children and family are
not private, isolated concerns, Giovanna Di Chiro has concluded from interviews
with women organizers in a variety of environmental justice movements. For
these activists, family health is always integrally connected to the larger context
of community and cultural/ethnic/racial survival, as well as to social issues such
as economic and civil rights (Di Chiro 1992, 115).

      Thus, acting in defense of themselves and their families, and as other-
mothers and protectors of communities at large, since the 1980s women of color
and poor women have lent their efforts to build the environmental justice
movement from the ground up. For example, Dollie Burwell mobilized rural
African American women, men, and children to lie down in front of the trucks
coming to dump PCBs in their home community of Warren County, North Carolina (Kaalund 2004). Across the continent in California, a multigenerational
group of Mexican American women assembled as the Mothers of East Los Angeles in order to prevent the siting of a state prison in their impoverished neighborhood, which had already been decimated by the construction of freeways
and the Dodgers Stadium (Gutierrez 1994). Hazel Johnson, who lived in a Southside Chicago housing project surrounded on all sides by toxic industrial development, began sponsoring "toxic tours" of the neighborhood in order to expose
the environmental hazards poisoning this poor, predominantly black community
(Kaalund 2004). On the Mohawk reservation along the border between New
York and Canada, a midwife named Katsi Cook began documenting the toxins
present in women's breast milk, acquired from their traditional diet of fish,
which were now polluted by industries that lined the St. Lawrence waterway
(LaDuke 1999). In northeastern cities such as Boston and New York City, mothers and other family members struggled to treat and prevent the growing epidemic
of environmental illnesses such as lead poisoning and asthma that are most
prevalent in poor urban children of color (Medoff and Sklar 1994; Sze 2004).

In these and other environmental justice causes, women act as the vigilant caretakers who sound the alarm and call attention to the threats when all is not well in their families, neighborhoods, and workplaces; the dreamers who dare to envision and demand safe surroundings and flourishing communities; the steadfast movers and shakers who rouse endangered peoples to challenge hostile corporate interests and negligent government agencies; the omnipresent membership who carry out the everyday tasks that keep movements rolling forward toward their goals. In fact, the second National People of Color Environmental Justice Leadership Summit (organized in large part through women's efforts), which assembled in Washington, D.C., in October 2002, hosted a special dinner, entitled "Crowning Women," to honor the powerful and pervasive contributions of women to these causes (Bullard 2003).[1]

While several studies have emphasized the ways that women's traditional gender roles have launched their environmental justice activism, it is crucial to note that women often fulfill those roles in creative and unconventional ways. This grassroots political engagement can lead to transformative, often radicalizing effects upon gender roles and upon the larger society. Cynthia Hamilton writes that as women commit themselves to grassroots campaigns, their family structures often must be rearranged to allow for this political work to take precedence over more traditional responsibilities. Furthermore, as women work together with other women against corporations and political structures, the sexism of our institutions becomes clear, and women recognize that their oppression is due to gender as well as to race/ethnicity and class (Hamilton 1994, 216). Hamilton also concludes that women in environmental justice movements may be such a strong force for social justice because they are less vested in the status quo than are men, less convinced by the arguments presented to them by authorities, and more committed to their own visions of positive futures for their communities: "These women were all guided by their vision of the possible: that it was possible to stop completely [polluting industries], that it is possible in a city . . . to have reasonable growth, that it is possible to humanize community structures and services" (Hamilton 1994, 214).

This vision of enlarged possibilities makes women a force to be reckoned with once they are set in motion, since they are unwilling to believe empty promises and unwilling to accept poor compromises that do not fulfill their images of genuine environmental and social justice. Similarly, Giovanna Di Chiro argues that environmental justice activism challenges and reconstitutes the basic social terms of our culture: "When these women assume leadership positions in the community and demand changes in the family expectations as they 'leave the house and enter the trenches' they break down traditional constructions of gender, race, class and construct new empowered identities and political agencies" (Di Chiro 1992, 118). Thus grassroots groups of engaged women push toward radical changes as they challenge the unequal and unjust structures of our society and work to rebuild them in the image of their dreams, block by block and brick by brick, from the ground up.[2]

In tribute to the predominance of women in this field, this anthology focuses upon issues of gender and sexuality as pertinent to environmental justice perspectives and activism. Dorcetta Taylor explains why so little overt attention has been directed to date to gender equality as an aspect of environmental justice:

> The absence of large numbers of environmental justice campaigns based solely or primarily on gender equality is no denial of the importance of the issue; it is the result of a strategy to mobilize a broad and effective coalition to help people and communities survive. In many instances, the struggles in which environmental justice groups are engaged are about survival. The language is about survival because it tells about life and death struggles. Consequently the language of gender equality is embedded within the language of survival. (Taylor 1997, 64)

While environmental justice groups do not work for women's rights as divorced from needs for racial and class equality and equal protection and representation, the remarkable fact that the movement is largely composed of women, particularly women of color, calls for further analysis of this gendered pattern, as Jael Silliman suggests: "So far, despite the strong role of women in the movement, the relationships between environmental discrimination and its particular gender impacts have not been made explicit" (Silliman 1997, 125).[3] Even though the muting of gender concerns may have been a strategic choice, *New Perspective on Environmental Justice: Gender, Sexuality, and Activism* serves to highlight issues of gender equality and sexual equality that have been embedded within environmental justice work and to make these aspects of the movements more visible. Early movement theorists realized that articulating environmental racism as a phenomenon distinct from but aggravating environmental classism would be a powerful tool for first exposing and then organizing against the insidious environmental harms directed towards vulnerable communities of color. Likewise we have found it illuminating to define the particular terms of women's (and men's) exposure to environmental ills and to analyze the ways that gender may inflect activism. Our intent has not been to exclude men (in fact, several articles do look at men and activism, and we hope that future work on gender and environmental justice will focus far more gender analysis upon men's involvement in the movements as well), but we offer here an analysis of how gender might function to expose women to environmental injustices, how these issues might affect women differently, and how gender roles might influence the forms of activism in which they engage.

The contributors to *New Perspectives on Environmental Justice* have sought to answer the following questions: How might environmental justice activism be gendered in ways that have not yet been theorized? What draws women, particularly women of color and poor women, into these movements, in contradiction to standard assumptions about which citizens are likely to be the most politically active? What sustains women working against high odds for social and environmental justice? How might gender shape the visions and understandings that women bring to the issues? How do race, class, and gender intersect in their praxis? How might womanist, feminist, or ecofeminist theory illuminate women's environmental justice work, and, conversely, how might women's activism help us to expand womanist, feminist, and ecofeminist theories? How might problematic constructions of gender, race, class, and nature underlie environmental injustices? How, then, do environmental justice activists reconstruct the relationship of women, race, class, and nature?

If discussion of gender oppression and environmental justice has been muted, discussion of the intersections between sexuality and environmental justice has been nearly inaudible as a topic for scholarship; however, contributors to this volume demonstrate the productivity of applying environmental justice principles and perspectives to this aspect of human identity and behavior, which overlaps to a great extent with gender identities and roles. Sexuality has been an aspect of human life quite vulnerable to social and environmental injustices, particularly for poor women and women of color, and is therefore a topic of growing importance for environmental justice studies.

Historically, the sexuality and reproductivity of women of color have been targeted for exploitation and control in the name of environmental needs and protections. We can see this interlocking history from the time of the European conquest and colonization of the indigenous peoples of the Americas, which was justified in part by their diverse sexual practices; through the enslavement of Africans and the legal construction of enslaved women as breeders whose children would be not kin, but simply more chattel property to increase the prosperity of the land owners; to the present debates about overpopulation and environment that focus on the fertility of Third World women of color rather than on overconsumption of resources by the First World (Silliman and King 1999; Stein 1997). Negative associations of women of color with overpopulation still underlie contemporary problems such as the coercive use of birth control, forced sterilization, and concerns over possible eugenics misuses of genetic research or biogenetic manipulation of environmentally stricken populations (Silliman and King 1999). Also, we continue to learn that certain environmental hazards affect female sexual/reproductive systems in particular, and growing attention is now being focused upon health concerns such as environmental toxicity and pregnancy, toxicity of human breast milk, environmental links to breast cancer, and sexually transmitted epidemics such as HIV/AIDS (LaDuke 1999; Steingraber 1997; 2001). We have found it useful to apply environmental justice perspectives to these health concerns in order to explore the social contexts and physiological reasons that put women's sexed bodies at especial risk of environmental harms.

Furthermore, because divergent sexual identities and practices have historically been condemned and punished as "unnatural" expressions of desire, environmental justice theory and perspectives offer us a useful set of principles to adopt for struggles for sexual justice. By analyzing how discourses of nature have been used to enforce heteronormativity, to police sexuality, and to punish and exclude those persons who have been deemed sexually transgressive, we can begin to understand the deep, underlying commonalities between struggles against sexual oppression and other struggles for environmental justice. By reframing sexuality issues as environmental justice concerns, we can argue that people of differing sexualities have the human right to bodily sovereignty and the right to live safely as sexual bodies within our social and physical environments.

Perhaps more importantly, incorporating issues of sexual oppression into the study of environmental justice also paves the way for us to form alliances between these related movements and to develop a more complex understanding of how environmental injustices may also target certain populations because of sexual identities and practices, or strike the sexed/sexual parts of our bodies. Finally, if sexuality has been a target of oppression and environmental exploitation, it has also been used historically as a site of resistance, as women and men of varied sexualities wield sexual/reproductive decisions that challenge the colonization of their peoples and lands, that subvert enslavement, genocide, and heterosexism. As contemporary lesbian, gay, bisexual, and transgender liberation movements and AIDS activism for adequate health care employ environmental justice tactics and principles, this creates the possibility of forging alliances and enlarges the scope of all of these movements.

As the scholar activists in this collection analyze intersections of sexuality and environmental justice we seek to answer questions such as the following: How were constructions of "unnatural" sexual practices used to justify persecution of women and homosexuality, and the colonization of indigenous peoples? How do movements for sexual justice challenge such toxic ideologies and reclaim the right to safe environments for persons of all sexual identities? How might movements for sovereignty of homelands be extended to sovereignty of our sexed bodies and our sexual identities? What risks are posed to communities of color and poor communities by new sexual/reproductive technologies such as invasive contraceptives and biogenetic testing and manipulations? How might our conception of environmental justice be expanded so as to foster alliances and help promote queer ecologies?

In order to address these questions, *New Perspectives on Environmental Justice* brings together practitioners, scholars, and activists from a range of fields, organizations, and geographical locations who approach our topics from these varied perspectives. The anthology is arranged into four sections, described below.

Part One: Gender, Sexuality, and Environmental Justice: Historical and Theoretical Roots

This anthology works to create an expansive understanding of environmental injustice that emphasizes the structural interconnections between race, gender, and sexual oppressions as historically related forms of the domination of nature that are once again erupting and converging within current environmental ills. Once we understand that these oppressions have common roots, we may understand why issues of gender and sexuality are now emerging so prominently within environmental justice work and why they strike us as necessitating the same attention that race has already received. In the opening essay for this collection, "Toward a Queer Ecofeminism," Greta Gaard urges us to think about these conjunctions in order to form wider political alliances: "The future of progressive organizing may well depend on how effectively scholars and activists can recognize and articulate our many bases for coalition" (21). Equally important to our analysis of gender and sexuality within contemporary environmental justice struggles is our attention to the proud historical legacy of women, particularly women of color, who have resisted such abuses of land and people by using environmental expertise and control of their sexuality/reproduction to struggle against colonization and control: contemporary activists are building upon this strong foundation.

Gaard uses tenets of ecofeminist theory to offer a compelling overview of the shared roots of racism, sexism, and heterosexism in Western culture's domination of persons negatively associated with nature. During the Inquisition and the simultaneous conquest of the Americas, certain European women and homosexuals were persecuted as unnatural, and similar negative views of gender equality and sexual openness "played a prominent role in the rhetoric and justification of colonial conquest" of the indigenous peoples of the New World. Extrapolating from this past, Gaard suggests that our understanding of these interlocking historical structures of racial, gender, and sexual exploitation could prompt more productive contemporary political alliances that would create effectively inclusive strategies for positive change. *New Perspectives on Environmental Justice* moves in that direction by exploring the integral relevance of gender and sexuality to environmental justice movements, and by expanding environmental justice principles so they encompass struggles for gender and sexual rights and equality.

During the centuries of conquest of the native inhabitants of this continent, of importation of enslaved Africans, and the immigration of other settlers to the Americas, gender and sexuality continued to serve as vectors by which colonial powers exercised power over peoples of color and communities of the poor, but which also became a means of resistance for women to exert control over their bodies, their cultures, and the natural environments. In "Women, Sexuality, and Environmental Justice in American History," Nancy Unger presents examples of individual North American women of various races whom we might view as precursors of contemporary environmental justice activists. Surveying pre-Columbian Native American women, enslaved African American women, early urban reformers and birth-control advocates, environmentalist Rachel Carson, lesbian back-to-the-land movements, and Women of All Red Nations, Unger argues that such women approached environmental issues and sexuality/reproductivity as interlocking in varied ways, and pursued these intersections as a means of resisting oppression and struggling for greater self-determination and social and environmental justice.

Part Two: Gender, Sexuality, and Activism

Margarita, a New Mexico environmental justice organizer quoted by Diane-Michele Prindeville in her essay for this section, describes how gender/sexual roles, including reproduction, may impel women into activism: "The people that now are taking leadership are women . . . the ones with the guts are women . . . I also think the bearers of children feel more angered and are more willing to put their necks on the chopping block. In general, women are more concerned about the welfare of the future generations" (100). While biological motherhood is certainly not a prerequisite for activism, Margarita's emphasis on the courage of women leaders, the urgency with which they address issues, and their visionary commitment to activism as they attempt to assure future generations of their peoples challenges us to rethink standard assumptions about the motivations and modes of activism by writing gender and sexuality into this equation. It is by now a truism that environmental justice activism defied corporate and institutional expectations that poor and people of color communities, unlike their wealthier and whiter counterparts, would fail to defend themselves from toxic pollution or deprivation of natural resources. It seems to have been a particular reversal to those assumptions that poor women and women of color—who often carry the additional burdens of household and family responsibilities on top of paid work responsibilities—would mobilize against these injustices. In "Feminist Theory and Environmental Justice," Robert Verchick suggests that whether or not environmental justice activists would label themselves as feminist, these grassroots organizations do employ feminist tactics of exposing social inequalities and challenging unequal structures of power. Environmental justice movements dislodge the false neutrality of scientific and legal systems based on white male privilege by applying feminist legal practices such as unmasking biases in environmental protection, using contextual reason to expand the definitions of environmental harms, employing consciousness-raising techniques to identify environmental problems and educate communities about issues, and creating grassroots, democratic structures for activism.

Although the influx of women into environmental justice activism is sometimes remarked upon as a new phenomenon within environmental politics, women of color have long-standing roles as public activists working for the well-being of communities under attack from racism, poverty, and a host of other threats. In "Witness to Truth: Black Women Heeding the Call for Environmental Justice," Valerie Kaalund suggests that although gender has often been overlooked as a factor prompting environmental justice activism, black women have made tremendous contributions to these movements, and this political work is a deeply rooted expression of black womanist or feminist ideologies, authorized by women's ethical/spiritual consciousness of themselves as moral agents of their communities. As illustration, Kaalund presents testimonies from black women active in rural North Carolina movements, who describe intolerable conditions of environmental degradation that prompt them to "heed the call" to defend their communities. Pursuing similar issues within different geographical and ethnic contexts, in "The Role of Gender, Race/Ethnicity, and Class in Activists' Perceptions of Environmental Justice" Diane-Michele Prindeville draws upon interviews with New Mexican Native American and Hispanic women leaders of environmental justice organizations to explore the motivations and modes of their work. As the quotation at the opening of this essay illustrated, in contrast to their counterparts in mainstream environmental organizations, the women interviewed by Prindeville practice a "politics of care" on behalf of families and communities and approach environmental concerns as integral to ethnic/cultural survival.

If environmental justice principles articulate the right of all humans to safe, healthy environments, then surely lesbians and persons living with AIDS (PWAs) should be assured safe spaces and welcoming environments in which they might live free from sexual oppression and exploitation. Because the dominant culture has historically deemed homosexuality as "unnatural," as Gaard argues, various movements for sexual freedom and health care have had to challenge these historical misconceptions and reframe positive relations between lesbians and nature, or between PWAs and the national landscape through a politics that we might consider to be a queer environmental justice. "Sexual Politics and Environmental Justice: Lesbian Separatists in Rural Oregon," by Catriona Sandilands, applies environmental justice theories to lesbian back-to-the-land communities who settled in Oregon in the 1970s and 1980s and are still in existence. Through interviews with members of these subsistence farm communities, Sandilands documents the principles of a queer environmental justice enacted by the communities, such as opening rural land to all classes and races of women, reclaiming rural pastoral nature from heterosexual North American culture, politicizing rural lesbian identity, and withdrawing land from patriarchal production and reproduction. Addressing a different form of heterosexism, Beth Berila's "Toxic Bodies? ACT UP's Disruption of the Heteronormative Landscape of the Nation" extends environmental justice analysis of the racism and classism that channel toxicity into vulnerable environments to consider how heterosexism and AIDS phobia have marked PWAs as toxic bodies that threaten the purity of the heteronormative national body. ACT UP's cultural activism exposed the insidious workings of this ideology, in much the same way that environmental justice groups expose the unfair environmental burdens borne by their communities.

Part Three: Gender, Sexuality, and Environmental Health Concerns

Women are often the caretakers, the daily observers who are the first to notice what is amiss in the family, community, and local environment; so it is often female relatives or caregivers who mobilize in order to protect children and other loved ones from ills such as asthma or lead poisoning that are aggravated by environmental factors. These women challenge political leaders and health experts who ignore or belittle their suffering while blaming mothers for poor care. Women's sexed bodies are also particularly vulnerable to environment ills, due to the way that toxins accumulate in fatty tissues such as breasts, and due to the way that hormones such as estrogen may be affected or mimicked by many of the pesticides and chemicals that we are releasing into the larger environment. In fact, as Arlene Plevin suggests in her essay in the final section of this book, many women's bodies and family homes are now so permeated by toxic threats that they no longer offer safe space to inhabitants: "The womb, the first home of the child, often a symbol of sanctuary, and the familial home outside of that, is vulnerable, recast—and one might argue usurped—as the site of corporate earnings" (230).

One of the largest tasks of environmental health movements is to expose this "usurpation" and to challenge our prevailing paradigm of disease, which, ironically, often blames victims of environmental illnesses for their own suffering in a pattern that is often raced/classed/gendered/sexualized in problematic ways. Through the laborious process of detecting and documenting patterns of illness, discussing medical and environmental factors with scientists and political authorities, and questioning the efficacy of social policy and laws, activists struggle to create a new paradigm based on precautionary principles and human rights of health and wellness, which might shift responsibility for environmental illness from the victims onto the larger society that allows the damages to occur. Yet as new biomedical and technological advances occur in our increasingly globalized world, grave new threats to environmental gender/sexual health continue to arise.

Giovanna Di Chiro traces potentially ominous new directions of this paradigm struggle between scientific experts and community activists in "Producing Round-Up Ready Communities? Human Genome Research and Environmental Justice Policy," which is based on interviews about the Environmental Genome Project that she conducted with government scientific researchers, independent geneticists and developmental biologists, and a number of environmental justice activists who live in communities burdened with excessive rates of environmental illness. In light of the genome project's focus upon genetic interventions into environmental illnesses, women activists from affected communities of color fear that such research could revive eugenics arguments about the genetic inferiority of minority and poor populations, stigmatizing populations who are at risk while normalizing toxic environmental threats. In contrast, Marcy Newman's article, "Public Eyes: Investigating the Causes of Breast Cancer," focuses upon a more productive relationship between lay activists and scientific experts. She suggests that the documentary film *Rachel's Daughters: Searching for the Causes of Breast Cancer*, directed by Allie Light and Irving Saraf, presents a positive paradigm shift in the public discourse of breast cancer. The film portrays a diverse group of women with breast cancer who treat this illness as a form of homicide and become the lay investigators, or "public eyes," researching environmental issues and working cooperatively with medical and environmental experts to uncover and expose the many possible environmental factors behind the growing epidemic from which they suffer.

Children's environmental illnesses highlight some of the dangerously ironic contradictions of gender/sexuality issues within the current paradigm, where, on the one hand, caretakers are blamed for their children's environmentally induced illnesses, such as asthma, yet on the other hand, mothers are offered no protections from toxic threats to infant health, such as breastmilk contaminated with persistent organic pollutants. In "Gender, Asthma Politics, and Environmental Justice," Julie Sze focuses upon the gendered components of community activism in response to the growing problem of childhood asthma in minority neighborhoods in New York City. While medical experts have continued to hold mothers responsible for the illness by emphasizing poor home sanitation as the primary cause, activists insist that the exponential increase of asthma among children of color is instead due to the growth of external urban pollutants and substandard housing. Addressing a similar struggle of toxicity and motherhood from a legal perspective, in " No Remedy for the Inuit: Accountability for Environmental Harms under U.S. and International Laws" Anne Lucas explores the insufficiencies of current legal protections for Inuit women living near the Arctic Circle whose breastmilk has been contaminated with the carcinogen dioxin that was released by factories in the midwestern United States. Using ecofeminist theory, Lucas deconstructs the predominant legal perspective and posits a framework that would value the health of native women and their communities above the profits of industrial countries.

Part Four: Gender, Sexuality, and Environmental Justice in Literature and Popular Culture

Expressive arts offer individuals and communities creative media through which to explore the intricate intersections of gender and sexuality with environmental justice. Artists act as Cassandras: seers who uncover problems that the rest of us have refused to witness and who voice the unspeakable, making known discomforting truths such as sexual/reproductive manipulation of women of color in the name of environmental protection or the widespread misuse of DES hormones on pregnant women. By representing sexed and gendered speakers and protagonists who live inside the issues, the artists give us an honest emotional sense of the complicated costs of environmental ills for those who dwell within affected communities. They also provide an appreciation of the complex and often conflicted positions of the women and men who act against these ills, incurring daily difficulties and real dangers to do so. The artists inspire us to hope for a truly just world by helping us envision positive resolutions to current disasters and the possibility of forming creative, nontraditional alliances that recreate an enlarged sense of "home," "family," or even "body" beyond current divisions and borders. To these ends, artists employ a range of genres to imaginatively explore issues and bring them before the public—poetry and essays, speculative fiction, detective fiction, and film—in order to represent serious concerns to audiences outside of affected communities, sometimes using unexpected tactics such as humor to entice viewers into openness toward issues to which their responses may have become deadened. However, in some instances the artistic products of mainstream media continue to misrepresent issues of environmental justice and gender and sexuality issues: children's popular culture, while apparently environmentally conscious, still conveys the old colonialist message that has proven problematic for so long.

While the idea of alien invasion of our bodies has long been a staple of science fiction, environmental justice health campaigns have shown us how permeable we are to external sources of harm. Environmental justice speculative fiction and film twists this notion in provocative directions by exploring women's bodies as the targets of biopiracy and DES poisoning; however, bodily vulnerability also becomes a source of radicalization, mobilizing strange new forces for change. My "Bodily Invasions: Gene Trading and Organ Theft in Octavia Butler and Nalo Hopkinson's Speculative Fiction" examines two contemporary black authors' novels that articulate the way that the bodies of women of color may be directly manipulated or harvested as environmental resources for those in power through the practices of forced gene trading and organ theft. Black female protagonists must grapple with societies that use situations of environmental degradation to authorize the colonization and exploitation of women's bodies as natural resources. Exploring related issues of female bodily vulnerability in a different medium, Arlene Plevin's "Home Everywhere and the Injured Body of the World: The Subversive Humor of *Blue Vinyl*" suggests that Judith Helfland's autobiographical documentary film, *Blue Vinyl*, uses humor to draw connections between the poisoning of mothers' bodies and the toxic production of materials such as vinyl that are widely used in the construction of family homes. Plevin traces Helfland's development as an environmental justice activist as Helfland, a DES daughter who underwent a radical hysterectomy, uses the funds from her suit against a DES manufacturer to explore the toxic consequences of manufacturing the vinyl that sides her parents' home.

Lesbian and gay writers express models of environmental justice that encompass sexual justice along with other issues in the manner that Greta Gaard calls for in her essay. "'Lo que queiro es tierra': Longing and Belonging in Cherríe Moraga's Ecological Vision" by Priscilla Ybarra explores the complex ways in which Chicana lesbian writer Cherríe Moraga articulates a more expansive form of environmental justice that confronts sexism and heteronormativity along with the more standard problems of racism, classism, and environmental exploitation. Condemning the parallel exploitations of land and of queer, dark-skinned women, Moraga dreams of a homeland to which she could truly belong, with all parts of her complex identity intact. Ybarra argues that as Moraga expands the definition of "land" to include our work sites, housing, and physical bodies, she also extends the definition of "sovereignty," which underlies many land struggles and land claims, so that it includes the rights of women, gays and lesbians, and people of color to "inhabit" their own bodies.[4] Analogously, Katie Hogan's "Detecting Toxic Environments: Gay Mystery as Environmental Justice" applies environmental justice theories to the gay detective novel *Night Work* written by Joseph Hansen in 1984. Hogan suggests that Hansen's novel juxtaposes the environmental and social costs of toxic dumping and toxic heterosexuality, which posits the pure natural world to be the realm solely of wealthy, white heterosexual men, and relegates people of color and homosexuals to the impure urban realm. Hansen's gay private eye exposes the destructiveness of this toxic ideology and forms multicultural allegiances that work toward justice.

We would hope that accurate portrayals of gender/sexuality and environmental justice would filter into mainstream popular culture as well, but Noël Sturgeon's "'The Power is Yours, Planeteers!' Race, Gender, and Sexuality in Children's Environmental Popular Culture" detects dangerously stereotypical values pervading U.S. kids' environmentally themed films and cartoon shows, which portray homosexuals as evil environmental destroyers and white male heterosexuals as heroic environmental protectors. While the shows do feature multi-cultural casts, Sturgeon notes that girls and people of color are usually imaged in terms of passive natural phenomena while white boys take the dynamic leadership to right environmental ills. Thus these programs provide misleading images of the roots of environmental injustices and distort children's understanding of people's real struggles to set them right.

New Perspectives on Environmental Justice: Gender, Sexuality, and Activism seeks to foster an expansive understanding of environmental justice that incorporates issues of gender and sexuality: one that crowns women on a continual basis by acknowledging their tremendous contributions to this movement; one that includes the long history of women of color and working-class women who used gender/sexuality and environmental knowledge in order to serve as defenders of homelands, cultures, and future generations; one that addresses the particular ways that environmental ills strike women's sexed bodies; one that acknowledges the complex situation of lesbians and gay men within stricken communities who seek to incorporate sexual freedoms and bodily sovereignty within their work for just societies, and the allied position of other lesbians, gay men, or PWAs who apply principles of environmental justice to issues of sexual justice or health care for stigmatized communities.

New Perspectives on Environmental Justice offers a vantage point from which to examine how gender and sexuality inflect environmental justice issues, activism, and arts. By doing so, we help make the field of environmental justice studies even more inclusive—acknowledging the contributions that women have made to these movements as well as the crucial needs of others who could also benefit from this form of justice—in order to build the alliances that would pull all of our multiple struggles together. As we expose the deep, historic conjunctions between gender/sexuality and environmental justice, we highlight the radical force imbuing environmental justice work, pointing out the huge odds against which activists work, the overwhelmingly stubborn forces they challenge. We, the contributors to this collection, are filled with awe, admiration, and acclaim for the hard-won, steadfast activism of the poor women, women of color, and sexual minorities who strive to recreate our world into an enlarged vision of environmental justice, and who, through doing this work, themselves become transformed. Margarita, the New Mexico environmental justice organizer interviewed by Diane-Michele Prindeville, commented on this process of radicalization: "Being a woman in a position of always having to fight, there are some gains but also lots of losses. Feeling oppressed . . . radicalizes me . . . I'm who I am because of my involvement" (101).

NOTES

1. In an article entitled "Crowning Women of Color and the Real Story Behind the 2002 EJ Summit," published on the Internet site of his Environmental Justice Resource Cen-

ter at Clark University, the renowned environmental justice scholar Robert Bullard candidly discusses struggles with sexism within the leadership of the environmental justice movement that came to a head during the planning and implementation of the 2002 Second National People of Color Environmental Leadership Summit. He notes, "Untimely resignations from the Summit II Executive Committee and Planning Committee by some of the male EJ leaders left the bulk of Summit II work on the shoulders of the women EJ leaders. It is ironic that the women solidified their leadership role in Summit II by default—when many of the men who had been in leadership roles walked away. The women would probably not have been able to achieve this level of visibility and power in an otherwise sexist, male-dominated society—which also extends to the environmental justice movement and Summit II planning—had the men stayed." He goes on to detail the successful efforts of women leaders to get the stalled committees moving forward toward a successful summit. His website also published the biographies of all of the women honored at the summit during the "Crowning Women" event.

2. Although some feminists and queer theorists might view women/mothers working to preserve families/environments as a conservative, even essentialist form of activism that plays into the hands of the right, communities of color in America historically have been denied the right to parent their own children, as in the cases of enslaved Africans whose children were sold as chattel, colonized Native Americans whose children were forcibly removed to boarding schools or adoptions, or Asian immigrant men forbidden by law from bringing their families to this continent. So a "politics of care"—in which mothers and others strive for cultural survival by working to assure the viability of future generations—strikes me as a radical politics, rather than a reactionary one. I would argue, furthermore, that this embattled form of parenthood/family/relationship/care/community places women of color in similar positions to sexual minorities who are working to create safe environments for themselves and loved ones, and so environmental justice ought to encompass sexual justice issues as well.

3. Silliman goes on to list pertinent topics for gender/sexuality analysis: "for example, while the environmental justice movement has highlighted the risks workers face on the job they have not articulated the fact that women, due to gender discrimination, are concentrated in certain types of low paying jobs that expose them disproportionately to environmental hazards and risks. The increasing connections being made between environmental poisons and reproductive health hazards would be natural place for greater collaboration between women's health and environmental justice movements. The relationship between environmental pollutants and the epidemic of breast cancer that is now documented is another excellent venue for activism" (Silliman 1997, 125). These are exactly the sort of concerns that this anthology does address, particularly in part three, on gender, sexuality, and environmental health. A number of contributors to this anthology have also published substantial contributions on such topics or have projects in process on related issues.

4. I would like to thank Priscilla Ybarra for introducing me to *The Last Generation: Prose and Poetry* by Cherríe Moraga, and for introducing me to Moraga's formulation of "land," which enriches our understanding of why environmental justice must encompass sexual justice, too.

REFERENCES

Bullard, Robert. 1994. *Unequal Protection: Environmental Justice and Communities of Color.* San Francisco: Sierra Club.

———. 2003. "Crowning Women of Color and the Real Story Behind the 2002 EJ Summit." *http://www.ejrc.cau.edu/SummCrowning04.html.*

Di Chiro, Giovanna. 1992. "Defining Environmental Justice: Women's Voices and Grassroots Politics." *Socialist Review* 22, no. 4: 93–130.

Gutierrez, Gabriel. 1994. "Mothers of East Los Angeles Strike Back." In Bullard 1994.

Hamilton, Cynthia. 1994. "Concerned Citizens of South Central Los Angeles." In Bullard 1994.

Kaalund, Valerie. 2004. "Witness to Truth: Black Women Heeding the Call for Environmental Justice." In *New Perspectives on Environmental Justice: Gender, Sexuality, and Activism*, ed. Rachel Stein. New Brunswick: Rutgers University Press.

Krauss, Celene. 1994. "Women of Color on the Front Line." In Bullard 1994.

Medoff, Peter, and Holly Sklar. 1994. *Streets of Hope: The Fall and Rise of an Urban Neighborhood.* Boston: South End Press.

Silliman, Jael. 1997. "Making the Connections: Women's Health and Environmental Justice." *Race, Gender, and Class* 5, no. 1: 104–29.

Silliman, Jael, and Ynestra King. 1999. *Dangerous Intersections: Feminist Perspectives on Population, Environment, and Development.* Boston: South End Press.

Stein, Rachel. 1997. *Shifting the Ground: American Women Writers' Revisions of Nature, Gender, and Race.* Charlottesville: University Press of Virginia.

Steingraber, Sandra. 1997. *Living Downstream: A Scientist's Personal Investigation of Cancer and the Environment.* New York: Vintage.

———. 2001. *Having Faith: An Ecologist's Journey to Motherhood.* Cambridge: Perseus.

Sze, Julie. 2004. "Gender, Asthma Politics, and Environmental Justice." In *New Perspectives on Environmental Justice: Gender, Sexuality, and Activism*, ed. Rachel Stein. New Brunswick: Rutgers University Press.

Taylor, Dorcetta. 1997. "Women of Color, Environmental Justice, and Ecofeminism." In *Ecofeminism: Women, Culture, Nature*, ed. Karen Warren. Bloomington: Indiana University Press.

PART ONE

Gender, Sexuality, and Environmental Justice

Historical and Theoretical Roots

1

Toward a Queer Ecofeminism

GRETA GAARD

Although many ecofeminists acknowledge heterosexism as a problem, a systematic exploration of the potential intersections of ecofeminist and queer theories has yet to be made. By interrogating social constructions of the "natural," the various uses of Christianity as a logic of domination, and the rhetoric of colonialism, this essay finds those theoretical intersections and argues for the importance of developing a queer ecofeminism.

Progressive activists and scholars frequently lament the disunity of the political left in the United States. Often characterized as a "circular firing squad," the left or progressive movement has been known for its intellectual debates and hostilities, which have served to polarize many groups that could be working in coalition: labor activists, environmentalists, civil rights activists, feminists, animal rights activists, indigenous rights activists, and gay/lesbian/bisexual/transgender (GLBT) activists. Meanwhile, it is observed, the conservative right in the United States has lost no time in recognizing the connections among these various liberatory movements and has launched a campaign (most recently articulated in the "Contract with America") to ensure their collective annihilation. As a result, the future of progressive organizing may well depend on how effectively scholars and activists can recognize and articulate our many bases for coalition. In theory and in practice, ecofeminism has already contributed much to this effort.

At the root of ecofeminism is the understanding that the many systems of oppression are mutually reinforcing. Building on the socialist feminist insight that racism, classism, and sexism are interconnected, ecofeminists recognized additional similarities between those forms of human oppression and the oppressive structures of speciesism and naturism. An early impetus for the ecofeminist movement was the realization that the liberation of women—the aim of all branches of feminism—cannot be fully effected without the liberation

of nature, and, conversely, the liberation of nature so ardently desired by environmentalists will not be fully effected without the liberation of women: conceptual, symbolic, empirical, and historical linkages between women and nature
as they are constructed in Western culture require feminists and environmentalists to address these liberatory efforts together if we are to be successful (Warren 1991). To date, ecofeminist theory has blossomed, exploring the connections
among many issues: racism, environmental degradation, economics, electoral
politics, animal liberation, reproductive politics, biotechnology, bioregional-
ism, spirituality, holistic health practices, sustainable agriculture, and others.
Ecofeminist activists have worked in the environmental justice movement, the
Green movement, the antitoxics movement, the women's spirituality movement, the animal liberation movement, and the movement for economic justice.
To continue and build on these efforts toward coalition, I would like to explore
in this essay the connection between ecofeminism and queer theory.

"We have to examine how racism, heterosexism, classism, ageism, and sexism are *all* related to naturism," writes ecofeminist author Ellen O'Loughlin
(1993, 148). Chaia Heller elaborates: "Love of nature is a process of becoming
aware of and unlearning ideologies of racism, sexism, heterosexism, and able-
ism so that we may cease to reduce our idea of nature to a dark, heterosexual,
'beautiful' mother" (1993, 231). But as Catriona Sandilands astutely comments,
"It is not enough simply to add 'heterosexism' to the long list of dominations
that shape our relations to nature, to pretend that we can just 'add queers and
stir'" (1994, 21).[1] Unfortunately, it is exactly this approach that has characterized ecofeminist theory to date, which is the reason I believe it is time for
queers to come out of the woods and speak for ourselves.[2]

The goal of this essay is to demonstrate that to be truly inclusive, any
theory of ecofeminism must take into consideration the findings of queer
theory; similarly, queer theory must consider the findings of ecofeminism. To
this end, I will examine various intersections between ecofeminism and queer
theory, thereby demonstrating that a democratic, ecological society envisioned
as the goal of ecofeminism will, of necessity, be a society that values sexual
diversity and the erotic.

Sexualizing Nature, Naturalizing Sexuality

The first argument linking ecofeminism and queer theory is based on the observation that dominant Western culture's devaluation of the erotic parallels its
devaluations of women and of nature; in effect, these devaluations are mutually
reinforcing. This observation can be drawn from ecofeminist critiques that
describe the normative dualisms, value-hierarchical thinking, and logic of domination that together characterize the ideological framework of Western culture.
As Karen Warren explains, value dualisms are ways of conceptually organizing

the world in binary, disjunctive terms, wherein each side of the dualism is "seen as exclusive (rather than inclusive) and oppositional (rather than complementary), and where higher value or superiority is attributed to one disjunct (or, side of the dualism) than the other" (1987, 6). Val Plumwood's 1993 critique of Western philosophy pulls together the most salient features of these and other ecofeminist critiques in what she calls the "master model," the identity that is at the core of Western culture and that has initiated, perpetuated, and benefited from Western culture's alienation from and domination of nature. The master identity, according to Plumwood, creates and depends on a "dualized structure of otherness and negation" (1993, 42). Key elements in that structure are the following sets of dualized pairs:

culture	/	nature
reason	/	nature
male	/	female
mind	/	body (nature)
master	/	slave
reason	/	matter (physicality)
rationality	/	animality (nature)
reason	/	emotion (nature)
mind, spirit	/	nature
freedom	/	necessity (nature)
universal	/	particular
human	/	nature (nonhuman)
civilized	/	primitive (nature)
production	/	reproduction (nature)
public	/	private
subject	/	object
self	/	other (Plumwood 1993, 43)

Plumwood does not claim completeness for the list. In the argument that follows, I will offer a number of reasons that ecofeminists must specify the linked dualisms of white/nonwhite, financially empowered/impoverished, heterosexual/queer, and reason/the erotic.[3]

Ecofeminists have uncovered a number of characteristics about the interlocking structure of dualism. First, ecofeminist philosophers have shown that the claim for the superiority of the self is based on the difference between self and other as manifested in the full humanity and reason that the self possesses but the other supposedly lacks. This alleged superiority of the self, moreover, is used to justify the subordination of the other (Warren 1990, 129; Plumwood 1993, 42–47). Next, ecofeminists have worked to show the linkages within the devalued category of the other, demonstrating how the association of qualities from one oppressed group with another serves to reinforce their subordination. The conceptual linkages between women and animals, women and the body, or women and nature, for example, all serve to emphasize the inferiority of these categories (Adams 1990; 1993). But while all categories of the other share these qualities of being feminized, animalized, and naturalized, socialist ecofeminists have rejected any claims of primacy for one form of oppression or another, embracing instead the understanding that all forms of oppression are now so inextricably linked that liberation efforts must be aimed at dismantling the system itself.

There is a theoretical gap, however, when we find that those few ecofeminists who do mention heterosexism in their introductory lists of human oppressions have still not taken the dualism of heterosexual/queer forward to be analyzed in the context of their lists of dualized pairs, and consequently into the theory being developed. In some cases, the same could be said for the dualism of white/nonwhite. This omission is a serious conceptual error, for the heterosexual/queer dualism has affected Western culture through its "ineffaceable marking" of these normative dualisms, according to queer theorist Eve Kosofsky Sedgwick (1990, 11). In her book *Epistemology of the Closet*, Sedgwick finds that these normative dualisms (or "symmetrical binary oppositions") "actually subsist in a more unsettled and dynamic tacit relation according to which, first, term B is not symmetrical with but subordinated to term A; but, second, the ontologically valorized term A actually depends for its meaning on the simultaneous subsumption and exclusion of term B; hence, third, the question of priority between the supposed central and the supposed marginal category of each dyad is irresolvably unstable, an instability caused by the fact that term B is constituted as at once internal and external to term A" (1990, 10). Sedgwick's findings bear a neat resonance with Plumwood's theorizing of the linking postulates that connect such dualisms both "horizontally" (one member of a dyad with the other) and "vertically" (groups of dyads with each other; my terms). These linking postulates include

1. Backgrounding, in which the master relies on the services of the other and simultaneously denies his dependency;
2. Radical exclusion, in which the master magnifies the differences between self and other and minimizes the shared qualities;
3. Incorporation, in which the master's qualities are taken as the standard, and the other is defined in terms of her possession or lack of those qualities;
4. Instrumentalism, in which the other is constructed as having no ends of her own, and her sole purpose is to serve as a resource for the master;

5. Homogenization, in which the dominated class of others is perceived as uniformly homogeneous (Plumwood 1993, 42–56).[4]

Queers experience backgrounding, radical exclusion, incorporation, and homogenization. As Sedgwick argues, the heterosexual identity is constituted through a denied dependency on the homosexual/queer identity (backgrounding). In terms of radical exclusion, queers find that the erotic (a particularly perverse erotic) is projected onto queer sexuality to such a degree that this quality is seen as the only salient feature of queer identities. When queers come out, heterosexuals frequently conclude they know everything there is to know about us once they know our sexuality. In terms of incorporation, it is clear that heterosexuality and its associated gender identities are taken as the standard in dominant Western culture, and queers are defined primarily in relation to that standard, and our failure to comply with it.

But the problem of oppression based on sexuality is not limited to the heterosexual/queer dualism. As queer theorists have shown, the larger problem is the erotophobia of Western culture, a fear of the erotic so strong that only one form of sexuality is overtly allowed, only in one position, and only in the context of certain legal, religious, and social sanctions (Hollibaugh 1983, 1989; Rubin 1989). The oppression of queers may be described more precisely, then, as the product of two mutually reinforcing dualisms: heterosexual/queer, and reason/the erotic.

As Plumwood has ably demonstrated, Western culture's oppression of nature can be traced back to the construction of the dominant human male as a self fundamentally defined by its property of reason, and the construction of reason as definitionally opposed to nature and all that is associated with nature, including women, the body, emotions, and reproduction (Plumwood 1993). Feminists have also argued that women's oppression in Western culture is characterized by our association with emotion, the body, and reproduction, and feminists have responded to these associations in different ways. Some have rejected these associations and attempted to align themselves with the public male sphere of rationality (liberal feminists); others have reversed the valuation and embraced these associations while devaluing the male rational culture (cultural feminists). In contrast, ecofeminists have argued for a "third way," one that rejects the structure of dualism and acknowledges both women and men as equal parts of culture and nature (Warren 1987; King 1989; Plumwood 1993; Gruen 1993; Gaard 1994b). As a logical development of ecofeminism, a queer ecofeminist theory would build on these analyses using both queer theory and feminist theories about the oppression of the erotic. Though the reason/erotic dualism seems to be an aspect of the original culture/nature dualism, the heterosexual/queer dualism is a fairly recent development, as it is only in the past century that the concept of homosexual and heterosexual identities has developed

(Smith 1989; Katz 1990). A queer ecofeminist perspective would argue that the reason/erotic and heterosexual/queer dualisms have now become part of the master identity, and that dismantling these dualisms is integral to the project of ecofeminism.

Bringing these dualisms into the list of self/other and culture/nature dualisms offered by Plumwood is one step toward queering ecofeminism. With this added perspective, ecofeminists would find it very productive to explore "vertical" associations on either side of the dualisms: associations between reason and heterosexuality, for example, or between reason and whiteness as defined in opposition to emotions and nonwhite persons; or associations between women, nonwhite persons, animals, and the erotic. From a queer ecofeminist perspective, then, we can examine the ways queers are feminized, animalized, eroticized, and naturalized in a culture that devalues women, animals, nature, and sexuality. We can also examine how persons of color are feminized, animalized, eroticized, and naturalized. Finally, we can explore how nature is feminized, eroticized, even queered.

The critical point to remember is that each of the oppressed identity groups, each characteristic of the other, is seen as "closer to nature" in the dualisms and ideology of Western culture. Yet queer sexualities are frequently devalued for being "against nature." Contradictions such as this are of no interest to the master, although they have been of great interest to feminists and queer theorists alike, who have argued that it is precisely such contradictions that characterize oppressive structures (Frye 1983; Mohr 1988; Sedgwick 1990).

Before launching into a discussion of queer sexualities as both "closer to nature" and "crimes against nature," it is crucial to acknowledge that sexuality itself is a socially constructed phenomenon that varies in definition from one historical and social context to another. As scholars of queer history have shown, there was no concept of a homosexual identity in Western culture before the late nineteenth century (Faderman 1981; Greenberg 1988; Katz 1990; Vicinus 1993). Until then, people spoke (or did not speak) of individual homosexual acts, deviance, and sodomy; the persons performing those acts were always presumed to be "normal" (the word "heterosexual" had no currency). Those homosexual acts were castigated as sinful excesses, moral transgressions of biblical injunctions.

The shift from seeing homosexual behavior as a sin to seeing it as a "crime against nature" began during the seventeenth century. As early as 1642, ministers in the American colonies began referring to the "unnatural lusts of men with men, or women with women," "unnatural acts," and acts "against nature" (Katz 1983, 43). "After the American Revolution," however, "the phrase 'crimes against nature' increasingly appeared in the statutes, implying that acts of sodomy offended a natural order rather than the will of God" (D'Emilio and Freedman 1988, 122). The natural/unnatural distinction had to do with procreation, but even "natural" acts leading to procreation could be tainted by lust and thus not free from sin. Procreative lust was preferable to "unnatural" lust, however (Katz 1983, 43). Finally, a third shift in the definition of homosexuality occurred toward the end of the nineteenth century. Through the work of sexologists such as Havelock Ellis, Magnus Hirschfeld, and Richard von Krafft-Ebing, the sexual invert became a recognizable identity, and the origins of sexual inversion were believed to lie in an individual's psychology. The word heterosexual first appeared in American medical texts in the early 1890s, but not in the popular press until 1926 (Katz 1983, 16).[5]

Today, nearly thirty years after the Stonewall rebellion, which launched the movement for gay liberation, the definition of queer identities is still evolving. "Homosexual" has changed to "gay," and "gay" to "gay and lesbian"; bisexuals have become more vocal; and most recently, transgender liberation has also reshaped queer communities, changes that have prompted many organizations to replace "gay and lesbian" with "gay/lesbian/bisexual/transgendered" or simply "queer" in their self-definitions. The recognition of varying sexual identities and practices has inspired a rereading of not only straight history or queer history but the history of sexuality itself. Based on these historical developments, queer theorists have determined that queer sexualities (both practices and identities) have been seen as transgressive in at least three categories: as acts against biblical morality, against nature, or against psychology. Thus, queer sexualites have been seen as a moral problem, a physiological problem, or a psychological problem (Pronk 1993). Though all three arguments are used against all varieties of queer sexuality today, the "crime against nature" argument stands out as having the greatest immediate interest for ecofeminists.

Queer theorists who explore the natural/unnatural dichotomy find that "natural" is invariably associated with "procreative." The equation of "natural" with "procreative" should be familiar to all feminists, for it is just this claim that has been used in a variety of attempts to manipulate women back into compulsory motherhood and the so-called women's sphere. From a historical perspective, the equation of woman's "true nature" with motherhood has been used to oppress women just as the equation of sexuality with procreation has been used to oppress both women and queers. The charge that queer sexualities are "against nature" and thus morally, physiologically, or psychologically depraved and devalued would seem to imply that nature is valued—but as ecofeminists have shown, this is not the case. In Western culture, just the contrary is true: nature is devalued just as queers are devalued. Here is one of the many contradictions characterizing the dominant ideology. On the one hand, from a queer perspective, we learn that the dominant culture charges queers with transgressing the natural order, which in turn implies that nature is valued and must be obeyed. On the other hand, from an ecofeminist perspective, we learn that Western culture has constructed nature as a force that must be dominated if culture is to prevail. Bringing these perspectives together indicates that the "nature" queers are urged to comply with is none other than the dominant paradigm of heterosexuality—an identity and practice that is itself a cultural construction, as both feminists and queer theorists have shown (Chodorow 1978; Foucault 1980; Rich 1986).

There are many flaws in the assertion that queer sexualities are "unnatural." First among them is that such an assertion does not accurately reflect the variety of sexual practices found in other species. For example, female homosexual behavior has been found in chickens, turkeys, chameleons, and cows, while male homosexual behavior has been observed in fruit flies, lizards, bulls, dolphins, porpoises, and apes (Denniston 1965; Pattatucci and Hamer 1995). An examination of insect sexual behavior reveals that the female scorpion kills the male after mating, the black widow spider eats the male after mating, and the praying mantis may eat the male while mating. Some animals are hermaphrodites (snails, earthworms), while other species are entirely female (toothcarp). Mating behavior also varies across mammal species. "Some pairs mate for life (jackals), some are promiscuous (zebras, most whales, chimpanzees). In some species, males and females travel together in herds, packs, or prides (musk ox, wolves, lions); in others, family groups are the basic unit (coyotes, gibbons); in others, males and females spend most of their time in same-sex groups and get together only for mating (hippopotamuses); in still others, all are loners who seek out members of their species only for the purpose of procreation (pandas)" (Curry 1990, 151).

The equation of "natural" sexual behavior with procreative purposes alone is conclusively disproven by both the evidence of same-sex behaviors and the observations of sexual activity during pregnancy, which have been reported for chimpanzees, gorillas, rhesus macaques, stumptailed macaques, Japanese monkeys, and golden lion tamarins (Pavelka 1995). In his study of the bonobo (pygmy chimpanzee), a species that, together with the chimpanzee, is the nearest relative to *Homo sapiens*, Frans de Waal (1995) found that sexual behavior served a variety of reproductive and nonreproductive functions. In effect, research on nonhuman primate sexual behavior indicates that nonhuman primates "engage in sexual activity far more than they need to from a reproductive point of view and thus much of their sexuality is nonreproductive" (Pavelka 1995, 22). As Jane Curry concludes, "If we look to nature for models of human behavior, we are bound, are we not, to value tolerance and pluralism" (1990, 154). This, however, is the second flaw in the assertion that queer sexualities are "unnatural": norms for one species cannot be derived from the behaviors and seeming norms of other species.

By attempting to "naturalize" sexuality, the dominant discourse of Western culture constructs queer sexualities as "unnatural" and hence subordinate. As Jeffrey Weeks writes in *Against Nature*, "appeals to nature, to the claims of the natural, are among the most potent we can make. They place us in a world of apparent fixity and truth. They appear to tell us what and who we are, and where we are going. They seem to tell us the truth" (1991, 87). Arguments from "nature," as feminist philosophers of science have repeatedly argued, are frequently used to justify social norms rather than to find out anything new about nature (Bleier 1984; Fausto-Sterling 1985; Hubbard et al. 1982; Keller 1985; Lowe and Hubbard 1983). Attempts to naturalize one form of sexuality function as attempts to foreclose investigation of sexual diversity and sexual practices and to gain control of the discourse on sexuality. Such attempts are a manifestation of Western culture's homophobia and erotophobia.

Returning to the list of dualisms that ecofeminists have shown to characterize Western culture, and examining how qualities are distributed across each side of the disjuncts to enhance that disjunct's superiority (that is, the association of culture, men, and reason) or subordination (the association of nature, women, and the erotic), we can see that the eroticization of nature emphasizes its subordination. From a queer ecofeminist perspective, then, it becomes clear that liberating women requires liberating nature, the erotic, and queers. The conceptual connections among the oppressions of women, nature, and queers make this need particularly clear.

Erotophobia and the Colonization of Queer(s)/Nature

The rhetoric and institution of Christianity, coupled with the imperialist drives of militarist nation-states, have been used for nearly two thousand years to portray heterosexuality, sexism, racism, classism, and the oppression of the natural world as divinely ordained. Today, although twentieth-century Western industrialized nations purport to be secular, those countries with Christian and colonial origins retain the ideology of divinely inspired domination nonetheless. This section will first examine how Christianity has been used to authorize the exploitation of women, indigenous cultures, animals, the natural world, and queers. It will conclude by examining twentieth-century colonial practices.

Many feminists and ecofeminists who have examined Western culture's hierarchical and oppressive relationship with nature date the problem of human separation from nature (the necessary precedent to hierarchy and oppression) back to 4000 b.c.e., the Neolithic era, and the conquering of matrifocal, agricultural, goddess-worshiping cultures by militaristic, nomadic cultures that worshiped a male god (Eisler 1987; Spretnak 1982; Starhawk 1979). The agriculturalists' view—that spirit was immanent in all of nature, that sexuality and reproduction were like the earth's fertility, and that both were sacred—was replaced by a worldview that conceived of divinity as transcendent, separate from nature, with humans and nature as God's creation rather than as equal parts of God. The female, bisexual, or hermaphroditic Goddess was replaced by the male, heterosexual God

the Father, and the matrifocal trinity of Maiden, Mother, and Crone became the
patriarchal trinity of Father, Son, and Holy Ghost (Evans 1978; Sjoo and Mor
1987). Thus, in searching for origins of the conceptual linkages among women,
nature, persons of color, and queers, along with their collective oppression,
many feminists and ecofeminists would argue that it is more relevant to look at
the shift in social organization from matrifocal to patriarchal structures and
values than to explore how a particular form of patriarchal religion (historically
antecedent to that shift by centuries or even millennia) has authorized the subordination of women, nature, and their associates.

For other ecofeminists, however, the theories of a matrifocal past remain just
that—anthropological theories rather than historical facts. So much of anthro-
pology is based on a few pieces of broken pottery, scattered bones, and the remnants
of buildings that some ecofeminists are reluctant to develop additional ecofeminist theory based too heavily on these interpretations alone. All ecofeminists
who have addressed the topic of spirituality, however, have observed that Christianity has been used as both an authorization and a mandate for the subordination of women, nature, persons of color, animals, and queers—and it is this
agreement that I will take as my point of departure.[6]

Christianity orginated as a small, ascetic cult, one among many such cults
in the Roman Empire. It was from the start an urban religion, shaped in the context of urban, secular philosophies rather than in the context of earth-based,
rural agriculturalism. The beliefs of the early Christians included the conception of Adam as both male and female, and of Christ as the restored androgynous
Adam (Ruether 1983, 100); and the critical opposition between reason and passion (Greenberg 1988, 225), with the power of reason (*logos*) as the unique characteristic distinguishing humans from animals (Evans 1978, 86). Comparing some
of those beliefs with the context in which they originated, one can surmise that
the proponents of Christianity were influenced both by the beliefs of earlier,
earth-based cultures and by popular philosophies of their time, such as Stoicism
and Gnosticism. Moreover, their ability to incorporate aspects of these other
popular beliefs into Christianity may have enhanced its appeal and ensured its
survival.

The early Christian perspective on sex and the erotic also suited the tem-
per of the time. Christianity appeared during a time of increasing militarization
in the Roman state. It was preceded by a "wave of grim asceticism" (Evans 1978,
41). For Stoic and Epicurean philosophers of the period, sex and other erotic
pleasures were seen as distractions from the contemplative life. Stoic morality
held out chastity as an ideal, with heterosexual intercourse allowed only for
procreation within marriage; other Greek and Roman writers also held that procreation was the only legitimate reason for intercourse (Greenberg 1988, 219).
According to David Greenberg, "To be like the angels was to be spiritual; to be
carnal, unspiritual. Sex was the essence of carnality, hence the antithesis of

spirituality" (1988, 224). During the first two centuries of Christianity, leading bishops and theologians required celibacy of all Christians, but later recanted (possibly from fear of alienating potential converts) and allowed limited sexual behavior within marriage for the sole purpose of procreation (1 Corinthians 7:1–2, 9; Greenberg 1988, 216, 228; Ranke-Heinemann 1990). From the second through the fourth centuries c.e., church leaders gave the topic of sex more attention and rejected it more vehemently than did the authors of the New Testament (Greenberg 1988, 223). Thus it would be inaccurate to argue that Christianity opposed queer sexuality per se; rather, Christianity opposed all sexual acts that were not purposely procreative (Ranke-Heinemann 1990). What distinguished Christianity from the many other ascetic cults of its time was the severity of its asceticism, its complete intolerance of other religions, and the high degree of organization among its adherents (Evans 1978, 42).

Hierarchy—the organizational structure and religious belief that characterized Christianity—may also have contributed to its survival because this belief matched that of the Romans, who praised "the virtues of self-sacrifice to the state, obedience to hierarchical authority, and suspicion of pleasure and sex" (Evans 1978, 37). As Elizabeth Dodson Gray has observed, the two accounts of creation in Genesis have been used in Christianity to legitimate both human/nonhuman hierarchy (the human dominion over nature, as described in Genesis 1) and anthropocentrism (man as the center of creation, as described in Genesis 2). Gray reminds us, moreover, that *hierarchy* itself means *holy order* (1979, 7). Her work shows that Christianity originally interpreted all social or economic ranking as reflecting a holy order, as the Apostle Paul explained: "Let everyone obey the authorities that are over him, for there is no authority except from God, and all authority that exists is established by God" (Romans 13:1–2). The conceptual symmetry between Christianity and the Roman state made it possible for Christianity to spread gradually throughout the Roman army, where it incorporated additional elements of a contending religion (Mithraism). Finally, under Emperor Constantine, "the cross was adopted as a military symbol and placed on shields and banners" (Evans 1978, 43). In the fourth century c.e., the Roman Empire became the Holy Roman Empire, and the union of church and state as representing the reign of God's will on earth was sealed. The inferiority and subordination of women, animals, the body, nature, the erotic, and all their associates was proclaimed by law, decreed by religion, and relentlessly enforced. From the fourth through the seventeenth centuries, all those perceived as "nature" were persecuted through a series of violent assaults: the Inquisition, the Crusades, witch burnings, and the "voyages of discovery."

In his underground classic, *Witchcraft and the Gay Counterculture*, Arthur Evans writes of the similarities between the Inquisition and the witch burnings, particularly in their pursuit of victims. From the fourth through the thirteenth centuries, the church was plagued with pagan influences, resurgences of the old religions attempting to combine with some of the tenets of Christianity: Gnosticism, Manichaeism, Massalianism, Bogomilism, Catharism, the Free Spirit, and others. According to Evans, these movements displayed five prominent features: "(1) belief in more than one deity; (2) a prominent leadership role for women; (3) a pagan sense of asceticism, including both self-denial and self-indulgence; (4) hostility to the wealth and power of the church; and (5) a tolerance for Gay sex" (1978, 61).

Unable to repress these continual resurgences, the church declared such beliefs heresy and commanded their eradication. The Holy Inquisition was created by Pope Gregory IX between 1227 and 1235, and in 1233 one of his famous bulls, the *Vox in Rama*, accused heretics of practicing sex rites that were "opposed to reason" (Evans 1978, 91–92). The Inquisition used the property of the accused to pay for the costs of trial and execution, and heresy hunting became a major industry in the Middle Ages. Economic motivations surely explain the persecution of a particular monastic military order of crusaders, the Knights Templars. In 1307, King Philippe of France brought charges of same-sex sexual behaviors against the entire order. Five thousand of its members were arrested, and over the next few years, those remaining free were hunted down all over Europe until the order was abolished. As Evans explains, the Knights Templars had accumulated vast amounts of wealth and had become the chief bankers of the Middle Ages: "Both Pope Clement and Philippe were in debt to them" (1978, 92–94). In this one example of many, the church can be seen as using antierotic and homophobic rhetoric to mask the economic motivations of church and state.

If the *Vox in Rama* was the launching point of the Inquisition, the appearance of the *Malleus Maleficarum* in 1486 was surely the codification for witch burnings. Written by two Dominican monks, the "hammer of witches" explicitly links witchcraft to women and women's "inferior nature," claiming that women are "more carnal" than men (Ruether 1983, 170). The spiritual practice of witchcraft was popularly seen as implicitly sexual: persons arrested on suspicion of witchcraft were always questioned about their sex lives, for witches were thought to hold wild and bawdy rituals that culminated in the witches kissing the devil's anus or having intercourse with the devil (Merchant 1980, 132–40). Same-sex sexual behaviors and gender nonconformity were also linked to witchcraft: the phrase "women with women" recurs throughout the Inquisition's reports on witches' sexual behaviors, and because the majority of witches were women, the charge of "wild orgies" in effect suggests that women were engaging sexually with one another (Grahn 1984, 96). Men who engaged in same-sex behaviors were often strangled and burned on bundles of sticks called "faggots," which were tied and stacked in the kindling at the "witches'" feet (Grahn 1984, 218; Evans 1978, 76). And in the earliest notorious example of what might today be called transgender persecution, nineteen-year-old Joan of Arc was burned at the stake as a witch in 1431, condemned to death for the sin of wearing men's clothing (Evans 1978, 5–8).[7] Older, economically independent women and those unprotected by a man were especially vulnerable to accusations of witchcraft. Like those convicted by the Inquisition, their property and assets were seized and used to pay the cost of their executions (Starhawk 1982, 185–88). Estimates of the number of witches executed range between one hundred thousand and 9 million; some say that approximately 83 percent of those executed as witches were women (Merchant 1980, 138).

What is known of the linkages between the "burning times" and the colonization of the Americas? Arthur Evans unequivocally asserts, "The widespread homosexuality of the North American Indians was given as an excuse by the invading Christian whites for their extermination" (1978, 101). In *Gay American History*, Jonathan Ned Katz writes, "the Christianization of Native Americans and the colonial appropriation of the continent by white, Western 'civilization' included the attempt by the conquerors to eliminate various traditional forms of Indian homosexuality—as part of their attempt to destroy that Native culture which might fuel resistance—a form of cultural genocide involving both Native Americans and Gay people" (1976, 284). And in his study of *The Zuni Man-Woman*, Will Roscoe finds, dating back to the sixteenth century, numerous reports on the "sinfulness" of native sexual behavior—the lack of inhibition, the prevalence of sodomy, and the tolerance or even respect for transgendered persons—all of which fueled the Spanish explorers' argument for the colonization of native peoples and their lands in the name of Christianity.[8]

It is interesting that both the monarchs and the explorers felt the need to justify their colonialist desires for more land, more wealth, and more slaves. From medieval theologians, Christianity had inherited the message that the "fruits of any conquest could only be legitimate if the war that won them had been just"; conveniently, through the Crusades, Christianity developed the principle that "war conducted in the interests of the Holy Church was automatically just" (Jennings 1975, 4). Because the church had been engaged in persecuting the erotic since its inception, choosing the sexual behaviors of indigenous peoples as proof of their heathenism and lack of civilization seemed adequate justification for their colonization.

Katz's valuable research in *Gay American History* offers numerous observations of native sexual practices, dating from the sixteenth-century explorers on. These records clearly express the explorers' erotophobic, imperialist attitudes. "The people of this nation [the Choctaw] are generally of a brutal and coarse nature," wrote Jean Bernard Bossu. "They are morally quite perverted, and most of them are addicted to sodomy. These corrupt men . . . have long hair and wear short skirts like women" (Katz 1976, 291). "The sin of sodomy prevails more among them than in any other nation, although there are four women to one man," wrote Pierre Liette about the Miamis in 1702 (Katz 1976, 288). The role of the *nadleeh*, or transgendered person, particularly offended western European sensibilities.[9] Of the Iroquois, the Illinois, and other tribes in the Louisiana area, Jesuit explorer and historian Pierre François Xavier de Charlevoix wrote in 1721, "these effeminate persons never marry, and abandon themselves to the most infamous passions" (Katz 1976, 290). When Jesuit father Pedro Font found "some men dressed like women" among the California Yumas, he inquired about their clothing and learned that "they were sodomites, dedicated to nefarious practices." Font concluded, "there will be much to do when the Holy Faith and the Christian religion are established among them" (Katz 1976, 291). The Franciscan missionary Francisco Palou reported with shock that "almost every village" in what is now southern California "has two or three" transgendered persons, but prayed "that these accursed people will disappear with the growth of the missions. The abominable vice will be eliminated to the extent that the Catholic faith and all the other virtues are firmly implanted there, for the glory of God and the benefit of those poor ignorants" (Katz 1976, 292). In the rhetoric of Christian colonialism, the Europeans filled the role of benevolent culture "civilizing" savage nature—and this "civilizing" involved taking the natives' homelands, eliminating their cultural and spiritual practices, and raping and enslaving their people.

A specific example of the role erotophobia played in authorizing colonization may be of use. In his book *The Elder Brothers: A Lost South American People and Their Wisdom*, Alan Ereira reports on the Kogi, who live deep in Colombia's Sierra Nevada mountains, and who may be "the last surviving high civilisation of pre-conquest America" (1992, 1). In 1498, the land around what is now the Colombian city of Santa Marta was discovered by the Spanish in their search for gold, and on June 12, 1514, a Spanish galleon arrived and began the process of colonization. That process involved reading a decree declaring the natives' new servitude to King Ferdinand and the Christian God, in both Spanish and Carib languages, although the native people did not speak either one. The Spanish conquistador Pedrarias Davila concluded his proclamation with the warning that if the native people did not submit to this rule,

> I assure you that with the help of God I will enter powerfuly against you, and I will make war on you in every place and in every way that I can, and I will subject you to the yoke and obedience of the church and their highnesses, and I will take your persons and your women and your children, and I will make them slaves, and as such I will sell them, and dispose of them as their highnesses command: I will take your goods, and I will do you all the evils and harms which I can, just as to vassals who do not obey and do not want to receive their lord, resist him and contradict him. And I declare that the deaths and harms which arise from this will be your

fault, and not that of their highnesses, nor mine, nor of the gentlemen who have come with me here. (Ereira 1992, 74)

The Spanish invasion proceeded accordingly.

As Ereira observes, gender and sexuality played a prominent role in the rhetoric and the justification of colonial conquest. "The Spanish could not endure the Indians' relationship between the sexes," he writes. "It was so fundamentally different from their own as to be an outrage. The men did not dominate the women" (Ereira 1992, 136). The Spanish were horrified, moreover, by the acceptance of homosexual behaviors and transgendered identities: "it was an inner fear, a fear of their own nature. And so they set out to eliminate sodomy among the Indians" (137, emphasis added). After nearly a century of colonial enslavement and missionary zeal, the Spanish concluded their most vicious assault on the native population in 1599. The governor of Santa Marta called together all the native chiefs at the base of the Sierras and told them he would put an end to their "wicked sinfulness" (138). The native population planned a revolt, but news of their plans was leaked to the Spanish through two missionaries, and the Spanish were prepared. For three months, the Spanish carried out their own plan of torture and genocide against the indigenous people. When it was over, the governor declared, "And if any other Indian is found to have committed or to practice the wicked and unnatural sin of sodomy he is condemned so that in the part and place that I shall specify he shall be garrotted in the customary manner and next he shall be burned alive and utterly consumed to dust so that he shall have no memorial and it is to be understood by the Indians that this punishment shall be extended to all who commit this offense" (Ereira 1992, 140). Those persons "who wish to live" were required to pay a fine of "pacification" amounting to fifteen hundred pounds of gold (Ereiera 1992, 140). Gender-role deviance and the accepted presence of nonheterosexual erotic practices had become the rhetorical justification for genocide and colonialism.

Not only did transgender practices and sodomy disturb the colonizers; even heterosexual practices devoid of the restrictions imposed by Christianity were objectionable. Among the Hopi of the Southwest, for example, those who had been successfully converted to Christianity were forbidden to attend the traditional snake dance because there, "male cross-dressing, adultery, and bestiality could be observed publicly" (D'Emilio and Freedman 1988, 93). Missionaries objected to the heterosexual practices of the Pueblo Indians, calling them "bestial" because "'like animals, the female plac[ed] herself publicly on all fours'" (Gutiérrez 1991, 72–73). What became known as the "missionary position" was advocated by the seventeenth-century Spanish theologian Tomás Sánchez, in his *De sancto matrimonii sacramento*, as the "natural manner of intercourse. . . . The man must lie on top and the woman on her back beneath. Because this manner is more appropriate for the effusion of male seed, for its reception into the female vessel" (Gutiérrez 1991, 212). Sánchez likened the phallus to a plow and the woman to the earth; the missionary position would be the one most conducive to procreation and hence the most "natural." In contrast, the *mulier supra virum* (woman above man) position was "absolutely contrary to the order of nature" (Gutiérrez 1991, 212).

Appeals to nature have often been used to justify social norms, to the detriment of women, nature, queers, and persons of color. The range of colonial assaults on sexuality—from gender role to same-sex behaviors to heterosexual practices—is the reason I name the colonizers' perspective erotophobic rather than simply homophobic. This colonial erotophobia remained intact through the arrival of the Pilgrims, the establishment of the United States, and the waves of westward expansion that followed. In the twentieth century, narratives of colonialism and exploration continue to bear the stamp of erotophobia, as feminist critiques reveal.

In her study of race and gender in international politics, Cynthia Enloe finds important connections between the conceptions of nationalism and of masculinity. In colonialist discourses of the nineteenth and twentieth centuries, the subordinated countries are feminized, the subordinated men are emasculated, and the colonized women are often depicted as sex objects by foreign men. One male writer described colonialism as the condition wherein a man's women are "turned into fodder for imperialist postcards. Becoming a nationalist requires a man to resist the foreigner's use and abuse of his women" (Enloe 1989, 44). In her study of U.S. polar expeditions, Lisa Bloom finds that "the explorations symbolically enacted the men's own battle to become men," and the recorded narratives left by the explorers present "U.S. national identity as essentially a white masculine one" (Bloom 1993, 6, 11).

Both Enloe's and Bloom's texts reprint popular colonial postcard images of naked or partially clothed native women reclining on the ground in what Bloom calls the "odalisque pose" (Bloom 1993, 104). Like the colonizers of three and four centuries past, the explorers and imperialists of the nineteenth and twentieth centuries used the perceived eroticism of native peoples as a justification for their colonization.

Serving as a foundation for all imperialist exploits, colonial nationalism offers a definition of identity that is structurally similar to the master identity. Enloe defines a nation as "a collection of people who have come to believe that they have been shaped by a common past and are destined to share a common future. That belief is usually nurtured by a common language and *a sense of otherness* from groups around them" (Enloe 1989, 45; emphasis added). Nationalism, then, is "a set of ideas that sharpens distinctions between 'us' and 'them'. It is, moreover, a tool for explaining how inequities have been created between 'us' and 'them'" (Enloe 1989, 61). Similarly, the editors of *Nationalisms and Sexualities* explain that "national identity is determined not on the basis of its own intrinsic properties but as a function of what it (presumably) is not" (Parker et al. 1992, 5). Inevitably "shaped by what it opposes," a national identity that depends on such differences is "forever haunted by [its] various definitional others" (Parker et al. 1992, 5).

Looking at these definitions of nationalism from an ecofeminist perspective, it becomes apparent that national identity bears a structural similarity to the master model as defined by Plumwood. National identity participates in two of the five operations characteristic of the master identity—radical exclusion and incorporation. Colonialist nationalism, however, depends on all five operations of the master model, including the linking postulates of backgrounding, instrumentalism, and homogenization. Throughout the documents of explorers and colonists, native peoples are constructed as animallike: they are perceived as overly sexual, and their sexual behaviors are described as sinful and animalistic. The indigenous women are eroticized while the men are feminized—and all these associations are used to authorize colonization.

The feature of masculine identity that Enloe and Bloom seem to overlook and that Plumwood does not explicitly address is sexuality. Here again, feminist and ecofeminist theories fall short without a queer perspective. As Gayle Rubin has noted, "Feminism is the theory of gender oppression. To automatically assume that this makes it the theory of sexual oppression is to fail to distinguish between gender, on the one hand, and erotic desire, on the other" (1989, 307). Queer theorist Eve Sedgwick argues that gender and sexuality are "inextricable . . . in that each can be expressed only in terms of the other . . . in twentieth-century Western culture gender and sexuality represent two analytic axes that may productively be imagined as being as distinct from one another as, say, gender and class, or class and race" (1990, 30).

From a queer ecofeminist perspective, then, it is clear that notions of sexuality are implicit within the category of gender. Simply stated, the masculinity of the colonizer and of Plumwood's master identity is neither homosexual, bisexual, nor transgendered. Heterosexuality—and a particular kind of heterosexuality as well, a heterosexuality contained within certain parameters—is implicit in conceptions of both dominant masculinity and Plumwood's master model. In the preceding examples, the discourse of nationalist colonialism contains specific conceptions not only of race and gender but also of sexuality. The native feminized other of nature is not simply eroticized but also queered and animalized, in that any sexual behavior outside the rigid confines of compulsory heterosexuality becomes queer and subhuman. Colonization becomes an act of the nationalist self asserting identity and definition over and against the other—culture over and against nature, masculine over and against feminine, reason over and against the erotic. The metaphoric "thrust" of colonialism has been described as the rape of indigenous people and of nature because there is a structural—not experiential—similarity between the two operations, though colonization regularly includes rape.

Western ecofeminists have repeatedly argued against the feminization of nature in metaphors such as "Mother Nature" because of the subordination implicit in these gendered constructions given the context of Western patriarchal culture. Elizabeth Dodson Gray may be the first ecofeminist writer to challenge the "tyranny of the straight white male norm," in her book *Green Paradise Lost*, when she shows how the "Mother Nature" metaphor leads to subordination. In patriarchal Western culture, Gray explains, masculinity is defined not only as independence but as "not-dependent." The process of socializing boys into men involves denying dependence on the mother; that dependence is then transferred to the wife. Male superiority is preserved by the social construction of a "wife" as "submissive . . . economically impotent, and in many other ways . . . inferior and non-threatening to her man. In short, a wife is to be *below* her man, *not above*" (1979, 41; emphasis added). According to Gray, the same transference is at work in Western culture's relationship with nature. "Men have done with Mother Nature this same dominance/submission flip-flop. They have by their technologies worked steadily and for generations to transform a psychologically intolerable dependence upon a seemingly powerful and capricious 'Mother Nature' into a soothing and acceptable dependence upon a subservient and nonthreatening 'wife.' This 'need to be above' and to dominate permeates male attitudes toward nature" (Gray 1979, 42).[10] As I have argued elsewhere, when nature is feminized and thereby eroticized, and culture is masculinized, the culture-nature relationship becomes one of compulsory heterosexuality (Gaard 1993). Colonization can therefore be seen as a relationship of compulsory heterosexuality whereby the queer erotic of non-Westernized peoples, their culture, and their land, is subdued into the missionary position—with the conqueror "on top."[11]

Toward a Queer Ecofeminism

Salient events in Western history reveal the foundations for a queer ecofeminism. More than any other period, the sixteenth and seventeenth centuries clarify the conceptual links between the oppression of women, the erotic, and nature. As Carolyn Merchant (1980), Susan Griffin (1978), and Evelyn Fox Keller (1985) have so clearly demonstrated, in a patriarchal system that conceives of nature as female, there is a clear and necessary connection between the development of science as the rational control of a chaotic natural world and the persecution of women as inherently irrational, erotic, and therefore evil creatures. Such connections have provided the conceptual foundations for ecofeminist theories. The foundations for queer ecofeminism, then, are established by restoring and interrogating other aspects of that historical period: that women

accused of witchcraft were accused not only for their gender but for their perceived sexuality and erotic practices; that such women were frequently burned
with men who had sex with other men; that the colonial conquest of indigenous
peoples in the Americas was authorized partly on the basis of the natives' sexual behaviors. I am not suggesting that "co-occurrence equals causality"; rather,
I am arguing that a careful reading of these several movements of domination—
the persecution of women through the witch burnings, of nature through science, and of indigenous peoples through colonialism—which reached a peak
during the same historical period in western Europe, will lead to the roots of an
ideology in which the erotic, queer sexualities, women, persons of color, and
nature are all conceptually linked.

Today, all those associated with nature and the erotic continue to experience the impact of centuries of Western culture's colonization, in our very bodies and in our daily lives. Rejecting that colonization requires embracing the
erotic in all its diversity and building coalitions for creating a democratic, ecological culture based on our shared liberation.

To create that culture, we must combine the insights of queer and ecofeminist theories. As feminists have long argued, the way out of this system of
endemic violence requires liberating the erotic—not in some facile liberal
scheme, which would authorize increased access to pornography or child sexual encounters, but through a genuine transformation of Western conceptions
of the erotic as fundamentally opposed to reason, culture, humanity, and masculinity. A queer ecofeminist perspective would argue that liberating the erotic
requires reconceptualizing humans as equal participants in culture and in
nature, able to explore the eroticism of reason and the unique rationality of the
erotic. Ecofeminists must be concerned with queer liberation, just as queers
must be concerned with the liberation of women and of nature; our parallel
oppressions have stemmed from our perceived associations. It is time to build
our common liberation on more concrete coalitions.

NOTES

Written during my 1995–1996 sabbatical, and originally published in *Hypatia* (winter
1997), published by Indiana University Press, this essay responds to social justice
questions in both theory and activism. As an ecofeminist member of the Green Party,
I had listened to the distress of Lavender Greens who felt alienated by our premature
presidential candidate, Ralph Nader, whose cavalier responses to questions about
queer rights undermined the four pillars of the Green movement. (Nader has since
become more educated on this issue, and many queers see him as an ally.) Three
years after the passage of Proposition 2 in Colorado, Lavender Greens from Boulder
and Denver were still quick to detect any lack of commitment to their human rights
at the August 1995 presidential nominating convention of the U.S. Greens, and some
debated whether to stay in the movement or withdraw in order to spend more time
working directly on civil rights. As members of a queer caucus within the Greens, we
were holistic, multi-issue activists with a clear "first emergency" of survival as gays,

lesbians, bisexuals, and transgendered people fighting for our lives and our rights—
and yet we had developed no argument for explaining our conflicting commitments
to other Greens. What we needed, I felt, was a clear, systematic exploration of the
potential intersections of ecofeminist and queer theories. By interrogating social constructions of the "natural," the various uses of Christianity as a logic of domination,
and the rhetoric of colonialism, this essay exposes those theoretical intersections and
argues for the importance of developing queer ecofeminisms.

In 2003, progressives of all kinds still struggle to build a cohesive movement
capable of confronting corporate globalization, defending environmental justice, and
reclaiming the earth. They ask each other, "Why can't we sustain the kind of unity in
diversity that we saw in Seattle, at the 1999 World Trade Organization protests?" And
they are given an answer over and over again—but are these progressive activists
really listening? What is it that prevents progressives from working together?

As part of the national "Rolling Thunder Down Home Democracy Tour" intended
to energize and unite progressives of all types on Labor Day 2002, the St. Paul Area
Trades and Labor Assembly hosted a Labor Day Picnic on Harriet Island, inviting
activists and pundits of local and national fame to converse on panels and mobilize
participants. Author Barbara Ehrenreich joined Mark Ritchie from the Institute for
Agriculture and Trade Policy, Larry Weiss of Minnesota's Fair Trade Coalition, former
legislator Tom Hayden, Senator Paul Wellstone, poet and indigenous activist John
Trudell, and over a thousand activists committed to social and environmental justice.
During the panel discussion on "Building a Progressive Movement," a woman from
the audience challenged the three privileged male panelists—Cornel West, a scholar
in history and African American studies from Princeton; Joel Rogers, founder of the
New Party; and Tom Hayden, activist and former legislator—to put their progressive
democratic theory into practice by refusing speaking invitations unless they were
assured that other places on their panels would be given to less dominant groups
such as women of color, gays and lesbians, and youth. Cornel West, whose talk had
focused on the importance of building a multigenerational movement, replied that
what was most important on these panels was the democratic ideology of the speakers, and not the specific features of their embodiment. Here, as a community, we lost
another practice opportunity for "Building a Progressive Movement," and the audience discussion dissolved into shouting after West's reply.

The conceptual, economic, and historic links between the oppression of queers,
people of color, and the earth can readily be detected using the analytic frameworks
of ecofeminism, environmental justice, and other inclusive movements for a radical,
economic, and ecological democracy. Yet these movements fall short, in practice, of
delivering the democracy they espouse in theory. This essay is still as urgently relevant in 2003 as it was when it was written in 1995.

1. The May 1994 special issue of the Canadian journal *UnderCurrents* was the first to
    address the topic of "Queer Nature." In addition to Sandilands, two other contribu-
    tors to this special issue explicitly recognize a relationship between ecofeminism and
    queer theory. In "Lost Landscapes and the Spatial Contextualization of Queerness,"
    Gordon Brent Ingram writes that "an understanding of the intensifying juncture of
    environmentalism, radical ecology, ecofeminism, and queer theory is becoming cru-
    cial for the expansion of political activism in the coming decade" (5). And J. Michael
    Clark compares ecofeminism and ecotheology in his essay, "Sex, Earth, and Death in
    Gay Theology," asserting that "we can construct a gay ecotheological analysis in con-
    tradistinction to primarily male 'deep ecology' and as a further extension of ecofem-

inism" (34). The essays in the special issue initiate explorations of a queer ecofeminist geography and a queer ecofeminist theology, respectively; none, however, develops the connections between queer theory and ecofeminism.

2. I use the term queer as a shorthand for gay/lesbian/bisexual/transgender, but I use more specific terms as the context warrants. I use first-person plural pronouns when speaking of queers (us and we) to make my subject position clear. I am fully aware that queer is a contested term, generally popular among urban, under forty, academic queers, but generally unpopular among rural, over forty, community-based people; again, I use the term to reflect my own situatedness in a particular historical moment and geographic and cultural location.

3. Two definitions are in order. First, I define the dualism as heterosexual/queer rather than heterosexual/homosexual in order to reference and to emphasize the many and various combinations of gender and sexual identity that are constructed as aberrant under the hegemony of heterosexuality; I do not believe that a dualism of monosexualities (hetero/homo) captures my meaning quite as precisely. Second, by erotic I refer not exclusively to sexuality but also in a more general way to sensuality, spontaneity, passion, delight, and pleasurable stimulation; I also expect the erotic to be variously defined in accordance with specific historical and cultural contexts.

4. I use the pronoun his for the master self and her for the subordinated other because these identities are gendered; I do not mean, however, to essentialize either position. Many privileged women benefit from participating in various structures of oppression, and many men are subordinated through those structures.

5. According to Smith, the word homosexual was coined in 1869 by a little-known Hungarian doctor, Karoly Maria Benkert (1989, 112); according to Katz, heterosexual was first used publicly in Germany in 1880 (1990, 12). In the United States, the words heterosexual and homosexual were first used in 1892 by a Chicago medical doctor, James G. Kiernan (Katz 1990, 14).

6. Note that my argument rests on the ways Christianity has been used or interpreted historically; I leave for others the actual interpretation of Christianity as a religion.

7. I am defining transgender as persons who feel that their gender identity is different from their biological sex. Some transgender persons wish to change their anatomy to be more congruent with their self-perception. Others do not have such a desire. There is no correlation between sexual orientation and transgender issues. Transgender persons can be heterosexual, gay, lesbian, or bisexual (Zemsky 1995).

8. Roscoe's earlier work has been criticized for focusing on indigenous sexuality to the exclusion of race (Gutiérrez 1989). Roscoe addresses these criticisms in a concluding chapter of his 1991 book.

9. The more common term, berdache, I reject here on the basis of its original meaning as "a boy kept for unnatural purposes." The word originated with the European colonizers, and reflects their erotophobic perspective just as it erases the various cultural, spiritual, and economic aspects of this particular gender role. Male and female transgenders have been found in more than 130 North American tribes (Roscoe 1991, 5), and have been named accordingly in each culture. I prefer the Navajo term *nadleeh* both for its indigenous rather than colonial origins and because the Navajo used the same term for both men and women transgenders (Gay American Indians 1988).

10. This excerpt should not be read to imply that all men are heterosexual and have wives; rather, as Gray's context makes clear, she is referring to the construction of

masculine identity as a category, and as I argue here, the normative definition of masculine gender includes the presumption of heterosexuality.

11. Suzanne Zantop has arrived at a similar conclusion in her study of a German debate regarding the colonization of the Americas. The debate took place in the years following 1768 between the Dutch canon Cornelius de Pauw and the Prussian royal librarian Antoine Pernety. Zantop finds that "by imposing a gender framework on the encounter between colonizer and colonized, and by grounding this gender structure in a particular biology, de Pauw render[ed] the violent appropriation of the New World natural and inevitable, even desirable" and that "the power relationship of colonizer to colonized [became] the model for a successful matrimony" (1993, 312–13).

REFERENCES

Abramson, Paul R., and Steven D. Pinkerton, eds. 1995. *Sexual Nature/Sexual Culture.* Chicago: University of Chicago Press.

Adams, Carol. 1990. *The Sexual Politics of Meat: A Feminist-Vegetarian Critical Theory.* New York: Continuum.

———. 1993. "The Feminist Traffic in Animals." In Gaard 1993.

Bleier, Ruth. 1984. *Science and Gender: A Critique of Biology and Its Theories on Women.* New York: Pergamon Press.

Bloom, Lisa. 1993. *Gender on Ice: American Ideologies of Polar Expeditions.* Minneapolis: University of Minnesota Press.

Chodorow, Nancy. 1978. *The Reproduction of Mothering: Psychoanalysis and the Sociology of Gender.* Berkeley: University of California Press.

Clark, J. Michael. 1994. "Sex, Earth, and Death in Gay Theology." *UnderCurrents* (May): 34–39.

Curry, Jane. 1990. "On Looking to Nature for Women's Sphere." In *And a Deer's Ear, Eagle's Song and Bear's Grace: Animals and Women*, ed. Theresa Corrigan and Stephanie Hoppe. San Francisco: Cleis Press.

De Waal, Frans B. M. 1995. "Sex as an Alternative to Aggression in the Bonobo." In Abramson and Pinkerton 1995.

D'Emilio, John, and Estelle B. Freedman. 1988. *Intimate Matters: A History of Sexuality in America.* New York: Harper and Row.

Denniston, R. H. 1965. "Ambisexuality in Animals." In *Sexual Inversion: The Multiple Roots of Homosexuality*, ed. Judd Marmor. New York: Basic Books.

Enloe, Cynthia. 1989. *Bananas, Beaches, and Bases: Making Feminist Sense of International Politics.* Berkeley: University of California Press.

Ereira, Alan. 1992. *The Elder Brothers: A Lost South American People and Their Wisdom.* New York: Random House.

Evans, Arthur. 1978. *Witchcraft and the Gay Counterculture.* Boston: Fag Rag Books.

Faderman, Lillian. 1981. *Surpassing the Love of Men: Romantic Friendship and Love between Women from the Renaissance to the Present.* New York: William Morrow.

Fausto-Sterling, Anne. 1985. *Myths of Gender: Biological Theories about Women and Men.* New York: Basic Books.

Foucault, Michel. 1980. *The History of Sexuality.* Vol. 1, An Introduction. New York: Vintage Books.

Frye, Marilyn. 1983. "Oppression." In *The Politics of Reality.* Trumansburg, N.Y.: Crossing Press.

Gaard, Greta. 1994a. "Domestic Partnership Benefits at the University of Minnesota." *Concerns* 24, no. 3: 25–30.

———. 1994b. "Misunderstanding Ecofeminism." *Z papers* 3, no. 1: 20–24.

——, ed. 1993. *Ecofeminism: Women, Animals, Nature.* Philadelphia: Temple University Press.

Gay American Indians. 1988. *Living the Spirit: A Gay American Indian Anthology.* New York: St. Martin's Press.

Grahn, Judy. 1984. *Another Mother Tongue: Gay Words, Gay Worlds.* Boston: Beacon Press.

Gray, Elizabeth Dodson. 1979. *Green Paradise Lost.* Wellesley, Mass.: Roundtable Press.

Greenberg, David F. 1988. *The Construction of Homosexuality.* Chicago: University of Chicago Press.

Griffin, Susan. 1978. *Woman and Nature: The Roaring Inside Her.* New York: Harper and Row.

Gruen, Lori. 1993. "Dismantling Oppression: An Analysis of the Connection between Women and Animals." In Gaard 1993.

Gutiérrez, Ramón A. 1989. "Must We Deracinate Indians to Find Gay Roots?" *Out/Look* 1, no. 4: 61–67.

——. 1991. *When Jesus Came, the Corn Mothers Went Away: Marriage, Sexuality, and Power in New Mexico, 1500–1846.* Stanford: Stanford University Press.

Hollibaugh, Amber. 1983. "The Erotophobic Voice of Women." *New York Native* 7 (Sept. 26–Oct. 9): 33.

——. 1989. "Desire for the Future: Radical Hope in Passion and Pleasure." In Vance 1989.

Hubbard, Ruth, Mary Sue Henifin, and Barbara Fried, eds. 1982. *Biological Woman: The Convenient Myth.* Cambridge, Mass.: Schenkman Publishing Co.

Ingram, Gordon Brent. 1994. "Lost Landscapes and the Spatial Contextualization of Queerness." *UnderCurrents* (May): 4–9.

Jennings, Francis. 1975. *The Invasion of America: Indians, Colonialism, and the Cant of Conquest.* New York: W. W. Norton.

Katz, Jonathan Ned. 1976. *Gay American History: Lesbians and Gay Men in the U.S.A.* New York: Penguin.

——. 1983. *Gay/Lesbian Almanac: A New Documentary.* New York: Harper and Row.

——. 1990. "The Invention of Heterosexuality." *Socialist Review* 20, no. 1 (Jan.–Feb.): 7–34.

Keller, Evelyn Fox. 1985. *Reflections on Gender and Science.* New Haven: Yale University Press.

King, Ynestra. 1989. "The Ecology of Feminism and the Feminism of Ecology." In *Healing the Wounds: The Promise of Ecofeminism*, ed. Judith Plant. Philadelphia: New Society Publishers.

Lorde, Audre. 1984. "Uses of the Erotic: The Erotic as Power." In *Sister Outsider: Essays and Speeches.* Trumansburg, N.Y.: Crossing Press.

Lowe, Marion, and Ruth Hubbard, eds. 1983. *Woman's Nature: Rationalizations of Inequality.* New York: Pergamon Press.

Merchant, Carolyn. 1980. *The Death of Nature: Women, Ecology, and the Scientific Revolution.* New York: Harper and Row.

Mohr, Richard D. 1988. *Gays/Justice: A Study of Ethics, Society, and Law.* New York: Columbia University Press.

Parker, Andrew, Mary Russo, Doris Sommer, and Patricia Yaeger, eds. 1992. *Nationalisms and Sexualities.* New York: Routledge.

Pattatucci, Angela M. L., and Dean H. Hamer. 1995. "The Genetics of Sexual Orientation: From Fruit Flies to Humans." In Abramson and Pinkerton 1995.

Pavelka, Mary S. McDonald. 1995. "Sexual Nature: What Can We Learn from a Cross-species Perspective?" In Abramson and Pinkerton 1995.

Plumwood, Val. 1993. *Feminism and the Mastery of Nature.* New York: Routledge.

Pronk, Pim. 1993. *Against Nature? Types of Moral Argumentation Regarding Homosexuality.* Trans. John Vriend. Grand Rapids: William B. Eerdmans.

Ranke-Heinemann, Uta. 1990. *Eunuchs for Heaven: The Catholic Church and Sexuality.* Trans. John Brownjohn. London: Andre Deutsch.

Rich, Adrienne. 1986. "Compulsory Heterosexuality and Lesbian Existence." In *Blood, Bread, and Poetry.* New York: W. W. Norton.

Roscoe, Will. 1991. *The Zuni Man-Woman.* Albuquerque: University of New Mexico Press.

Rubin, Gayle. 1989. "Thinking Sex: Notes for a Radical Theory of the Politics of Sexuality." In Vance 1989.

Ruether, Rosemary Radford. 1983. *Sexism and God-Talk: Toward a Feminist Theology.* Boston: Beacon Press.

Sandilands, Catriona. 1994. "Lavender's Green? Some Thoughts on Queer(y)ing Environmental Politics." *UnderCurrents* (May): 20–24.

Sedgwick, Eve Kosofsky. 1990. *Epistemology of the Closet.* Berkeley: University of California Press.

Smith, John H. 1989. "Abulia: Sexuality and Diseases of the Will in the Late Nineteenth Century." *Genders* 6 (fall): 102–24.

Starhawk. 1982. *Dreaming the Dark: Magic, Sex, and Politics.* Boston: Beacon Press.

Vance, Carole S., ed. 1989. *Pleasure and Danger: Exploring Female Sexuality.* London: Pandora Press.

Vicinus, Martha. 1993. "'They wonder to which sex I belong': The Historical Roots of the Modern Lesbian Identity." In *The Lesbian and Gay Studies Reader*, ed. Henry Abelove, Michele Aina Barale, and David M. Halperin. New York: Routledge.

Warren, Karen J. 1987. "Feminism and Ecology: Making Connections." *Environmental Ethics* 9, no. 1: 3–21.

———. 1990. "The Power and the Promise of Ecological Feminism." *Environmental Ethics* 12, no. 2: 125–46.

———. 1991. "Feminism and the Environment: An Overview of the Issues." *APA Newsletter on Feminism and Philosophy* 90, no. 3: 108–16.

———, ed. 1994. *Ecological Feminism.* New York: Routledge.

Weeks, Jeffrey. 1991. *Against Nature: Essays on History, Sexuality, and Identity.* London: Rivers Oram Press.

Zantop, Suzanne. 1993. "Dialectics and Colonialism: The Underside of the Enlightenment." In *Impure Reason: Dialectic of Enlightenment in Germany*, ed. W. Daniel Wilson and Robert C. Holub. Detroit: Wayne State University Press.

Zemsky, Beth. 1995. Personal communication, Nov. 6.

2

Women, Sexuality, and Environmental Justice in American History

NANCY C. UNGER

The modern environmental justice movement emphasizes the right to a safe and healthy ecological, physical, social, political, and economic environment for all people. Issues of race and class are regularly addressed in environmental justice studies as characteristics that increase people's chances of being subjected to injustice, but these characteristics have also served to unify and mobilize those same people in their struggles against that injustice. Only limited scholarly attention, however, has been paid to the vital function of gender and its role in people's environmental vulnerability and empowerment (Blum 2001). Issues of sexuality, especially as they relate to reproduction, have played a leading role in subjecting women to a variety of environmental injustices. Native American women in the 1970s, for example, protested that uranium mining on their lands led to high levels of miscarriages and cancers of the reproductive organs, while at the same time Indian women were the targets of an aggressive government-funded mass sterilization program as part of the effort to take over resource-rich Indian lands. However, women have also used their unique strengths and experiences based on their gendered identities and sexualities to benefit themselves and oppressed others. Certainly women have taken part in more conventional environmental justice campaigns, such as community-based organizations protesting local environmental hazards brought on by major corporate polluters. But women's less conventional methods of seeking environmental justice (such as Margaret Sanger's insistence in the early twentieth century that birth control devices for women could end the sexual subservience of working-class women to men and the resultant overcrowding and cycle of poverty) remain underappreciated. Through a sampling of women's contributions that highlight sexuality issues, the relationship between gender, race, class, and environmental justice activism proves to be not just occasionally and peripherally a part of recent American history, but rather a varied, pervasive force from the pre-Columbian period to the present.

Pre-Columbian Native American Women: Agriculture, Sexuality, and Environmental Sustainability

The old stereotype concerning pre-Columbian Native Americans, environmental impact, and gender is the belief, reflecting the gender biases of the early European chroniclers, that Indian men did all the *real* providing for their people. In this view, anything that impacted the land was carried out solely by Indian men, because it was they who decided and set the controlled burns that created clearings that made grazing, and therefore hunting, easier and destroyed pests as well. Men were the hunters and the fishers, thereby impacting wildlife populations and habitat. The women, according to this view, remained within the villages caring for the children and doing the "drudgery" appropriate to their subordinate social status, producing finished goods (especially clothing and food that would not spoil) from the raw materials provided by the men (see Forsyth 1827, 20). This old stereotype has been partially replaced more recently by the popular glorification of Indians as all leading nomadic lifestyles, living totally off the land but having virtually no impact upon it.

The truth is quite different, although it is as dangerous to generalize about Americans in the pre-Columbian period as it is about Americans today. In what is now the United States there were not just varieties of Indian tribes, but entire Indian nations. For example, prior to the mission period, California was home to some 300,000 Indians who spoke at least 135 different languages and had an equally large diversity of customs, belief systems, and ways of life. Because natural food supplies were generally abundant, only the Mojaves, Yumas, and Cahuillas, who lived primarily in the extreme southeastern portion of the state's modern boundaries, practiced agriculture to any meaningful degree. The rest lived by hunting, fishing, and gathering as the incredible diversity of California's environment determined the diversity of its original peoples. The "grunt" work many missionaries incorrectly assumed to be indicative of women's inferior status was in fact a centuries-old attempt at an equitable division of labor, one facilitating women's ability to feed and care for children while simultaneously carrying out various tasks communally. Such gendered divisions of labor were rarely rigid. While California Indian men, for example, were the primary hunters and fishers and the women the primary gatherers and food preparers, men sometimes aided in the gathering (such as knocking acorns off oak limbs) while women hunted, fished, and trapped small game. Gender relations were equally variable, in California and elsewhere. The hierarchy of tribes in many places was determined less by gender and more by age and lineage. Some tribes were matrilineal. In others, women served as advisers and sometimes as leaders, as shamans, and as warriors.

It remains true, nonetheless, that in Indian societies throughout what is now the United States, men did frequently manipulate the environment by burning, hunting, and fishing. Women, however, made their own, and not always subtle, manipulations as they provided via gathering and/or farming much of their communities' total food. In areas where tribes practiced agriculture, women were usually the primary distributors of the crops they planted, weeded, and harvested. In southeastern New England, for example, since about 1000 A.D., the corn alone produced by women provided about 65 percent of their tribes' caloric input. Instead of planting corn in neatly plowed rows bereft of all other vegetation, they planted each hill with four grains of maize (corn) and two of pole beans that would twine around the cornstalks. Between the hills they grew squash and pumpkins so that as their vines grew and spread, they smothered any late-sprouting weeds. By not leaving the soil totally exposed, they shielded it from excessive sun and rain and cut down drastically on the amount of weeding that European farming methods necessitated (Merchant 1995, 92–95).

The ability of women to provide for their people combined with their abilities and contributions as mothers gained them a place of respect and value within their society, but this reverence was by no means shared by the Europeans who were to come. Understanding native women's reluctance to relinquish their respected position within their traditional cultures helps solve the puzzle of why missionaries intent on imposing patriarchal values frequently complained that it was easier to convert men than women (see Devens 1992). Outsiders misunderstood other aspects of Indian life as well. Colonists in New England, for example, were horrified rather than impressed by the practicality of the solution local Indians took to the problem of soil depletion. Native American crops, especially because they were so varied, did not leach nutrients from the soil at the same pace or to the same degree as did the Europeans' more monocultural methods of farming. Nonetheless, even those soils cultivated under native women's methods tired and crop yields lessened. Indian peoples then moved onto new, untilled soils. Europeans, stunned at this flagrant "waste," urged the fertilization of the land already under cultivation, especially since it could be done with relative ease due to the abundance of local fish. Indians, in view of the small numbers of their people combined with the seemingly endless amount of easily accessible untilled land, rejected this solution as both wasteful and absurdly labor intensive. These contrasting approaches to the problem of soil depletion highlight the two cultures' dramatically different land values, which were, significantly, ultimately based on population issues (Cronon 1983, 45, 151–52).

Indians did not live in total harmony with nature. They did on occasion cause the loss of entire local plant and animal species. More often, however, they were able, with relative ease and minimum of labor, to transform their physical environment without destroying it. The key to their ability to carry out what William Cronon calls "living richly by wanting little" was that they controlled their own numbers so that this "rich" lifestyle was sustainable and could be enjoyed by all tribal members. Native American women's greatest environmental impact came not through their gathering, irrigation projects, horticulture, fishing, herding, or ability to preserve foods. Instead, it came through their nearly universal practice of prolonged lactation.

Breast-feeding was very common in the first three years after childbirth, but among some tribes it lasted for four years and sometimes even longer. Certainly breast-feeding in the first two years had enormous practical benefits, primarily convenience and mobility. It was also valued because it decreased fertility. Because Native American women actively sought to control their populations, breast-feeding was routinely extended past the period where children could easily thrive on solid foods, and frequently more than twice as long as their European counterparts (Forsyth 1827, 20). Along with prolonged lactation, Native American women, like their European counterparts, also practiced infanticide and abortion (Thorton 1987, 31). To guarantee population control, breast-feeding was sometimes combined, as in the case of the Huron and California's Ohlones, with sexual abstinence, a practice also used by many indigenous peoples worldwide, including those who lived along the Amazon and in Africa's Congo basin (Hochschild 1999, 73; Thorton 1987, 31). By carefully controlling their populations, keeping them below the land's "carrying capacity," Indian women made a crucial contribution to their peoples' ability to live easily sustainable lifestyles. Their populations were also periodically checked by factors including wars, droughts, and floods. In addition, they endured "lean" winters, during which limited stores of food ensured that the weakest people did not survive. But these latter factors alone cannot account for the remarkably stable (although larger than previously believed) numbers of Indians estimated to have populated what is now the United States (Mann 2002).

If prevailing gender relations had prohibited Indian women from employing measures of population control, their numbers would have grown unchecked, compromising their people's ability to share resources easily and equitably, to move on to fresh lands for farming or hunting when the old ones had been depleted. The area where a "controlled" burn had flamed out of control could not have simply been abandoned in the confidence that fresh and fertile lands were readily available nearby. The species hunted into local extinction would not have been a provincial problem but a widespread catastrophe. Native American women's active and welcome role in limiting population reflects Indian perceptions of partnership with, rather than stewardship over, the land. It also reflects Indian gender relations, in that women shared more of a sense of control and partnership with their men than did their European counterparts.

Recognition of the role of Native American women's sexuality highlights the crucial, central, and far too frequently overlooked impact of population density in environmental justice. This factor has consequences that carry into the twenty-first century. In 1968 the American Indian Movement (AIM) was created to help Indians displaced by government programs into urban ghettos. AIM's environmental justice goals quickly expanded to encompass not only revitalization of traditional culture, autonomy over tribal lands, and restoration of lands illegally seized, but recognition of traditional native ways as potential solutions to environmental problems nationwide, goals that continue to be sought by various Indian groups today (Banyacya 1993; LaDuke 1999). If the significance of the powerful role pre-Columbian women played in limiting their people's environmental impact is ignored, then traditional Indian practices can (incorrectly) be understood to have been just as environmentally reckless and shortsighted as those of whites (see Krech 1999). According to that perception, modern efforts to protect Indian lands and Indian land-use traditions are pointless exercises that should be abandoned. If Indians were not the "first environmentalists," why should the federal government continue to protect Native American lands and resources, declaring, for example, a moratorium on mining in the Black Hills of northern Cheyenne, Blackfeet, and Crow territory or allow Indians in Washington State to hunt whales? The belief that Indians were no less guilty than whites of negatively impacting the environment "seeks to absolve Europeans of blame [for environmental problems] and ultimately can be used to help fuel a backlash of anti-Native sentiment in this country," particularly when it comes to issues of environmental justice and definitions of "wise use" of resources (Pennybacker 2000, 31).

Enslaved Women: Limiting Population, Forcing Expansion of Land Cultivation

The land-use and population practices of European settlers quickly rendered Indian ways of living obsolete in much of what is now the United States, shattering many traditional links between gender, sexuality, and environmental sustainability. Two examples suggest the spectrum of experiences: Indians in the Great Lakes region turned to the fur trade as their means of survival, while in California Indians supplied the labor for the Spanish missions. In both cases, Indian women did not respond passively to the obliteration of their sustainable land inhabitation practices and the incursions into their peoples' traditions, but, through reproductive choices, practiced cultural self-determination in a number of powerful ways. Susan Sleeper-Smith notes how native women in the western Great Lakes region frequently married French fur traders but strove to maintain their Indian identities. They served as cultural mediators and negotiators of change, largely through extensive kin networks they created and sustained as mothers, grandmothers, and godmothers. These networks facilitated their access to valuable pelts while empowering women to negotiate positions of prominence. But even as women of the Great Lakes used variations of motherhood to enhance female autonomy, in the harsh conditions of many California missions, Indian births were outpaced by deaths not only due to disease, inadequate food supplies, and overwork, but because women consciously limited their reproduction through sexual abstinence, abortion, and infanticide. Sometimes pregnancies were terminated because they were the result of rape, other times because unwed mothers who had engaged in consensual sex would be subjected to questioning and punishment by priests (Hurtado 1992, 384). For a variety of reasons, native women were not complicit in producing large supplies of future mission workers who, bereft of their native culture, would perpetuate their own people as a permanent laboring class carrying out unsustainable environmental practices. And these women were not the only ones in American history to use their very bodies to resist oppression.

The dramatic changes to the relationship between Native Americans and the environment were frequently facilitated by the peoples the invading Europeans brought with them as forced labor. Like the Indians on the missions, the enslaved were not merely passive agents of European desires. They used their environmental knowledge and sexuality to subtly undermine the institution that bound them. Recent studies emphasize the knowledge of abortion and contraception enslaved peoples brought from Africa and the Caribbean (Fett 2002, 65, 176–77; Perrin 2001). Methods used previously to control local populations to their own benefit were adapted in their new situations as forms of resistance to slavery. The demands of forced field labor precluded most enslaved women's ability to breast-feed with sufficient frequency to suppress ovulation. Instead, the environmental knowledge gained in their homelands concerning the use of a number of medicinal plants also available in the New World as abortifacients (especially cotton root) was used. Such practices not only reduced their masters' supplies of new generations of forced laborers, but also served as a kind of strike, since reproduction was considered an important enslaved women's role, contributing to higher prices for women considered to be promising "breeders" (Perrin 2001, 258–59, 263, 266). Enslaved women used their environmental knowledge concerning production to combat the injustice of slavery in other ways as well.

Because most slave owners shared the gendered perception that all men were smarter and more easily trained than women, enslaved men were granted the majority of available "skilled" work. Like the more elite enslaved men, enslaved women also carried out a variety of tasks as house servants, but an additional variety of occupations remained almost exclusively within the male domain: stable worker, blacksmith, driver, horse breaker, cooper, carpenter, and so on. In the nineteenth century, a disproportionate number of women (almost 90 percent) worked in the field, regularly outnumbering their male counterparts. While slave owners may have considered the field work carried out by women to be unskilled labor left to them by default, they nevertheless benefited from the gendered expertise of female field hands. Women's agricultural expertise in rice, indigo, corn, and cotton production stemmed back to specialized knowledge and hand-tool experience gained in their native lands. In turn, observes historian Judith Carney, "subordinated peoples used their own knowledge systems of the environments they settled to reshape the terms of their domination" (2001, 162).

Agricultural experience and wisdom combined with gender roles to empower enslaved women. All family members were, of course, subject to the will of the master, but within the cabins of the enslaved, women generally enjoyed greater gender equity than did their white counterparts. Limiting their masters' supplies of new slaves was only one of many forms of resistance to white tyranny. Another was the passive refusal of field workers to fertilize increasingly depleted cotton fields or to terrace untilled hillsides. Field workers, disproportionately women, rarely refused outright to increase their masters' crop yields, but the expensive tools required were ill used, forever breaking or disappearing mysteriously. Costly fertilizers were applied improperly. So widespread were these actions that slave owners preferred to view them as further proof of their slaves' laziness and stupidity rather than as calculated forms of resistance, and quickly abandoned terracing and fertilizing efforts (Genovese 1993, 238). As the soils became exhausted and cotton yields shrank, expansion onto fresh lands became imperative if King Cotton was to thrive, or even survive.

Prior to the Civil War, many northerners, including Abraham Lincoln, professed not to oppose slavery where it existed, but wished "only" to prevent its spread. To cotton-growing southern whites, because of the crucial issue of soil depletion, to prevent the spread of slavery *was* to bring about its demise. The actions of enslaved field workers, disproportionately female, hastened the necessity for the geographic expansion of slavery. A series of political compromises opened some new territories to the institution, delaying but ultimately not preventing the day of reckoning: the Civil War. In other words, enslaved women's environmental knowledge empowered them to indirectly facilitate their own freedom. Certainly slaves were aware that if they successfully fertilized their masters' fields and increased arable lands by terracing, production would increase, as would white profits and power. Because that increased production would have taken place within southern lands where slavery had long been accepted, even by most in the North, the Cotton South and the institution of slavery would have continued to thrive with little outside opposition. Instead, the passive resistance of women working the fields led to dwindling production as their actions threatened the wealth and position of their white owners, setting off a chain reaction. Fresh soils had to be acquired if the Cotton South and its peculiar institution were to be saved. Northerners, willing to tolerate slavery but not its spread, resisted, and the conflict culminated in the war that freed all

slaves, including those female field workers who had contributed to the urgency
of expansion. Like the Native American women who were considered powerless
due to their gender, race, and status, enslaved women in fact asserted considerable control over the production of lives and of crops, effectively resisting an
oppressive institution. (Not surprisingly, the same people who were so inept as
slaves managed tools and fertilizers quite effectively once they attained their freedom, but only in instances where such expensive resources could be acquired.)

Sexuality Issues in Early Twentieth-Century Foundations of the Modern Environmental Justice Movement

As the United States became increasingly urbanized and industrialized, women
of middle- to upper-class backgrounds played a central leadership role in urban
organizations that promoted reforms including civic cleanliness and sanitation,
smoke and noise abatement, and pure food and drugs, making clear the "absolute
necessity of combating health hazards and pollution for the safety of all citizens" (Melosi 2000, 54). Women's educational programs to promote public
health ranged from persuading citizens not to spit on city sidewalks (thereby
preventing the spread of diseases, including tuberculosis) to alerting tenement
dwellers to the dangers of lead poisoning. They also addressed concerns specific
to women in economically oppressed neighborhoods, promoting healthful food
preparation and proper baby and child care. While the much celebrated "John
Muirs, Gifford Pinchots, and Teddy Roosevelts of the conservation movement
gave little mind to the quality of urban life," lesser-known and frequently female
activists including Alice Hamilton, Jane Addams, and Ellen Swallow Richards
"struggled with the blight of pollution, health hazards, and the physical degradation of cities" (Melosi 2000, 53).

Labor activist Rose Schneiderman railed against hazardous workplace environments where property was held so dear and human lives, especially the lives
of "working girls," so cheap that tragedies like the Triangle Factory fire in New
York City (which killed 146 women, mostly young and Jewish) were common-
place. However, Schneiderman's immigrant and working-class origins as well as
her emphasis on corporate responsibility for urban suffering set her apart from
most of her sister urban reformers. While Schneiderman defended the rights
of working women, other female reformers expressed their concern for these
working "girls" as the future mothers of the race. For example, Elizabeth Beard-
sley Butler, assistant secretary of the Socialist Party's Rand School in New York
City, argued that "the greatest danger was not to the 'girls' but to 'racial vitality' in the form of 'nervous exhaustion,'" ultimately resulting in "undervital-
ized" children (in McClymer 1998, 4–5). As working women's capacity as future
mothers garnered the most attention and sympathy, other issues of sexuality

and reproduction figured prominently in the goals of many female urban reformers.

Many middle- and upper-class reformers associated having large numbers of children with a lack of self-control, a succumbing to animal passions signaling general weakness. Birth control advocate Margaret Sanger, one of eleven children, took a different view. She attributed her mother's premature death to the rigors of frequent childbirth and poverty. She avoided a similar fate for herself, attaining the skills to be financially self-supporting as a practical nurse before marrying and limiting her own family to three children. Working as a visiting nurse among the immigrants in New York City's Lower East Side, Sanger decried the toll of venereal disease, miscarriage, self-induced abortion, and frequent childbirth on the health of poor urban women. She was appalled by impoverished women's sexual subservience to men and the resultant overcrowding and cycle of poverty. Awakened to the connection between contraception (rather than sexual abstinence) and working class women's empowerment by anarchist and feminist Emma Goldman, "Sanger became convinced that liberating women from the risk of unwanted pregnancy would effect fundamental social change" (Katz 2000). Sanger's monthly publication asserting the right of every woman to be "absolute mistress of her own body" resulted in her being charged with violating postal obscenity laws. While in exile in England to escape prosecution, Sanger was profoundly influenced by sexual theorist Havelock Ellis. In 1916, seeking to promote the socioeconomic and sexual empowerment of poor urban women by freeing them both from unwanted pregnancies and the inequality of sexual experience, Sanger opened the nation's first birth control clinic in Brooklyn.

However, as the number and influence of conservative supporters increased, "Sanger's initial focus on women's personal autonomy and empower-ment was subordinated to an emphasis on selective population control," including forced sterilization of the mentally incompetent "and the maintenance of traditional middle-class values" (Katz 2000). Although Sanger never advocated forcibly limiting reproduction based on race, class, or ethnicity, her beliefs in "scientific eugenics" and assertions that some people were more fit than others and therefore worthier of procreation contribute to the assessment that many early urban environmentalists were tainted by contemporary cultural beliefs and values.

The middle- and upper-class status of early urban environmental reformers frequently led them not only to ignore or neglect issues of class and race, but to openly exhibit hostility to various ethnic groups and peoples of color, judging them as inferiors who were as much the cause as the victims of disease and sanitation problems. However, leading environmental scholar Martin Melosi concludes, "The fairest assessment to make about the turn-of-the-century urban environmentalism is that it provides a partial legacy for modern environmental justice activists, rather than no legacy at all" (2000, 55). The role of gender and sexuality in toxic urban environments is evident in this early period, as women were recognized as both unique victims of urban environmental dangers (at home and in the workplace) as well as uniquely qualified to offer relief from some of those burdens.

Heterosexist Backlash to Rachel Carson's Challenge of Postwar Patriarchal Resurgence

Even women's suffrage did not bring an end to American traditions of patriarchy. However, the upheavals caused by two world wars and the intervening depression forced enduring challenges to the traditional gender stereotypes and prescribed spheres. With the Cold War, however, came new, stricter, and more rigid prescriptions. The perception of communism as a powerful threat to American freedoms and ways of life produced a pervasive fear. Patriarchy, Christianity, and especially the heterosexual nuclear family were prescribed as not only socially desirable but politically necessary if the nation was to survive—and to triumph over—the communist menace (May 1988). The ideal American family, glorified as the greatest bulwark against communism, featured a husband and father who produced the family's single income and a wife and mother whose sole occupation was caring for her family, especially catering to her husband's needs and raising a large brood of good patriotic Americans. The lesbian and gay organizations that emerged out of World War II were forced into retreat in the 1950s as homosexuals were widely declared to be especially dangerous to the American social fabric. Individuals identified as homosexual suffered a variety of forms of discrimination, including both housing and employment.

In 1962, with the publication of *Silent Spring*, pioneer ecofeminist Rachel Carson challenged the government's misplaced and ineffectual paternalism. Specifically, she questioned governmental wisdom concerning industrial waste and the vast reliance upon pesticides, especially DDT. *Silent Spring* appeared just one year before Betty Freidan's assault on patriarchy, *The Feminine Mystique*. Both books were roundly criticized. *Silent Spring* was denounced as "hysterically overemphatic" in a scathing review in *Time* magazine. The many denunciations in the popular press of Carson's work as overly emotional reinforced the long-held view of women as unreasoning and inherently hysterical (a word derived from the Greek word "hystera" for womb) (Corbett 2001, 728). She was dismissed contemptuously by most in the scientific community as well. Ezra Taft Benson, an elder in the Mormon church who had been secretary of agriculture in the Eisenhower administration, suggested in a letter to Eisenhower that Carson's unnatural status (her perceived lack, as a never-married woman, of sexual activity) disqualified her from making inquiries in the first place. Benson wondered "why a spinster with no children was so worried about genetics" and settled on the only possible conclusion. Most likely unaware of Carson's private but long-term intimate relationship with Dorothy Freeman, Benson accused her not of lesbianism but of one of the few things possibly even worse: Carson was "probably a Communist" (Graham 1970, 60; Udall 2000, 105).

Carson and Freeman strove to protect their privacy, labeling certain letters in their voluminous correspondence as destined for "the strong box," their code for immediate destruction (Freeman 1995, xvi). Although few people knew of their relationship, numerous stories in the popular press focused on Carson's marital status. She was variously described as "unmarried," "never married," and "a shy female bachelor." Her obituary in *Time* quotes a friend who called her a "nun of nature." Even without charges of lesbianism, such references served to "desex Carson and brand her as not-quite-woman" (Corbett 2001, 729). Carson's defenders, however, also used arguments that hinged on widely held perceptions of gender and sex. In a January 16, 1963, letter to the *Virginia Pilot*, one woman praised Carson for denouncing the highly touted postwar notion that "Father Knows Best" (the title of one of the era's popular TV shows in which a happy, nuclear family is shepherded through life's hazards by a wise and benevolent patriarch): "'Papa' does not always know best. In this instance it seems that 'papa' is taking an arbitrary stand, and we, the people are just supposed to take it, and count the dead animals and birds" (in Norwood 1994, 318). Carson's critique of the country's dependence on chemical pesticides has since been widely recognized as one of the most influential books of the century. Rejecting prevailing sexual stereotypes in her personal and professional life, Carson has been credited with making the public aware of attempts by the scientific-industrial complex to manipulate and control nature, thereby inspiring the environmental movements of the 1960s and 1970s.

Lesbians Create an Alternative Environment

Rachel Carson did not identify as a lesbian, but even her contemporaries who did remained, for the most part, discreet about their sexuality. Advances in population control throughout the 1960s, however, led to the increasing acceptability of nonreproductive sex outside of marriage, weakening the charge that lesbian sexual pleasure was wrong because it did not lead to reproduction (Faderman 1991, 201). In 1969, the Stonewall riots gave birth to the modern gay and lesbian movement. Lesbians claimed the right to their sexuality, rejecting the long-held beliefs that sex was primarily for men's pleasure and that "real" sex took place exclusively between a man and a woman.

A trickle of people, many lesbian, began moving to rural communities across the nation to take part in the back-to-the-land movement, determined to transcend the sexism, homophobia, violence, materialism, and environmental abuse afflicting mainstream society. The proliferation of ecological problems and the ongoing and fruitless war in Vietnam significantly contributed to a radical lesbian-feminist vision of an American nation in such deep trouble that only drastic measures could reverse its course. Women convinced that the root causes of America's problems were the result of male greed, egocentrism, and violence believed that only a culture based on superior female values and women's love for each other could save the nation. Others embraced separatism for different reasons: some lesbians insisted that "women-only" spaces were the only way to ensure that lesbians' needs came first. Living in the country was considered superior to living in cities created and dominated by men because in urban centers both lesbian sexuality and efforts to transform society were constantly oppressed and diverted. Separatism and/or country life were considered crucial in the creation of models that would allow women to reclaim their sexual and environmental rights (Faderman 1991, 216).

In southern Oregon in 1972, the trickle of members of the back-to-the-land movement became "a wave of women immigrants" (Corinne 1998). In their efforts at transvaluation, women erected (or adapted from existing shacks and cabins), small housing units that were easy to build and manage. These tiny residences (frequently less than ten by twelve feet—smaller than Thoreau's cabin at Walden) represented safety, economy, and autonomy. These structures did not dedicate space to entertaining or child rearing due to the conscious rejection of traditional women's roles. The emphasis tended to be collective rather than communal. One resident recalls, "So much of the back to the land movement was about coming out, and coming into our power and identities as Lesbians. We intuitively knew we had to get out of the patriarchal cities, and redefine ourselves and our lives. We actually tried to build a new culture . . . not [just] back to the land but back to ourselves" (in Corinne 1998).

This new culture included "a desire to live lightly on Mother Earth and in sympathy with nature" (Corinne 1998) and was marked by a rejection of the postwar celebration of unbridled human and material production. It de-emphasized permanence and valued salvaged, recycled, and handcrafted materials over those industrially produced and store-bought. Sophisticated technology, heavy machinery, and animal products were eschewed by these women in favor of solar power, hand tools, and vegetarian organic foods in their desire to protect the environment as part of a larger effort to combat the evils of patriarchy and heterosexism.

Sexuality Issues in Modern Environmental Justice Campaigns by Women of All Red Nations

Women of All Red Nations (WARN) was established in the 1970s by Native American women to strengthen themselves and their families in the face of ongoing attacks on Indian culture, health, and lands. Cofounder Lorelei DeCora Means argued that while tribal people as a whole suffered the ongoing injustices of colonization, "On reservations Indian women and children bore the greater burden of poor nutrition, inadequate health care, and forced or deceptive sterilization programs; Native women and children also faced higher levels of domestic violence resulting from poverty, joblessness, substance abuse, and hopelessness" (in Zheng 2002). Many WARN members were motivated by a variety of factors in addition to maternal concerns, including rights and responsibilities in regard to values based in gendered traditions such as matrilineal inheritance of property and women's spiritual power. In addition, many native men had died as a result of their work as miners (the risk of lung cancer for miners increased by a factor of at least eighty-five), leaving their widows to band together seeking compensation (Barry 1979, 25–28).

Since the 1950s, in a series of actions later denounced as "Plundering the Powerless," lands held by Chicanos and especially by Native Americans had been aggressively gutted for uranium (Robinson 1979, 3). In 1980, one of WARN's activities was to draw attention to health concerns involving reproduction, specifically the fantastically high increase in miscarriages, birth defects, and childhood deaths due to cancer on affected Indian reservations in western South Dakota, Nebraska, and the Southwest. WARN noted, for example, that on the Pine Ridge reservation the miscarriage rate for the previous five years averaged 6.35 times higher than the U.S. average (Lifsey 1980). WARN's emphasis on the drastic increase in childhood cancers of the reproductive organs (at least fifteen times the national average) made the demands for action by mothers particularly compelling. But efforts were also made to use the issue of motherhood to undermine the women's campaign. When asked in a public meeting by Indian Health Service officials to comment on health issues important to women in 1980, Lakota women reported alarming statistics of miscarriages and high cancer rates, which they attributed to contaminated water supplies. Government officials changed the subject to fetal alcohol syndrome, implying that in fact mothers were to blame for a variety of the birth defects (Battese 1980).

WARN repeatedly emphasized the importance of reproduction in cultural self-determination. Its members saw their reproductive rights threatened by their contaminated surroundings as well as by more direct efforts to curtail their populations. WARN worked to inform Native American women of their rights to resist an aggressive government-funded mass sterilization program WARN termed genocidal, citing a 1973 General Accounting Office study showing that more than 50,000 Indian women had been sterilized either without their knowledge or under duress, rendering infertile 23 percent of all Indian women of childbearing age west of the Mississippi. "The plan of sterilization is one way that the government has of weakening our nations," the organization warned. "To get control of our land it would be much easier if our numbers got smaller.

We must think hard about keeping our right to bring life to the next generation."
WARN stressed the current generation's responsibility: "We must preserve
our rights for the next generation to live the way we want to—SOVEREIGN!"
(WARN document n.d.). At a WARN sovereignty workshop, Indian women were
told they "must lead." Activists urged them, "Control your own reproduction:
not only just the control of the reproduction of yourselves . . . but control of
the reproduction of your own food supplies, your own food systems" to rebuild
traditional native cultures and ways of living with the earth (WARN Report 2
1979).

Conclusion

Toxic waste facilities, pollution emissions, and health risks from air pollution
disproportionately affect communities of color, setting the stage for the modern environmental justice movement. Concerned with a variety of issues,
including those surrounding reproduction, African American women and Latinas
in particular continue to play a prominent role in organizations in these communities, waging campaigns against environmental dangers in the workplace
and the home, especially in areas known as "brown fields" because of their toxicity (Bolton and Unger 2002). They are part of a rich and varied history.
Women's perspectives on their environments and their contributions to environmental reform have changed dramatically across time and space, especially
as affected by class, race, and prescribed gender roles. Yet the impact of women's
sexuality, ranging from cultural self-determination to environmental sustainability, pervades environmental justice issues throughout American history.

NOTES

A presidential grant and a research grant from the Center for Science, Technology,
and Society at Santa Clara University supported the research for this essay, portions
of which were delivered as Gonzaga University's William L. Davis, S.J., Lecture (Feb. 1,
2001), and to the EPA, Section 10, in Seattle, Washington (Mar. 20, 2002). Don White-
bread and Mary Whisner provided editing expertise.

REFERENCES

Banyacya, T. 1993. "Hopi Leaders on the Desecration of Their Sacred Lands, 1970." In
    Major Problems in American Environmental History, ed. Carolyn Merchant. Lexing-
    ton, Mass.: D.C. Heath.
Barry, T. 1979. "Bury My Lungs at Red Rock." Progressive (Feb.): 25–28.
Battese, J. 1980. "Health Study Presentation in Pierre." LAND Papers, Box 7, file 14. Wiscon-
    sin Historical Society, Madison. Mar. 27.
Blum, E. 2001. "Linking American Women's History and Environmental History: A Prelimi-
    nary Historiography." *H-Environment* (May 28) *http://www2.h-net.msu/edu/~envi-
    ron/historiography/*.

Bolton, M., and N. Unger. 2002. "Pollution, Refineries, and People." In *The Modern Demon: Pollution in Urban and Industrial European Societies*, ed. Christoph Bernhardt and Geneviève Massard-Guilbaud. Clermont-Ferrand: l'Universite Blaise Pascal.

Carney, J. 2001. *Black Rice*. Cambridge: Harvard University Press.

Corbett, J. 2001."Women, Scientists, Agitators: Magazine Portrayal of Rachel Carson and Theo Colborn." *Journal of Communication* 51: 720–49.

Corinne, T. 1998. "Little Houses on Women's Lands." *http://lib.usc.edu/~retter/tee-houses.html*.

Cronon, W. 1983. *Changes in the Land: Indians, Colonists, and the Ecology of New England*. New York: Hill and Wang.

Devens, C. 1986. "Separate Confrontations: Gender as a Factor in Indian Adaptation to European Colonization in New France." *American Quarterly* 38: 461–80.

———. 1992. "'If We Get the Girls, We Get the Race': Missionary Education of Native American Girls." *Journal of World History* 3, no. 2: 219–37.

Faderman, L. 1991. *Odd Girls and Twilight Lovers*. New York: Columbia University Press.

Fett, S. 2002. *Healing, Health, and Power on Southern Plantations*. Chapel Hill: University of North Carolina Press.

Forsyth, T. 1827. "Manners and Customs of the Sauk and Fox Nations of Indians." Thomas Forsyth Papers. Lyman Draper Manuscripts. 9T. Wisconsin Historical Society, Madison.

Freeman, M., ed. 1995. *Always, Rachel: The Letters of Rachel Carson and Dorothy Freeman, 1952–1964*. Boston: Beacon Press.

Genovese, E. 1993. "Soils Abused." In *Major Problems in American Environmental History*, ed. Carolyn Merchant. Lexington, Mass.: D.C. Heath.

Graham, F. 1970. *Since Silent Spring*. Boston: Houghton Mifflin.

Hochschild, A. 1999. *King Leopold's Ghost*. New York: First Mariner Books.

Hurtado, A. 1992. "Sexuality in California's Franciscan Missions: Cultural Perceptions and Sad Realities." *California History* 72 (fall): 370–85.

Katz, E. 2000. "Sanger, Margaret." *American National Biography Online*.

Krech, S. 1999. *The Ecological Indian: Myth and History*. New York: Norton.

LaDuke, W. 1995. "The Indigenous Women's Network: Our Future, Our Responsibility." *http://www.igc.org/beijing/plenary/laduke.html*.

———. 1999. *All Our Relations: Native Struggles for Land and Life*. Cambridge: South End.

Lifsey, E. 1980. "WARN Findings Confirmed: McGovern's Office 'Misled.'" *Black Hills Report*.

Mann, C. 2002. "1491." *Atlantic Monthly* Mar.: 41–53.

May, E. 1988. *Homeward Bound: American Families in the Cold War Era*. New York: Basic Books.

McClymer, J. 1998. *The Triangle Strike and Fire*. Orlando: Harcourt Brace.

Melosi, M. 2000. "Environmental Justice, Political Agenda Setting, and the Myths of History." *Journal of Policy History* 12, no. 1: 43–71.

Merchant, C. 1995. *Earthcare: Women and the Environment*. New York: Routledge.

Norwood, V. 1994. "Rachel Carson." In *The American Radical*, ed. Mari Jo Buhle. New York: Routledge.

Pennybacker, M. 2000. "The First Environmentalists." *Nation* (Feb. 7): 29–31.

Perrin, L. 2001. "Resisting Reproduction: Reconsidering Slave Contraception in the Old South." *Journal of American Studies* 35: 255–74.

Robinson, G. 1979. "Plundering the Powerless." *Environmental Action* (June): 3–5.

Sleeper-Smith, S. 2000. "Women, Kin, and Catholicism: New Perspectives on the Fur Trade." *Ethnohistory* 47, no. 2: 423–52.

Thorton, R. 1987. *American Indian Holocaust and Survival: A Population History Since 1492.* Norman: University of Oklahoma.

Udall, S. 2000. "How the Wilderness Was Won." *American Heritage* (Feb.–Mar.): 98–105.

WARN document. n.d. LAND Papers, Box 7, file 14. Wisconsin Historical Society, Madison.

WARN Report 2. 1979. "The Sovereignty Workshop." June–Dec. LAND Papers, Box 7, file 14. Wisconsin Historical Society, Madison.

Zheng, R. 2002. "Women of All Red Nations: Female Leadership and Initiatives." Mar. 4. *http://manila.cet.middlebury.edu/rzheng/stories/storyReader$26.* (Aug. 14, 2002).

PART TWO

Gender, Sexuality, and Activism

3

Feminist Theory and Environmental Justice

ROBERT R. M. VERCHICK

It may be surprising to learn that the environmental movement's next revolution is now being plotted around kitchen tables. In inner cities, in rural poverty pockets, and on Indian reservations, poor people and people of color are meeting in kitchens and living rooms, organizing coalitions, and speaking out against pollution that threatens their families and communities. These campaigns, collectively called the "environmental justice movement," challenge traditional environmental policy, which has too often benefited the affluent at the expense of the poor.

What is more, many of America's most visible and effective environmental justice organizations are led by and consist mainly of women (Austin and Schill 1994, 62; Birkeland 1993, 51; Setterberg and Shavelson 1993, 265). Thus, while "environmental justice" describes an environmental movement and a civil rights movement, it also describes a *women*'s movement, and, I suggest, a *feminist* movement as well.

This essay examines how female activists and feminist legal theory have shaped the environmental justice movement. It shows how methods associated with feminism have contributed to the movement's primary concerns for family safety and social equality, and how the movement has so far prompted creative ways to identify and attack a broad range of environmental threats.

Women in the Movement

It is almost impossible to discuss the environmental justice without considering the participation of women. Sometimes the names of the organizations underscore their leadership: the "Mothers of East Los Angeles," for instance, or "Mothers' Air Watch" of Texarkana, Arkansas. Women's participation is also obvious on organization membership rolls and on the streets. From homemakers organizing against toxic incinerators, to Native American women fighting nuclear waste, to rural farmworkers challenging the use of dangerous pesticides, women are everywhere in the environmental justice movement.

Why are women so active in such campaigns? The best answers come from female activists themselves, who often describe their motivations in terms of family roles and social connections. Many activists, as the primary caretakers of young children in the home, attribute their work to a special concern for family health and safety. They see their work as the natural extension of the nurturing and parenting role (Farenthold 1988, xxii).

Other activists speculate that women are more likely to challenge existing institutions in order to redress a wrong. Bernice Kaczynski, who spearheaded an opposition movement against the siting of a General Motors plant in her Polish American neighborhood, told an interviewer: "[W]omen are more aggressive, really. I think we find it more natural to go out and fight for what we think is right. I think the men, a lot of the time, just let go. They figure it's a lost cause. But that's not the attitude to take" (Garland 1988, 29–30). Some commentators speculate that men are more likely to lay down the sword because they are more likely to hold large stakes in the economic and political institutions that create environmental harms. Women, in contrast, may be more likely to associate misfortune with an illegitimate system, and thus be more likely to rebel against it (Farenthold 1988, xii). Law professor Carrie Menkel-Meadow has argued that women in general appear especially adept at networking and advising people (Menkel-Meadow 1985, 57). Perhaps these skills have helped organizers put environmental justice on the map.

Feminist Legal Theory in the Movement

The environmental justice movement can be described as a feminist movement in two senses. First, the movement pursues goals important to women's lives. To the extent that women remain the primary caregivers in their homes and communities, the responsibility over family health remains an immediate and primary goal for them. Because women may be more vulnerable than men to some environmental dangers, concern for their own health and that of their family is a primary concern.

Second, environmental justice activists have generally pursued their goals in ways that reflect "feminist legal methods" developed by women's rights activists and feminist legal scholars in the late 1960s and early 1970s. Although descriptions vary, the fundamentals of feminist legal methods include unmasking patriarchy, contextual reasoning, and consciousness raising (Bartlett 1990, 836–37). Each of these methods appears prominently in environmental justice campaigns.

Unmasking Patriarchy

Feminists often begin their critique of law with a series of questions designed to reveal male biases that lie beneath supposedly "neutral" law. By attempting to "unmask" patriarchy in this way, feminists seek to identify the gender implications of society's laws and show that such effects are not inevitable. Implicit is the argument that even the most seemingly neutral aspects of law conceal "the substantive way in which man has become the measure of all things" (Mackinnon 1987, 34).

Just as feminists challenge the inevitability of employment benefits by exposing male biases in, say, workplace management, environmental justice activists challenge the inevitability of distributional unfairness by unmasking biases in environmental protection. The process of exposing these biases begins by asking a variation of what law professor Kathleen Bartlett calls "the woman question," namely, How does law (in our case, environmental law) fail to take into account the experiences and values of women, particularly those whose daily lives are afflicted with environmental problems? And, to follow up: How might some features of the law reflect nonneutral values associated with white patriarchy?

In answering these questions, environmental justice advocates have composed a litany of the ways in which the poor, people of color, women, and other marginalized groups bear the brunt of environmental harm (Rechtenshaffen and Gauna 2002, 65). This inequality in exposure to environmental harm flows directly from a failure to consider the experiences and values of these groups. Examples come readily. A county board votes to allow a hazardous waste incinerator in a town of mainly Latino farm workers without furnishing the means for non-English-speaking residents to read or comment in Spanish on the impact studies (Cole 1993–94, 74–77). A report suggests that inspectors for the U.S. Environmental Protection Agency (EPA) prefer to inspect waste-generating facilities in the suburbs, rather than ghettos, which then leads to slower cleanups at sites in poor communities and communities of color (Lazarus 1993–94, 5). Or a battery manufacturing plant allows levels of workplace contaminants that appear safe for male workers but not female workers *(International Union, UAW v. Johnson Controls)*. Inattention to these groups' experiences and values is buttressed by the false, but widespread, belief that many marginalized groups do not care about environmental issues.

Yet despite the similarity between the critiques of feminism and grassroots environmentalism, a significant difference calls attention to itself at almost every turn: the critical lens of environmental justice focuses not only on patriarchy, but on all the intersections of bias (including racism, classism, and ageism) that surround and permeate environmental issues. This suggests that while feminist theory may throw light on grassroots environmental activism, feminist theories may also be made richer and more sophisticated through an analysis of environmental justice.

Contextual Reasoning

Feminist theory is, at its core, an exploration of the actual. Whatever the appeal of broad principles or abstract rules, such tools cannot lead to justice unless they are understood and applied in ways that acknowledge the real-life experiences of those affected. Thus, when examining legal or social issues, feminists pay special attention to the personal and social history of the parties, relative perceptions among the parties, and overall context.

As law professor Mari Matsuda writes, "who makes breakfast, who gets a paycheck, who gets whistled at in the street—all the experiences of daily life are a part of the distribution of wealth and power in society" (Matsuda 1986, 618).

Grassroots environmental movements grow from the values and experiences of real people. Environmental justice activists, mainly women and people of color, bring previously unheard "bottom-up" perspectives to environmental issues. Drawing from both intuition and empirical analysis, these activists see connections between social welfare and the environment, pollution and the home, and connections between pollution and discrimination that have gone unnoticed (or ignored) by mainstream environmentalists. These connections expand the scope of environmentalism, supplement the ways in which we identify environmental problems, and propose new explanations for them.

Traditional environmentalists often promoted an image of "environment" as something removed from everyday experience. The word conjured images of undeveloped, exotic, and sometimes faraway places—Yellowstone, the Oregon Coast, or the Florida Everglades. Similarly, environmental "harm" suggested harm to these places or to the wildlife that inhabited them. This telescopic view of environmentalism significantly influenced the direction of environmental policy in the United States.

Environmental justice activists expand this view of environment. For them environment also means the places where they live and work—an Indian reservation, an African American neighborhood in Dallas, or the barrios of South Central Los Angeles. Harm to that environment includes not only the contamination of natural resources (toxic soil, poisoned water, dirty air), but anything in the environment that threatens human health and safety. Thus, lead poisoning of children, traditionally seen as a "health" or "housing" issue, is now described by many activists as an "environmental" problem (Calpotura and Sen 1994, 234). Similarly, activists now use the language of environmental harm to describe human exposure to harmful chemicals in enclosed manufacturing plants (Nelson 1990, 178), and even infestations of rats in low-income housing (Cole 1992, 679–82).

If local context enables activists to expand the definition of environmental harm, it also allows them to better identify such harms when they appear. Scientific experts and government officials, far removed from a contaminated site, are sometimes slow to link health problems or property damage to environmental contamination. In contrast, residents of polluted communities, who every day tend the gardens, do the laundry, and care for their children, are much more likely to notice the first clues of environmental threat.

Consider Cathy Hinds, a mother turned activist who discovered well-water contamination in her rural community in Maine. Her first evidence involved a series of observations in the home, including laundry stains, dizzy spells among family members, and warm bath water that felt scalding hot on the skin (Garland 1993, 90–105). Grassroots activists across the country have similarly found clues to environmental harm from rat infestations, a child's earaches, ulcers, or miscarriages (Setterberg and Shavelson 1993, 45–46).

Sometimes the connections that residents draw between problems in the household and pollution are first minimized by experts or government officials (Krauss 1993, 111–13). When Hinds first expressed concern about her well water to her doctor, he first "dismissed the idea and prescribed tranquilizers" (Garland 1993, 91). Activists respond by adopting a "dual" strategy in which they accumulate the scientific data and form technical arguments to persuade their listeners while continuing to confront them with the faces of real people who are being harmed.

Contextual reasoning also enables activists to link environmental threats to racism, sexism, and other forms of discrimination. The dynamic of oppression, after all, is something many female and minority activists experience every day. Living in a society in which race and gender play a role in determining what we earn, how we are educated, and where we live, it is hardly surprising that women and people of color would view their sometimes alarming exposure to pollution as related to other forms of discrimination. In this way, their reasoning recalls the efforts of earlier feminists who used women's experiences of past discrimination to develop theories that described sexual harassment and the denial of abortion services in terms of sex discrimination. Environmental justice advocates have also employed contextual reasoning, combining personal stories and empirical data, to convince others of the connection between pollution and discrimination.

Consciousness Raising

Consciousness raising describes the process by which individuals share personal experiences with one another in an effort to derive collective significance or meaning from those experiences (Bartlett 1990, 863–64). Its catalysts are what Virginia Woolf called "the arts of human intercourse; the art of understanding other people's lives and minds, and the little arts of talk" (Woolf 1938, 34). Through consciousness raising, women begin to view what otherwise might appear as isolated instances of insensitivity or chauvinism as symptoms of broader societal oppression.

A common environmental justice motto is "We speak for ourselves" (Cole 1995, 11). The words suggest unity, autonomy, and, of course, communication. The sharing of ideas—among activists and with outside groups or institutions—is essential to the movement's ambitious goal of mobilizing neglected communities and transforming the meaning of environmental protection. By speaking for themselves, grassroots environmental groups promote consciousness raising both in the ways in which they organize and in the procedural solutions they seek in environmental law.

Just as feminists in the 1970s and 80s discovered the prevalence of domestic violence and sexual harassment through informal discussion groups, grassroots activists today discover the prevalence and institutional character of environmental inequities. Often activists begin to identify local environmental threats by noting a common health problem and then searching for a potential cause.

Identifying the problem and causes by group exploration sets the foundation of future activism. Frances Farenthold writes, "After talking and listening comes education—educating oneself and the community about the issues. Becoming expert and establishing credibility are closely associated with this process, and they become foundations for action" (Farenthold 1988, xx). The need for personal contact and feedback is constant. Also, grassroots activists emphasize the importance of rewarding themselves for good efforts and making activities "fun."

Hierarchical structures, common in many mainstream environmental groups and governmental agencies, have little presence here. Professor Cynthia Hamilton, for instance, notes that for more than a year the Concerned Citizens of South Central Los Angeles functioned "without a formal leadership structure." News reporters, she writes, "were disoriented when they asked for the spokesperson and the group responded that everyone could speak for the neighborhood" (Hamilton 1994, 214).

Such democratic and interactive organizing methods produce a number of advantages. The continual sharing of information and ideas promotes a "self-reflexive" learning style that acknowledges the positional nature of knowledge and includes diverse perspectives. Such interaction also helps maintain momentum in efforts that will span months or years. Finally, an openness to new perspectives and a downplaying of hierarchy helps build local and national coalitions, which are essential for a sustained commitment to environmental justice.

Consciousness raising allows activists to create a new kind of environmentalist. Here we find not Edward Abbey, a lone voice mourning the loss of Southwestern deserts, or the anonymous face of bureaucracy but rather a dynamic and interactive network of citizen-activists struggling together to protect their homes. This impulse toward discussion and deliberation typifies the solutions that environmental justice advocates seek from governmental institutions. For instance, social scientist Robert Bullard advocates more participation for minority community members in the land-use planning process, so that community concerns can be communicated to and considered by decision makers (Bullard 1993, 13). Deeohn Ferris, executive director of the Washington Office of Environmental Justice, urges Congress to allow local communities more participation in fashioning remedies under the Superfund laws (Ferris 1994, 673). Law professor Eileen Gauna argues that federal citizen-suit provisions should be interpreted so as to allow greater involvement of poor and minority communities in the enforcement of environmental laws (Gauna 1995, 22). Indeed, opening lines of communication and opportunities for joint decision making between local communities and government is a primary solution sought by environmental justice advocates.

In addition, advocates also urge changes in agencies themselves. Deeohn Ferris recommends the creation of a federal interagency council that would be responsible for meeting regularly with community organizations to identify and address environmental problems (Ferris 1993–94, 115). Law professor Richard Lazarus argues for more decentralization in environmental policy making. With a looser, flatter hierarchical structure, he hopes that agency officials will be better able to educate themselves about community concerns. Commentators also seek more diversity in such agencies as the EPA so as to better include the perspectives of women and people of color (Lazarus 1993, 850–52). These recommendations can be seen as attempts to formalize consciousness raising in government structure.

An Illustration: Feminist Theory, Environmental Justice, and the Assessment of Risk

Because risk assessment plays an essential role in environmental protection, it provides a useful setting for examining the relationship between feminist theory and environmental justice. As classically defined, risk is a product of "the severity of the threatened harm, and the probability of its occurrence" (Folk 1991, 187). Federal agencies use assessment of risk to determine acceptable levels of toxins in setting environmental and occupational safety standards (ibid.). Thus the process of assessing risk and determining minimum levels of risk influences a broad gamut of health issues, including the location of polluting facilities, the designation of "Superfund sites," the cleanup standards for Superfund sites, and the speed with which such facilities are cleaned up. Laws regulating solid waste, pesticides, water quality, and air quality similarly incorporate health assessments to define the minimum standards of human safety.

Many reasons exist to doubt the efficacy of risk assessments as currently employed. Much of the risk assessment data are manipulable and could easily be used by "captured" agencies to satisfy corporate or political goals. The acceptability standards applied to such findings are often inconsistent among safety and environmental laws and serve to protect some groups more than others. Further, many EPA programs fail to collect or consider data on potentially exposed people and instead rely on more generalized findings.

For the purposes of this essay, I will focus on two other very significant criticisms that directly affect feminism and environmental justice: (1) most health studies do not consider the variation in vulnerability to environmental threats among different groups, and (2) the process of identifying and evaluating risk does not sufficiently incorporate community perceptions and fears. Analysis of these topics illustrates how the feminist methods of unmasking, contextual reasoning, and consciousness raising can be used. These methods point to a framework that could be adopted by policy makers working to address environmental justice issues.

Risk Assessment: Beyond "One Size Fits All"

All people do not respond to environmental insults in the same way. As many scientists and environmental agencies acknowledge, the likelihood of suffering adverse health effects from exposure to pollutants is significantly greater for members of some groups (Nelson 1990, 176–78). Women, for instance, may be more susceptible to PCBs, dioxins, and other dangerous chemicals that bioaccumulate in fatty tissue (Swanston 1994, 592). Evidence suggests that certain chemical exposures are more likely to damage women's immune systems (Nelson 1990, 176–77). Women in childbearing years may be more susceptible to ozone exposure (Fox et al. 1993, 242–44). Environmental degradation also threatens women's capacity to bear and nurse healthy children (Eggen 1992, 848–51).

Biological and social factors also make other groups more susceptible to certain environmental threats. Some of these differences, such as smaller average lung capacity in African Americans as compared with whites, are, in fact, reflected in occupational safety standards (Swanston 1994, 589). The fact that minority groups and the poor suffer disproportionately from asthma, anemia, cardiovascular disease, and are more likely to give birth to low-weight babies also makes them more vulnerable to the cumulative effects of toxic exposure (ibid.). Similarly, young children and the elderly may also be at higher risk from certain levels of exposure (ibid., 595).

Most environmental agencies recognize the existence of such variations, but have done little to protect these more sensitive groups in any consistent way. Citing the lack of information about sensitive subgroups, the EPA often falls back on analysis based on toxic exposures to the "average" person (ibid., 590). This "average" person, of course, cannot reflect the higher sensitivity levels of certain minorities, young children, fetuses, or women in childbearing years. Indeed, this "average" person is usually a white man (Latin 1988, 140).

Although the lack of data on subpopulations may explain why the EPA does not currently incorporate more particularized information into its risk analysis, it does not explain why greater strides in this direction are not being contemplated for the future (Swanston 1994, 599–600). I suggest two related reasons. First, as environmental justice advocates have pointed out, the mainstream environmental movement has always shown more concern for reducing environmental degradation in the aggregate than for distributing the resulting gains and losses equitably among society's members. Second, this arrangement is not likely to be challenged by policy makers because the "average" susceptibility level on which protective regulations are based is not an average at all, but rather a level based on the vulnerabilities of those making policy, namely white men. (This effect may not be intentional.) Thus we return to the feminist notion that beneath society's normative or "average" standards, "man is the measure of all things." To solve the problem, we must collect more information about the variations in susceptibility among groups and enact stricter baseline protections for all.

Community Perception: Beyond Neutrality

Because risk assessment is based on statistical measures of risk, it is often thought to be an accurate and objective tool in establishing environmental standards. Feminism challenges this model of scientific risk assessment on at least three levels. First, feminism questions the assumption that scientific inquiry is value neutral, that is, free of societal bias or prejudice.

Second, even if scientific inquiry, by itself, were value-neutral, environmental regulation based on such inquiry would necessarily contain subjective elements. Environmental regulation, like any other product of democracy, inevitably reflects elements of subjectivity, compromise, and self-interest. The technocratic language of regulation serves only to "mask, not eliminate, political and social considerations" (Bartlett 1990, 862).

Finally, feminists would argue that questions involving the risk of death and disease should not even aspire to value neutrality. Such decisions—which affect not only today's generations, but those of the future—should be made with all related political and moral considerations plainly on the table. In addition, policy makers should look to all perspectives, especially those of society's most vulnerable members, to develop as complete a picture of the moral issues as possible.

Debates about scientific risk assessment and public values often appear as a tug of war between the "technicians," who would apply only value-neutral

criteria to set regulatory standards, and the "public," who demand that psychological perceptions and contextual factors also be considered. Environmental
justice advocates, strongly concerned with the practical experiences of threatened communities, argue convincingly for the latter position.

But a feminist critique of the issue suggests the debate is more complicated. For feminists, value neutrality simply does not exist. The debate between
technicians and the public is not merely a contest between science and feelings, but a broader discussion about the methods, values, and attitudes to
which each group subscribes. The parties to this discussion divide into more
than two categories. Because one's worldview is premised on many things,
including personal experience, one should expect that subgroups within either
category will differ in significant ways from other subgroups.

This critique makes sense. Scientists disagree among themselves about the
hazards of nuclear waste, ozone depletion, and global warming. Many critics
have argued that scientists, despite their allegiance to rational method, are
nonetheless influenced by personal and political views (Cross 1994, 890 n. 5).
Similarly, one should not be surprised to see politicians, land developers, and
blue-collar workers disagreeing about environmental standards for essentially
nonscientific reasons. In order to better understand the diversity of risk perception and to see how attitudes and social status affect the risk assessment
process, we must return to a feminist inquiry that explores the relationship
between attitudes and identity.

A national survey, conducted by James Flynn, Paul Slovic, and C. K. Mertz,
measured the risk perceptions of a group of 1,512 people, which included pro-
portional numbers of men, women, whites, and nonwhites (Flynn, et al. 1994,
1101). Respondents answered questions about the health risks of twenty-five
environmental, technological, and "lifestyle" hazards, including such hazards as
ozone depletion, chemical waste, and cigarette smoking.

The researchers found that perceptions of risk generally differed on the
lines of gender and race. Women, for instance, perceived greater risk from most
hazards than did men (ibid., 1102–4). Furthermore, nonwhites as a group perceived greater risk from most hazards than did whites (ibid., 1105). Yet the most
striking results appeared when the researchers considered differences in gender and race together. They found that "white males tended to differ from
everyone else in their attitudes and perceptions—on average, they perceived
risks as much smaller and much more acceptable than did other people" (ibid.,
1101). Indeed, without exception, the pool of white men perceived each of the
twenty-five hazards as less risky than did nonwhite men, white women, or nonwhite women (ibid., 1103). Even after correcting for differences in income, education, political orientation, the presence of children in the home, and age, the
results remained clear: "Gender, race, and 'white male' [status] remained highly
significant predictors of the hazard index" (ibid., 1107).

From a feminist perspective, these findings suggest that risk assessors, politicians, and bureaucrats—the large majority of whom are white men—may be acting on attitudes about security and risk that women and people of color do not share. If this is so, white men, as the "measurers of all things," have crafted a system of environmental protection that is biased toward their subjective understandings of the world.

Flynn, Slovic, and Mertz speculate that white men's perceptions of risk may differ from those of others because in many ways women and people of color are "more vulnerable, because they benefit less from many of [society's] technologies and institutions, and because they have less power and control" (ibid.). Although Flynn, Slovic, and Mertz are careful to say that they have not yet tested this hypothesis empirically, their explanation appears consistent with the life experiences of less empowered groups and comports with previous understanding about the roles of control and risk perception.

Women and people of color, for instance, are more vulnerable to environmental threat in several ways. Such groups are more biologically vulnerable than are white men. People of color are more likely to live near hazardous waste sites, to breathe dirty air in urban communities, and to be otherwise exposed to environmental harm. Women, because of their traditional role as primary caretakers, are more likely to be aware of the vulnerabilities of their children. It makes sense that such vulnerabilities would give rise to increased fear about risk.

It is also very likely that women and people of color believe they benefit less from the technical institutions that create toxic by-products. People may be more likely to discount risk if they feel somehow compensated for the activity (Cross 1994, 926). Risk perception research frequently emphasizes the significance of voluntariness in evaluating risk. Thus a person may view water skiing as less risky than breathing polluted air because the former is undertaken voluntarily (ibid., 914). Voluntary risks are viewed as more acceptable in part because they are products of autonomous choice. A risk accepted voluntarily is also one from which a person is more likely to derive an individual benefit and one over which a person is more likely to retain some kind of control. Some studies have found that people prefer voluntary risks to involuntary risks by a factor of 1,000 to 1 (Morgan 1990, 21).

Although environmental risks are generally viewed as involuntary risks, white men are still more likely to exercise greater choice in assuming environmental risks than other groups. Communities of color face greater difficulty in avoiding the placement of hazardous facilities in their neighborhoods and are more likely to live in areas with polluted air and lead contamination. Families of color wishing to buy their way out of such polluted neighborhoods often find their mobility limited by housing discrimination, redlining by banks, and residential segregation (Bullard 1993, 27). Environmental hazards in the workplace similarly present workers (a disproportionate number of whom are minority) with impossible choices between health and work, or between sterilization and demotion.

Just as marginalized groups have less choice in determining the degree of risk they will assume, they may feel less control over the risks they face. For this reason, people often fear flying in an airplane more than driving a car, despite the fact that flying is statistically safer (Cross 1994, 921). If white men are more complacent about public risks, it is perhaps because they are more likely to have their hands on the steering wheel when such risks are confronted. White men still control the major political and business institutions in this country. They also dominate the sciences and make up the vast majority of management staff at environmental agencies. Women and people of color see this disparity and often lament their backseat role in shaping environmental policy. Thus many people of color in the environmental justice movement believe that environmental laws work to their disadvantage *by design*. The toxic air of Louisiana's "Cancer Alley," the extensive poisoning of rural Native American land, and the mismanaged cleanup of the weapons manufacturing site in Hanford, Washington, only promote the feeling that American environmentalism sacrifices the weak for the benefit of the strong.

In addition, the catastrophic potential that groups other than white men associate with a risk may explain the perception gap between those groups and white males. Studies of risk perception show that, in general, individuals harbor particularly great fears of catastrophe (Cross 1994, 921). Local environmental threats involving toxic dumps, aging smelters, or poisoned wells produce high concentrations of localized harm that can appear catastrophic to those involved.

Some commentators contend that the catastrophic potential of a risk should influence risk assessment in only minimal ways (ibid., 923–24). Considering public fear of catastrophes, they argue, will irrationally lead policy makers to battle more dramatic but statistically less threatening hazards while accepting more harmful but more mundane hazards (ibid., 921–22). At least two reasons explain why the catastrophic potential of environmental hazards must be given weight in risk assessment. First, concentrated and localized environmental hazards do not simply harm individuals, they erode family ties and community relationships. An onslaught of miscarriages or birth defects in a neighborhood, for instance, will create community-wide stress that will debilitate the neighborhood in emotional, sociological, and economic ways. To ignore this communal harm is to severely underestimate the true risk involved.

Second, because concentrated and localized environmental hazards tend to be unevenly distributed on the basis of race and income level, any resulting mass injury to a threatened population takes on profound moral character. For this reason, Native Americans often characterize the military's poisoning of Indian land as "genocide."

Flynn, Slovic, and Mertz challenge the traditional, static view of statistical risk with a richer, more vibrant image involving relationships of power, status, and trust (Flynn et al. 1994, 1107). "In short, 'riskiness' means more to people than 'expected number of fatalities'" (Slovic 1983, 285). These findings affirm the feminist claim that public policy must consider both logic and local experience in addressing a problem. Current attempts to "reeducate" fearful communities only through risk assessments and scientific seminars are, therefore, destined to fail. By the same token, even dual approaches that combine science and experience will fall short if the appeal to experience does not track local priorities and values.

If developers and government officials are ever to win the acceptance of less empowered groups, they must move beyond one-way conversation. Society must explore new methods of participation and power sharing. Such efforts must be pursued with the primary goal of engendering a relationship of trust among all participants; for only by gaining trust can one hope to persuade.

Legal commentators have also suggested ways to help promote a more equal distribution of environmental benefits and burdens. Some call for the diversification of state and federal agencies and mainstream environmental groups to better reflect the perspectives of women and people of color (Lazarus 1993, 820–21, 851). Others recommend reforming Superfund's community outreach mechanisms and increasing citizen participation in siting decisions (Freeman and Godsil 1994, 570–71; Folk 1991, 214–15). Regulatory agencies could also be required to consider the distributional effects that their actions have on women and children.

Conclusion

Solutions to environmental injustice, in the field of risk assessment and elsewhere, will ultimately be judged on their incorporation of the values and experiences of marginalized groups. Feminism can guide environmental policy makers by challenging them to unmask hidden biases in environmental law, to bring personal experience to the fore, and to remain committed to broad and open dialogue with the community.

If American environmentalism has been nurtured by the belief that in nature "everything is connected to everything else" (Commoner 1971, 39), the environmental justice movement, reflecting the process of feminist inquiry, now affirms that *everyone* is connected to everyone else. Until we heed the voices of the less powerful, environmental policy in America will always fall short.

NOTES

This chapter originally appeared as "In a Greener Voice: Feminist Theory and Environmental Justice," 19 *Harvard Women's Law Journal* 23 (1996). ©1996 by the President and Fellows of Harvard College and the Harvard Women's Law Journal.

REFERENCES

Austin, R., and M. Schill. 1994. "Black, Brown, Red, and Poisoned." In Bullard 1994.

Bartlett, K. 1990. "Feminist Legal Methods." *Harvard Law Review* 103: 829.

Birkeland, J. 1993. "Ecofeminism: Linking Theory and Practice." In *Ecofeminism: Women, Animals, Nature*, ed. G. Gaard. Philadelphia: Temple University Press.

Bullard, R., ed. 1993. *Confronting Environmental Racism: Voices from the Grassroots.* Boston: South End Press.

———. 1994. *Unequal Protection: Environmental Justice and Communities of Color.* San Francisco: Sierra Club.

Calpotura, F., and R. Sen. 1994. "PUEBLO Fights Lead Poisoning." In Bullard 1994.

Cole, L. 1992. "Empowerment as the Key to Environmental Protection: The Need for Environmental Poverty Law." *Ecology Law Quarterly* 19: 619.

———. 1993–94. "The Struggle of Kettleman City: Lessons for the Movement." *Maryland Journal of Contemporary Legal Issues* 5: 67.

———. 1995. "Foreword: A Jeremiad on Environmental Justice and the Law." *Stanford Environmental Law Journal* 14: 11.

Commoner, B. 1971. *The Closing Circle: Nature, Man, and Technology.* New York: Knopf.

Cross, F. 1994. "The Public Role in Risk Control." *Environmental Law* 24: 887.

Eggen, J. 1992. "Toxic Reproductive and Genetic Hazards in the Workplace: Challenging the Myths of the Tort and Workers' Compensation Systems." *Fordham Law Review* 60: 843.

Farenthold, F. 1988. Introduction to Garland 1988.

Ferris, D. 1993–94. "A Broad Environmental Justice Agenda: Mandating Change Begins at the Federal Level." *Maryland Journal of Contemporary Legal Issues* 5: 115.

———. 1994. "Communities of Color and Hazardous Waste Cleanup: Expanding Public Participation in the Federal Superfund Program." *Fordham Urban Law Journal* 21: 671.

Flynn, J., et al. 1994. "Gender, Race, and Perception of Environmental Health Risks." *Risk Analysis* 14: 1101.

Folk, E. 1991. "Public Participation in the Superfund Cleanup Process." *Ecology Law Quarterly* 18: 173.

Fox, S., et al. 1993. "Enhanced Response to Ozone Exposure During Follicular Phase of the Menstrual Cycle." *Environmental Health Perspectives* 101: 242.

Freeman, J., and R. Godsil. 1994. "The Question of Risk: Incorporating Community Perceptions into Environmental Risk Assessments." *Fordham Urban Law Journal* 21: 547.

Garland, A. 1988. *Women Activists.* New York: Feminist Press at the City University of New York.

Gauna, E. 1995. "Federal Environmental Citizen Suit Provisions: Obstacles and Incentives on the Road to Environmental Justice." *Ecology Law Quarterly* 22: 1.

Hamilton, C. 1994. "Concerned Citizens of South Central Los Angeles." In Bullard 1994.

International Union, UAW v. Johnson Controls, Inc., 499 U.S. 187 (1991).

Krauss, C. 1993. "Blue Collar Women and Toxic Waste Protests." In *Toxic Struggles: The Theory and Practice of Environmental Justice*, ed. Richard Hofrichter. Philadelphia: New Society Publishers.

Latin, H. 1988. "Good Science, Bad Regulation, and Toxic Risk Assessment." *Yale Journal on Regulation* 5: 89.

Lazarus, R. 1993. "Pursuing 'Environmental Justice': The Distributional Effects of Environmental Protection." *Northwestern University Law Review* 87: 787.

———. 1993–94. "The Meaning and Promotion of Environmental Justice," *Maryland Journal of Contemporary Legal Issues* 5: 1.

MacKinnon, C. 1987. *Feminism Unmodified: Discourses on Life and Law*. Cambridge: Harvard University Press.

Matsuda, M. 1986. "Liberal Jurisprudence and Abstracted Visions of Human Nature: A Feminist Critique of Rawls' Theory of Justice." *New Mexico Law Review* 16: 613.

Menkel-Meadow, C. 1985. "Portia in a Different Voice: Speculations on a Woman's Lawyering Process." *Berkeley Women's Law Journal* 1: 39.

Morgan, W. 1990. "Choosing and Managing Technology-Induced Risk." In *Readings in Risk*, ed. T. Glickman and M. Gough. Washington, D.C.: Resources for the Future.

Nelson, L. 1990. "The Place of Women in Polluted Places." In *Reweaving the World: The Emergence of Ecofeminism*, ed. I. Diamond and G. Orenstein. San Francisco: Sierra Club.

Rechtenshaffen, C., and E. Guana. 2002. *Environmental Justice: Law, Policy, and Regulation*. Durham: Carolina Academic Press.

Setterberg, F., and L. Shavelson. 1993. *Toxic Nation: The Fight to Save Our Communities from Chemical Contamination*. New York: Wiley, J.

Slovic, P. 1983. "Perception of Risk." *Science* 236: 280.

Swanston, S. 1994. "Race, Gender, Age, and Dispropartionate Impact: What Can We Do About the Failure to Protect the Most Vulnerable?" *Fordham Urban Law Journal* 21: 577.

Woolf, V. 1938. *Three Guineas*. New York: Harcourt Brace Jovanovich.

4

Witness to Truth

Black Women Heeding the Call for Environmental Justice

VALERIE ANN KAALUND

"O woman, woman! Upon you I call; for upon your exertions almost entirely depends whether the rising generation shall be anything more than we have been or not. O woman, woman! Your example is powerful, your influence great; it extends over your husbands and your children, and throughout the circle of your acquaintance."

–Maria W. Stewart

Maria W. Stewart (b. 1803–d. 1879), often accounted to be the first African American woman to speak in public about women's rights (Guy-Sheftall 1995) urged women as the moral center of their families and communities to fight against injustice. In Stewart's time injustice meant the continued enslavement and servitude of black people and women. She exhorted blacks and whites, male and female in her society to fight against the enslavement of blacks and for the uplift of women (Guy-Sheftall 1995; Richardson 1987). Today, black women in the environmental justice (EJ) movement use their power and influence to fight against an array of environmental injustices as if directly heeding Stewart's call and in much the same way their nineteenth-century counterparts did indeed heed her.

The purpose of this essay is threefold: first, to discuss black women's involvement in the EJ movement as framed by a concept of ethical consciousness reflected in black womanist/feminist ideology and spiritual authority; second, to demonstrate the link between black women's involvement in the EJ movement and black feminist activism; and third, to recount stories of individual black women in North Carolina involved in the EJ movement. My remarks in this essay derive from my participation in the EJ movement as an activist, educator, and scholar, where I have witnessed and shared the many testimonials concerning environmental injustice.

Heeding the Call—Twentieth/Twenty-first-Century Style

The clarion call for environmental justice as a national movement began in 1982 with the actions of Dollie Burwell and fellow residents of Warren County, North Carolina. They cried out in response to the siting in Warren County of 32,000 cubic yards of PCB-contaminated soil generated from the cleanup in 1978 of PCB-laden toxic waste materials illegally dumped along a 210-mile stretch of North Carolina highway (Burwell 2000, 2002; EJRC 2002). The danger this posed for residents in Warren County cannot be understated. Numerous studies document that exposure to PCB (polychlorinated biphenyl) mixtures can cause cancer and also have negative neurological, developmental, and reproductive effects on both human and animal populations (Lester 1999). Concerned with the physical, economic, emotional, and intellectual health of this predominantly black community whose members can trace their ancestry to enslavement on the Warren County land, Burwell and others fought to clean up this toxic site and advocate for economic development in the area. Even children participated in the many protests. In fact, Burwell's daughter, Kim, aged nine years old at the time, said to her mother that the illegal acts they were protesting against "looked like environmental racism" (Burwell 2001), a term whose currency is demonstrated by its ubiquitous use by EJ activists and others.

Also in 1982, Hazel Johnson (a grandmother), out of concern for the health of people in her southside Chicago community, became involved in environmental justice activism after learning that southeast Chicago had the highest incidence of cancer of any other area of the city (EJRC 2002). People in this area were suffering from asthma, cancer, skin rash, and kidney and liver problems all documented on complaint forms and attributable to environmental causes (EJRC 2002). Because of Johnson's tireless efforts in drawing attention to her community's problems by sponsoring "toxic tours" of the affected areas, hosting two environmental conferences, speaking at numerous colleges and universities, and holding workshops and training programs, in 1991 at the First National People of Color Environmental Leadership Summit, she was recognized as the "Mother of the Environmental Justice Movement"[1] (EJRC 2002).

These women and others, acting with moral agency, were instrumental in launching the national movement for environmental justice, advocating for fit communities in which to live, work, play, pray, and learn. This moral agency is based in part on an ethical consciousness that is an articulation of principles and values that affirms the activists' humanity and the humanity of those in their communities. Their advocacy also derives from an authority and confidence based on the moral validity of their cause and spiritual support for their actions, similar to the way Maria W. Stewart framed her call for political and economic action with a spiritual context.[2] This spiritual dimension of the EJ movement can be seen in part in the way meetings, roundtables, and summits usually open with prayer. For example, at a recent convening of the Academics, Communities, Agencies Network (ACA-Net)[3] Strategic Planning Roundtable, prayer was used to open and close each day's sessions drawing on either Christian, Muslim, or Native American religious traditions to frame our collective spiritual expression.

Another aspect of an expressed spirituality that carries with it strong moral advocacy is the public testimonial that many in the black Christian church tradition would understand as the act of "witnessing." To witness is to share publicly one's spiritual beliefs in the form of personal stories that attest to divine intervention and assistance. For many black people, the testimony is one of the key expressions of black spirituality, and the autobiographical information rendered serves as an exegesis for the entire community. In attending any number of meetings and summits on environmental racism I have heard testimony about thirteen-year-old girls in a community in Tennessee diagnosed with uterine cancer; I have spoken with residents in North Carolina still living in moldy, mildewy homes more than four years after surviving the onslaught of Hurricane Floyd; and heard report after report of miscarriages and assorted cancers found in women living in communities across the country located adjacent to landfills, toxic dumpsites, and uranium mining sites. The sincere, impassioned, and often heartbreaking public testimonies offered by black women (as well as other women of color) in the EJ movement are a witness to truth.

According to Katie Cannon, a black womanist theologian, black women who understand the prophetic tradition of the Christian Bible are empowered to "fashion a set of values on their own terms, as well as mastering, radicalizing, and sometimes destroying the pervasive negative orientations imposed by the larger society" (Cannon 1995, 56). For example, Reverend Carrie Bolton, in addressing the attendees at the Fifth Annual North Carolina Environmental Justice Summit (in Durham, North Carolina), contextualized her remarks with the following biblical passage: "The earth is the Lord's and everything in it, the world, and all who live in it: for he founded it upon the seas and established it upon the waters" (Psalm 24:1) aptly demonstrating Cannon's assertion. As Bolton talked about her struggle to make sure her community is not subject to regional landfills and economic underdevelopment, she reminded her audience of her belief in the power of God to effect change and overcome adversity. Bolton's reference to biblical texts also demonstrates that her "authority" to speak and witness is divinely sanctioned. Later at this same summit, Dollie Burwell prefaced her remarks, entitled "From Lemons to Lemonade: From Environmental Racism to Environmental Justice," with a quotation from Micah 6:8: "He has showed you, O man, what is good. And what does the Lord require of you? To act justly and to love mercy and to walk humbly with your God." In recounting the Warren County struggle against environmental racism, Burwell affirmed that their struggle was fundamentally a fight for justice, and in fighting for justice "the environmental will be taken care of" (Burwell 2002). This was accomplished through organized action, praying, and singing spirituals (Burwell 2002), methods still held to be effective today. Burwell gave as a reason to engage in the EJ fight her belief that God required that "I do all that I can do" (Burwell 2002). Such beliefs, as exemplified by Bolton and Burwell, demonstrate that in the face of seemingly insurmountable odds, reliance on a force greater than oneself is needed not just to overcome the obstacles but as a way to sustain one's ability to continue to mount opposition to those who oppress you.

In making direct reference to biblical texts, Bolton and Burwell also exemplify what Cannon considers part of black womanist tradition: using Scriptures to "learn how to dispel the threat of death in order to seize the present life" (Cannon 1995, 56). These women, like other black women preachers past and present (see Collier-Thomas 1998), understand the racist nature of the society in which they live and take their preaching opportunities to argue for racial advancement and social justice, emphasizing biblical women and the importance of black women's contributions and leadership for the advancement of the race as a whole. Their preaching also incorporates a witness to the experiences in their lives that mirror biblical stories, especially as they illustrate overcoming oppression. Just as black women preachers called on women in the Bible to explicate justice concerns and moral agency (Collier-Thomas 1998) so too do women like Burwell and Bolton draw from personal struggles with events such as the illegal and toxic dumping of waste materials in their neighborhoods or noxious odors emanating from yet another landfill in their community.

Biblical texts are not the only means for providing moral support and guidance. Cannon, in reviewing a variety of literary works by black women, identified an ethical sensibility that informs black women's actions and ideas.[4] This sensibility stems in large part from surviving within an oppressive society and out of that survival creating the means to be moral agents and arbiters in their communities. Akasha Hull draws our attention in *Soul Talk: The New Spirituality of African American Women* (2001) to the outburst of transformative spirituality among black women (and others) beginning around 1980 that reenergized both the civil rights and women's rights movements. Black women engaged, for example, in practices associated with the New Age (like crystal work, Eastern religions, and metaphysics) along with more traditional cultural spiritual expressions leading to what Hull describes as dramatic lifestyle changes and life directions that she found in her interviews with writers such as Lucille Clifton, Toni Cade Bambara, and Michelle Gibbs. As EJ activists engaged in a protracted struggle for justice, we draw upon these many spiritual sources and guidance for the support needed to help create meaningful improvements for our communities adversely impacted by environmental injustice.

EJ Activism within a Black Feminist Framework

In my office is a framed print of African American artist Varnette Honeywood's piece "She Who Learns Teaches." This point was brought home to me recently by a student who commented on the definition of environmental justice I had presented in class: "The pursuit of equal justice and equal protection under the law for all environmental statu[t]es and regulations, without discrimination based on race, ethnicity, and/or socioeconomic status."[5] The student, who earlier had taken a class with me on black women in America, appropriately asked why gender wasn't mentioned in this definition. Nonplussed for a moment, I collected my thoughts and replied that yes, on the surface this seems problematic especially since the leadership of the EJ movement in North Carolina is largely female. It is puzzling that we excluded explicit reference to gender in defining environmental justice even though leadership and participation in the movement was largely female. And in identifying incursions against communities as environmental racism, we put at the forefront of action and analysis race and class rather than gender. As I reflected more on this "teaching moment," I realized that this omission (and orientation toward "race") indicated the complexities involved in environmental justice activism. The EJ movement has been shaped largely by actions based on earlier civil rights campaigns for social justice, and in some ways it has inherited similar modes of omitting or diminishing the importance of women's participation in the movement.

It also is interesting to me that while we rail against an oppressive patriarchal hegemony as feminists (and rightly so)—often noting the way in which adherents to patriarchy pejoratively categorize the female as "natural," "animalistic," "earthy"—these same qualities are valued by mainstream "environmentalists" who until recently had all but ignored the plight of people of color with regards to environmental desolation and oppression. It then becomes understandable that an agenda largely associated with "mainstream" or "majority" populated movements (like "environmentalism" and "feminism") would be subsumed under an agenda or ideology based on race, ethnicity, and socioeconomic status when shaped by the experiences of people of color. However, by maintaining these separations through silence and reluctance to call out our own omissions, we unconsciously support the very same oppressive regimes we loathe.

In North Carolina we raise our voices to "Save the People" (the theme of the first North Carolina environmental summit), aware that on some level perhaps we do not need to draw attention to the gendered ways environmental injustices manifest themselves precisely because we have such a strong physical presence of women in the EJ movement. As Reverend Leo Woodberry, a leading environmental activist in South Carolina, observed recently, if not for women in the EJ movement, little if anything would have moved forward. An explicit feminist agenda may not always be identifiable, but in observing the actions of women in the North Carolina EJ movement (and elsewhere), I have observed an empowered consciousness that variously fell along a continuum of feminist consciousness. In other words, in workshops, meetings, organizing sessions, calls to action, community-based participatory research projects, writing, and all the footwork needed to keep a movement going, women of color are front and center. In this way the relationships formed while engaged in these actions help provide a "community for Black women's activism and self-determination" that Patricia Hill Collins (1991) states was first championed by Maria Stewart. As recently as the second convening of the People of Color Environmental Leadership Summit in Washington, D.C., public acknowledgement of the critical contributions of our elder activist women culminated in a celebratory dinner, "Crowning Women," honoring the women in the environmental justice movement.[6] What is interesting to note is that much of the work of these activists goes unnoticed in many instances, including in the academy. Black women like Dr. Mildred McClain, convener of the ACA-Net collaboration; Dr. May Samuels, associate director of the Environmental Science Program at Benedict College; Dr. Yolanda Banks Anderson, chair of the environmental science program at North Carolina Central University; and Dr. Beverly Wright, executive director of the Xavier University Deep South Center for Environmental Justice represent a very partial yet longstanding commitment of academic women in the EJ movement.[7]

Black women's participation in the environmental justice movement is indeed part of the continuum of feminist/womanist activism exemplified by the works and writings of women such as Maria Stewart, Anna Julia Cooper, and Ida B. Wells[8] who expressed moral outrage at social injustices (like enslavement, women's subjugation, and lynching) through their writing and speeches. In advocating for justice, black women as EJ activists call for a world in which all can coexist healthily and humanely. This ideology has at its foundation a vision of a world that allows for the peaceful, prosperous coexistence of all its peoples and justifies the fight against one's oppressor(s), whoever or whatever that may be. Their work also falls easily within core feminist themes discussed by Patricia Hill Collins in *Black Feminist Thought* (1991): legacy of struggle; realization of the interlocking nature of race, gender, and class oppression; replacement of denigrating images of black womanhood with self-defined images; belief in black women's activism as teachers, mothers and community leaders; and issues around sexual politics.

So when black women stand up and demand that there be clean air and clean water in their neighborhoods and follow those demands with actions (such as peaceful protests, rallies, legal action, work slowdowns, and so on), they make concrete the nexus between ideology, moral agency, and what is "real." The interlocking nature of oppression based on race, gender, age, class, and ability so aptly observed by black feminists and others[9] is integral to the lived experience of these activists. Black women as EJ activists understand that their communities are targeted because they are perceived as being inhabited by inferior, politically disenfranchised, economically disadvantaged people who do not have much social, political, or economic capital and so can be easily dispensed with or ignored. This is how, for example, the city of Detroit (which is 85 percent black) can be designated a brownfield site—an area contaminated with hazardous substances as a result of commercial, industrial, and/or military use—because of both neglect and deliberate action. It is little wonder that Detroit is home to two-thirds of Michigan's lead-poisoned children (Wendland-Bowyer 2003). But because of this economic and political disenfranchisement, black women like Donelle Wilkins, director of Detroiters Working for Environmental Justice, know that simply cleaning former toxic sites is not going to be enough to address the needs of people exposed to these health hazards.[10]

Black women as EJ activists link their local struggles for environmental justice with global environmental injustice through participation in various national and international summits and meetings (such as the World Congress Against Racism). Many activist women spend a considerable amount of time traveling around the United States as well as overseas generating support for their particular situation and for the movement at large. Personal time (whether for family, job, or their own pleasure) is often sacrificed in this activist work and these sacrifices mirror what previous black women feminists like Ida B. Wells and Josephine St. Pierre Ruffin experienced in their lives (Guy-Sheftall 1995). To paraphrase Dollie Burwell (2001), think what these women could have accomplished in their lives if they had not had to spend their time fighting to clean up a mess of someone else's making.

I maintain that today's environmental justice movement has been largely influenced by the work of black women (and other women of color) who, through their organizing efforts in local communities, their participation in national and international summits and conferences, and their continued leadership in all aspects of the EJ movement, bring to this movement an implicitly womanist/feminist activism.

Examples from the Ground

Our movement is not a reaction to the environmental movement. We have come here to define for ourselves the issues of the ecology and the environment. We have to speak these truths that we know from our lives to those participants and observers whom we have invited here to join us. We have come for you to hear our understandings from our mouths directly, so there will be no confusion and no misunderstandings.

—Dana Alston

We learn from feminist scholars and activists of color that one of the best means for understanding the experiences of women of color is through their stories. Anthologized collections such as Cherríe Moraga and Gloria Anzuldúa's *This Bridge Called My Back: Writings by Radical Women of Color* (1981, 1983) and D. Soyini Madison's *The Woman That I Am* (1994) provide a means for exploring and understanding the lives of women of color as revealed through their narratives. These revelations further enable us to better hear and accept what grassroots and community activists have to say about their lives and the world we all live in.

Connie Tucker, an EJ activist, organizer, and survivor of environmental racism, tells us we must go directly to the people suffering from the deleterious health effects of living in "toxic doughnuts" (what Hazel Johnson calls impacted communities) and learn what is happening to them from "their own lips." As Anna Julia Cooper, an African American feminist from North Carolina, stated in her 1892 book *A Voice of the South: By a Black Woman of the South*, "All I claim is that there is a feminine as well as a masculine side to truth; that these are related not as inferior and superior, not as better and worse, not as weaker and stronger, but as complements—complements in one necessary and symmetric whole" (Busby 1992, 140).

I present below three short cases representing three different areas in North Carolina and complementary aspects of a "symmetric whole." They provide a small glimpse into the complicated nature of environmental justice activism from "ground zero." These stories are from black women who, out of their own ethical sensibilities and within a womanist/feminist framework as described above, made the choice to act on behalf of their impacted communities.

Concerned Citizens of Edgecombe County-II

In first becoming acquainted with environmental racism in North Carolina, I was introduced to a few members of Concerned Citizens of Edgecombe County-II (CCE–2) by attorney and North Carolina EJ activist Savi Horne.[11] CCE–2 presents a compelling case regarding the disadvantages of living, working, playing, and praying in a community that includes a hog farm operation. For this community inhabited by a majority of black residents, the construction of a 6,000-head hog production operation adjacent to the Morning Star Missionary Baptist Church caused considerable consternation and resulted in organized opposition. Morning Star (founded in 1882 with a predominantly black congregation) and the surrounding community, also predominantly black, is located in Edgecombe County immediately northeast of the Battleboro community in the north end of the city of Rocky Mount, North Carolina.

Morning Star Missionary Baptist Church was remodeled more than twenty years ago, has an adjacent cemetery still in active use, and, prior to the development of the hog operation, had acquired additional land immediately behind the church grounds that was to be used as a children's play area. Also affected by this hog operation is a day care center owned and operated by Evelyn Powell, who when we met was president of CCE–2.

Powell and CCE–2 members (primarily black women) maintained that their community was in serious danger of being destroyed because of the contamination and destruction of the quality of residents' lives directly attributable to the noxious odors from the hog farm operation, seepage of hog waste (feces and urine) into the groundwater, and increased traffic. In meetings and subsequent conversations with CCE–2 members, several expressed their fear that there was the potential for an outright spill of stored hog waste to occur in the event of a break in the storage lagoons or a flood. Their fears regarding flooding and spills were realized in 1999 when, in the aftermath of Hurricane Floyd, widespread flooding washed carcasses of hogs and waste from the lagoons into area creeks and rivers.[12]

Prior to construction of the hog operation in the spring of 1996, local residents, church members, parents of children in the child care center, and supporters formed Concerned Citizens of Edgecombe-II (CCE–2) to oppose its construction. CCE–2 organized area residents, including a number of people in what was to become part of the city of Rocky Mount, tested their wells (at their own expense), and conducted a health assessment screening. With little support from county officials and the health department, the group found in 1997 that seventeen of twenty-two wells were contaminated with fecal matter and nitrates. In the previous year, prior to the operation of the hog factory, only one well out of the twenty-two tested was contaminated.[13] Their efforts culminated in a legal action against the hog factory and county officials. With additional support and assistance from Judith Thomas (who lives in a community not far from Battleboro) and Adora Lee, both environmental justice advocates with the United Church of Christ National Board,[14] CCE–2 has been able to pressure Edgecombe County officials into developing the necessary infrastructure to bring in piped water.[15]

Eubanks/Rogers Road Landfill

Similar problems are faced by a small community in Chapel Hill, North Carolina. Again, the well-being of this predominantly black, working-class community has been compromised by the ever growing regional landfill. Promises made nearly thirty years ago to close the landfill and redevelop the land into a green space have not been fulfilled. In expanding this landfill, residents report increased rates of cancer, presence of buzzards and other pests, increased truck traffic, and undrinkable local water. Most of the residents negatively impacted by the landfill are on well water and septic systems that are not part of the city of Chapel Hill's water and sewer infrastructure. This story is repeated in community after community of people living near a structure that affects the quality of their environment. Whether it is a quarry, landfill, or hog factory, one of the worst health problems that develops is the lack of potable water. People facing difficult economic decisions have to use a portion of their scarce resources to buy bottled water, as I witnessed in this neighborhood. For example, when visiting Reverend Mona Sampson,[16] a local resident and pastor of a church in this neighborhood, I was told emphatically not to drink the water from the tap. They gave me bottled water to drink, and I observed Sampson's daughter use several gallons of bottled water to prepare a spaghetti dinner for a church activity. I witnessed for myself the water clouded with flecks of sediment that came from the taps of people's homes and churches.

In the Eubanks/Rogers Road area, a coalition of community residents have had to address the problems with this regional landfill over a thirty-year period. Families such as the Belles, with Sarah Belle[17] in the lead, and church leaders like Mona Sampson have at various times been spokespeople for the community, pushing local officials to remedy the situation with their water and compensate them for the negative impact of a landfill that seems never to be filled.

Holly Springs

"It's amazing what can happen when a group of people gets together on their own behalf."

–Mary Beamon, Wake County chapter chair, North Carolina Fair Share

Membership in the North Carolina Environmental Justice Network has allowed me to meet people across the state of North Carolina working on EJ issues and form key relationships with a variety of black women in the network. Through network member Lynice Williams of North Carolina Fair Share, I learned of the situation in Holly Springs, Wake County, North Carolina, discussed below and more recently the lack of post–Hurricane Floyd flood remediation for people in Pender County, North Carolina.

Della McQueen Cross, Artris Woodard, and Leonara Carrington describe in the excerpts below a few of the problems faced by people in Holly Springs. The neighborhood of Sunset Acres, located at the northern end of Holly Springs, is primarily African American, with approximately two hundred mobile and frame homes and at that time no municipal services: residents were on well water and lucky to have septic tanks (Cole 1998). Also affected are the older communities of Old Pierce Place and Turner Village, which support about five hundred residents. Fifteen miles from the state capital of Raleigh, North Carolina, African American residents live a mostly rural lifestyle as descendants of sharecroppers who had farmed the land for decades (McDonald 2000).

Imagine turning on a faucet and seeing a foul, brown, and disgusting-to-smell fluid coming out of the tap. Out of 117 water wells tested in Sunset Acres, only 36 had water deemed safe to drink. Dangerous levels of *E. coli* bacteria contaminated 81 wells, and 10 wells contained significant levels of *E. coli*, making the water unsuitable even for washing vegetables (Cole 1998). Relief from their situation has been achieved primarily through organized action as members of North Carolina Fair Share.

DELLA MCQUEEN CROSS. The water was contaminated. My sister-in-law, who owns the daycare, they were wanting to close the daycare. And she kept calling and the water was contaminated and the health department kept coming out and testing the water and stuff and she had to haul water. The health department tested the wells. We can't really say if anyone got sick. Back in the sixties, we had a city dump down here I even checked and we've had several people down here die of cancer. We don't really know [if it was because of the water], if that caused it, could have, we don't know. My sister in law had put Clorox in her water and all. (Kerr 2000, 9–10)

ARTRIS WOODARD. We've been having trouble with our wells for a long time. The water would go from cloudy to smelly, from good to bad. When Della came by I decided to work on it. We tried to get the Health Department involved. I feel real good about getting water and sewer, but I know we have to stay close behind it. We have a verbal agreement with the town on how the money we got will be used, but maybe not everyone will go along with a verbal agreement. We need to work together to get a written agreement. (Kerr 2002, 11)

LEONORA CARRINGTON. Della went around putting flyers in people's mailboxes. I didn't know how to get involved, but I thought, if Della can do it, with the little bit that she could see, then I can do it too. I'm overjoyed for health reasons that the water and sewer is going in. We didn't know what kind of diseases the bad water was causing. There were lots of cancers in the same family. (Kerr 2002, 11)

The story in Holly Springs has not ended. Residents of a black neighborhood adjacent to the ones described above are currently in litigation to prevent the siting of another proposed landfill in the area.

These vignettes illustrate, I hope, the terrorist nature of the oppression faced by many, many people and should generate an interest in the EJ movement beyond the accidental or incidental encounters with people living in environmentally oppressive communities that are not of their making.

Conclusion

Gay McDougal of the International Human Rights Law Group urged the assembled body at the first annual North Carolina Environmental Justice Summit in October 1998 to use the language of human rights to frame any discourse on environmental justice. She maintained that people are empowered by this language and that it helps people remember that they have rights that must be protected and enforced. She wanted to leave the group with the understanding that it is possible to tell your story to a larger audience, an international audience. She could not promise that if grassroots groups go to the United Nations the toxic waste dump or hog farm is going to be cleaned up, but she does promise that "[we] are going to cause a different kind of a ripple" (McDougal 1998).

The black women working to fight environmental oppression and terrorism represent a diversity of class, religious background, ableness, educational achievement, sexuality, occupation, age, and even political affiliation, but they are united in their desire to create positive change in their communities and globally. Their feminism may be quite marked and conscious, or they may just be working in concert with other black women to fight injustice. Still, at the core, this body represents a humanist understanding of their condition and the willingness to take a moral stand against injustice. They try to create a world as envisioned by Mary Thomas Roberson, who asked of us, "Can we win in the battle of races? Can we get culture enough to fit all races to live in the world physically and socially with the respect for the rights of others? This will be the last great achievement."[18]

NOTES

In keeping with my spiritual traditions I first give honor and thanks to God the Creator for all her blessings. I thank Rachel Stein, our editor, for her guidance in this project, the faculty and staff in the African and Afro-American Studies department at University of North Carolina–Chapel Hill for their assistance and support, my colleagues in the North Carolina environmental justice movement, my family for their support, and especially the women of the environmental justice movement who have shared their "witness" with me.

1. By giving her the title "Mother of the EJ Movement," summit attendees recognized her contributions as an important elder more than relegating her to a strictly feminine space.

2. For instance, Maria W. Stewart said in a lecture delivered at Franklin Hall in Boston (Sept. 21, 1832): "Methinks I heard a spiritual interrogation—'Who shall go forward, and take off the reproach that is cast upon the people of color? Shall it be a woman?' And my heart made this reply—'If it is thy will, be it even so, Lord Jesus!'" (Guy-Sheftall 1995). Collier-Thomas (1998) noted in her study on black women preachers that starting with Stewart, when black women referred to the ideology of "true womanhood," they did so as a challenge to white supremacist beliefs and assumptions that African Americans (and especially African American women) were moral degenerates.

3. ACA-Net is an environmental justice action group directed by Dr. Mildred McClain under the auspices of the Citizens for Environmental Justice–Harambee House, Inc., Savannah, Georgia.

4. For a more elaborate discussion of the relationships between faith, ethics, and black women's literary traditions, see K. Cannon, "Moral Wisdom in the Black Women's Literary Tradition" (1995, 57–68).

5. G. Grant and N. Freeland remarks at the 1998 North Carolina Environmental Justice Network Summit Coordinating Meeting attended by the author.

6. The following women were honored on Friday, October 25, 2002, at this dinner: Charon Asetoyer, executive director and founder of the Native American Community Board, Yankton Sioux Reservation; Rose Augustine, founding member and cochair of the Southwest Network for Environmental and Economic Justice, Tucson, Arizona; Dollie Burwell, Warren County, North Carolina; Willie Faye Bush, executive director, Newtown Florist Club, Gainesville, Georgia; Mayor Emma R. Gresham, Keysville, Georgia; Hazel Johnson, founder of People for Community Recovery, southside of Chicago; Pam Tau Lee, founding member and board chair of APEN, one of nine environmental justice networks in the United States, San Francisco Bay area; Alicia Marentes, director of social services and pesticides training coordinator at the Farm Worker Center, Texas; Margie Eugene Richard, president and founder of Concerned Citizens of NORCO (New Orleans Refinery Company), New Orleans, Louisiana; Gloria Weaver Roberts, Deep South Center for Environmental Justice, Convent, Louisiana; Peggy Shepard, executive director and cofounder of West Harlem Environmental Action, Inc. (WE ACT), northern Manhattan, New York; Emelda West, one of the founders of the St. James Citizens for Jobs and the Environment, Convent, Louisiana; and Margaret Williams, leader of the Citizens against Toxic Exposure (CATE), Pensacola, Florida. The work of each of these women is extensive in scope and longevity in the EJ movement and cannot be fully explicated in a footnote.

7. For example, in an otherwise important and well-done collection on African American women's contemporary activism, *Still Lifting, Still Climbing: African American Women's Contemporary Activism* (Springer 1999), explicit reference to the work of black women in the current EJ movement is absent.

8. A review of anthologies such as *The Woman That I Am* (Madison 1994) and in the particular case of black women, *Women of Fire* (Guy-Sheftall 1995), represent the breadth and depth of feminist thought. The activists in the EJ movement are a diverse body— they are old and young, immigrants and those indigenous to this nation, of every racial and ethnic group, and range from very poor to very rich.

9. See works such as *Black Feminist Thought* (Collins 1991); *SisterOutsider* (Lorde 1984); *Still Lifting, Still Climbing: African American Women's Contemporary Activism* (Springer 1999) and very recently *Gender Talk* (Cole and Guy-Sheftall 2003).

10. Donelle Wilkins, director of Detroiters Working for Environmental Justice, from remarks made to the ACA-Net Strategic Planning Roundtable, Meharry Medical College, Nashville, Tennessee, January 24, 2003.

11. Savi Horne's work in EJ largely involves activism around land-loss issues. As an attorney with the nonprofit legal assistance organization Land Loss Prevention Project (based in Durham, N.C.), Horne has fought against the discriminatory practices and mechanisms designed to dispossess people from their land and, in the case of farmers of color, their livelihoods.

12. Personal communication with Powell, September 1999.

13. Author's notes from CCE–2 meeting, May 25, 1998.

14. The United Church of Christ (UCC) has long been involved in the environmental justice struggle as evidenced by the 1987 release of the now famous report *Toxic Wastes and Race in the United States* (the first national study to correlate waste facility siting and race). Considerable resources have been allocated by the UCC National Board to assist local grassroots organizations in their activism around environmental justice.

15. Personal communication with Judith Thomas, November 2002.

16. This name is a pseudonym.

17. This name is a pseudonym.

18. This is an excerpt from the valedictorian's address made by my maternal grandmother, born to Kizzie Elizabeth Davis and Thomas Roberson, in Augusta, Georgia, October 15, 1901, at Haines Institute School in Augusta on May 24, 1921.

REFERENCES

Alston, Dana. 1991. Speech given at the National People of Color Environmental Leadership Summit, Washington, D.C., Oct. 1991. *http://www.ejrc.cau.edu/dana_speech.htm.*

Burwell, D. 2000. Speech given at the North Carolina Environmental Justice Summit, Nov., Franklinton Center at Bricks, Whitakers, N.C.

———. 2001. "Environmental Justice for All," UNC–Chapel Hill School of Public Health 23rd Annual Minority Health Conference: 'Race, Class, and the Environment: The State of Minority Health,' Minority Health conference.

———. 2002. "From Lemons to Lemonade: From Environmental Racism to Environmental Justice." Plenary session, North Carolina Environmental Justice Summit, Oct. 18–19, Durham, N.C.

Busby, M. 1992. *Daughters of Africa: An International Anthology of Words and Writings by Women of African Descent: From the Ancient Egyptian to the Present.* New York: Pantheon Books.

Cannon, K. 1995. *Katie's Canon: Womanism and the Soul of the Black Community.* New York: Continuum Publishing Co.

Cole, S. 1998. "Community Wins Clean Water, Targets Dumpsite." *Prism,* Feb., Triangle Area, N.C.

Collier-Thomas, B. 1998. *Daughters of Thunder: Black Women Preachers and Their Sermons, 1850–1979.* San Francisco: Jossey Bass Publishers.

Collins, P. H. 1991. *Black Feminist Thought: Knowledge, Consciousness, and the Politics of Empowerment.* New York: Routledge.

Environmental Justice Resource Center. *http://www.ejrc.cau.edu/(s)heros.html*; http://www.ejrc. cau.edu/dana_speech.htm.

Guy-Sheftall, B., ed. 1995. *Words of Fire: An Anthology of African-American Feminist Thought.* New York: New Press.

Hull, A. 2001. *Soul Talk: The New Spirituality of African American Women.* Rochester, Vt.: Inner Traditions.

Kerr, M. L., ed. 2002. *The Holly Springs Story.* Revised ed. Raleigh, N.C.

Lester, S. 1999. "Still Toxic After All These Years: An Update on the Toxicity of PCBs." *Everyone's Backyard* (spring): 15.

Lorde, A. 1984. *SisterOutsider.* Freedom, Calif.: Crossing Press.

Madison, D. S. 1994. *The Woman that I Am: The Literature and Culture of Contemporary Women of Color.* New York: St. Martin's Press.

McDonald, T. 2000. "Housing Disparity Still Lives in Triangle." Raleigh, N.C., *News and Observer.* Sept. 7, p. 1A.QQQfmt

McDougal, G. 1998. Keynote address. North Carolina Environmental Justice Summit, Oct., Franklinton Center at Bricks.

Moraga, C., and G. Anzuldúa 1981, 1983. *This Bridge Called My Back: Writings by Radical Women of Color.* New York: Kitchen Table: Women of Color Press.

Richardson, M., ed. 1987. *Maria W. Stewart: America's First Black Woman Political Writer: Essays and Speeches.* Bloomington: Indiana University Press.

Springer, K., ed. 1999. *Still Lifting, Still Climbing: African American Women's Contemporary Activism.* New York: New York University Press.

Wendland-Bowyer, W. 2003. "LEAD'S TOXIC TOLL: Wanted: A Leader who says 'enough is enough.'" *Detroit Free Press*, Jan.

Wilkins, D. 2003. Remarks to the ACA-Net Strategic Planning Roundtable, Meharry Medical College, Nashville, Tenn.

5

The Role of Gender, Race/Ethnicity, and Class in Activists' Perceptions of Environmental Justice

DIANE-MICHELE PRINDEVILLE

This is my purpose: not just to help people–that sounds too patronizing–
to motivate. You're part of something bigger than yourself. Everyone has
this ability, but we put limitations on people. . . When I was thirty-five, I
realized, looking back, that my whole life was preparation to assume the
responsibility of the matriarch. I was prepared for it by my grandmother. . . . I had a good grounding in tribal values. It's my way of giving
back.

—Lorna, Native American activist

I hope my efforts have led to a few people acknowledging that Chicanos
are players, too.

—Susana, Latina public official

The political leadership and activism of Native American and Hispanic women
in New Mexico's environmental justice movement can be differentiated from
that of mainstream environmentalists. Unlike mainstream environmentalists,
these leaders are mobilized to political action by a desire to empower their
communities, preserve their cultures, and achieve racial, ethnic, and gender
equality, in addition to conserving the environment. Identifying themselves as
"Third World" and "indigenous" environmentalists, the women who lead New
Mexico's grassroots organizations pursue a political agenda based on social and
economic justice, and racial and gender equity.

This essay explores how race, ethnicity, gender, and class shape Native
American and Hispanic women's motives for participating in politics, the role
that these aspects of identity play in the formulation of these activists' environmental beliefs, and how these factors affect leaders' conceptions of environ-

mentalism. First, however, it will be helpful to consider briefly the historical, social, and economic influences that have led to the growth of the environmental justice movement in New Mexico, and to women's leadership within it.

Colonization of the Southwest, first by Spain and later the United States, determined the composition of the culture, economy, and politics of the region today. This is especially true of New Mexico, where long-standing disputes over rights to land and water involving Indian sovereignty, Spanish land grants, the federal government, and private developers persist and contribute to racial/ethnic tensions. Rich in coal, gas, oil, and timber, the state's economy was built on the extraction of natural resources, and, in the 1940s, New Mexico became a center for the development and testing of nuclear weapons by the United States government. Dependence on these particular industries has contributed to human suffering and environmental degradation, the burden of which has been borne largely by Native and Hispanic residents of the state. To illustrate, a Native activist relayed the following experience. "A metal alloy plant was in [our pueblo] for twenty years, then shut down. The company was international. They were exploitive of people and the environment. It made welding rods, those kind of things. It created tailing piles there. The kids would play in it. Workers were coughing stuff up. The company challenged tribal taxes. They were not a good neighbor. So when their lease ran out and the environmental problems were more visible, the tribe didn't renew it. There's a cleanup underway now" (Karen).

Navajo and Pueblo peoples whose tribal lands are rich in mineral resources have suffered much of the impact of often fatal health problems and the environmental damage associated with extractive industries. For years, excavation of uranium was a critical component of U.S. military research. Most of the uranium was located on Indian reservations and mined by Navajos and Pueblos. Hispanic communities around the state have also been adversely affected by large commercial mining operations that have harmed wildlife and resulted in significant soil and water pollution. Furthermore, despite considerable protests from a broad range of interests across the state, the U.S. Department of Energy has opened the Waste Isolation Pilot Project in southeastern New Mexico. While it provides little benefit to the local economy, WIPP serves as a national depository for medium- and low-level radioactive wastes collected from sites across the country. In protest, environmental justice groups unwilling to see New Mexico host such undesirable land uses erected a billboard near the Albuquerque airport that proclaimed, "Welcome to the only nuclear colony in the United States!"

These activities—harmful mining practices, weapons testing, and the large-scale storage of nuclear waste—have a considerable impact on the state's economy, politics, and environment. As a result, environmental health and safety are issues especially salient for New Mexicans. Residents have organized to protect the health, safety, and well-being of their communities, building coalitions and forming a dynamic and politically important movement for environmental justice. Led largely by Native American and Hispanic women, the grassroots organizations that comprise the movement are active in local, state, and tribal politics and public policymaking.

Historically, women have effectively used community-based organizing as a forum for making demands on political and economic institutions and for seeking social change (West and Blumberg 1990). As an expression of dissent or as the voice of marginalized groups' interests, grassroots activism is vital to the development and maintenance of democracies. Besides providing an outlet for groups traditionally excluded from formal politics (such as women of color), participation in grassroots organizations affords individuals opportunities for gaining valuable experience and knowledge of political processes and institutions.

Women's participation in grassroots organizations is motivated, shaped, and informed by their roles and identities as mothers, workers, community residents, members of racial and/or ethnic minority groups, or by a combination of these identities (Di Chiro 1992; Orleck 1997; Pardo 1990; Prindeville and Bretting 1998; West and Blumberg 1990). Within their communities, Native American and Hispanic women play an integral role in creating and employing networks that provide resources, support, and communication links to residents. Informal and familiar, these networks build on existing relationships developed by women in their neighborhoods, children's schools, workplaces, churches, and clubs or civic groups (Ford 1990; Hoikkala 1995; Pardo 1990). Using these informal networks, Native American women have struggled for policy reforms to maintain their cultures, tribal sovereignty, and control over their native lands and natural resources (Ford 1990; Gunn Allen 1986; Jaimes 1992). And, from the early days of the labor movement in the United States, Hispanas have organized for workers' rights, equitable pay, safe working conditions, and fair treatment (Kingsolver 1989; Marquez 1995).

Today, Native American and Hispanic women in New Mexico's environmental justice movement continue to engage in struggles to remedy social and economic concerns. Whether they are Mexican American mothers organizing against the placement of undesirable land uses such as waste incinerators in their barrio (neighborhood), or Native women fighting the federal government over the deployment of nuclear weapons on tribal lands, these women share common approaches to leadership, and their activism is often motivated by similar reasons (see Pardo 1990; Redhouse 1984). Building on the goals of the civil rights and women's movements, Native American and Hispanic leaders work to achieve social justice, economic equity, and environmental quality for their communities, and to transform social and political institutions and environmental conditions. In particular, they seek to ensure that potentially hazardous or otherwise undesirable land uses are not disproportionately located in poor and minority neighborhoods or on Indian lands, and that these communities are not targeted for placement of such facilities.

New Mexico groups, like environmental justice organizations around the country, include various environmental and economic concerns on their political agenda such as pollution, neighborhood safety, workplace hazards, and job opportunities (Marquez 1994; Prindeville and Bretting 1998). Movement leaders believe that poverty and the inequitable distribution of resources pose threats, not only to public health and the environment but also to the stability of social and political systems. They already know what a growing body of research has revealed: that racial/ethnic minorities and the poor face a disproportionate risk of exposure to environmental hazards (see, for example, Adeola 1994; Bretting and Prindeville 1998; Cable and Cable 1995).

My research project seeks to add to the knowledge gained from earlier studies about women of color and the environmental justice movement. I undertook this study to better understand why Native American and Hispanic women in New Mexico engage in environmental politics. What motivates them to become involved in grassroots organizing? What do they wish to accomplish? How do these leaders perceive themselves and their relationship to their communities vis-à-vis their racial/ethnic identity and their role as women, mothers, wives, and workers? To what extent do they identify as environmentalists? What methods do they use, as leaders in the state's environmental justice movement, to influence politics and public policy in New Mexico?

During the late 1990s, I conducted personal interviews with women who were community organizers and political activists in twenty environmental justice organizations across New Mexico. Twenty-six leaders participated in my research, including twelve Native North American women and one Native Hawaiian who comprise the indigenous sample, and twelve Hispanas who identify as either Mexican Americans or mestizas (of mixed Native American and Spanish heritage). Due to their relatively small number, high level of political activity and coalition building, and membership in the political elite of the environmental justice movement, many of the activists knew each other. To protect their identities, I have used pseudonyms rather than their real names whenever they are quoted.

Description of the Leaders

Table 1 provides a breakdown of the racial/ethnic identity of the leaders and their organizational role. As we can see, equal numbers of activists were employees or volunteers in environmental justice organizations in New Mexico. Twenty-three women or 88 percent were directly affiliated with one or more grassroots groups. Four women were independent activists who were not formal members

TABLE 1
Racial/Ethnic Identity of Activists and Position Held

Race/Ethnicity	Staff	Volunteer	Total
Indigenous	6	7	13
Hispanic	7	6	13
Total	13	13	26
Percent	50%	50%	100%

of any single organization but spent considerable time and resources as volunteers for a number of different groups. With the exception of the "independents," all of the activists worked through their grassroots groups to effect changes in environmental and social policy. In general, volunteers served on their organizations' board of directors or steering committees. Both volunteers and staff demonstrated leadership by participating in the development of organizational goals, identifying policy and program directives, setting budget priorities, and formulating issue campaigns.

The independent activists also exercised leadership, although their situations were somewhat different. For example, Donna, who was a vocal advocate of tribal sovereignty and worked with several groups to change environmental policy, was establishing an organization for environmental justice in her pueblo when I interviewed her. Carmen, a semiretired Native rights leader, remained politically active by providing technical assistance and valuable organizing experience to fledgling environmental groups in New Mexico, Arizona, and Nevada. Karen's knowledge of environmental law, her advisory role to the tribal governor, and her advocacy on behalf of her pueblo during critical negotiations placed her in a leadership position as an environmental activist for her community. In varying ways, these activists influenced public policy both within Indian tribes and the state of New Mexico.

Of the twenty-six leaders, twenty-two or 85 percent chose to pursue environmental justice through nongovernmental organizations (NGOs). In fact, ten leaders played key roles in founding their groups. As table 2 indicates, their groups varied in scope as well as focus. Organizations with a local scope served a particular neighborhood or an entire city. Some groups worked throughout the state of New Mexico while others were limited to serving the members of particular Indian tribes. Some NGOs had a larger geographic scope that included several states within the southwestern region of the United States. A few NGOs represented groups throughout the nation, while others reached across national boundaries to serve even broader constituencies.

TABLE 2

Focus and Scope of Activists' Organizations

Organizational Focus	Organizational Scope						
	Local	State	Tribal	Regional	National	Int'l	Total
Indigenous Environmental Rights	1	1	0	2	0	2	6
Environmental Protection	0	0	0	2	1	0	3
Sustainable Economic Development	2	0	0	0	0	0	2
Political Empowerment	1	0	0	0	1	0	2
Health & Safety	2	3	2	0	0	0	7
Total	6	4	2	4	2	2	20

The majority of the activists' organizations (fourteen or 70 percent) maintained a local, state, or regional scope focusing on indigenous environmental rights and/or issues pertaining to public health and safety (thirteen or 65 percent). However, environmental protection, sustainable economic development, and political empowerment of community members were also important goals for several groups (seven or 35 percent). In general, the NGOs existed outside of, but interacted with, formal political institutions such as legislative bodies, the courts, and executive agencies.

Activists' Motives for Political Action

Racial/ethnic identity and class figured prominently in the leaders' political activism. This was evidenced in their shared goals of preserving cultural practices, traditions, languages, and life-ways for future generations, despite tremendous pressure to assimilate into the dominant Anglo-American culture. Activists sought to revive centuries-old artistic or agropastoral (farming and sheep raising) traditions, to repatriate native lands or artifacts, to prevent the commercialization of indigenous cultures, to preserve water and soil quality, and to politically empower their peoples. As Marta explained,

> In northern New Mexico we have one of the few pastoral cultures left in this country. And when a pastoral culture loses its land, it becomes an artifact. And I was really very worried that with development pressures, people were going to have to sell their land. . . . Can anything be done to

TABLE 3

Activists' Motives for Political Participation

Motive*	Indigenous	Hispanic	Total	Percent
Cultural preservation	13	12	25	96%
Personal experience/rage	5	5	10	38%
Health/environment	12	13	25	96%
Advocate for children	5	10	15	58%
Advocate for women	2	7	9	35%

*Leaders could indicate multiple reasons for their political participation.
The reasons are not ranked in any way.

bring rural residents together around not losing their culture and their resources as opposed to desperately saying "yes" to jails, to radioactive dumps, to resorts, to whatever? A lifelong question of mine is "How do you even the odds for rural residents that have these cultural relationships and that we're losing in this country?" We're losing that diversity, and the science, and the arts that go with it.

Marta initiated a highly successful economic development project based on traditional agropastoral practices, which was largely owned and operated by women in the community (Pulido 1993). Besides invigorating the local economy, the project had a significant and positive impact on the lives of the women who participated in the project.

Cultural preservation motivated the overwhelming majority of activists (twenty-five or 96 percent) to become politically involved. Like Marta, leaders found that working to achieve cultural preservation often resulted in additional benefits such as the empowerment of residents, increased autonomy in decision making, and material/economic benefits to the community.

Characteristic of the environmental justice movement, numerous leaders identified relationships among people of color, their land and labor, and environmental health issues. For equal numbers of Native women and Hispanas, participation in politics stemmed from personal experiences that politicized them or sufficiently enraged them to mobilize for justice or social change. One leader, Donna, was mobilized into action against the company that had mined her tribe's land for years, leaving the water and soil severely contaminated. Furthermore, she believed that the industry's mining of uranium on the reservation was directly responsible for the unusually high rate of cancer in the community. A cancer survivor herself, and previously apolitical, Donna had begun to make connections between patterns she saw in the siting of hazardous facilities and

Native lands. For Monica, inequalities based on race/ethnicity, gender, and class became visible as a result of her experience as a worker in the microchip industry. The vast majority of the assembly workers in the industry, and, therefore, those most affected by dangerous working conditions, were working-class women of color like her.

Their gendered roles—as women, mothers, wives, and workers—influenced the politics and activism of the New Mexico leaders. After all, women are socialized into the role of caregiver, responsible for the well-being and maintenance of the family and home. For many American Indian and Hispanic women, identity is deeply rooted in their relationship to family, culture, community, and spirituality. As women, they fulfill "harmonious roles in the biological, spiritual, and social worlds. . . . Biologically, they [value] being mothers and raising healthy families; spiritually, they [are] considered extensions of the Spirit Mother and keys to the continuation of their people; and socially, they [serve] as transmitters of cultural knowledge and caretakers of their children and relatives" (LaFramboise et al. 1990, 457; also see Hoikkala 1995). This experience was shared by both the Native and Hispanic leaders, some of whom described themselves as "a Chicana feminist," "an independent Comanche woman, an Indian activist," a "Hispanic woman professional, a single mother," "not your typical Pueblo woman" (laughing heartily), and "a Chicana working mother, a grandmother, a strong woman."

In fulfilling their role as nurturers and providers, women find themselves practicing a "politics of care," which in turn may lead to their political activism and leadership. Researchers note that "for many women in cultures around the world, motherhood is a powerful political identity around which they have galvanized broad-based and influential grassroots movements for social change" (Orleck 1997, 7). Indeed, a number of the New Mexico activists believed that women's gendered roles make them especially suited to organizing and leading. Salina's comments reflect these views: "The world would be much better if more women were in leadership positions. I have a lot of strong women friends. Women have a more nurturing orientation. We're much more helping. . . . I think even in leadership development and empowerment, women naturally know how to do that more." Margarita expressed a similar opinion: "The people that now are taking the leadership are women. . . . The ones with the guts are the women. . . . I also think the bearers of children feel more angered and are more willing to put their necks on the chopping block. In general, women are concerned about the welfare of the future generations." Emphasizing human relationships, the politics of care are characterized by traditionally feminine concerns such as health, safety, housing, and education, issues central to the environmental justice movement (Sidel 1995; Tronto 1993). Terri explained, "Women are life-givers, their connection to Mother Earth is important. Women feel the impact of environmental issues more because they are in the home.

Women look after the health and safety of the family and, by extension, the community." It is no surprise, then, that nearly all of the activists (twenty-five or 96 percent) cited concerns for public health and the environment as motives for their political participation.

Tied closely to the leaders' interest in issues of community health and safety, and to preservation of the natural environment, was concern for the well-being of the next generation. This sentiment is expressed poignantly by Donna: "Everywhere you look there are all kinds of Native American Indians . . . dying of cancer . . . We see the scars the [mining] company left . . . I'm scared about the future for my grandkids. What will there be left for them?" For leaders such as Donna, concern for the well-being of women and children corresponded with the need to respect all life and to maintain harmony in all aspects of life. Preserving environmental quality, conserving natural resources, and respecting "Mother Earth" were themes that emerged frequently, and that were directly related to concerns over the future of the planet. Representing women's and children's issues, protecting their rights, and advocating for their empowerment were motives for political participation articulated twenty-four times by the leaders. For example, Toni said, "I'd like to talk more to women's groups to empower, [to explore] what solutions/changes can you make? To bring a sense of empowerment for self and children's sense of pride in self, in their heritage." Similarly, Salina explained, "I try to push a feminist agenda. In the organization, I look at ways we can involve more people: having meetings in the evening, providing child care, that kind of stuff. Bringing up feminist dialogue in our organizational meetings because it's a good way to educate ourselves about our own internalized oppression. There are real obvious reasons why we need to be feminist. We're still earning sixty cents to the dollar."

Whether or not the activists cited advocacy for women as a motive for their political involvement, however, they all expressed support for equality and the empowerment of women. As Margarita related, "Community activism becomes a part of you, becomes dominant in your life, part of my psyche. Being a woman in a position of always having to fight, there are some gains but also lots of losses. Feeling oppressed . . . radicalizes me. As we move into the twenty-first century and compete for resources it's more of a challenge. . . . I'm who I am because of my involvement." Shaped by their gendered identities as women, mothers, and workers, and by their racial/ethnic identity as indigenous and Hispanic women, the New Mexico leaders were motivated to engage in the politics of environmental justice.

Formulation of Activists' Environmental Beliefs

The activists defined environmentalism in different ways, depending on their personal orientation. Their orientation, or point of view, was based on complex

TABLE 4

Basis of Activists' Environmental Beliefs

	Indigenous	Hispanic	Total*	Percent
Preservation	12	4	16	62%
Sustainable use	11	12	23	88%
Environmental justice	13	13	26	100%
Spiritual beliefs	10	3	13	50%

*Leaders could indicate multiple bases for their environmental beliefs. These are not ranked in any way.

systems of beliefs that may be organized into four broad categories: preservation, sustainable use, environmental justice, and spirituality. Proponents of preservation value wilderness and biodiversity for their own sake, whether or not human beings benefit directly from their existence. Preservation is concerned with maintaining the integrity of "the whole geosphere and biosphere, including man himself" over the long term (Caulfield 1989, 49). In contrast, sustainable use (also known as conservation) involves the development and "wise use" of natural resources, and places human needs above those of nonhuman life. An underlying principle of sustainable use is "the greatest good, for the greatest number, for the longest time" (Caulfield 1989, 20–21). As a belief system, environmental justice incorporates social, economic, and racial- and gender-equity goals. Environment is defined as "where we live, work, and play." Spirituality and traditional religious values were interwoven with the environmental beliefs of several women. In the context of the leaders' spiritual beliefs, the natural environment and nonhuman life are sacred and valued for their own sake; all life is seen as a harmonious interconnected web.

Of the New Mexico activists, sixteen or 62 percent based their environmental beliefs, in part, on preservation. Like mainstream environmentalism, "preservation" stresses the value of maintaining wilderness areas and biodiversity because nature has value in and of itself. The role of humans was seen as stewards of the earth. Nearly all of the indigenous leaders (twelve or 92 percent) and one-quarter of the Hispanas (four or 31 percent) supported preservation. The difference between preservation and conservation was not always clear-cut, however. Lucia, who saw a need for preserving the balance among all living things, sought to protect both endangered species and the life-ways of human communities indigenous to New Mexico. Leaders who similarly incorporated elements of both preservation and conservation into their environmental belief systems were able to bridge effectively the political and ideological differences between the mainstream environmental groups and local grassroots organizations that worked for environmental justice and advocated sustainable use.

Sustainable use, also referred to as "conservation," promotes the "wise use" of natural resources and places human needs above those of nonhuman life. The environmental approach preferred by 88 percent (twenty-three) of the New Mexico activists, sustainable use favors forms of economic development and lifestyles that seek a balance between the human and natural environments. The considerable support for conservation by the New Mexico activists may be explained, in part, by its strong cultural component. Advocates of sustainable use emphasized the historic ties to the land that both Native people and Spanish descendants share. Historic practices such as ritual field burning to replenish the soil, the maintenance of *acequias* (irrigation canals), sheep herding and weaving, and the cultivation and use of indigenous medicinal plants by *curanderas* and *curanderos* (healers) are rich cultural traditions unique to New Mexico. Sustainable use promotes maintenance of traditional agrarian and/or pastoral life-ways, which was seen as especially important to this group of leaders for preserving New Mexico's indigenous and Spanish cultures. Such views tie in directly with the political goals of the environmental justice movement, to obtain social justice and economic parity for women and communities of color.

All twenty-six leaders based their environmental beliefs on principles fundamental to the environmental justice movement, which include such goals as achieving social and economic justice and racial and gender equity, as well as improving or maintaining environmental quality. Environmental justice advocates promote social and economic equity among racial/ethnic and socioeconomic groups by ensuring that both the costs and benefits of development and environmental policies are shared across society.

The New Mexico leaders' spirituality and religious beliefs also shaped their environmental ideology. Half of the New Mexico leaders included spirituality as a basis for their environmental beliefs. Three Hispanas (23 percent) and a majority of indigenous women (ten or 77 percent) exhibited spiritual-environmental beliefs. Key to these beliefs was the principle that the natural environment and all life, whether human or not, is equally sacred and, therefore, equally valued. All of life forms an interconnected web, which must be held in balance and respected in order to be maintained.

The interconnectedness among Native spirituality, environment, and tribal sovereignty has been prominently illustrated by an ongoing struggle between development interests and Native peoples in the state. In recent years, Indian tribes across New Mexico have allied with both grassroots environmental justice organizations and national environmental groups to litigate against the U.S. Forest Service, the Bureau of Land Management, and municipal authorities to protect religious sites such as Petroglyph Park near Albuquerque from encroaching urban development. The issues of tribal sovereignty and cultural preservation have come up against economic interests and political concerns in this and similar disputes, which mirror the larger struggle of the environmental justice movement: to improve the quality of life for the poor and for people of color by empowering women and communities of color. As Native American scholar Paula Gunn Allen notes, "If American society judiciously modeled the traditions of the various Native Nations, the place of women in society would become central, the distribution of goods and power would be egalitarian, the elderly would be respected, honored, and protected as a primary social and cultural resource, . . . the destruction of the biota, the life sphere, and the natural resources of the planet would be curtailed, and the spiritual nature of human and nonhuman life would become a primary organizing principle of human society" (Gunn Allen 1986, 211).

Activists' Conceptualizations of Environmentalism

Although they espoused values that included respect for nature and conservation of the earth's resources, most of the New Mexico activists did not consider themselves to be environmentalists. As we can see from table 5, only a minority (nine or 35 percent) of the twenty-six leaders actually called themselves "environmentalists."

In the tradition of the mainstream environmental movement, environmentalists demonstrated values such as preservation of wilderness areas and maintaining biodiversity, and saw the appropriate role of human beings as stewards of the earth. This perspective is exemplified in Erica's comments: "I believe in preserving, in respecting the use of resources. Respect for the environment is essential. If you take care of the earth and you take care of the heavens—important things in life—that will always be there to sustain your life."

The majority of the leaders described themselves as "Third World" or "indigenous" environmentalists. As Linda explained, "An indigenous environmentalist is one who believes in the spiritual value of nature. One who sees nature not only in a patch of forest, but also in the middle of downtown. An indigenous environmentalist does not see anything 'wild' about nature." Equal numbers of indigenous and Hispanic leaders (sixteen or 62 percent of the total) identified themselves as what I call a Third World environmentalist. Third World environmentalists advocated participatory decision making and locally determined priorities that reflect the concerns and values of women, indigenous, and Third World peoples. The leaders who identified with the environmental justice movement sought to incorporate the cultural beliefs of Third World peoples regarding sustainable use (conservation) into contemporary environmentalism. Belief in the value of indigenous people's knowledge and experience of the earth is central to the environmental justice movement. Winona LaDuke, an indigenous environmentalist, ties environmental protec-

TABLE 5

Activists' Conceptualization with Environmentalism

	Indigenous	Hispanic	Total	Percent*
Environmentalist	4	5	9	35%
Non-environmentalist	1	0	1	4%
Third World environmentalist	8	8	16	62%

* Total is greater than 100% due to rounding.

tion to cultural preservation and economic autonomy for her tribe (Orleck 1997).

Proponents of the environmental justice movement were concerned with the economic and political empowerment of women and Third World communities. Third World environmentalists differentiated their perspective from that of the mainstream environmental movement, claiming that the latter is out of touch with the economic and social realities of the poor, the working class, women, and people of color (Di Chiro 1992). Indeed, the problems that Third World environmentalists face are far more immediate and personally threatening than the traditional environmental concern for preservation of wilderness areas and nonhuman species, which the Third World environmentalists regarded of less consequence than the survival of their people and their communities (Austin and Schill 1994; Marquez 1994). As a result, political activism was often highly personal because threats to the environment were interpreted as threats to their families and communities. For example, several New Mexico leaders shared the opinion that "our land is being ripped off with the help of the top ten mainstream environmental organizations that have colluded with industry, the military, and government, and agribusiness" (Juana).

Activists like Juana believe that government and industry specifically select communities of color for siting hazardous or otherwise undesirable land uses. Juana and other activists view these efforts as "environmental racism," a form of genocide that targets racial/ethnic minority groups and economically disadvantaged communities to bear a disproportionate burden of society's wastes. Environmental racism is a dominant theme in the narratives of many minority women activists (Churchill and LaDuke 1992; Jaimes 1992).

Conclusions

"I've learned to use every strategy in the book, from female wiles to crying—if that will help. [Laughs] We've joined boycotts, picketed, marched. Our leadership training program prepares the next generation. . . . We've created a network of people nationwide to help, mainly activists but [some are] in government. . . . Changing institutions is so hard. What's most effective is changing individuals to become change agents. I cultivate people, contacts; then I can call them for help" (Lorna).

As leaders in the environmental justice movement, Native American and Hispanic women work to influence public policy and politics in villages and towns across New Mexico. Whether at the local, state, tribal, or regional level, these activists build coalitions among like-minded groups and empower community residents to affect environmental, social, and economic changes. Their political ideology and policy goals are shaped by their experiences as women, as workers, as members of racial and/or ethnic minority groups, and by their socioeconomic position in the dominant society.

Nearly twice as many of the New Mexico activists identified as Third World environmentalists as environmentalists, preferring an ideology that takes into account the beliefs, cultural values, and life-ways of racial/ethnic minorities. While these leaders may share some of the precepts, goals, and strategies of the mainstream environmental movement, they create an alternative approach and political agenda that addresses the particular needs of communities of color. Third World environmentalism seeks to do much more than maintain or improve environmental quality and protect wildlife. As a political and social movement, it is clearly distinguished from mainstream environmentalism by its goals of cultural preservation, the attainment of racial and gender equality, and empowering community members to take an active role in politics and public decision making.

New Mexico's history of colonization, substantial Native American and Hispanic populations, political culture, and economy contribute to the vitality of the environmental justice movement within the state. The impact of the mining and nuclear industries on New Mexico's environment has no doubt contributed to the proliferation of grassroots environmental justice organizations in the state. Headed by Native and Hispanic women, these organizations provide excellent opportunities for community members to gain valuable leadership experience and to become involved in politics and public policymaking. And as conflicts over rights to resources, development, and political influence persist among the state's various interests—Hispanic and Anglo communities, Indian nations, federal agencies, farmers, ranchers, developers, and corporations—activists will continue to play an important role.

The political involvement of Native American and Hispanic women leaders is motivated by their identification with their racial/ethnic group, their desire to improve the status of women, and by their concern for the rights of socioeconomically disadvantaged individuals. This illustrates an important distinction from Anglo-American women leaders in that racial/ethnic identity and culture have tremendous salience for both Native women and Hispanas whose concerns range from battling environmental racism, to preserving their native language, to maintaining tribal sovereignty. By advocating for and empowering politically marginalized and economically disadvantaged groups within the state, Native and Hispanic women activists promote democratic values and processes. They are devoted political actors who advocate universal participation in public decision-making processes as they work to improve social, environmental, and economic conditions in their communities. Their activism is animated by the overarching goal of achieving economic equity and social justice for their communities.

The politics of these Native American and Hispanic women leaders are heavily influenced by their racial, ethnic, and gender identity. They represent the interests of their ethnic communities, advance the position of women in society, and motivate individual citizens to participate actively in public life. Gender, race/ethnicity, and class inform and shape their leadership and public policy agendas. Through their work in New Mexico's environmental justice movement, Native American and Hispanic women demonstrate love, courage, strength, and vision. Their efforts to empower others, to protect the environment, and to improve the lives of their people help to make the state a land of enchantment.

REFERENCES

Adeola, F. O. 1994. "Environmental Hazards, Health, and Racial Inequity in Hazardous Waste Distribution." *Environment and Behavior* 26, no. 1: 99–126.

Austin, R., and M. Schill. 1994. "Black, Brown, Red, and Poisoned." *Humanist* 54, no. 4: 9–16.

Bretting, J. G., and D. M. Prindeville. 1998. "Environmental Justice and the Role of Indigenous Women Organizing Their Communities." In *Environmental Injustices, Political Struggles: Race, Class, and the Environment*, ed. D. Camacho. Durham: Duke University Press.

Cable, S., and C. Cable. 1995. *Environmental Problems, Grassroots Solutions: The Politics of Grassroots Environmental Conflict.* New York: St. Martin's Press.

Caulfield, H. P. 1989. "The Conservation and Environmental Movements: An Historical Analysis." In *Environmental Politics and Policy: Theories and Evidence*, ed. J. P. Lester. Durham: Duke University Press.

Churchill, W., and W. LaDuke. 1992. "Native North America: The Political Economy of Radioactive Colonialism" In *The State of Native America: Genocide, Colonization, and Resistance*, ed. M. A. Jaimes. Boston: South End Press.

Di Chiro, G. 1992. "Defining Environmental Justice: Women's Voices and Grassroots Politics." *Socialist Review* 22, no. 4: 93–130.

Ford, R. L. 1990. "Native American Women Activists: Past and Present." Master's thesis. Southwest Texas State University.

Gunn Allen, P. 1986. *The Sacred Hoop: Recovering the Feminine in American Indian Traditions.* Boston: Beacon Press.

Hoikkala, P. H. 1995. "Native American Women and Community Work in Phoenix, 1965–1980." *Dissertation Abstracts International*, vol. 56–06A: 2382. Item No. AAI95–33382.

Jaimes, M. A. 1992. "American Indian Women: At the Center of Indigenous Resistance in North America." In *The State of Native America: Genocide, Colonization, and Resistance*, ed. M. A. Jaimes. Boston: South End Press.

Kingsolver, B. 1989. *Holding the Line: Women in the Great Arizona Mine Strike of 1983*. Ithaca: ILR Press.

LaFramboise, T., A. Heyle, and E. Ozer. 1990. "Changing and Diverse Roles of Women in American Indian Cultures." *Sex Roles* 22, no. 7/8: 455–76.

Marquez, B. 1994. "The Politics of Environmental Justice in Mexican American Neighborhoods." Paper presented at the annual meeting of the Western Political Science Association in Albuquerque, N.M., Mar. 10–12.

———. 1995. "Organizing Mexican-American Women in the Garment Industry: La Mujer Obrera." *Women and Politics* 15, no. 1: 65–87.

Orleck, A. 1997. "Tradition Unbound: Radical Mothers in International Perspective." In *The Politics of Motherhood: Activist Voices from Left to Right*, ed. A. Jetter, A. Orleck, and D. Taylor. Hanover: University Press of New England.

Pardo, M. 1990. "Mexican American Women Grassroots Community Activists: 'Mothers of East Los Angeles.'" *Frontiers* 11, no. 1: 1–7.

Prindeville, D. M., and J. G. Bretting. 1998. "Indigenous Women Activists and Political Participation: The Case of Environmental Justice." *Women and Politics* 19, no. 1: 39–58.

Pulido, L. 1993. "Sustainable Development at Ganados del Valle." In *Confronting Environmental Racism: Voices from the Grassroots*, ed. R. D. Bullard. Boston: South End Press.

Redhouse, J. 1984. "The Seven Sisters: Native Women in Struggle." Unpublished memoir.

Sidel, R. 1995. "Toward a More Caring Society." In *Race, Class, and Gender*, ed. P. S. Rothenberg. 3rd ed. New York: St. Martin's Press.

Tronto, J. 1993. *Moral Boundaries: A Political Argument for an Ethic of Care*. New York: Routledge.

West, G., and R. L. Blumberg. 1990. "Reconstructing Social Protest From a Feminist Perspective." In *Women and Social Protest*, ed. G. West and R. L. Blumberg. New York: Oxford University Press.

6

Sexual Politics and Environmental Justice

Lesbian Separatists in Rural Oregon

CATRIONA SANDILANDS

In her essay "Ecological Legitimacy and Cultural Essentialism" (1998), Laura Pulido makes an interesting argument about cultural politics and environmental justice. Describing Ganados del Valle, a Hispano community project in northern New Mexico, Pulido argues that the group's deployment of a strategically essentialist connection between Hispano culture and environmental sustainability was an effective strategy to make changes that were both ecologically and culturally beneficial for the community. Set against a dominant Anglo representation of Hispanos as ecologically irresponsible, the counterdiscourse of Hispanos as inherent nature stewards created what Pulido calls "ecological legitimacy" in the political realm as well as a cultural pride important to community involvement with the project. Apart from the important observation that environmental and cultural issues are strongly linked in environmental justice struggles, Pulido's analysis demonstrates that the creative act of weaving a collective identity, a new or hybrid culture of nature, can have profound environmental significance.

The leap between Hispano environmental organizing in New Mexico and lesbian land communities in Oregon is a large one, but in this respect they share an agenda: they are marginalized communities crafting new cultures of nature against dominant social and ecological relations of late capitalism. Where the environmental justice movement has, however, described the organizing co-relations of power between racism and environmental degradation, there has been little attention paid to the fact that sexuality might also be a dimension of power worth investigating for its environmental significance. What I propose here is that the social relations of nature clearly include sexuality, and indeed, that there may then be fruitful collaborations between gay/lesbian/bisexual/transgendered/queer (GLBTQ)[1] and environmental politics. To the lesbians living in intentional land-based communities in the southern Oregon, of course, this proposition is intuitively obvious. At the height of lesbian feminism in the 1970s and 1980s, lesbian separatists who moved to rural settings to live collectively away from urban heteropatriarchy had a clear idea about the importance of nature in their culture, and the importance of their culture to ecology. One of the most famous separatist texts of the period, Sally Gearhart's utopian novel *The Wanderground* (1979), exemplified this position; it argued that women are not only naturally allied to nature (in opposition to male-constructed capitalist cities), but that women-identified-women living in self-sufficient communities in nature could develop new sensual and social relations that are truly in tune with natural processes.

As a political movement, lesbian separatism gained prominence during the 1970s and 1980s. As Arlene Stein (1997) describes, its origins are generally traced back to fury at the ways mainstream feminists distanced themselves from lesbian struggles and purged lesbians from their organizational ranks. In response, separatists sought to establish lesbianism as a radical political position through an active strategy of women's *separation* from male culture. Borrowing from the nationalist identities and strategies of black and aboriginal civil rights movements, lesbian separatists argued that women needed to withdraw support from the heteropatriarchy and develop communities away from the oppressive influence of men. To be sure, separatism had its share of problems. It called on women to prioritize their sexual-gender identity over all others and to break solidarities that might have been based on race or class but that tied women to men. As a result, separatism was a largely white and middle-class movement; it also discouraged affinities with gay men's struggles. At its height, lesbian separatism—and here I simplify critiques offered by Stein, Sally Munt (1998), and Dana Shugar (1995), among others—tended toward ahistorical, essentialist, and biologically determinist analyses of sexuality and identity. As a cultural nationalism, however, lesbian separatism was importantly about creating a libratory space for radical transformation.

Although it is, twenty-odd years later, customary to condemn separatism out of hand for its more "extreme" essentialist elements, it was actually a more complex politics than most critiques allow. For example, lesbian separatists were among the first white (second wave) feminists to include explicit analyses of class and race in their political visions. In this light, much separatist rhetoric can be understood as *strategically* essentialist;[2] with strategic consciousness came a recognition of diversity that was quite powerful for the time and place. A closer historical view suggests that, for all its problems, separatism acted in particular times and places as a form of locally specified political culture.

I would argue that rural lesbian separatism is also a locally specified form of *queer ecology*, a cultural-political-social analysis that interrogates the co-relations between the social organization of sexuality and ecology and is allied with both environmental justice and ecofeminism. Although seldom discussed explicitly, queer ecology has been indicated in at least two contexts. First, a number of recent texts in "queer geography" call attention to the ways sexualities are organized spatially, including such issues as queers' access to—and particular sexual, cultural, political, and other uses of—public nature spaces; the discursive-ideological sexualization of ideas of wilderness, urbanity, and rurality; and the importance of particular landscapes for the formation and organization of particular queer cultures and experiences (see Bell and Valentine 1995a; Ingram et al. 1997; Phillips et al. 2000). For example, urban nature spaces have been significant hives of sexual and other activity for many urban gay men and lesbians. For another, medicalized discourses of "natural" sexuality have had, at least since the late nineteenth century, a strong impact on the ways in which individuals understand and organize their sexualities and communities.

Second, ecofeminist writers Greta Gaard (1997) and Stacy Alaimo (2000) have suggested interesting trajectories of analysis.[3] For Gaard, the crucial point is that the conceptual organization of hierarchical dualism in Western thought similarly justifies both the dominance of heterosexuality over other sexualities and the elevation of (rational, disembodied) culture over (erotic, embodied) nature. She thus concludes that "the native feminized other of nature is not simply eroticized but also queered and animalized, in that any sexual behavior outside the rigid confines of compulsory heterosexuality becomes queer and subhuman" (130). Alaimo, building on such insights, demonstrates that writers such as Canadian novelist Jane Rule actively disrupt this configuration, creating a textual-cultural politics that articulates ecological with lesbian concerns. She notes that Rule's influential *Desert of the Heart* (1964), for example, "complicates the natural to such a degree that it can no longer serve as the bedrock of heterosexuality" and "(de)naturalizes the desert, transforming nature into a space for lesbian desire" (2000, 166 and 167).

It is in a combination of these two currents that one can find a useful place from which to think of a genuinely queer ecology. Parallel to Pulido, who sees Hispano culture at Ganados del Valle as a strategic intervention into Hispano social and ecological community creating a counterhegemonic culture of nature, I see an ecology framed by the spatial-discursive power relations of nature and sexuality and by an active cultural politics to displace the interstructured power relations of heterosexism and ecological degradation. That these two may not be separate projects is also indicated by Pulido: cultural intervention may, in many cases, have a strong impact in the organization of nature space. Such is the case with the lesbian separatist land communities of southern Oregon, whose struggles over nearly thirty years indicate this kind of impact.

This essay thus springs from the question "what do the experiences of Oregon lesbian separatist land communities show us about possible relations between sexuality and ecology?" In the context of recent condemnations of separatist essentialism, this analysis also seeks to tell a more complex tale about lesbian separatists' ideas of nature, including the facts that lesbian essentialism is often also strategic and that separatism itself has changed a great deal since the 1970s. Although this examination is a very partial (in all senses of the word) representation of the southern Oregon communities and their complex ideas and practices of nature, it ultimately seeks to suggest that these communities offer a political program of "queering" ecology that is very important to contemporary understandings of sexual and environmental justice.

From the 1970s until the present, hundreds of women moved to southern Oregon, as they moved to lesbian intentional communities or "women's lands" all over North America. Many "landdyke" communities were disbanded over the years; others have survived in various forms, and new communities have come into being. Despite the persistence of these communities, few academic works have even recognized rural separatism, and the few that do (Valentine 1997; Shugar 1995) tend to render it as a politics belonging to another age entirely. This study, in contrast, begins with the premise that the rural lesbian separatist intentional communities are alive and, particularly along the southern Oregon stretch of Interstate 5, quite well. The "community" of lesbian communities there is a porous and fluid entity, comprised of a variety of lesbians, a variety of separatist and nonseparatist philosophies, and a variety of institutional arrangements. As Summerhawk and Gagehabib describe:

> The Southern Oregon Lesbian Community is a loose network of intentional, rural collectives and individual women living in the small towns or in the country who consider themselves part of it. The intentional land communities range from a well-organized WomanShare collective, to the individually controlled Rootworks, to the buy-share arrangement of Rainbow's End. The community has several gatherings each year to celebrate itself or natural events such as the Equinox, or to produce workshops around a common theme. (2000, 115)

By and large, the lesbians to whom I spoke (and the archival sources I consulted) agreed that there were, over the years, five or six "core" collective women's lands plus various other institutions (newsletters, properties, support groups, and educational resources) and individuals/households who had some relationship to this core. The network of rural lesbians and institutions currently extends south into Jackson County and particularly into Ashland, and north into Eugene and even to the We'Moon lands near Portland. My research focused on the still-inhabited intentional communities, but necessarily included a broader historical consideration of the others and of the experiences of some of the women who had left the communities at various points but were still part of the larger southern Oregon network.

A Rural Idyll? Early Separatist Nature Imaginings

In 1974, three women—Dian, Billie, and Carol—got out of their van in southern Oregon and bought "23 acres with two houses overlooking a beautiful view of the surrounding mountains" for $27,000 (Womanshare Collective 1976, 64). They sought a life on the land, "to live near the healing beauty of nature," and to have, in a sanctuary carved outside of urban patriarchy, "a safe space to live, to work, to help create the women's culture [they] dreamed of" (62). From the very beginning, nature had played an important role in lesbian separatist politics. Gill Valentine notes that generally the women who moved to the land drew "upon stereotypical representations of the rural as a healthy, simple, peaceful, safe place to live while also imagining their 'rural idyll' in a very different (and very politicized) way from traditional white middle-class understandings of rurality" (1997, 109). In early separatist rhetoric, male culture was exemplified by the city, and a movement of women into "new" and more innocent space, a nature not yet written upon by male culture, would facilitate the founding of a new lesbian culture.

Thus, when Dian, Billie, and Carol arrived at Womanshare, they brought with them a desire to create a lesbian existence that articulated these ideas of nature with the politicized tenets of separatism. They wanted to exclude themselves from patriarchal institutions, developing as self-sufficient an existence on the land as possible. They wanted to make decisions and own the land collectively, to transform middle-class financial privilege into working-class women's solidarity. They wanted to practice nonmonogamy, removing the institution of "ownership" from their sexual and emotional lives, and to share all forms of labor, enabling each woman to gain a diversity of land skills and allowing her time and space for creative pursuits. They wanted to grow food organically, live simply, challenge consumer culture, and engage in ecologically appropriate lifestyles. They wanted to include spirituality and ritual practice in their lives, including veneration for women's bodies and cycles. Eventually, they wanted more—and more diverse—women to join them on their land, and they worked hard toward greater accessibility. In this context, part of the separatist desire for land was as a space of freedom for women to become themselves; another part was for land as a space of experiment in which women could become something else.

Difficult though it was, this separatist desire for rural collectivity proved popular in the 1970s and 1980s for many (mostly white) women. Partly because of the growing visibility of the lands generated by publications like *Country Women* and *WomanSpirit*, other women began to move to southern Oregon either to look for land or join existing communities. Cabbage Lane, founded as a gay/bisexual mixed-sex commune in 1972, was divided in 1973 into a sixty-acre women's parcel and a twenty-acre "men's parcel up the hill" (Nelly in Corinne n.d., 6). In a less friendly split, Jean and Ruth Mountaingrove left the mixed-sex commune at Golden and founded the smaller Rootworks (seven acres) in 1975. Further north, a couple took possession of the forty-seven acres that became Rainbow's End on January 1, 1976. Halfway in between and after a difficult search, Fly Away Home (forty mountaintop acres) became women's land in 1976. Perhaps most importantly, the Oregon Women's Land Trust (OWLT) established the 147-acre OWL Farm as "open wimmin's land" in 1976 (they saw it as the first of many such purchases). As an information pamphlet from that period described,

> *Oregon Woman's* [sic] *Land* is a nonprofit corporation, founded to acquire land for women and preserve it in perpetuity. Women need to have the time and space and resources to develop their own culture. Recognizing that most women are confined in cities with no access to land, we are attempting to acquire and provide access to land in as many ways as women want it. . . . We want to be stewards of the land, treating her not as a commodity but as a full partner and guide in this exploration of who we are. (OWLT 1976, n.p.)

By the late 1970s, these "core" lesbian communities had been joined by others. In addition, a network of lesbian relationships and institutions had begun to form around the lands, ranging from the editorial collective of *WomanSpirit*, now produced at Rootworks; to aspiring- or ex-landdyke individuals living in nearby towns; to workshops drawing women to Womanshare from San Francisco and Portland, among other places; to rituals, dances, and potlucks; to a writers' group and photography seminars (Corinne n.d.; Summerhawk and Gagehabib 2000). In short, the community as a whole was so culturally vibrant that the I–5 corridor between Eugene and the California border came to be known as "The Amazon Trail."

At the same time, the communities were conflict ridden; many of the collectively held lands went through intense and painful struggles. OWL Farm erupted quickly: the vision of land open to all women, the equal valuing of all labor, and the commitment to collective decision making proved a particularly incendiary combination. Other collectives found that no amount of well-intentioned lesbian labor could compensate for a poor water supply in August or a lack of knowledge about production gardening. Still others were torn apart by interpersonal jealousies, financial difficulties, and lack of commitment. The tensions of polyamory were intensified by constant interaction. Thus, Valentine is correct when she argues that "lesbian separatist attempts to establish 'idyllic' ways of living appear to have unraveled because, in common with traditional white middle-class visions of 'rural community,' attempts to create unity and common ways of living also produced boundaries and exclusions" (1997, 119).

But she is not correct in proclaiming the dissolution of the *communities*; they have survived, albeit in much changed forms.

Tenets of a Separatist Ecology

After nearly thirty years of existence, the southern Oregon separatist community as a whole can be characterized by an ongoing dynamic between a separatist utopian ideology and an everyday practice of subsistence culture located in its particular geographic place. This dynamic is especially important when describing the community's ecological views; separatist principles have been rethought and reworked in the particular places and activities that are the everyday life of the community. Apart from the influential sociopolitical specificity of the state, it is fair to say that Billie, Carol, and Dian's choice of southern Oregon had an ecological impact on the communities' development. The relatively mild weather allowed considerable latitude in building design and quality in addition to year-round agriculture, but the relatively poor soil necessitated a creative array of soil augmentation technologies and the dry summers spelled water shortages. The mountains allowed for a greater sense of isolation and privacy than would be possible in a flatter landscape, thus affording a much greater lesbian sexual freedom (even with the abundant poison oak); they also created problems of access for women with disabilities and—crucially now—for women worried about aging.

The landscape has truly had a profound influence on the ways in which separatism became a "local" political-ecological culture. First, separatist philosophy actively included a philosophy of nature and promoted a particular awareness of the landscape and ecological relations that has grown over the years. Second, the physical rigors of life on the land intensified conflicts, but they also brought the women who stayed on the lands into particular kinds of contact with natural processes that many women—including many rurally born women—were not familiar with; these interactions allowed for "new" experiences of nature. Third, the land itself became a tie that bound community members when separatist ideology came apart; in the absence of utopia, the realities of survival came to occupy an important role in collective life. Out of these nature-culture interactions, a sophisticated series of social ecological principles and practices has emerged.

The following six principles, gleaned from both documentary and interview materials, serve as particularly rich indicators of a thriving separatist ecological culture in southern Oregon. I offer them neither as a complete picture of rural lesbian separatism nor as a template for a queer ecology. Rather, they are descriptions of an ecological culture that has emerged, through conflict and change, over time; my descriptions thus include both historical and contemporary dimensions. Although not all principles are currently shared by all members, all, I think, are recognizable elements of the community's collective identity. Given space constraints, I can only outline them briefly; what they indicate, separately and together, is a distinct body of separatist-ecological culture, to be discussed as such in the final section.

1. Opening rural land to all women by transforming relations of ownership

Rural separatist politics were founded on the idea that land should be made accessible to as many women as possible. OWL Farm was explicitly "founded to acquire land for women who would otherwise not have such access" (OWLT 1977, n.p.) and sought to remove the criterion of property ownership from the possibility of living a rural life. Nearly all of the communities began with this desire: to acquire rural spaces and invite women of all classes and races to come and stay, thereby (1) allowing women to live in nature as equal members of a women's community (and not as a man's "property") and (2) removing class and race privileges from this nature experience. OWL Farm was particularly important in this respect; it was the only land that never had residents who were also owners, and it sought to enshrine a distinctly classless relation to landscape in its "reservation" of land for all women. Still it, and all the other lands, held contradictions of ownership; most of the women are profoundly aware of them and saw themselves as using their privileges of ownership for a redistributive good.

The women remain committed to this strategy. For example, Bethroot[4] stated:

> Women's land, lesbian land . . . [is] land that women have purchased and are living on or [is] in a Land Trust context. It is intended to serve lesbians, not only the ones who live here, and it is intended to be lesbian land evermore. It's not imagined that someday it will be bought and sold and it will be on the open market again. It's land that we always have assumed other lesbians will live on after we go.

Beverly added:

> In some ways [Womanshare] really was like a Lesbian National Park. I love that analogy. It was very cheap; it was safe; there was a tremendous amount of access but there were enough rules to give it structure, and a level of sanitation that people didn't get sick, and it was consciously creating access for working class women.

2. Withdrawing the land from patriarchal-capitalist production and reproduction

From its beginnings, the separatists understood that the rural landscape was a site of domination. On one level, they sought to alter the subjection of women to capital (through wage labor) and to men (through daily reproduction) by enabling women to choose a life free from both and to live a self-sufficient rural existence with other women. On another level, separatists also sought to alter the relations by which rural nature is dominated in capitalism, by privileging relations to nature outside of commodity production and exchange. Even in the 1970s, country lesbians were concerned about the increasing organization of agricultural lands by corporate interests, the exploitation of farm workers, the effects of chemical farming, and the massive loss of diverse knowledges of agricultural and natural processes. Wresting control of farmland from agribusiness was a gesture of refusal; working that land in noncorporate ways offered to create a landscape—and a women's culture—in an alternative mode.

The communities continue to practice subsistence agriculture as part of their anticapitalist intention. Although on such a small scale this shift to subsistence has little effect on surrounding corporate practice, it does have an effect on the women's culture as a microcosm of possibility. For example, growing their own food has changed the ways many women think about and live in the landscape. Nearly all of the women I spoke to understood gardening as a crucial practice of coming to respect and understand the land; certainly, part of their craft was born of necessity, but it also became a visceral pleasure and ethical principle. As La Verne described, "We started immediately to pick over the garden because the women [at Golden] had just let it go, they were too busy to do the garden. So [my partner] and I started caring for the garden. . . . I enjoyed it, getting my hands in the soil. . . . I had a certain respect for the land [before I came] but I learned more when I was there." In addition, agricultural and other life relations to the land were and are organized along strong principles of nonviolence. Jean, for example, refuses to fuel an antagonistic relationship to the poison oak that is one of the banes of southern Oregon existence. Rather, she welcomes the plant into her spirituality through contemplation and ritual, into her body by ingesting small but progressively larger amounts of it to increase (along homeopathic principles) her body's acceptance of the poison, and into her life by learning to think of poison oak as as much a part of the landscape as herself.

3. Feminizing and reacculturing the landscape, symbolically and physically

Rural separatists' resistance is strongly oriented to reinscribing gender and nature, to living a life among women and for women that could conceivably allow new forms of gender to come into being alongside nature. The utopian elements of separatism's earliest articulations were not just ideological statements about the ecological future that would come into being if only women ruled the world; they were imaginative leaps that opened the world to the possibility of living gender and nature differently. As a result, apart from the physical changes to the landscape wrought by low-impact agricultural and living practices, there was also a definite "feminizing" trend in the lands' aesthetic organization. Some of these interventions are obvious; Rootworks has a vulva-shaped garden, there are assorted goddesses placed in strategic locations at Fly Away Home, and there is a decided preference for simple, low, roundish buildings. At OWL Farm, the cleared land takes the shape of a dancing woman; the map of the land posted on the front of the main house is thus also a portrait of the spirit the land is to evoke. True, there are fences (practical). But there are also places where boundaries are intentionally blurred: a garden specifically for the deer, outdoor kitchens and outhouses, inedible flowers in the same patch as food. In this feminization, the women demonstrate that nature is a "like" place or actor, not an Other to be tamed or feared but a friend, a sister, a lover. In turn, of course, nature has written into feminism; the trees at OWL encroach on the dancing woman, changing her shape; the goddess in the garden is barely visible above the undergrowth; cleared land is reclaimed by encroaching root systems.

These movements of nature into lesbian culture are not simply physical, but spiritual, metaphoric, and creative; almost all of the women have taken nature into creative writing, and many have been published. For example, relatively recent Rootworks arrival Helen invokes in this excerpt from her poem "bare" the idea of nature as a space of sensual pleasure and renewal alongside a feminist "we" that gestures toward struggle and solidarity:

> can't you see?
> we *deserve* this—to have
>   april rain greet our skin
>   bare as tulips
> shot from darkness into
>   this tender light—
> knowing spring
> fat with promise— . . . .
> (2001, 5)

4. Developing a holistic and gender-bending physical experience of nature

Many women demonstrated a complex understanding of how the separatist community's reorganization of mainstream gendered divisions of labor actively changed experiences of living on the land, and perceptions of nature as a result. Their insistence on lesbian identity as a challenge to prescribed gender roles, combined with the particular physical rigors of living on the land without elaborate infrastructure, led to a situation in which even women who were not previously adept at tree felling and mechanical repairs developed skills in these areas. As each woman participated in multiple forms of work, each was exposed to physical experiences of the landscape in a way far less gendered than is typically the case in mixed-sex communities. Some articulated a belief that separatists had a richer and more complex understanding of nature for the simple reason that they had a richer and more complex *working* knowledge of it. More

generally, they understood that their knowledge of the land derived from physical work, creative production, and spiritual reflection; these were and are understood as part of an integrated life in nature.

This understanding includes a feminist commitment to extend women's
lives beyond mainstream gender roles, the fact of subsisting on the land without a socially supported model of male expertise, a lack of easily available services for hire, a commitment to low-technology living, and the presence of a
community of like-minded women offering resources and guidance. NíAóda-
gaín told a wonderful story about her first major building project at OWL Farm:
replacing the heavy beam that supported the porch roof on the main house. She
avoided the task for weeks, afraid of the beam and not confident that she could
fix it if she tried. Committed separatist though she was, she admitted that "if
there had been a man there, he would have done it . . . but there was only me
and when I finally did it, it was one of the greatest accomplishments of my life."
Similarly, she told me that another woman who had lived at OWL Farm "was
elated because she had cooked a pot of beans on her own stove with wood she
had cut herself and water she had hauled in buckets." Indeed, she indicated
that some of the women felt they were able to "become" lesbian more fully on
the land than they would have in a city, meaning that their identities as lesbians were strongly tied to their transcendence of *gender* roles and that such
roles were more likely broken on the land. She saw this process as distinctly
ecological: "women coming down to their simplest place: do you understand
the relationship between your life and the land, what it does to the earth, where
the water and wood come from?"

5. *Experiencing nature as an erotic partner*

For some of the women, one of the most significant ways the land shapes their
rural lesbian identity is in the weaving together of sexual-erotic with rural-natural
elements. Some have actively appropriated a normative idea of "nature" for a
lesbian sexuality societally deemed "unnatural." Others have carved out an idea
of "natured" female sexuality in defiance of what they see as an urban-mascu-
line patriarchal sexuality. The idea of nature as a normative ideal for a rural lesbian sexuality is widespread and carries with it some interesting inflections.
One of the most self-conscious proponents of this view is Tee Corinne, who has
spent much of her artistic career advocating for and creating representations of
lesbian sexuality in which lesbian sex is beautiful *because* natural. These representations allow lesbian "nature" to be "art" against aesthetic conventions
that would insist on, for example, shame or perversion. She understands this
"wholesomeness" specifically against other representations of lesbian sex that
celebrate, for example, sexual roles, self-conscious perversity, and fetishism;
she wrote to me that she has "sought to present lesbian sexuality as loving,
lovely and natural. In thinking about this I considered how 'unnatural' many of

the images in [the lesbian erotic journal] *On Our Backs* appear and how this shift in goals from early lesbian feminism (1970–1985) coincides with a shift to images of dildo sex, bondage, flagellation, etc."

Others of the separatists I spoke to were aware that they were not discovering a "natural" sexuality in a pristine natural space but were actively *creating* a lesbian sexuality in and for their communities in this time and place. Indeed, although Tee's presence certainly mobilized the community's erotic conversations and literary outputs in the 1990s, many considered sex an important dimension of existence from the outset. Nonmonogamous, nonpossessive sex was one of the grand experiments with which the communities began; even if this ideal did not produce anything like a total sexual revolution, it certainly inspired a willingness to experiment with erotic possibilities as an important part of living in the separatist landscape. As Madrone described:

> I have the experience of making love with the land, that the land is my lover, and that lovemaking is a lesbian lovemaking with herself and it is very specifically inspired by the landscape. . . . I am very aware that I do have that erotic experience and that it is very specifically inspired by something that's happening on the landscape. This would never happen to me in the city. . . . I'm talking about making love because the landscape is asking me to. . . . The trees are watching me make love, the sky is listening to me, the earth is holding me and we're all having this experience together and we're all full of joy.

6. Politicizing rurality and rural lesbian identity

The final principle concerns a longstanding commitment among the Oregon communities to the politicization of rural space and identity. One of the clearest early articulations of these views was published as part of a debate in *Woman-Spirit*. In 1976, five women (Cohen et al. 1976) wrote a series of reflections about the tensions between feminist spirituality and radical feminist politics. In the next issue, Sally Gearhart responded by explicitly tying spiritual politics to rural separatism. In an argument about the need for both rural enclaves of lesbian community *and* urban political struggle, she argued that a rural separatist community is the only place where what she called "politicized psychic energy" can be gathered (1976, 43). While this construction of rural space reifies it as a space "away" from the front lines of the battle against the patriarchal enemy, it also *politicizes* rural space by arguing that rurality engenders particular *kinds* of political practice.

More recently, Beverly, one of the women most strongly committed to the politicization of lesbian rurality, insisted on disrupting more Arcadian ideas of rural nature and emphasized the prior existence of multinational resource corporations in the region and the damages wrought by agricultural monocultures.

She also indicated that there were uniquely "lesbian" inflections to some of the communities' resistances to these political and ecological issues: "There were conflicts between the environmental community and some of the rest of us who wanted to look at it from a social perspective. . . . [T]he lesbians were definitely on the social side. . . . I'm not sure if it's because we were lesbians but because we had a network we were talking to each other and the social links overlap and become very important." Although none would now, I think, argue that lesbians are the only or even best resisters to rural environmental devastation, many of the separatists have thus kept their political *desire* for the land. In this context, even "creative" groups such as the Southern Oregon Women Writers Group, Gourmet Eating Society, and Chorus can be understood as creating a *rural lesbian public sphere*. The rounds of potluck discussions, writing groups, and Land Trust meetings are important sites through which the community comes to constitute itself as politically distinct. Community discussions operate to clarify opinions and disagreements; histories and aspirations are shared, allowing individual troubles to become community issues. In turn, these community knowledges support individual endeavors; important as the presence of a gay/ lesbian rural social network may be, the presence of a discernible community with shared public traditions also gives life and legitimacy to the existence of a lesbian rural *public*.

In addition, the idea of a distinct rural lesbian public had a great deal to do with the fact that many of the women understood their relationship to *nature* as central to their identities. Some women saw their particular rural location in agricultural, natural resource, and other environmental issues as shaping their lesbian identities differently from urban lesbians. For some, this meant a carefully worked out understanding of the place of rural Oregon in world capitalism; for others, this meant a thorough knowledge of forestry issues in the region; for others, this meant an aesthetic or spiritual orientation to the Oregon landscape; for still others, this meant a strong connection with agricultural cycles and traditions. In all cases, these centrally rural elements of identity were woven into the idea of being a lesbian so much that some women felt they had very little in common with urban lesbians, even of the same generation. As Tee put it, "I think my life on the land has kept me from getting involved with the intellectual controversies that heavily influenced [lesbian] artists in the 1980s and 1990s. I have done what I wanted to do. Not much pay, but a great sense of joy, and that joy is fed every time I look out a window or walk out of doors."

Conclusions: Separatist Ecology, Queer Environmental Justice

In the continuing development of their reflections on and practices in the unique landscape of southern Oregon, these separatists demonstrate that their culture of nature is both shifting and particular, both complex and limited. In other words, it is a living and *situated* tradition of resistance. But how does one speak, from this particularity, of a separatist ecology? A queer environmental justice? I would like to suggest that this lesbian culture not only demonstrates the contextually specific intersectionality of the power relations of sexual orientation with ecology (entwined with but not reducible to race, class, and gender)[5] but also the importance of politicizing these relations in order to understand and transform social ecological relations. Like Pulido, then, I suggest that the cultural politics of environmental justice take shape and have resonance in very particular contexts; it is precisely in the concrete specificities of Ganados del Valle and the Amazon Trail that one finds a transformational politics of ecocultural justice.

In this context, it is important to point out some of the separatists' political and cultural accomplishments. First, and perhaps most obviously, the women challenge the essentialized narrative by which rural, pastoral nature has been heterosexualized in North American culture. Although as Shuttleton has written (2000), there is a diverse queer history to rural sexuality including a distinct gay pastoral tradition, there remains a pervasive assumption that all gay culture is urban and all rural culture is straight. Apart from the self-fulfilling quality of this assumption, the lack of a strong representation of queer rurality impoverishes both ecological and GLBTQ culture and reinforces an articulation of queer-urban-artifice against straight-rural-nature. Country lesbians, who are publicly queer *and* rural and have a well-developed sense of their collective presence, disrupt the articulation. In addition, they also disrupt conventional understandings of rurality by practicing alternative forms of family, community, and ownership. Other environmental justice advocates have pointed to the inequalities and exploitations of rural life and challenged the ways they are hidden behind a screen of pastoralism. Although these critiques have focused on race and class, the rural idyll also perpetuates a heterosexist narrative that impacts both queers and others whose lives are constrained by a monolithic rural heterosexuality. Focusing attention on the sexual diversity of rural communities draws attention to the conditions of sexual organization in rural communities and demonstrates that there are ways of living one's life sexually in rural nature that do not replicate heterosexism.

Second, these women have lived their lives as an experiment in lesbian vision: what does rural nature look like when it is seen and experienced in a very self-consciously lesbian way? The fact that this culture has ended up as a hybrid of lesbian feminism and local ecological knowledge is not just interesting; there are also normative implications. On the one hand, the particularities of place have intruded on the utopian aspirations of lesbian feminism. On the other hand, the intentions of lesbian feminism have intruded in the unfolding of the landscape. In fact, the Oregon separatists themselves understand the precept that nature is a realm of interaction among a variety of human and nonhuman actors. That their separatist aspirations have changed in and for the place and *remain separatist principles* suggests a tremendous openness to the influence of the land *as well as* an affirmation of lesbian politics.

Finally, the Oregon separatists highlight the importance of a public realm to the negotiation of sexual and ecological identity, and to the democratic potential of environmental justice politics. The communities were founded with a central idea of publicity; however impossible the original vision of processing and continual consciousness raising might have been, this tradition of public discussion has continued in a variety of ways. I understand this rural lesbian public sphere as a crucial component of the communities' survival; it is a mode through which their ideas of sexuality, identity, creativity, ecology, and nature are presented and *contested as a central dimension of their lesbian culture*. Their identity and history as lesbian separatists call them together as a meaningful and distinct group, but the meaning of that group shifts and changes because their culture has a series of built-in mechanisms through which to negotiate its ideas.

This ongoing negotiation of rural lesbian culture included a variety of definite disagreements over nature and ecological politics. One clear disagreement concerned the relative merits of a scientific understanding of forestry versus an animistic understanding of trees as individuals experiencing pleasure and pain; another concerned the relative merits of a more materialist view on agrarian capitalism versus a more spiritual one on women's empowerment in land communities. In addition to these active disagreements, it is clear that "nature" in general is an important topic of conversation in and for the rural lesbian community. Nature knowledges are shared from remedies and recipes to profound spiritual and erotic relationships; the systemic degradation of rural nature is also an ongoing subject of discussion, and information sharing across the lands helps to map the social-ecological impact of extractive industry.

The Oregon separatists have contributed to a queer environmental justice by actively inserting the social relations of sexuality into the spatial relations of rural North American society, by consciously developing a lesbian nature episteme that includes the varied and active influence of nonhuman natures, and by insisting on the negotiation of nature ideas and opinions as part of the public realm of a lesbian community. But they also offer interesting insights about culture, ecology, and "strategic" essentialism more broadly. In particular, I would like to suggest that the transformation of rural separatism over time—especially its hybridization of ideological elements with local cultures and ecologies—demonstrates the considerable significance of cultural creativity in the success of alternative ecological communities, and also the limits of an overfocus on strategic essentialism as a conception to describe the political dynamics of culturally based environmental justice movements.

To be sure, many of the rural lesbian separatists of southern Oregon maintain elements of an essentialist feminist politics, and proudly so. Essentialist under-standings of gender and nature were strongly present in 1970s rural lesbian separatist ideologies, and some are still strongly imbricated in the women's ongoing negotiations of gender. However, many of the separatists' essentialist understandings of gender and nature should be read as "strategic" in the most politically precise sense of the word; there seems a fairly clear and self-aware orientation among some of the women to essentialist principles as modes of political intervention. In other words, as many of the women gave up the idea that women were (if only left alone) nurturant and peaceful beings, they main-tained separatist organizational principles by declaring them to be necessary conditions for the creation of a nonalienated women's mode of being in the natural world. In fact, many of the women indicated this kind of gender under-standing: if gender is a social relation, (essentialist) separatist practices are social relations that change gender. As La Verne put it, for example, "the word 'separatist' is not our word. . . . For us, I think we need another name. But I do believe we need our space . . . [so] I have to call it [separatism] a tool because a tool is something you fix something with. . . . I haven't given up on it."

Clearly, the revolutionary fervor of the 1970s has died down; the communi-ties did not create a separatist utopia. It would be a stretch to speak about "open" women's land with the same passionate belief in its possibility as was expressed in the 1970s. But the women were successful in generating a life based on a principled attention to the dynamics of power, gender, and nature in late capitalism and also on an experiential recognition of the sustaining material importance of nature in everyday life, through the experiences of work, sexual-ity, creative production, and spiritual reflection. Part of this success derives from the personal reflexiveness that separatism has always demanded; part derives from the vibrancy of the cultural institutions they have created because of the particular rural community in which they live. A further part derives from the skill with which many community members have taken on the worlds of written and artistic creative production. In these successes—and in the fail-ures as well—the lesbian separatist communities of southern Oregon offer a rich and interesting environmental justice tradition that challenges us to think about and live differently the relations of sexuality, gender, and nature upon which the tradition bases its principles and practices. In the end, its contradic-tions give it life and relevance; as Beverly put it, "it's an awkward place to be, but then, living on the planet is awkward as well." Ultimately, however, under-standing the struggles and experiences of the Oregon landdykes as a form of queer environmental justice does not require that we accept the success of their strategically essentialist experiment in separatist ecology. It is enough, I think, that these women chose to live their lives, consciously and politically, in active resistance to dominant currents that link sexual with environmental power relations.

NOTES

This paper is a revised and considerably abbreviated version of "Lesbian Separatists and Environmental Experience: Notes Toward a Queer Ecology," *Organization and Environment* 15, no. 2 (June 2002): 131–63. I acknowledge, with thanks, copyright permission. Readers interested in the historical development of the southern Oregon communities, the methodological and epistemological issues that frame the paper, or the "flesh" of the six ecological principles I sketch here should consult this longer work.

1. I use this unwieldy term to highlight the diversity of views and positions within the queer political community, even though it can also be read as homogenizing what are, in fact, conflicting experiences and perspectives. Transgendered folk and lesbian separatists, for example, may disagree hotly on issues of gender. In addition, many separatists are actively hostile to the moniker "queer," refusing ideas of political alliance with gay men and transgendered folk. At the other end, many queer thinkers are among the most vocal critics of lesbian philosophy and politics. My slippage from separatist to queer is, in this context, entirely intentional; disagreement is part of our history.

2. Most queer commentators assume that lesbian separatists were and are simply essentialist; my argument is that their deployments of essentialism were and are uneven and often highly strategic. For an extended discussion of feminist essentialism and antiessentialism, see Fuss 1989.

3. I have also written at some length about queer and ecological affinities from a perspective that is deeply indebted to ecofeminism (e.g., Sandilands 2001).

4. All quotes identified with a first name in the rest of the paper are from women I interviewed in the spring of 2000. Their ideas and opinions are supplemented and reinforced by materials gleaned from archival sources housed at the University of Oregon and from the women's own published writings (of which there are, delightfully, many).

5. I must note here that the separatists' culture is significantly founded on particular class and racialized relations of nature and ecology, ranging from the racism and class utopianism underscoring their Arcadian imaginings (see Shuttleton 2000) to the fact that almost all the separatists were and are white. Racism and anti-Semitism are significant issues in rural Oregon more generally; the separatists' ability to settle these lands and carve out a distinct separatist space is clearly influenced by their whiteness, as was the particular shape of their articulation of sexuality with ecology. Although one of the women to whom I spoke at length was both African American and a committed rural separatist, it is still necessary to argue that rural separatism has a particularly racialized history and practice of rurality. Still, to the extent that many of the separatists have moved significantly away from Arcadian understandings, they have also come to understand the race relations of their rural politics.

REFERENCES

Alaimo, S. 2000. *Undomesticated Ground: Recasting Nature as Feminist Space*. Ithaca: Cornell University Press.

Bell, D., and G. Valentine, eds. 1995. *Mapping Desire: Geographies of Sexualities*. London: Routledge.

Cohen, S., A. Yarabinee, L. Norwood, T. C. Tinder, and J. Mendelsohn. 1976. "View of the Moon from the City Streets." *WomanSpirit* 3, no. 9: 17–21.

Corinne, T., ed. (n.d.). *Community Herstories: Living in Southern Oregon.* Sunny Valley, Ore.

Fuss, D. 1989. *Essentially Speaking: Feminism, Nature, and Difference.* New York: Routledge.

Gaard, G. 1997. "Toward a Queer Ecofeminism." *Hypatia* 12, no. 1: 114–37.

Gearhart, S. 1976. "Another View of the Same Moon from Another City's Streets." *Woman-Spirit* 3, no. 10: 41–44.

———. 1979. *The Wanderground: Stories of the Hill Women.* London: Women's Press.

Ingram, G. B., A. M. Bouthillette, and Y. Retter, eds. 1997. *Queers in Space: Communities/Public Places/Sites of Resistance.* Seattle: Bay Press.

Laurence, Helen. 2001. "Bare." *Women and Environments International Magazine* 52/53 (fall): 5.

Munt, S. 1998. *Heroic Desire: Lesbian Identity and Cultural Space.* New York: New York University Press.

Oregon Women's Land Trust. 1976. Oregon Women's Land (Information Sheet). Eugene, Ore.

Phillips, R., D. West, and D. Shuttleton, eds. 2000. *De-Centring Sexualities: Politics and Representation Beyond the Metropolis.* London: Routledge.

Pulido, L. 1998. "Ecological Legitimacy and Cultural Essentialism: Hispano Grazing in the Southwest." In *The Struggle for Ecological Democracy: Environmental Justice Movements in the United States,* ed. D. Faber. New York: Guilford Press.

Rule, J. 1964. *Desert of the Heart.* Tallahassee: Naiad Press.

Sandilands, C. 2001. "Desiring Nature, Queering Ethics: Adventures in Erotogenic Environments." *Environmental Ethics* 23, no. 2: 169–88.

———. 2002. "Rainbow's End? Lesbian Separatism and the (Ongoing) Politics of Ecotopia." In *Feminist Utopias: Visions for the Millennium,* ed. M. Eichler and J. Larkin. Toronto: Inanna Press.

Shugar, D. 1995. *Separatism and Women's Community.* Lincoln: University of Nebraska Press.

Shuttleton, D. 2000. "The Queer Politics of Gay Pastoral." In Phillips et al. 2000.

Stein, A. 1997. *Sex and Sensibility: Stories of a Lesbian Generation.* Berkeley: University of California Press.

Summerhawk, B., and L. Gagehabib. 2000. "Circles of Power: Issues and Identities in a Lesbian Community." *Bulletin of Daito Bunka University* 38: 115–37.

Valentine, G. 1997. "Making Space: Lesbian Separatist Communities in the United States." In *Contested Countryside Cultures: Otherness, Marginality and Rurality,* ed. P. Cloke and J. Little. London: Routledge.

Womanshare Collective. 1976. *Country Lesbians: The Story of the Womanshare Collective.* Grants Pass, Ore.: Womanshare Books.

7

Toxic Bodies?

ACT UP's Disruption of the Heteronormative Landscape of the Nation

BETH BERILA

When former President George Bush said that "the American way of life is not negotiable," he articulated in most blatant terms a particularly hegemonic ideology of the U.S. nation. This construct includes an insatiable level of conspicuous consumption that produces a high degree of waste, much of which is funneled into vulnerable communities.[1] This definition of the "American way of life" also refuses responsibility and accountability to the rest of the world for the high cost of that lifestyle. The United States has demonstrated this refusal numerous times: when it walked away from the Kyoto agreement, and when it ignored staunch opposition from the international community toward U.S. plans to bomb Iraq. Environmental justice activists have long argued that we need to pay more attention to the environmental implications of this "American way of life," implications that have racial, gender, and economic dimensions. But I argue that there is another layer here: the way in which the rhetoric of the nation is mobilized to protect and propagate this particular "American way of life." It is no accident that nationalist discourse is deployed in these instances. Indeed, this narrow nationalism has only intensified since the tragic events at the World Trade Center on September 11, 2001, as George W. Bush urges Americans to show their patriotism by consuming products.

This brand of nationalism operates in powerful ways in both environmental justice issues and in AIDS issues, both of which involve identifying what and who counts as "toxic" to the "purity" of the national body. Both the environmental justice and ACT UP movements have publicly challenged these constructs by revealing that decisions about access to medical and governmental resources are fueled by complex intersections of heterosexism, racism, sexism, classism, and AIDS phobia that are deeply embedded in constructs of the nation. While environmental justice movements focus on the dangers that contaminants pose to the bodies of individuals and the earth, ACT UP battles mainstream public perception that people living with AIDS are somehow toxic to public health, at both the individual and national levels. Environmental justice activists point out that marginalized communities are also often marked as threats to national "purity." Whereas texts such as Richard Hofrichter's *Toxic Struggles* and scholars such as Winona LaDuke, Vandana Shiva, and Robert Bullard highlight the toxicity that puts vulnerable communities most at risk, ACT UP members reveal that AIDS phobia has historically co-opted these concepts to perpetuate fears of contamination around people living with AIDS, or PWAs. While queerness is often disparaged as "unnatural," what is considered "natural" and "unnatural" is a cultural construction, so that nature is made to do the work of a heteronormative culture (Gaard 1997; Evans 2003). The appropriation of environmental discourse in this context serves to uphold narrow constructs of the heteronormative—and thus "pure"—national body. ACT UP's actions both created and highlighted "strange encounters" with "toxic others" in ways that reveal audience members' participation in that production (Ahmed 2000). That is, ACT UP revealed that passersby are implicated in the production of some bodies (usually those who are healthy, white, not poor, and straight) as the "general population" of the nation precisely by marking others (usually those who are queer, poor, HIV positive, or people of color) as stained and toxic, and therefore as "contaminants" of the nation.[2] Certain bodies thus become the landscape on which the boundaries of the heteronormative nation are inscribed and upheld.

As activists move to meet the current challenges of environmental justice issues, I suggest that we pay close attention to this construct of the nation, both to deconstruct it and to rework it for different, more socially just ends. This essay examines the idea of the hegemonic nation as it is used to produce a particular sense of national "purity." Specifically, I juxtapose a discussion of ACT UP's activism around AIDS issues in the early eighties with environmental justice perspectives in order to analyze how the "purity" of the nation is constructed.[3] Of course, there are many different models of nation, some of which are much more congruent with an ethics of social justice. But the hegemonic model of the nation is operating in insidious and powerful ways and thus deserves a great deal of attention. While much environmental justice work explores the racism and classism that channel toxicity into particular communities, this essay extends this analysis to consider the heterosexism and AIDS phobia that mark certain bodies as toxic. If, as Greta Gaard argues in her chapter in this volume, "Toward a Queer Ecofeminism," heterosexism is a fundamental ecofeminist issue, then by extension AIDS is also an environmental justice issue (Gaard 2004). ACT UP's cultural activism in the early eighties problematized constructs of contamination and staining as they play out in U.S. national identity. In doing so, they revealed not only that such constructs require the participation of average citizens, but also that such constructs can be altered if average citizens begin to transform our understandings of particular issues.

There are several useful parallels between ACT UP and environmental justice movements. Both movements use the media in savvy ways to get their messages out, and both simultaneously target public perception and pressure government officials and scientists to stop ignoring the urgency of the issues. Both work to break down false public/private divides to expose the links between "private" health and "public" actions, and both critique the lack of quality health care for affected communities. As they do so, both groups redefine who counts as "experts" about their own bodies and their own communities.

First, some background about ACT UP. The AIDS Coalition to Unleash Power formed in New York in March 1987 to combat inadequate attention towards the AIDS crisis (Crimp and Ralston 1990). In the 1980s and 1990s, ACT UP branches around the country targeted both local and national policies that inadequately addressed the needs of PWAs, though the group eventually also branched out to issues of homelessness, access to medical care, inadequate drug research, and the particular needs of women and people of color living with AIDS.[4] Most ACT UP graphics were created by Gran Fury, a self-appointed group of about fifteen ACT UP members who became experts at rapidly producing witty and powerful graphics aimed at targeting particular issues in a timely way and then massproducing them for broad distribution.

The group's widespread use of witty graphics was intended to revise problematic representations of people living with AIDS (Crimp and Ralston 1990). This focus on representation and interpretation is crucial, both for AIDS issues and for environmental justice movements, since who and what count as toxic depends on the political perspective one holds. Indeed, many environmental justice activists work to trouble the assumptions behind corporate and governmental policies that construct poor communities as expendable. They also critique the denial of dangerous leakages of waste dumps that are often placed in poor communities because politicians know that wealthier communities have the political and financial resources to prevent the dumps from coming into their neighborhoods. This battle of definitions is not merely pedantic—it has very real consequences and is an important demonstration of environmental justice concerns, as well as in AIDS activism. For instance, in the recent debate over whether to drill for oil in Alaska, the notion of "sustainability" was used in multiple and conflicting ways. While environmentalists talked of sustaining national ecosystems and wildlife, as well as protecting the people who would deal with the fallout from the drilling, the Bush administration talked of "sustaining" the American lifestyle, which meant the need for sources of fuel that could support a high level of conspicuous consumption. Thus to reveal the processes through which meaning is produced can help trouble concepts of toxicity and contamination that too often seem self-evident.

It is also no accident that toxicity gets relegated to certain neighborhoods that are then marked as polluted, or that early AIDS discourse explicitly conflated AIDS with gays, marking both as sites of contamination to be shunned and contained. Environmental dangers, like AIDS, are too often seen as invisible "intruders" that can have lasting and unforeseen consequences (Luke 2000, 242). Rhetoric of AIDS phobia, as well as much mainstream discourse around toxicity, reflects fears that "contamination" will "seep into" the heterogeneous and contained nation. Environmental discourse is thus appropriated in ways that uphold narrow constructs of the heteronormative—and thus "pure"—national body. If the nation is too often constructed through the idea of keeping outsiders out, it also, suggests Ahmed, follows a metaphor of a healthy body, where healthy is read as homogeneous and self-contained: "a good or healthy neighborhood [or nation] does not leak outside itself, and hence does not let outsiders (or foreign agents/viruses) in" (Ahmed 2000, 25). Since the bodies of particular others, usually people of color, queers, women, or people from other nations, are repeatedly targeted as threats to the nation, the reading of which bodies are marked as toxic seems particularly important in any discussion of the landscapes of nation and national identity.

Purging the Stain: A Revision of Contamination Discourse

In hegemonic discourses of the nation, references to the "public" usually refer to the "general population" from which queers, people of color, the poor, women, and people living with AIDS have presumably already been purged. However, this othering is crucial to constructions of a homogeneous nation state, since, as Ahmed argues in a different context, "there is no body as such that is given in the world: bodies materialize in a complex set of temporal and spatial relations to other bodies, including bodies that are recognized as familiar and friendly, and those that are considered strange" (Ahmed 2000, 40). Who and what counts as toxic, then, is a construction that is deeply contested ground. To reveal the contested meanings, and to reveal the ways that social relations between bodies are produced through those contested meanings, opens possibilities for valuable activism. For instance, blood plays a significant role in AIDS discourse, as that which can be the source of both purity and contamination. That is, blood can be the site of the transmission of HIV, but it has also played an important role in discourses of racial and national purity. Historically, for instance, the one drop-rule marked African Americans as unworthy of citizenship in the nation, both during slavery and its aftermath, at the same time that many white citizens were profiting from the labor of African American men and women.[5] The definition of an "other" was integral—economically and racially—to a particular hegemonic construct of the U.S. nation. Indeed, heteronormativity, homophobia, racism, and sexism have often fueled acts of imperialism in the name of the hegemonic nation (Gaard 1997).

ACT UP's cultural activism worked to redefine the processes of meaning production that have made such violent binaries of stained/unstained and impure/pure integral to the interlocking projects of nation building and heteronormativity. If heteronormativity involves the cultural and social structures and ideologies that privilege heterosexuality, then, as scholars Lauren Berlant and Michael Warner suggest, "National heterosexuality is the mechanism by which a core national culture can be imagined as a sanitized space of sentimental feeling and immaculate behavior, a space of pure citizenship" (Berlant and Warner 1993, 355–56). Thus, heteronormativity enforces the privilege and "rightness" of heterosexuality that plays a key role in defining insiders of a nation. ACT UP helped uncover and trouble the link between heteronormativity and nation making by revealing the fissures in the "coherence" so often assigned to heternormativity. Similar fissures also exist in environmental justice movements, as, for example, local residents argue that materials and policies are toxic to their communities even as governmental and health officials refuse to acknowledge that toxicity. Again, though, that denial is not accidental, as it serves to protect wealthier communities and to construct certain bodies as "pure."

The fear of contamination through blood or simply through fears of contact became hypervisible during a well-publicized ACT UP demonstration at the White House on June 1, 1987, during the Third International Conference on AIDS. Activists who were protesting the Reagan administration's policy of inaction in the AIDS crisis were arrested by police wearing bright yellow rubber gloves. The police presence and the extensive press coverage the event received added fire to already unfounded fears about how HIV is transmitted (Crimp and Ralston 1990, 33). ACT UP challenged this treatment and produced fliers that linked this discrimination with hegemonic constructs of the nation. One flyer read, "In one day the Pentagon spends more than the total spent for AIDS research and education since 1982. By 1991, more Americans will die from AIDS each year than were killed in the entire Vietnam War" (Crimp and Ralston 1990, 33). These statistics provocatively link attempts to protect national security with attempts to ban contact with people living with AIDS. Not coincidentally, AIDS and national security are too often collapsed, as are environmental justice issues. The Clinton administration, for instance, passed a law in 1993 allowing AIDS to be a factor in immigration and citizenship applications, thus codifying attempts to "protect" national "purity" (ACT UP 2003). It is also no accident that many of the people targeted as a "threat" to national "purity" are poor people and people of color, both from within the United States and abroad.

In both cases, the "purity" of the hegemonic nation is seemingly preserved by "purging" the "toxic" body. That model, however, overlooks something absolutely crucial in this rhetoric, which is the fact that that which is marked "toxic" is actually integral to the hegemonic nation. That is, the heteronormative nation can only be constructed by marking queers and people living with AIDS as alien others, and by collapsing the two categories into "threats of contamination." In a different but parallel way, while certain marginalized communities are considered expendable and exposable to toxic waste, that waste exists as a direct by-product of the lifestyle of consumption that the hegemonic nation is designed to protect. This inherent dependence has been a major site of oppression, but it can be an important site for activists to target in order to trouble and revise who and what counts as "toxic" to the nation. If that waste is the result of a way of life that many will fight wars to protect, then either we should take responsibility for the waste, instead of dumping it on marginalized communities, or we should revise our lifestyle so that such waste does not exist. The discourse of "pure" national bodies is too often used to avoid either of these responsibilities.

Metaphorically, the notion of staining emphasizes the contaminated body, the body that fears contamination, and occasionally the act of contamination—the spread of the stain. But perhaps this is not the most useful way to think about staining—one that sets up a binary between pure/impure, stained/ unstained. The way in which different subjects are defined in relation to each other define not only individuals but also their social relations.[6] The act of differentiation between self and other is not a given; it must be constantly reproduced, not just at the level of the nation-state but also through the actions of individuals within that state. If acts of differentiation hold such a key role, then playing on the acts that reveal the permeability of public spaces and the bodies that move within them hold radical potential. Far from being separate or distant, notions of stained/unstained, contaminated/pure absolutely depend on each other. Activists can capitalize on this relationality between the binaries to help destabilize the presumption of coherence and homogeneity too often attached to the heteronormative nation. In doing so, they can reveal the contestation that always exists around understandings of toxic bodies.

Toxic Constructions of the National Body

Toxicity and contamination are not unexamined concepts in environmental justice movements, and many environmental justice scholars have evaluated how toxicity gets defined and, in turn, how officials determine risk factors of particular materials. Once again, contesting interpretations exist, and "risk" is partly determined by which communities are most affected and the degree of political and financial clout they are perceived to have. But toxicity is not a simple, objective quality of a substance: it is as much textual as it is technical, depending on moments of interpretation to assess risk (Luke 2000, 240). The interpretations are, of course, shaped by the political investments of those who are doing the interpreting as well as the context in which they are read.[7] ACT UP members revealed similar textual contingencies of interpretation around the AIDS crisis, by first insisting in the face of governmental neglect that it was indeed a crisis, and then challenging scientists' methods of researching the virus and developing effective treatments. Like many community members working on environmental justice issues, ACT UP members became experts, educating themselves on various experimental treatments and challenging scientific perspectives in ways that redefined what counted as credible knowledge (Epstein 1996). In doing so, they revealed insights about the politics of knowledge that carry over to environmental justice issues.

Indeed, one of the most important elements of ACT UP's defamiliarizing tactics is this creation of public moments of meaning production that illustrate those processes to be interactive and open to multiple interpretations. This multiplicity revealed the culture around us to be rife with difference that the heteronormative nation too often obscures under a cloak of sameness. While Eve Sedgwick has taught us that "coming out" of the closet is an act that can never be fully accomplished under heteronormativity, Foucault has taught us that the presumed privatization of sexuality obscures its highly regulated nature that is constantly produced through the interdependence of public and private spaces (Sedgwick 1990; Foucault 1990). The public spectacles and controversies that many of ACT UP's works created revealed meaning production to be a process in flux—one that holds very real material consequences for both queers and people living with AIDS. In fact, many of ACT UP's actions highlighted that there were contested understandings of the nation that are *always* circulating in public spaces, though they are not often immediately recognizable.

ACT UP's Wall Street action, for instance, played on the fear of contamination by queerness by revealing the inability to effectively read some bodies as "queer." On September 15, 1989, several ACT UP members, dressed in conservative suits, infiltrated Wall Street and entered the stock exchange, passing unnoticed among other similarly suited stockbrokers who probably read them as familiar, not noticing that they were engaged in another "strange encounter" in which queers were "passing," so to speak, right under their noses. A similar action occurred at Burroughs Wellcome, where ACT UP activists entered unnoticed and handcuffed themselves to furniture in an office to demand that Burroughs Wellcome lower the price of the drug AZT. They remained there until police knocked down the office door and arrested the activists (Crimp and Ralston 1990). Both "infiltrations" gained widespread media attention, thus highlighting the activists' demands for less profiteering around AIDS drugs (*Voices from the Front* 1991).

They also, significantly, highlighted some people's inability to "read" bodies around them. In both actions, ACT UP members played on the assumption that people in Wall Street and Burroughs Welcome would identify with them, assuming them to be "normal" or part of the norm, and thus absorbing them into the construct of the "general population." This identification was rapidly subverted when ACT UP members revealed themselves as activists and challenged the identificatory assumptions of workers in the public spaces—thus revealing that people cannot so easily read and mark bodies in such daily encounters. By troubling people's ability to "read" the bodies around them, ACT UP revealed interpretations to be political acts deeply embedded in heteronormativity. Unfortunately, such tactics are not so easily adopted by environmental justice activists, many of whom are women, people of color, and/or poor people who cannot so easily "pass." However, the strategy of creating public reading moments in which passersby are made aware of their roles in producing meaning about issues that are not static or self-evident is useful, particularly when such reading moments can reveal the contested interpretations that *always* circulate in our communities and that hold very real material consequences. If national identity depends on marking "alien" others as outsiders in order to mark "citizens" as insiders, then unsettling the ability to accurately make this distinction helps to challenge the production of the insider/outsider binary. Moreover, revealing the *constant production* that is necessary to maintain constructs of the nation helps challenge any presumption of its omnipresent "naturalness."

While ACT UP gained virtually unprecedented attention for AIDS issues and instigated some very tangible and important changes in AIDS care, there are also very real limitations to their tactics, not the least of which is the fact that the movement, at least initially, was led by middle- to upper-class white men who actively used their privilege in their tactics. While many groups formed within ACT UP to better address the needs of women and people of color living with AIDS and to address issues such as poverty and medical care in prisons, some of their tactics could not be easily used by environmental justice proponents, many of whom lack the privilege that some ACT UP members so successfully used in some of their actions. Nevertheless, ACT UP does shed some interesting insight into the heteronormativity of the nation. Simultaneously, environmental justice movements offer more solidly developed strategies for addressing racial, gender, and economic oppression, and have the potential to effectively address issues of sexuality as well, so that a combination of the tactics could prove quite useful. Indeed, given the groups who now bear the brunt of AIDS, which includes people of color and poor people as well as GLBT communities, environmental justice strategies are likely to prove more effective than early ACT UP tactics. Environmental justice movements that fully integrate critiques of heteronormativity with critiques of racial, gender, and economic oppression are in many ways better equipped to deal with racial and economic differences in AIDS policies and the communities they affect. But both movements illustrate that to challenge or transform structural inequalities into a more environmentally just equation will require more than just a shift in resources; it will require a deep transformation of structures and meanings that shape how the very landscapes of bodies and nation are produced.

NOTES

1. Special thanks to Rachel Stein, whose editorial generosity and insight made this article possible. A version of this paper was presented at the Association for the Study of Literature and the Environment conference in Boston, Massachusetts, on June 5, 2003. Thanks also to Margaret Himley and Susan Edmunds for their thoughtful comments on earlier versions of this piece, which is part of a larger project entitled *The Art of Change: Experimental Writing, Cultural Activism, and Feminist Social Transformation.*

2. Here I am tweaking Sara Ahmed's terms a bit. Whereas Ahmed talks mostly about embodiment and postcoloniality, the concept applies in provocative ways to AIDS and environmental justice issues.

3. While ACT UP continued its protests through the 1990s and into the present, the 1980s marked the period of greatest public exposure and controversy, as well as the high point of the group's activist membership, and therefore serves as a useful focus for my argument.

4. Many critics rightly point to the limits of ACT UP's emphasis on public policy and mainstream social institutions such as the government and the church—tactics that necessarily involve working within the system. Nevertheless, the material changes that ACT UP produced, including better access to drug trials and quicker federal approval of new drugs, were urgent necessities for PWAs. Moreover, the group's emphasis on the ideologies and power systems that shaped governmental and medical policies that negatively affected PWAs parallels the work of many environmental justice activists, who also target social institutions such as the government and corporations that enact problematic policies.

5. As Cynthia Enloe argues, nationalism is "a set of ideas that sharpens distinctions between 'us' and 'them.' It is, moreover, a tool for explaining how inequities have been created between 'us' and 'them'" (Enloe 1989, 61). Of course, there are many other examples of racial discourse around blood and citizenship. The fact that constructs of citizenship are so often racialized is precisely my point here, and I would argue that those constructs are also deeply gendered and heteronormative.

6. Ahmed writes that "an emphasis on the dialectic between self and other is insufficient; it is the very acts and gestures whereby the subjects differentiate between others that constitute the permeability of both social and bodily space" (Ahmed 2000, 15). This focus on how we create distinctions between self and other that result in particular sets of social relations is precisely the point here, in part because it suggests the possibility for alternative ways of defining that can produce different social relations.

7. Luke argues that "all too often the type and quantity of evidence needed to assess environmental risk is treated as purely scientific data secure on allegedly pure technical grounds, when, in fact, determining the qualities of the toxicity often is a *social act of political interpretation*" (Luke 2000, 240, emphasis in original).

REFERENCES

ACT UP. 2003. http://www.actupny.org/.

Ahmed, S. 2000. *Strange Encounters: Embodied Others in Post-Coloniality.* New York: Routledge.

Berlant, Lauren, and Michael Warner. 1993. "Sex in Public." In *The Cultural Studies Reader,* ed. Simon Darling. 2nd ed. New York: Routledge.

Bullard, Robert. 1993. "Anatomy of Environmental Racism." In Hofrichter 1993.

Crimp, Douglas, and Adam Ralston. 1990. *AIDSDemographics.* Seattle: Bay Press.

Enloe, Cynthia. 1989. *Bananas, Beaches, and Bases: Making Feminist Sense of International Politics.* Berkeley: University of California Press.

Epstein, Steven. 1996. *Impure Science: AIDS, Activism, and the Politics of Knowledge.* Berkeley: University of California Press.

Evans, Mei Mei. 2003. "Queer(y)ing Nature." Paper presented at the Association for the Study of Literature and the Environment conference. Boston, Mass. June 5.

Foucault, Michel. 1990 [1978]. *History of Sexuality.* Vol. 1, *An Introduction,* trans. Robert Hurley. New York: Vintage Books.

Gaard, Greta. 1997. "Toward a Queer Ecofeminism." *Hypatia* 12, no. 1: 114–37.

Hofrichter, Richard, ed. 1993. *Toxic Struggles: The Theory and Practice of Environmental Justice.* Philadelphia: New Society Publishers.

LaDuke, Winona. 1999. *All Our Relations: Native Struggles for Land and Life.* Cambridge, Mass.: South End Press.

Luke, Timothy W. 2000. "Rethinking Technoscience in Risk Society: Toxicity as Textuality." In *Reclaiming the Environmental Debate: The Politics of Health in a Toxic Culture,* ed. Richard Hofrichter. Cambridge, Mass.: MIT Press.

Sedgwick, Eve K. 1990. *Epistemology of the Closet.* Berkeley: University of California Press.

Shiva, Vandana. 2002. *Water Wars: Privatization, Pollution, and Profit.* Cambridge, Mass.: South End Press.

Voices from the Front. 1991. Directed by Robin Hunt, David Meieran, and Sandra Elgear. 90 minutes. Testing the Limits.

PART THREE

Gender, Sexuality, and Environmental Health Concerns

8

Producing "Roundup Ready®" Communities?

Human Genome Research and Environmental Justice Policy

GIOVANNA DI CHIRO

> [E]nvironmental justice advocates . . . need to be informed and proactive about the science, the politics, and the ethical, legal and social issues if we are to be knowledgeable players *at the forefront, not the back of,* the genomics "revolution."
>
> – Swati Prakash, Julie Sze, Julia Chance, and Peggy Shepard

The recent flurry of research into gene-environment interactions and their role in disease causation, a feature of the genetics "revolution" spawned by the sequencing of the human genome in late 2000, has captured the attention of many environmental justice organizations across the country. Some environmental justice activists and concerned scientists are investigating how modern advances in biotechnology might help to identify, develop treatments for, and/or repair defective genes that are thought to contribute in part to the high incidences, in low-income communities of color, of environmental illnesses such as respiratory disease, cancer, and birth defects. In the spirit of technoscientific possibilism, these groups are keeping a watchful eye out for the good news that may come from the pathbreaking advances in scientific research on human genetics. Other scholars and activists, expressing more skepticism, are uneasy about the optimistic rhetoric underlying genetic science reporting and worry about some of the research practices already underway in human genome studies. Moreover, these critics question whether the recent spate of government-initiated research projects on the interplay between genes, environmental toxins, and factors such as age, gender, race/ethnicity, and behavior might not represent the resuscitation and reemergence in new forms of widely discredited eugenic arguments that associate disease and other problems in minority and poor populations with genetic inferiority.[1]

The analysis in this chapter is based on interview responses to the launching of a recent research initiative by the National Institutes of Health (NIH) called the Environmental Genome Project (EGP). The interviews were conducted with several groups of people interested in this most recent foray into high-tech approaches to environmental problem solving: (1) government researchers involved in the EGP, (2) nongovernmental geneticists and developmental biologists who are advocates for environmental justice (what some have called "oppositional scientists"), and (3) environmental justice activists who live in the communities burdened with disproportionately high rates of environmental illnesses. This chapter examines the responses from these interviews through the analytical lens of environmental justice, and focuses on the critiques raised by women environmental justice activists that expand the debate about how best to solve environmental health problems at the turning of the "century of the gene."[2] Among many other issues, the activists and concerned scientists I interviewed raised questions about the potential effects of the growing attention, even fixation, on the genetic basis of environmental illness, the social impacts of the widening gap in scientific and technical expertise between scientific and lay communities in environmental decision making, and the arguments about what constitutes democratic participation in future directions of science and technology.[3]

The Brave New World of Environmental Genome Research

The first genetic revolution that ushered in the "biotech century," many argue, was the introduction of genetic engineering into the field of agriculture (c.f. Doyle 1985; Krimsky and Wrubel 1996; Lappé and Bailey 1998). The "new genetics," especially the offspring of the Human Genome Project such as the EGP, aims to reach beyond agriculture and "revolutionize" all aspects of the life sciences, including biomedicine and public health. The title of this chapter, "Producing 'Roundup Ready®' Communities?," imagines a future dystopic scenario where corporate agricultural biotechnology has infiltrated the domain of environmental and public health. What might such a future look like? A glance at the agricultural genetics research agenda of one of the largest self-described "life sciences" conglomerates, the Monsanto Corporation, suggests one possibility. Monsanto has for a number of years successfully marketed a very potent, broad-spectrum herbicide known as Roundup®. Farmers use Roundup® to prepare their fields for planting to eliminate an array of invasive weeds that outcompete and overgrow their commercially valuable crops. But one of the problems with the widespread application of herbicides is that these chemicals also endanger and sometimes kill the emergent young shoots of the farmer's intended crop. To solve this problem, and, incidentally, improving the vertical integration of the company, Monsanto's agro-scientists have bioengineered Roundup Ready® crop seeds: varieties of economically important plants such as canola, corn, soybeans, cotton, and sugar beets that are resistant to the company's widely used herbicide, Roundup®. A farmer can now purchase Monsanto's Roundup Ready® soybeans and confidently apply Monsanto's highly effective herbicide Roundup® without imperiling the health of the young, genetically modified soybean shoots.

Among other things, the Monsanto Corporation promotes the marketing of its Roundup Ready® technology with an environmental rationale: farmers who buy Roundup Ready® seeds would now be able to minimize the application of broad-spectrum herbicides that ordinarily require multiple sprayings over the course of a particular crop's life cycle. Now, just one application of the potent herbicide suffices to kill any offending weeds. Biotechnology thus allows Monsanto's business to proceed as usual while the company promotes its product lines as "compati[ble] with more sustainable agricultural practices."[4]

Why devote this attention to the Monsanto corporation and its attempts to corner the market for its chemical herbicides by bioengineering seeds that can survive contact with these herbicides? The development and especially the marketing of Roundup Ready® technology in agriculture demonstrates a new approach to biological problems, one where genetic solutions are foregrounded. This approach, taken from the field of agricultural genetics, is being *translated* into new ways to solve human environmental health problems, and is evident in some of the latest NIH-sponsored human genome research projects. Many public health scientists and policy makers at the NIH are interested in encouraging the "geneticization" the biomedical fields of toxicology and epidemiology to "fill a long- standing gap in the sciences" (Schmidt 2000, 1) that, when accomplished, would enhance their explanatory and productive capacities (Olden and Wilson 2000). Given these scientific and political commitments, it is conceivable, if presently only in the world of speculative fiction, that the technological transfer of genetic research from agriculture to public health might be envisioned as a desire to engineer the ultimate "biotechnological fix": the production of Roundup Ready® people or communities. I will return to this point later.

The Environmental Genome Project in Focus

One of the functional genomic spin-offs of the National Human Genome Research Institute (NHGRI) is the Environmental Genome Project (EGP), a new human genomic research program that claims to be on the path to solving environmental health problems at their core by zeroing in on the innate flaws in the human genome. The EGP intends to uncover these defects, which may show up disproportionately in particular subgroups of the population and which are associated with an increased susceptibility to a range of environmentally related illnesses. Ultimately, EGP scientists hope to provide the medical and pharmacological professions with the genetic information necessary to repair or treat a defective gene or gene product, thereby eliminating what they consider to be the fundamental cause of diseases such as cancer, asthma, and heart disease: the breakdown of the body's genetically controlled defense mechanisms in the event of exposure to an environmental agent such as a toxic chemical, a treatment drug, or UV light from the sun. Many scientists and activists question this premise of genetic reductionism, that is, the single-minded focus on the flawed or defective "environmental disease genes" as the basis of environmental illness. They wonder whether this is the best way to improve environmental health, or, as the above dystopic scenario portends, whether this research prophesies a future of genetically resistant "Roundup Ready® communities" living, working, and playing happily alongside the toxic effluent of American industry.

An Overview of the Environmental Genome Project

The Environmental Genome Project is a joint venture by the NIEHS and the Human Genome Institute at the NIH and was launched in 1997 as one of the first "functional genomic studies" emerging from the technological advances on human genetic variation generated by the Human Genome Project and is said to be "the genomics of the future" (Carrano 1998, 1). In recent years, the consensus in modern biomedical science has concluded that illnesses are the outcome of a "complex array of factors" including genetic susceptibility, environmental exposures, and aging. Until now, according to government scientists, the largest information gaps in knowledge needed to accurately assess human disease risk have been located in the arena of human genetics, and consequently, the EGP aims to close those gaps. To increase the precision of our understanding of human variation in sensitivity or resistance to disease, EGP researchers are developing a catalogue of all the genetic variances, or single nucleotide polymorphisms (SNPs), that may render certain populations "more susceptible to, or more resistant to, substances they may encounter at work, at home, or more generally, in the environment."[5]

Project researchers intend to collect blood samples from "approximately 1,000 Americans from five ethnic groups—Asian American, African American, Hispanic, Caucasian, and Native American—in order to learn what the allelic variations and frequencies of these 'environmental disease' genes are in the U.S. population overall and within ethnic groups" (Albers 1997, 2). NIEHS director Dr. Kenneth Olden asserts that this pathbreaking research will help his office identify "susceptible subgroups" and will "provide more precise information for regulators, such as the Food and Drug Administration and the Environmental Protection Agency, who now arbitrarily apply large safety margins to cover what is not known about the variations in human susceptibility. More precise information would permit the best protection at the least cost."[6]

During its initial phase, the EGP is cataloguing relatively common sequence variations, or SNPs, in genetic samples taken from different populations. At present, scientists in the EGP and the Genome Institute have assembled a "DNA Polymorphism Discovery Resource," which is a set of 450 immortalized cell lines[7] taken from 450 U.S. citizens whose ancestry represents all the major geographic regions of the world—Europe, Africa, Asia, and the Americas.[8] Although the popular discourse about genetic variation research (for example, the Human Genome Diversity Project) appeals to the multicultural rhetoric of race/ethnicity, that is, "equal scientific resources and attention for all racial/ethnic groups," NIH scientists, invoking the contemporary scientific retreat from the idea of race as a legitimate object of biological investigation, assert that race or ethnicity is not a valid basis for genetics research.[9] Rather, they adopt the more rigorous and biologically acceptable concept of "ancestral lineage" and assert that the Polymorphism Discovery Database contains most of the genetic variation, or genetic archetypes, that exist in human beings. From these 450 cell lines, all obtained with strict institutional review board approval, scientists intend to discover the normal range of SNP variations for the so-called environmental response genes that exist in the human species.[10] The project scientists acknowledge, however, that given the melting pot or mixed-blood composition of the U.S. population, the notion of a pure line of genetic archetypes is unrealistic. This means, of course, that the Polymorphism Discovery Resource will be unable to "cover all the sources of polymorphisms in the U.S. and thus be a comprehensive survey of the range of sensitivities in the U.S." since its limited samples could not possibly account for the genomic diversity inherent in a nation of immigrants with immeasurable mixed racial/ethnic backgrounds.[11]

Project scientists have targeted approximately five hundred environmental response genes, or "susceptibility genes," that code for proteins critical in the body's response to environmental agents and that appear to be associated with increased risk for disease. The environmental response genes of interest to EGP scientists include, for example, DNA repair genes, cell cycle control genes, cell signaling and receptor genes, and the cytochrome P450 family of genes, which produce enzymes that metabolize or detoxify chemical toxins. Polymorphisms in these environmental response genes are thought to play a role in causing disease or in susceptibility to disease and "might determine how a person responds to and metabolizes drugs or carcinogenic compounds after exposure" (Olden and Wilson 2000, 150). Kenneth Olden and Samuel Wilson explain the EGP's focus on the "environmental response genes" and their relation to the environment:

> Every organism is exposed to hazardous agents in its environment on a continual basis. As a result, organisms have evolved sophisticated pathways that can minimize the biological consequences of hazardous environmental agents. These pathways constitute "the environmental response machinery." All human genes, including those that encode components

of the environmental response machinery, are subject to genetic vari-
ability, which can be associated with the altered efficiency of a biological
pathway. So a person's risk for developing an illness as a result of an environmental exposure might be dependent on the efficiency of their own
unique set of environmental response genes. (2000, 150)

After accomplishing the resequencing and cataloguing of all the possible polymorphisms contained in the 500 selected environmental response genes, phase
2 of the EGP will determine the functional significance of those allelic variants.[12]
In other words, phase 2 will study how, if at all, one or more polymorphisms in
these candidate environmental response genes predispose an individual to
contracting a disease whether or not the individual is exposed to an environmental "trigger." This phase of the project will study the association of particular SNPs with particular diseases by conducting population studies examining
the "frequency with which given alleles occur in a population of affected people,
compared with the frequency of the same alleles in a population of unaffected
people" (Olden and Wilson 2000, 152). For example, if a group of people has a
sequence variation, or a combination of sequence variations, in one or more of
the histocompatibility genes that code for proteins that resist damage from the
toxic substance beryllium, then if those individuals are exposed to beryllium,
will they be more susceptible than others to developing berylliosis, a deadly
lung disease?[13]

Finally, phase 3 of the EGP will develop animal models to increase our
understanding of human susceptibility to disease and the precise mechanisms
leading to disease. After identifying and isolating a particular polymorphism
that appears to increase an individual's susceptibility to environmental illness,
scientists will then investigate the exact function of that SNP variation by conducting so-called knockout and knock-in experiments on laboratory animals.
These studies will help scientists determine the biological outcomes, or the phe-
notypic expression that surfaces, when a specific gene is removed from or added
to the organism under experimental conditions (Olden and Wilson 2000, 152).[14]

An allied project of the EGP, also sponsored by the NIEHS, is the National
Center for Toxicogenomics (NCT). The promise of toxicogenomics lies in determining at a molecular level exactly how a particular toxic substance damages
the DNA itself. Using new genetic methodologies and technologies, scientists
can expose experimental samples of certain target genes or gene fragments to
a carcinogenic chemical like trichloroethylene (TCE), for example, in order to
determine exactly how those target environmental response genes are impaired
or altered as a result of exposure. Toxicogenomic research aims to develop
computer-assisted genetic assays that might identify protein biomarkers of
exposure and effect, enabling scientists to detect specific genetic "signatures"
for a given pathway of toxicity. These signatures might help "identify the agent

and dose to which individuals or populations have been exposed," which will, according to the NCT, "dramatically change our understanding of human disease risk . . . provid[ing] new opportunities for the nation (and individuals) to protect human health and prevent disease."[15]

Environmental Health Policy Implications

By collecting information on the genetic basis of environmentally associated diseases and increasing our knowledge of gene-environment interactions, the EGP's (and NCT's) environmental health goals are to help with more accurate assessments of disease risks, thereby increasing multifold the explanatory and predictive power of environmental health risk assessment and epidemiology. The EGP scientists argue that due to our incomplete knowledge about disease causation, standard epidemiological studies are largely based on educated guesses, an imperfect decision-making process that forces government agencies, such as the EPA or the FDA, to either underregulate or overregulate. By linking the power of molecular studies to epidemiology, scientists argue, regulators can increase the scientific validity of the government's environmental health policies.[16] Furthermore, the EGP's SNP catalogue will provide information to the pharmacogenetics industry, which, when armed with this new knowledge of susceptible subpopulations, can design action-specific drugs. A drug may be designed, for example, to supply lung tissue protection from the damaging effects of beryllium exposure that the aforementioned hypothetical subpopulation's particular genome doesn't provide.

The EGP also hopes to aid in earlier diagnosis of disease or to screen populations at higher risk of disease, thereby "taking the guesswork out of risk assessment" (Olden and Guthrie 2001, 9). Armed with this new monitoring tool, regulators would have access to the potential range of sensitivities to a particular environmental agent and would be able to control it with greater accuracy, or to develop better preventative measures. According to Kenneth Olden and Janet Guthrie, the precision afforded by this new information will allow regulators and medical professionals to "reduce risk . . . by several mechanisms: (i) eliminating or reducing exposure, (ii) pharmacological intervention, and (iii) gene therapy" (2001, 9). Indeed, this list represents the primary risk-preventative measures that were enumerated during my interviews with EGP geneticists. The first line of defense consists of cautioning at-risk individuals that they should keep themselves out of harm's way, an admonition that might proceed as follows: "If you have the SNP that makes you genetically sensitive to, say, beryllium, you are advised not to work in the Brush-Wellman defense contracting plant in Tucson, Arizona, because there you may be exposed to beryllium, which is vital to the manufacture of nuclear weapons and to the aerospace industry." Other second-order "preventative" measures that were mentioned during my interviews included manufacturing and prescribing genome-specific drug and gene therapies, and DNA screening for "susceptibility genes" to use in genetic counseling on heritability and reproduction.[17]

Labeling these post-exposure measures as "preventative" is what's known in environmental regulation parlance as an "end of pipe" solution—not in fact what most environmentalists would consider *prevention*. Prevention of environmental health problems usually means not producing the pollution, or the environmental "trigger," in the first place.

More in line with what is generally understood as prevention, the EGP scientists also pointed to the significance of the role of genomic research on susceptibility genes for the development of more effective environmental regulations designed to protect "susceptible" individuals. However, these policy decisions concerning the use of the new genetic knowledge is decidedly not the role of the scientists themselves. Rather, it will be up to the government to decide whether or not the scientific fact that, say, 5 percent of the population is susceptible to a particular substance such as, for example, beryllium, warrants that substance being removed from production and use. Of course, this begs the question of what in fact does it mean to be "susceptible"? That is, can or should someone be labeled "susceptible," or genetically disadvantaged, *before* they are exposed to a toxin that most would argue they should not be exposed to in the first place? If an individual carrying a specific "faulty" genetic variation or variations is *not* exposed to a potential environmental "trigger," they most likely would not become ill. The discourse of susceptibility assumes that we *will* live with environmental toxins—it naturalizes environmental toxicity and pathologizes some genomic subsets of the human population. The idea of inherent genetic susceptibility to environmental illness makes sense only if it is accepted that environmental pollution is a given, or a "natural" and inevitable component of modern society. Ultimately, this approach to environmental health policy is about placing the responsibility for ameliorating risk squarely on the shoulders of the individual and away from the larger social, legal, and economic factors that are essential to the production of both illness and health.

Questions of Ethical, Legal, and Social Implications

Echoing the sentiments of scientists from many other disciplines, the EGP geneticists and molecular biologists maintain a distinction between the production of scientific knowledge and its use after it leaves the laboratory and enters civil society, the recognized domain of environmental and public health policy. On the question of the potential dangers of the research on genetic variation, which might include enabling genetic profiling and stigmatization and discrimination against those people marked as members of genetically "susceptible subpopulations," one geneticist explained: "How the information about susceptibility is used is a little bit more uncertain; I have no idea. There's a potential for wrongdoing at any level. That's beyond what we, the scientists, can do. It's not our role to stop science in that way. The EGP is all about knowledge. But is it better to have knowledge or to lack knowledge?"[18] While distancing themselves from responsibility relating to the potential uses and abuses of the findings that may emerge from the EGP, the NIH scientists I spoke with were clear about what constituted their role in the ethical, legal, and social implications of the research process itself. The scientists expressed great sensitivity concerning several issues: Would genetic samples from target populations be collected with legally assured informed consent? Would the privacy and confidentiality of the participants be respected and guaranteed? Would the moral, spiritual, and cultural considerations of a group of people be addressed in terms of the use, distribution, and disposal of their donated bodily materials?

To address the thorny issues of privacy and the ethics of human genome research, approximately 5 percent of the budget of the HGP and the EGP funds a program known as ELSI (ethical, legal, and social implications).[19] The ELSI program conducts research on the potential impacts of human genome research on Native American, African American, Asian American, and Latino communities and funds conferences, workshops, and dialogue groups for public education and assistance in the development of public health policy recommendations. Heedful of the appalling history of racist practices in medical experimentation by government scientists on unwitting African American subjects during the Tuskegee syphilis study, the ELSI program was established to provide a "new approach to scientific research" that can anticipate potential legal, ethical, and social problems before they actually occur "at the same time that the basic scientific issues are being studied."[20] Referring to the priority of ELSI issues to the EGP, Olden and Wilson state: "The EGP is promoting research projects and broad-based discussions on [ELSI] issues, and will try to ensure that the public is adequately protected. *This is essential even to allow the EGP to move forward to completion*" (2000, 153; my emphasis). One might argue that this sentiment contradicts the presumed objectives of the ELSI program: the people who participate may, among other things, question whether research projects like the EGP should in fact move forward to completion and, if so, with what kinds of modifications. This raises questions about the extent to which the ELSI program can, or is willing to, implement its stated goals, which presumably include the promotion of more democratic approaches to scientific research in human genetics.

Environment, Genes, and Justice: Democratizing
Human Genome Research

To gain other perspectives on the promises and limitations of human genome research, I also interviewed two geneticists allied with environmental justice organizations who are interested in genetic research on gene-environment interactions that may be of use to communities suffering from high rates of environmental diseases. Trained in genetics and molecular biology, both Dr. Paul Billings (GeneSage and Council for Responsible Genetics) and Dr. José Morales (Biotechnology in the Public Interest) support the growth of scientific research initiatives, such as the EGP and the NCT, that study how allelic polymorphisms confer resistance or susceptibility to a particular environmental agent. For Morales, such advances in biotechnology help us to understand how the diverse mechanisms creating disease pathways are encoded in the genomes of different populations and, more important, he argues, this new knowledge will provide powerful "informational weapons" to arm impacted communities with the scientific tools necessary to fight for environmental justice.[21] While both scientists insist that genetics research greatly adds to our understanding of human health, they argue strongly against the genetic reductionism embedded in the promotion of technologies such as genetic testing and screening as the key to preventing environmental diseases. Billings emphasizes this point:

> One of the things that annoys me about [the HGP] is that people are talking about the causation of disease as being present in the genome. That's incorrect. The *mechanism* of disease is in the genome, in the sense that much of what disease is is an aberrant physiological response to an environmental agent. So the bacteria gets into your lungs, you pour out all these white cells . . . all that stuff is in genetic control. But that doesn't mean the causation of the illness was the genes. The causation of the illness was the bacteria. In the same sense, [in the EGP] the environmental agent will be the causation. There may be genes that alter our responses and there may be damage that the environmental agent actually produces to the gene—all possible. But it's still the environmental agent that causes the problem.[22]

Genetic reductionism oversimplifies what Morales and Billings, and many of the EGP scientists themselves, identify as the real causes of disease. Although there are some diseases that are highly associated with particular genes, such as Tay-Sachs disease or cystic fibrosis, most diseases have their roots in multiple causes, whether it be the involvement of multiple genes or exposures to multiple environmental toxins. But increased risk for disease is also linked to other factors including inadequate nutrition, poverty, and lack of quality health care. Furthermore, as Morales and Billings explain, although some diseases, like cystic fibrosis, are caused by a single, recessive, highly penetrant allelic variation, most environmental diseases, like cancer, are "polygenic," that is, they are the result of the complex interactions of several genes that will modify an individual's health risks only in the event of exposure to specific environmental agents. Therefore, as these "oppositional" scientists imply, the most rational and simplest measure to improve the health of low-income populations would be to prevent the dumping, incineration, or release of environmental contaminants into their, or anyone else's, communities, one of the central goals of the environmental justice movement.

Although most geneticists, including those at the NIH, argue vehemently against the genetic reductionism perspective and explain that our genes are only part—albeit an important part—of the story, the discourse of "susceptible subpopulations" remains at the core of research projects like the EGP. This discourse of genetic disadvantage is hard to displace, especially when it is linked to the associated discourse of genetic resistance, a rhetorical binary that assumes the notion of greater robustness or even the idea that resistant genomes might be better adapted to modern environmental conditions. Again, this view is repudiated by the scientists working on the EGP, but it is inescapably embedded in the twin discourses of susceptibility and resistance. For example, at a recent conference at the University of California at Berkeley, Max More, president of the Extropy Institute, exclaimed in a public letter to Mother Nature: "You have raised us from simple self-replicating chemicals to trillion-celled mammals. What you have made us is glorious, yet deeply flawed. We will no longer tolerate the tyranny of aging and death. Through genetic alterations, cellular manipulations, synthetic organs, and any necessary means, we will endow ourselves with enduring vitality and remove our expiration date" (in Deneen 2000, 22). This unabashed technological optimism verges upon my earlier fantasy of the "brave new world" stratagem to produce Roundup Ready® communities using the knowledge generated from the EGP—could the more robust SNPs isolated from the more resistant subpopulations be engineered into a biotechnological fix to cure diseases like cancer or berylliosis?[23] If that were the case, exposure to beryllium at the Brush Wellman plant in Tucson would not be viewed as a significant health hazard after all. This is the liberal humanist vision of Man's recovery of his lost mastery over nature; biotechnology can fix the people/communities, in this case by making them Beryllium Ready, so that the business of industrial production of nuclear weapons can proceed, unimpeded, as usual.

Whose Science? Whose Environmental Health Research Agenda?

Presumably, one of the purposes of ELSI's commitment to community-based human genome research is to increase public education and participation in this research. This would suggest that the research foci selected by project scientists would overlap with those of the impacted communities. Why then the preoccupation in this chapter with the health effects of exposure to beryllium? Are communities who are experiencing environmental injustices calling for more research into the genetic origins of berylliosis? In my conversations with the NIH scientists, the example of beryllium exposure was consistently put to use in helping to explain the goals of the EGP. I had first heard about beryllium during a research trip to Tucson, Arizona, to interview women environmental justice activists working on the U.S.-Mexico border. One of these activists, Rose Augustine, invited me on a "toxic tour" of the 85 percent Latino neighborhood of South Tucson where we visited the Brush Wellman factory, a defense contracting plant that uses beryllium to manufacture the trigger mechanisms for nuclear missiles.

Beryllium is a metallic element extracted from bertrandite and beryl mineral ores, and is chemically converted into a hard, lightweight metal that is three times lighter than aluminum and six times harder than steel (Roe 1999a). Because of these properties, and because it enables a more efficient chain reaction in the nuclear fission process, beryllium has become a "strategic metal," critical to the U.S. government's military policy and to the expansion of its nuclear arsenal. Beryllium was first produced for use in the Manhattan Project in factories in Cleveland and Lorain, Ohio and, by the mid–1940s, local doctors were treating dozens of beryllium workers and their families (including nuclear weapons scientists) who had become seriously ill with berylliosis, a respiratory disease that destroys the lung's delicate alveoli air sacs and is usually fatal. Alarmed at the rising incidences of berylliosis in factory workers and nuclear scientists, the newly formed Atomic Energy Commission realized it had both a public health and a public relations problem on its hands. Although the federal government knew that the metal was toxic at infinitesimally small doses, in the name of national security, it continued to support production, to overlook Occupational, Safety, and Health Administration (OSHA) inspections, and to kill plans to strengthen beryllium regulations. Despite considerable epidemiological evidence and a mounting death toll, only once in the last fifty years has OSHA tried to impose stricter exposure limits for beryllium. That was in 1975, and the then-head of the Department of Energy, James Schlesinger, warned that the new regulations would "seriously limit our ability to develop and produce weapons for the nuclear stockpile" (Roe 1999a, 7). Thus, with the endorsement of President Jimmy Carter, the OSHA plan to more tightly regulate beryllium was abandoned.[24]

As Rose Augustine and I stood outside the Brush Wellman factory in South Tucson, we saw the plant's stacks towering over an elementary school and a child care center. Augustine commented, "Many people in the neighborhood are sick with lung problems, and they [the Pima County Health Department] tell us it's our 'genealogy' or the chilies and beans that we eat."[25] Augustine expressed concern about how genetics arguments are used to explain the serious illnesses suffered by the low-income Latino communities who work in and live next to the plant. It became more clear to me that the scientific research issues of interest to the NIH geneticists were quite different from the environmental health concerns of the Latino residents and workers of South Tucson.

Today, in the name of defending the "free world" and the war against terrorism, the U.S. government is still in the business of nuclear weapons manufacturing and therefore requires a steady supply of beryllium and its alloys. It is in the interests of national security and military supremacy that the Department of Energy, the Department of Defense, *and* the NIH should be eager to determine how to prevent "susceptible" subpopulations, who might comprise the labor force in nuclear weapons production factories, from getting sick from exposure to beryllium.

Dilemmas of Participation in Human Genome Research

The environmental-justice-oriented scientists with whom I spoke argued that it is preposterous to locate the ultimate solution to environmental health problems in tinkering with genes, on the scientific grounds that genes are not us, or rather, are only partly us. However, even though these researchers warn against the genetic reductionist position, they also make the argument that greater knowledge, particularly knowledge about disease responses in minority populations, is a move towards greater social justice. Historically, biomedical research on disease susceptibility, therapies, and treatment have primarily been conducted on white males, and so the specific health needs of people of color have been ignored. These geneticists, who include Morales and Howard University researchers Dr. Georgia Dunston and Dr. Charmaine Royal, argue that genetic technologies should be understood as tools to help us understand how and why our bodies respond differently to exogenous agents in the environment in order to help with disease prevention and the development of cures.[26] Greater information about environmental illnesses in communities of color, even at the genetic level, is therefore a scientific advance consistent with the goals of environmental justice. For Morales, Dunston, and Royal, the genetics revolution, when spearheaded by scientists aware of and sensitive to racial biases, should galvanize communities of color in the United States to participate enthusiastically in research projects like the EGP.

Adopting a somewhat different stance on environmental justice and the potential of the "new genetics" to improve the health of communities of color, Debra Harry, a Northern Paiute activist from the Pyramid Lake Reservation in Nevada, questions the NIH's plans to collect genetic variation data on the different "races," and calls for greater scrutiny of the nature and quality of public participation in this new scientific research. Harry argues that participation in projects like the Human Genome Diversity Project (HGDP) and the EGP, which for Native Americans most often has been limited to donating blood or other body parts, must be predicated on the "return of the benefits of the genetic research to the donor community."[27] A number of indigenous groups, in North America and overseas, Harry explains, are offered an exchange value arrangement to remunerate them for their involvement in the research—either they are given a cash payment for their body material, provided with limited health care for conditions like diabetes, or promised royalty payments for future products that may be manufactured from their genetic materials.[28]

For Harry, human genome diversity research, like the EGP, represents the newest genre of race-based science couched in the benign and objective language of either "geographic lineage" or "environmental disease prevention." She argues that contemporary forms of eugenics and racialized science arise when researchers insist on "collecting and maintaining racial group or tribally identified labels on samples," a cataloguing practice that is paramount to "operating with a zookeeper's mentality" and that inherently invites "racialized outcomes" (Prakash et al. 2003, 22–23). Furthermore, Harry contends, the health problems of most indigenous peoples in North America and elsewhere are the outcome of the interconnected histories of colonialism, economic poverty, deteriorating infrastructure, and contaminated environments. The single-minded focus on genes obscures these fundamental causal factors and diverts attention away from the necessary actions to change them—actions that would call for political, cultural, and economic, not genetic, solutions to these preventable problems. Indigenous peoples around the globe, says Harry, must be fully informed about the goals and objectives of the most recent army of "bio-prospectors" to invade native peoples' lands and communities in order to decide for themselves whether they should participate in research projects like the EGP.[29] Confronting head-on the triumphalist discourse embedded in phrases such as "revolutionary science" and "the golden age of biomedical research,"[30] Harry urges all indigenous peoples to critically ponder the question, "Science needs us and wants us, but do we really need them?"[31]

With these caveats in mind, exactly what would meaningful participation in genetics research consistent with the goals of environmental justice look like? To respond to this question, the NIH's ELSI program offers grants for community-based initiatives that "promote public understanding of the social, ethical, and legal implications of conducting environmental health research involving human subjects in areas such as gene-environment interactions."[32] One of these initiatives, supported by a $1.2 million ELSI grant, involves a consortium of three universities: the University of Michigan, Michigan State University, and the Tuskegee Institute. The central aim of the "Communities of Color and Genetics Policy Project" is to "develop a process to engage communities of color, representing a range of socioeconomic backgrounds, in dialogues concerning genetic research and its resulting technologies."[33] The project convened "dialogue groups" of ten to fifteen people per group with African American and Latino communities in Michigan and Alabama and assembled their responses in a report to be developed into recommendations for laws, professional standards, and institutional policies regarding the use and application of genome research and technology.[34] The most oft-repeated concerns raised by participants in the dialogue groups were about privacy and control of access to one's genetic information, fears of stigmatization and discrimination by employers or insurance companies, and distrust of government and scientific agendas in terms of who will be the primary beneficiaries of genetics research.[35]

The apprehensions voiced by members of the Michigan and Alabama communities are situated within a broader social paradigm of "scientific inevitability," in this case, the inevitability of the forward progression of human genetics research. Given that the dialogue groups are funded with ELSI monies that are disbursed by the NIH, the very institution that is conducting the genetics variation research, there exists little opportunity for participants to raise questions that are outside the rhetorical universe of the forward advancement of this research. The participants in the ELSI community-based dialogue groups were limited to raising concerns about their taking part in genetic research projects exclusively within the context of how to minimize the potential dangers of the research process and its potential outcomes; it is assumed that the "human genome research ship" has already sailed out of the harbor. The predominantly African American and Latino respondents were not invited to question the research agendas themselves, nor to recommend other research agendas. This notion of "participation" is about reassuring the donors of genetic material (that is, members of minority communities) that their privacy will be protected, their culture will be respected, and that they will benefit somewhere down the line—all worthy goals—but it is not about strengthening the tools of participatory democracy that would enable community residents to contribute meaningfully to the discussion on how to solve environmental health problems. Debra Harry argues that these community-based ELSI studies are essentially designed to get communities of color to rubber-stamp the research and provide the informed consent required to proceed legally with the genetic studies. As the head of the NIEHS, speaking at the plenary session of a recent ELSI-funded conference, succinctly put it, "the research must not be stopped."[36]

For Debra Harry, Rose Augustine, and many other women environmental justice activists, the genetics research conducted by the EGP represents a tactic by government to divert attention and resources away from issues that are truly important to low-income communities and communities of color who receive few of the benefits, but bear the lion's share of the costs, of modern industrial society. These women activists call for research on how to remove pollutants from the environment and from people's bodies, on how to provide communities with adequate health care, nutrition, and clean air and water, and on how to develop more sustainable industries and jobs that do not pollute the environment. To

these women environmental justice activists, the EGP is asking all the wrong
questions.

What would constitute appropriate guidelines for meaningful participation in community-based genetic research projects? Meaningful participation
does not mean either donating one's blood or other body parts and then being
remunerated for these parts, what I call "exchange-value" participation, where
bodily material is a commodity that is exchanged for cash or other compensation. Nor does it mean, as in the case of ELSI-sponsored dialogue groups, first
assuming the inevitability of the implementation of the scientific project and
the risks that go along with it, and then laying out a set of limited, predeter-
mined options among which an at-risk community may choose. Genuine participation that supports environmental health democracy is consistent with environmental justice activists' concept of "community-driven" participatory research,
in contrast to the more commonly used "community-based research."[37] Conducting participatory research to improve a community's health problems
means establishing at the outset exactly what are the community's most urgent
health problems. Moreover, democratizing the research process would necessi-
tate a commitment to the centrality of the community's role in setting research
goals, in formulating and prioritizing research questions and protocols, and in contributing to decisions about use and dissemination of the research outcomes.

The environmental justice activists I spoke with were adamant about the
need for participatory research to be driven by community needs rather than
simply based in a particular community, as though it were the scientist's personal laboratory. These activists emphasized the importance of the community
members being in control of research questions, of budget allocations, of the
use and dissemination of the data, and even over publication of the research
results. But how would this paradigm of participation function in the arena of
genetic variation research? The issue of meaningful participation of communities with vast differences in expertise and access to the tools and methods of the
genetic sciences must confront the problem of considerable epistemic barriers.
Among these barriers are, for example, the high levels of specialized knowledge
and theoretical refinement and access to the sophisticated instrumentation
and techniques that are central to the field of genetics. Do these obstacles necessarily prohibit genuine community participation in the future directions of
human genome research?

The primary recommendations that concerned scientists and activists
suggested to confront these barriers of expertise include increased public education and a redoubling of efforts to train and credential members of under-
represented communities in the field of genetics.[38] In addition, many activists
discussed the need for building trust-based alliances between professional scientists and local communities; the "sympathetic" or concerned scientist would
thus be entrusted to represent the community's environmental health rights in

genetic technology assessments. The recent turn in government-sponsored studies toward "community-based research" (while taking into account activists' critique of this terminology) may, according to some activists, offer some promise in efforts to build collaborative research partnerships among environmental health scientists and members of communities of color. An assessment of the true collaborative nature of these studies will rest on the extent to which community residents' voices are heard *before* the genetics research ship sets sail.[39]

Expressing a restrained optimism toward the current trend in community-based research on environmental health genetics, many activists wonder whether this new focus on *partnerships* might not respond to the concerns of the environmental justice movement, and perhaps, as Debra Harry puts it, produce a genuine "science for the people." The success of these community-government partnerships depends, however, on the extent to which the NIEHS's research on "gene-environment interactions" takes seriously the interactive role of both genetic and environmental factors. Indeed, many government geneticists contend that the EGP's stated focus on the *interaction* between genes and the environment mitigates against the narrow, genes-as-root-cause explanation that characterizes the genetic reductionist paradigm. Destabilizing the reductionist standpoint by emphasizing interaction would also challenge the underlying assumptions that are associated with it: "inevitability" (of toxic pollution in the environment) and "susceptibility" (of genetically-disadvantaged subpopulations). While this sounds like a plausible argument, during my interviews with EGP scientists, references to the "environment" end of the equation rarely came up. "Environment" consistently falls out of the picture in EGP documents, except as the naturalized substratum on which genetic variation operates.

By combining a research focus on the interactive dynamics of genes and the environment together with a survey of the health status of specific communities or populations who live in particular *places*, the EGP would be capable of demonstrating that genetic "susceptibility" to environmental illnesses is place-specific and not an inherent quality of "genetically disadvantaged subpopulations" (Shostak 2003). The analysis that people are genetically susceptible in *places* (that is, polluted places) could bolster the environmental justice movement's assertion that where we live, work, and play impacts our health status and life chances.

Conclusion: Producing Genetically Informed Communities in the Age of Environmental Justice

The rhetoric of "revolution," so widespread in popular science reporting on human genome research, demands that we take notice. But what exactly are the promises of the genetics revolution to which we can look forward? Biotechnological advances in agriculture, such as Monsanto's Roundup Ready® line of seeds, for example, strive to manage the unpredictability of nature to produce higher and more marketable crop yields. Many agro-scientists refute such optimistic claims and argue that these genetic advancements, rather than *revolutionizing* the field, actually *preserve* a commitment to conventional practices in industrial agriculture by altering the genetic makeup of a farmer's crops instead of altering the methods we use to grow our food (Altieri 2001). Likewise, the proclamations of an imminent "golden age" of biomedicine that accompany recent trends yoking public health research to the new human genome bandwagon compel us to ponder just what is golden about this new age. Does cutting-edge genetic research in environmental health, such as the EGP, envision a nation of "Roundup Ready® Communities" resistant to the toxic emissions of the United States's military-industrial complex? As Rose Augustine quipped, "fix the people, rather than fix the industry!"[40]

Environmental justice activists, most of whom are women of color, contest the flawed logic of genetic reductionism, illustrated in the above examples, and the way it forecloses on and erodes commitment to solving environmental problems that are the result of social and economic injustices, *not* faulty genes.[41] Women activists like Debra Harry and Rose Augustine have become "proactive" technoscientific actors by increasing their scientific literacy and insisting on actively participating *at the forefront, not the back of,* decision making about scientific "revolutions" that affect their lives. Refusing to passively accept the gender, class, and race reductionism that has historically restricted women and minorities from access to the upper echelons of science, they have challenged the genetic reductionism that tends to locate the source of environmental health problems in our genes, rather than in our society's environmentally destructive activities that emit poisons into the earth and into the bodies of all living things.

Debra Harry and Rose Augustine both agree that, despite the government's stated intentions to "promote public acceptance" of human genome research by instituting community-based dialogue groups, the greatest stride toward achieving authentic participation in the future directions of science and technology is enabling all communities the opportunity to develop diverse scientific literacies, a prerequisite for a genuinely democratic society committed to environmental justice at the turning of the "century of the gene."

NOTES

Many thanks to Marcy Darnovsky, Debra Harry, Anne Wibiralske, Cate Sandilands, Lisa Bunin, Debbie Klein, and the volume editor, Rachel Stein, for helpful discussions and comments on prior drafts of this essay. An earlier, abbreviated version of this paper appeared in *Women and Environments* no. 52/53 (fall 2001): 40–43.

1. For thorough arguments mapping the eugenic underpinnings of the "new genetics," see Duster 1990, Hubbard and Wald 1993, Rothman 2001, Paul 1995, and Roberts 1997.

2. For discussions on the emergence of a new period in the history of modern science and technology that is driven by the discursive/material production and harnessing of the "gene," see Haraway 1997, Keller 2000, and Rifkin 1998.

3. Elsewhere, I have written on the intersections of lay and professional expertise in environmental problem solving. See, for example, Di Chiro 1997.

4. Monsanto's website explains how its Roundup Ready technology "can have added benefits for growers, consumers and the environment including a reduction in the number of pesticide sprays and reduced environmental exposure, reduced labor, higher yields and compatibility with more sustainable agricultural practices, while respecting the environment as well as regional and cultural diversity" (*http://www.monsanto.com*)

5. National Institutes of Health News Advisory, Oct. 10, 1997.

6. Ibid.

7. These are cell samples, usually taken from blood, that have been subjected to a series of chemical, bacterial, or genetic manipulations that promote continual replication, thereby providing the researcher a steady supply of the particular cell line.

8. Author's interview with Dr. Lisa Brooks, National Human Genome Research Institute (NHGRI), Bethesda, Md., Jan. 25, 2001.

9. Recent work by sociologist Troy Duster suggests that genomics research in law and medicine is at the same time rejecting the study of "race" and developing new "proxies for race," which he likens to "putting old wine into new bottles." For example, "Human Molecular Genetics and the Subject of Race: Contrasting the Rhetoric with the Practices in Law and Medicine," paper delivered at the Conference on Human Genetics, Environment, and Communities of Color, Columbia University, Feb. 4, 2002.

10. Author's interview with Dr. Lisa Brooks, NHGRI, Jan. 25, 2001.

11. Author's interview with Dr. Paul Billings, GeneSage, San Francisco, Feb. 16, 2001. There is considerable debate within the scientific community on the issue of the meaningfulness of the notion of "race" or "continental lineage" in medical research on health disparities. See Wade 2003.

12. Author's interview with Dr. José Velasquez, NIEHS, Research Triangle Park, N.C., Jan. 30, 2001.

13. A group of scientists has recently determined that approximately 97 percent of workers suffering from berylliosis carry a genetic susceptibility to the disease; see Z. Wang et al. 1999.

14. Martin Teitel, former director of the Council on Responsible Genetics, explained to me that "knockout" experiments regularly result in what is known as genome redundancy. That is, a gene is knocked out (i.e., chemically removed from the genetic material), and the associated trait or function that the scientist was expecting to disappear appears phenotypically anyway demonstrating that several genes may perform the same function. The far-reaching goals articulated by promoters of human genome research, including the EGP, assert a greater level of confidence in science's putative mastery of the workings of the human genome than the experimental data provide. Author's interview with Martin Teitel, Council on Responsible Genetics, Cambridge, Mass., Jan. 26, 2001.

15. National Center for Toxicogenomics website, *http://www.niehs.nih.gov/nct/impact.htm*. For an analysis of the intersections of biological and cultural meanings in toxicogenomics, see Shostak 2003.

16. Author's interview with Dr. José Velasquez, NIEHS, Jan. 30, 2001.

17. Author's interview with Dr. Lisa Brooks, NHGRI, Jan. 25, 2001.

18. Author's interview with Dr. José Velasquez, NIEHS, Jan. 30, 2001.

19. For more on the ethical implications of human genome research, see Zilinskas and Balint 2001.

20. National Human Genome Research Institute website, *http://www.nhgri. nih.gov/ELSI/ aboutels.html.* For more information about ELSI and the EGP, see Sharp and Barrett 2000.

21. Author's interview with Dr. José Morales, Biotechnology in the Public Interest, New York, Dec. 12, 2001.

22. Author's interview with Dr. Paul Billings, GeneSage, Feb. 16, 2001.

23. This racialized, technoscientific argument would suggest, for example, that if the bodies of one racial/ethnic group seem to be less able to resist the onslaught of various pollutants, then the facilities that release these chemicals or radiation emissions should be placed in the neighborhoods of those populations whose physiologies are more "robust." The concept of environmental justice, in the field of environmental health science, then becomes equal distribution of pollution based on one's natural resistance or inherent ability to absorb toxins. Armed with the EGP's knowledge of the genetic variations in different racial/ethnic groups that make up the US population, federal policy makers would be enabled to produce a fully rationalized/racialized geography of environmental impacts and allow the appropriate human bodies and their industrial toxin counterparts to coexist harmoniously, thereby guaranteeing business as usual.

24. See the reprint of the six-day series on the history of beryllium in the United States (Roe 1999b).

25. Author's interview with Rose Marie Augustine, Tucson, Ariz., June 13, 2001.

26. For example, Charmaine Royal, "Genetics Research and Communities of Color: The Good, the Bad, and the Ugly," Paper delivered at the Conference on Human Genetics, Environment, and Communities of Color, Columbia University, Feb. 4, 2002.

27. Author's interview with Debra Harry, Indigenous People's Council on Biocolonialism, Wadsworth, Nev., Jan. 23, 2001.

28. Ibid.

29. Ibid.

30. Kenneth Olden, "The Role of Gene-Environment Interaction in Health Disparities." Presentation at the Conference on Human Genetics, Environment, and Communities of Color, Columbia University, New York, Feb. 4, 2002.

31. Comments delivered for the panel discussion, "Opportunities and Challenges of Genetics Research for Communities of Color," Conference on Human Genetics, Environment, and Communities of Color, Columbia University, New York, Feb 4, 2002.

32. Request for Applications, RFA ES–02–005, "Environmental Justice: Partnerships to Address Ethical Challenges in Environmental Health." Program Administrator, Shobha Srinivasan, Ph.D., NIEHS, Research Triangle Park, N.C.

33. "Communities of Color and Genetics Policy Project: An Interview with Vence Bonham," *Alliance Alert*, Alliance of Genetic Support Groups, Washington D.C. (March 2001).

34. See the project website, *http://www.sph.umich.edu/genpolicy/index.html.*

35. Amy Schulz et al., "Focus Group Content Report," University of Michigan, School of Public Health, 2000.

36. Olden, "The Role of Gene-Environment Interaction in Health Disparities."

37. Author's interview with Carlos Porras, Communities for a Better Environment, Los Angeles, Jan. 30, 2001.

38. Author's interview with Dr. José Morales, Biotechnology in the Public Interest, Dec. 12, 2001.

39. For example, as coauthors of the RFAs for community-based research projects that the NIEHS has recently announced, see note 34.

40. Author's interview with Rose Marie Augustine, Tucson, Ariz., June 13, 2001.

41. Debra Harry and the Indigenous People's Council on Biocolonialism (IPCB) have published two booklets to educate communities, specifically indigenous communities, about the cultural, environmental, and health implications of the new wave of human genome research. See Harry et al. 2000 and 2001.

REFERENCES

Albers, Julie Wakefield. 1997. "Understanding Gene-Environment Interactions." *Environmental Health Perspectives* 105, no. 6: 1–2.

Altieri, Miguel A. 2001. *Genetic Engineering in Agriculture: The Myths, Environmental Risks, and Alternatives*. Oakland, Calif.: Food First/Institute for Food and Development Policy; Chicago: distributed by LPC Group.

Carrano, Anthony. 1998. "Genome Resources Help Scientists Explore Life-Environment Interactions." *Human Genome News* 9: 1–5.

Deneen, Sally. 2000. "Designer People." *E Magazine* 12, no. 1: 19–22.

Di Chiro, Giovanna. 1997. "Local Actions, Global Visions: Remaking Environmental Expertise." *Frontiers* 18, no. 2: 203–31.

———. 2001. "A New Biotechnological 'Fix' for Environmental Health? Examining the Environmental Genome Project." *Women and Environments* no. 52/53: 40–43.

Doyle, Jack. 1985. *Altered Harvest: Agriculture, Genetics, and the Fate of the World's Food Supply*. New York: Viking.

Duster, Troy. 1990. *Backdoor to Eugenics*. New York: Routledge.

Haraway, Donna. 1997. *Modest-Witness@Second-Millennium.FemaleMan-Meets-OncoMouse: Feminism and Technoscience*. New York: Routledge.

Harry, Debra, Stephanie Howard, and Brett Shelton. 2000. *Indigenous Peoples, Genes, and Genetics*. Nixon, Nev.: Indigenous Peoples Council on Biocolonialism.

———. 2001. *Life, Lineage, and Sustenance: Indigenous Peoples and Genetic Engineering, Threats to Food, Agriculture, and the Environment*. Nixon, Nev.: Indigenous Peoples Council on Biocolonialism.

Hubbard, Ruth, and Elijah Wald. 1993. *Exploding the Gene Myth*. Boston: Beacon Press.

Keller, Evelyn Fox. 2000. *The Century of the Gene*. Cambridge, Mass.: Harvard University Press.

Krimsky, Sheldon, and Roger Wrubel. 1996. *Agricultural Biotechnology and the Environment: Science, Policy, and Social Issues*. Urbana: University of Illinois Press.

Lappé, Marc, and Britt Bailey. 1998. *Against the Grain: Biotechnology and the Corporate Takeover of Your Food*. Monroe, Me.: Common Courage Press.

Olden, Kenneth, and Janet Guthrie. 2001. "Genomics: Implications for Toxicology." *Mutation Research* 473: 9–15.

Olden, Kenneth, and Samuel Wilson. 2000. "Environmental Health and Genomics: Visions and Implications." *Nature Reviews in Genetics* 1 (Nov.): 149–53.

Paul, Diane. 1995. *Controlling Human Heredity: 1865 to the Present.* Atlantic Highlands, N.J.: Humanities Press.

Prakash, Swati, Julie Sze, Julia Chance, and Peggy Shepard, eds. 2003. "Human Genetics, Environment, and Communities of Color: Ethical and Social Implications Conference Report." New York: Communications Department, West Harlem Environmental Action.

Rifkin, Jeremy. 1998. *The Biotech Century: Harnessing the Gene and Remaking the World.* New York: Jeremy P. Tarcher/Putnam.

Roberts, Dorothy. 1997. *Killing the Black Body: Race, Reproduction, and the Meaning of Liberty.* New York: Pantheon Books.

Roe, Sam. 1999a. "Decades of Risk: US Knowingly Allowed Workers to be Overexposed to Toxic Dust." *Toledo Blade*, Mar. 28–Apr. 2.

Roe, Sam. 1999b. "Deadly Alliance: How Government and Industry Chose Weapons Over Workers." *Toledo Blade*, Mar. 28–Apr. 2.

Rothman, Barbara Katz. 2001. *The Book of Life: A Personal and Ethical Guide to Race, Normality, and the Implications of the Human Genome Project.* Boston: Beacon Press.

Schmidt, Charles. 2000. "Populations and Polymorphisms: Building the New Science of Environmental Genomics." *Genome News Network*, Center for the Advancement of Genomics, Rockville, Md.: 1–3.

Sharp, Richard, and Carl Barrett. 2000. "The Environmental Genome Project: Ethical, Legal, and Social Implications." *Environmental Health Perspectives* 108: 279–81.

Shostak, Sara. 2003. "Locating Gene-Environment Interaction: At the Intersections of Genetics and Public Health." *Social Science and Medicine* 56, no. 11: 2327–42.

Wade, Nicholas. 2003. "Two Scholarly Articles Diverge on the Role of Race in Medicine." *New York Times*, Mar. 20, A26.

Wang, Z., et al. 1999. "Differential Susceptibilities to Chronic Beryllium Disease Contributed by Different Glu69 HLA-DPBI and-DPAI Alleles." *Journal of Immunology* 163: 1647–53.

Zilinskas, Raymond, and Peter Balint, eds. 2001. *The Human Genome Project and Minority Communities: Ethical, Social, and Political Dilemmas.* Westport, Conn.: Praeger.

9

Public Eyes

Investigating the Causes of Breast Cancer

MARCY JANE KNOPF-NEWMAN

"Whatdunit?"

Allie Light and Irving Saraf's documentary *Rachel's Daughters: Searching for the Causes of Breast Cancer* (1997) opens with a series of vehicles driving through a central California desert landscape accented with sparse wildflowers set against a vivid blue sky visible beyond the hills. The environment seems pure until a power line, which rests unobtrusively at the top of the camera's frame, enters the viewer's consciousness. The audience soon realizes that these cars are en route to a funeral. We see women crying, hugging as they gently place flowers on a casket. Though we do not know it yet, the body of a young woman lies inside that coffin. Throughout this opening sequence, we hear the voice of poet and ecologist Sandra Steingraber, setting the narrative in motion,

> We are a generation who was born and came of adult age during the most toxic and environmentally unregulated decade ever known. Whose baby food was contaminated with traces of DDT, PCBs, and DES. Our neighborhoods were sprayed with pesticides and filled with toxic waste. Most of these chemicals did not even exist before World War II. We are the generation whose early idealism opened the original generation gap. We didn't know that this gap would come to mean premature and early death in our thirties, forties, and fifties. We didn't know that the "in" generation was destined to become the cancer generation. We didn't know that so many of our mothers would bury us.

Steingraber's voice-over gives the first hints as to whatdunit? That is, what killed her? We may not know who died, but we have an idea what killed her. It also links the film to Rachel Carson in crucial ways. The audience who listens to these words—while witnessing people grieving over a death—will hear resonances with Carson's Silent Spring. Indeed, the film Rachel's Daughters is as much a daughter of Silent Spring as the women with breast cancer featured in the film are daughters of Rachel. They are Rachel's daughters because they inherited the environment laden with toxic chemicals that her generation exploited. They are Rachel's daughters because they pursue the research questions about the causes of cancer that Carson put into the public sphere with her landmark book. And they are Rachel's daughters because they show us how their narratives and the supporting scientific evidence can lead to change.

Perhaps the most famous claim Carson made public in *Silent Spring* was about the carcinogenic "biocide" DDT (dichloro-diphenyl-trichloro-ethane). Concerned that there was no safe dose since no long-term scientific studies proved otherwise, she alluded to future irreparable damage that could occur if no one researched the potential dangers. Ironically, she posits, "since so many people came into extremely intimate contact with DDT and suffered no immediate ill effects the chemical must certainly be *innocent* of harm" (Carson 1962, 21; emphasis mine). Such an entrenched belief system—that these "elixirs of death" would be considered innocent until proven guilty—struck her as tragic. With the unregulated use of DDT, she anticipated higher cancer rates and worried about the effect on future generations. The film suggests that the woman buried at the beginning of *Rachel's Daughters* may have died as a result of exposure to the contaminants Carson worked tirelessly to limit.

Thirty-five years after the publication of *Silent Spring*, Light and Saraf created a film that revisits and revives Carson's central questions through the lens of breast cancer. That they merge her work with this specific type of cancer is significant: Carson herself was dying of the disease while writing this last book, although the public was not aware of that fact.[1] In the spirit of Carson's life and work, *Rachel's Daughters* awakens viewers who are versed in breast cancer literature, science, or medicine to a paradigm shift. The film unravels three mythologies persistent in public discourse about cancer. First, the film represents a diverse body of U.S. women with breast cancer: working-class and middle-class; African American, Chinese American, Native American, white, Latina; lesbian and heterosexual; women diagnosed in their twenties, thirties, forties, and fifties; and women from the south, the east, the north and the west. Second, it minimizes the use of barren war metaphors. Third, rather than wonder "why me?"—which usually encourages women to blame themselves—the women in the film set out on a journey to discover answers to the more complex and productive questions why? and what causes the disease? Decentering the expected breast cancer discourse leads the film's protagonists and creators to investigate environmental links to the disease and discover why women are diagnosed and dying from breast cancer at alarming rates.

Propelling the film's narrative structure is a new mode of inquiry—one that blends investigative journalism with hard-boiled detective work. In the second scene of the documentary, each of the women with breast cancer gets labeled as an "investigator" or "detective" as they take on the role of private eyes who probe into what caused their breast cancer. There are eight such women, but I hone in on one in particular, Jennifer Mendoza, a thirty-two year old Latina nanny. Although her role in the documentary is the smallest of the group, her presence functions as the film's emotional core. Precisely halfway through *Rachel's Daughters*, we learn that the body in the casket in the opening scene was Jennifer's. Thus she embodies the warning that Carson sounded in the fable that begins *Silent Spring*. Jennifer's body becomes a testament to the need for laws regulating substances that *indicate* harm. For she believes that exposure to DDT led to her cancer, and by extension, to cancer in the farmworker community she grew up in. Her premature death feels like déjà vu; just like Carson, Jennifer dies of breast cancer while making the public aware of the dangers pesticides pose. Unlike Carson, Jennifer displays her deteriorating health before the camera. Light and Saraf situate Jennifer's death in ways that interrupt the film's narrative and motivate us—citizens and scientists alike—to intervene with a strategy and an argument for preventing breast cancer. The brevity of Jennifer's life and appearance on screen serves as a cautionary tale to propel viewers into action, action that promotes collaboration among women with cancer, scientists, and activists; action that includes and highlights poor women and women of color; action that investigates the environmental and the biological.

Just the Facts, Mam(m)

Typically detective narratives intimate a crime has taken place. Of course, *Rachel's Daughters* begins with death, though we do not yet know who has died nor how or why she died. Certainly something is out of synch; the natural order of the life cycle is suspended here because we are told mothers are burying their daughters. But a murder did not bring these women to the graveyard. Or did it? Janette Sherman provocatively posits this question while wondering why those who pollute the environment are not held responsible: "Dr. John Gofman said: 'I am aware of no instance in the civilian economy where we take it as a premise that injury and murder of members of the public are to be regarded as beneficent acts.' Yes, *murder* is the word he used. Think about it! If you or I cause harm, and are told we are causing harm, and don't stop, and it results in the death of a person, wouldn't we be put in prison before we could blink an eye? Why have corporations been allowed to escape punishment for the harm they have caused?" (Sherman 2000, 218) Gofman's provocative use of the term "murder" does not prove a direct cause-and-effect relationship between pollution and cancer. His hyperbolic language certainly implies wrongdoing and projects blame while he suggests that producers of toxic substances should be held accountable for the damage their products cause. Gofman's discourse positions the political nature of breast cancer—especially in one strand of dominant rhetoric that blames women's lifestyle choices rather than investigating larger systemic causes of the disease. For many farmworker families there is no agency in where one lives or what one does for a living. Therefore, blaming women with cancer for "choices" they make within the context of Jennifer's community is not attuned to the complex way that race and class factor into this equation. And this is one gesture the film makes: rather than pointing fingers at women's dietary or reproductive choices, it looks for answers in larger social, political, and institutional forces.

If the first scene of *Rachel's Daughters* suggests that a crime has occurred, the second scene shows us the detectives collecting theories about how and why it happened. Nancy Evans, a fifty-something white woman who is the lead detective, invites her cohorts to tell their stories: "We have come here today as women living with breast cancer to find out why, not just why me? or why us? but why so many of us have this disease." They first convene in a San Francisco house to share their individual cancer stories, each of which doubles as a clue: how they found out about their diagnosis, about their mothers' breast cancer, what course of treatment they chose, and how their physicians minimized their concerns. The camera pans the room following the women tightly as they speak while capturing knowing glances from their peers. Interspersed within each verbal telling of the story are images that the camera uses to reinforce theories of causation the speaker reports. For instance, Essie Mormon, a forty-something African American woman, shares with the group the story of her diagnosis and her theory of its cause: "I was raised in rural Mississippi where DDT was used to kill the bugs and stuff on plants. I remember the stuff flying around in the air like fog. I said to one of the doctors, 'I wonder if this exposure to DDT could be a cause of this breast cancer.' And the doctor said to me in this greater-than-thou attitude: 'Well, I don't think so.'" As she recounts these details, black-and-white footage of a truck spraying DDT in suburban neighborhoods fills the screen. As in Essie's case, in each of these narratives is a doctor who did not believe they had breast cancer or whom they had to fight to get a biopsy or mammogram. Personal narrative underscores the larger purpose of the film—to detect what causes breast cancer—but personal experiences also generate their research questions. They work collaboratively to collect facts from their stories and from scientists to postulate whatdunit? Each woman extrapolates from her story to decide what larger systemic questions she will investigate as they divide the detective work: pesticides, hormones (birth control, hormone replacement therapy [HRT]), genetics, electromagnetic fields (EMFs), polychlorinated biphenyls (PCBs), and radiation.

The new way the film approaches cancer is made clear by the way the women discuss it: there is no mistaking these women for scientists or reporters. They are novices. And this is part of the film's argument: their personal concerns guide their questions, and their emotions affect the way they arrive at conclusions. Their inexperience as scientists makes them, perhaps, more susceptible to an emotional perspective or to be easily persuaded. The documentary style, however, also follows some elements of the generic formula guiding hard-boiled detective stories, which legitimates the use of sentiment in this context. Heta Pyrhönen outlines the traditional plot of this subgenre, which hinges on "the story of the investigation, with a focus on what will happen next" (Pyrhönen 1999, 21). In other words, the crime does not take center stage. Because the primary subject is the detective and not the crime, Pyrhönen argues that "this subgenre evokes a more emotional form of reader participation than does the 'whodunit'" (Pyrhönen 1999, 22). Of course, in traditional detective films and novels, the successful investigator is devoid of emotions. Indeed, when s/he begins to feel or become personally involved in a crime, s/he begins to make mistakes; feelings cloud his/her objectivity and judgment. But in *Rachel's Daughters* the reverse is true.

As the emotional core of the documentary, Jennifer Mendoza's presence in the film elicits viewer participation. Unlike all the other investigators, she speaks of her illness in the present tense, and she wears a cap on her head because she is still bald from chemotherapy. Likely because she has less distance from cancer, she cannot speak about it without tearing up. And, as audience members watch her tell the story of her disease, it becomes increasingly difficult not to cry along with her:

> I was first diagnosed with breast cancer in 1993 at the age of twenty-eight. And I had known that I had breast cancer for five years, but nobody believed me. And I didn't want to believe that I had it either, so I kept letting doctors say "oh, you're too young." Eventually I found a surgeon who would do a biopsy, and it turned out that I did have a tumor. And my breast wasn't healing well and they found another tumor. And I did the strongest chemotherapy and a year and a half later I was diagnosed with cancer—with metastatic breast cancer—and now it's in my liver and my bones and I also had a brain tumor and that was pretty devastating. I never anticipated that I wouldn't get cancer again, but I always thought that I'd have a little more time.

As she speaks about her chemotherapy treatment, the camera cuts away to a close-up shot of a clear fluid dripping from an IV tube. Taken in concert with all of the environmental hazards shown during the narratives, this shot turns the drug into a suspect as well. Images of chemotherapy in this context juxtaposed with stories of a childhood surrounded by pesticides paints a bleak picture of a life sandwiched between chemicals treating cancer and chemicals that possibly caused cancer—and, significantly, a life in which few choices could be made to limit exposure to those substances. Racism, sexism, and classism converge as Jennifer's intuitive sense about her body gets silenced by medical professionals. Zillah Eisenstein blends all of these concerns about power: "breast cancer is more socially, economically, and racially constructed than it is genetically inherited. This means understanding a range of social factors: an increased number of women being exposed to toxicity in the workplace, shifting discourses about women's health, so-called science narratives with their masculinist and racialized assumptions, and global capital with its petro/chemical-pharmaceutical empire and postindustrial-medical complex" (Eisenstein 2001, 85–86).

In this sociopolitical context, Eisenstein offers a way of seeing how these often unarticulated factors contribute to increased exposure to carcinogenic substances for the most disenfranchised populations. Racism, sexism, and classism collide here in a couple of important ways. First, few studies focus on Latina women's health, let alone breast cancer incidence and mortality rates. Second, little attention is paid to the labor and health conditions of people like migrant farmworkers. Third, the way women's breasts get fetishized in U.S. culture privileges white women's bodies as valuable—if only to serve heterosexual male fantasies—in such a way that erases brown women's bodies. All of these elements play a role in the health care setting: the way Jennifer's concerns about her body were trivialized and silenced indicates that these dominant cultural ideologies seep into medical institutions as well.

The ways in which Latina bodies are devalued by agribusiness in the context of farmworker communities compels Jennifer to uncover the possible cause of breast cancer in her body and in her community. She knows who she wants to interview, in part, because she already has a strong suspicion of what caused her breast cancer at such an early age. As she volunteers, the film cuts from the first group meeting to follow Jennifer climbing a staircase into an office building as she explains her rationale for selecting her subject: "I'm interested in interviewing Marion Moses because she's an expert on the link between cancer and pesticides. She's been very active in the migrant farm community, and prior to my generation everyone was a migrant farmworker in my family. Down below my house they grew pesticide-laden soybeans, and I drank the water that ran off into the creek." Embedded in her story is the hypothesis that pesticides may cause cancer. Woven into her theory is the tangled web of racism, classism, and sexism that controlled both her home and her family's work environments.

Although Jennifer's story already puts forth a compelling and plausible theory about the link between breast cancer and pesticides, her visit with epidemiologist Marion Moses provides the audience with some facts that support her theories.[2] Both women sit down together, side by side, facing the camera, suggesting a collaborative dialogue; the camera angle encompasses both of them, indicating this process of inquiry. Jennifer poses questions that allow Moses to validate her intuitive sense of her body and illness in ways that the medical professionals she dealt with did not. The investigation commences when Jennifer asks a question reminiscent of Carson: "For those of us born in the sixties, how much DDT do we have in our bodies?" To respond, Moses historicizes DDT as a post–World War II product. While she relates this narrative, black-and-white archival footage shows farmers spraying cows with DDT, factory machines mixing the chemicals, and military planes preparing to spray urban and rural landscapes alike. The wartime marching band music in the background accents this propaganda footage. These film images document and allude to answers. Gradually Moses's narrating voice fades out to be replaced with a vintage news-reel voice who promises: "Today's target for this B–25 is Rockford, Illinois. A peacetime mission to spread five hundred gallons of DDT, the army's miracle insecticide, over the city stricken with an infantile paralysis epidemic. By spray-ing the city, authorities will test the theory that insects are carriers of the dread germ. A farmer turns to an instrument of peace, becomes an instrument of sci-ence, and may become the means of saving countless lives." This deep, male radio-announcer voice serves as an ironic reminder of the military's practices, practices intended to *protect* American citizens but that possibly harmed them instead. Those words and images sit uncomfortably in the mind of the viewer as Moses corroborates Jennifer's theories about what caused the cancer in her body. Moses links the current and historical situation to Rachel Carson, who called these chemicals "elixirs of death." The audience watches black-and-white footage of Carson serenely walking through the woods with her binoculars in hand as Moses reveals that she now calls these toxins "the Rachel Carson chemicals."

In this one-on-one interview, Moses teaches the audience that everyone has DDE, the substance DDT becomes once it breaks down in our bodies. This is due, in part, to postwar spraying described in the newsreel; after widespread government use, pesticides like DDT became popular agricultural tools. The danger for women is in the way DDT enters mammalian bodies and mimics the female hormone estrogen. With this information, Moses offers the audience its first important clue: DDT and similar chemicals become foreign invaders, mimic estrogen, and interfere with the body's hormone production: "Some of them are called xeno, xenoestrogens. Xeno means foreign; it's a Greek word, so it means chemicals that are foreign to the body. Our body works, our ovaries and the uterus and the testes, and all of our endocrine functions work because they are very finely tuned. Well, these chemicals—these environmental chemi-cals—can throw that out of balance. It's called disruption. And so they're called endocrine disruptors."[3] To demonstrate how ubiquitous these chemicals are, Moses shows Jennifer pesticides currently on the market that behave like estro-gen if they come into contact with our bodies. People store many pesticides similar to DDT in their homes: kelthane (more commonly known as insect or vegetable dust), methoxychlor, lindane. These are all chlorinated hydrocarbons that act like female hormones.[4] These products do not label their carcinogenic potential for consumers. Although DDT may not be on the U.S. market any longer, other chemicals interfere with our bodies in the same fashion, most notably PCBs, which, according to Moses, exist in "snow, wind, the arctic snow, wildlife, people's tissue, newborn babies, everywhere they've looked to test for these chemicals."

In what may appear to be a non sequitur, Jennifer pursues a concern about diet by asking, "What does it mean to eat low on the food chain?" Moses's answer, "Not eating things that come from animals," seems at the outset to support the dominant discourse suggesting women need to be responsible for their health by changing their diet. Implicit in this imperative is that she is to blame if she does not watch her diet with an eye toward "preventing" breast cancer.[5] This issue is significant, however, because when we eat, we do not just eat the food on our plates. Moses elaborates, "If everything is contaminated—if the seas are contaminated, if the lakes are contaminated, if the water where you lived is contaminated—everything has to go somewhere. In my work with farmworkers, you'll never convince me that any level of a cancer-causing pesticide is safe. People like Jennifer and farmworker children, I think, are paying the price." Identifying the risk of eating explains that when we eat meat, chicken, or fish we also take in the food eaten by those animals. If their food—other animals and plants—is contaminated, we incorporate all of their contaminated materials into our blood and tissue in addition to the contaminants we take in on our own. Light and Saraf splice in images of a damaged planet that we see as Moses explains the hazards of pollution on the animals that we consume. They juxtapose images of fish swimming near the ocean's floor in what appears to be clean water, a dark trash-filled wave crashing against the shore, and a helicopter spraying pesticides on a farm as workers harvest the crop. We all ingest pollution in some way, but, returning to Jennifer's initial concerns, Moses concludes by exposing the need for further studies on farmworkers and their families whose proximity to pesticides on a daily basis warrants further investigation.

The narrative frame of *Rachel's Daughters* asks viewers to participate in piecing together the clues as the investigation unfolds. The questions that arise in Jennifer's session with Moses may not be answered definitively, but they lead citizens and scientists in the direction of pursuing research that combines the study of the environment with an examination of power that structures unequal relations between agribusiness and farmworkers. Each meeting between the investigators and scientists builds on the previous one in ways that illustrate the complex landscape of studying cancer. For it is not just what a woman eats, or where she lives, or where she works that predicts a future cancer diagnosis. Nor will her blood relatives' history of breast cancer indicate a woman's chance of developing the disease. Light and Saraf make this clear by constructing a tight argument that demonstrates the role of the environment in increased breast cancer incidence and mortality. If one were to gather the story of breast cancer from the mass media, one might believe that the answers to "curing" the disease lie entirely in genetics. Steingraber also challenges the perception that diet alone explains the increased incidence rates when she echoes Moses's cau-tion about eating high on the food chain. Steingraber depicts this cumulative effect that can create problems in the breast: "If you've got herbicides in your drinking water and you're spraying some on your lawn, and you're getting a little in your diet. Those can all add up to something that's quite significant. And nobody's looking at that right now." Like Moses, she points to an area for further research. To support her claim, Steingraber tells her cancer story. In her home state of Illinois, some studies implicate the triazine family of herbicides in breast cancer in animals and humans. Regardless of whether or not pesticides get phased out, the nature of their chemical composition means that the substances we've already used remain in our soil, drinking water, fog, and rain. Her evocative words describe how contaminants saturate the soil and run off into the drinking water and evaporate into the rain: "A woman can be diagnosed with breast cancer, leave her doctor's office, stand in the rain at the bus stop, and there'll be breast carcinogens falling on her." While she illustrates this scenario, the camera turns to Essie opening her umbrella to walk to her first interview. Thus the film forces viewers to witness the shift not only from the visual image of a tractor in Illinois to Essie at a bus stop in the rain, but also from the abstract theories about chemical carcinogens to a real person in the documentary with whom viewers come to identify.

Forecasting breast cancer risk gets further complicated, however, depending upon the age of the woman. Menarche and menopause play a crucial role in this scenario, as epidemiologist Devra Lee Davis points out: "when you get to be an adolescent your breast is starting to actually grow. During the time the breast is growing it's getting hit with more DDT. Finally, you get close to the change of life, and your ovaries are no longer producing as much estrogen as they were. But guess what's in your fat in your body? All that DDT that you've been exposed to in your life and all the other xenoestrogens." These hormonal factors become important because one of the proven "vulnerability factors," as Davis refers to them, for breast cancer is a woman's lifetime exposure to estrogen. Davis backs up her scientific theories by reciting some of the mortality statistics of women who die from the disease in industrialized countries. To appeal to our sentiment, she concludes by saying, "These numbers, these statistics are human beings with the tears removed." This statement hits home as the film cuts abruptly to a weakened, emaciated, gaunt Jennifer speaking from a hospital bed.

Light and Saraf's gesture of moving from the findings that the investigators weave together about the pesticides, fat, and hormones to the startling reality of cancer mortality is crucial. It represents the way in which this film will not allow statistics to become abstract. It demonstrates how the film refuses to allow these stories to be perceived as merely anecdotal. The detective narrative is interrupted when the film cuts to the startling scene of Jennifer's hospitalization for neutropenia, which makes us add up all the clues about the suspect

DDT. From her bed, she tells the audience that her neutropenic fever originated as an "illness created by a broken-down immune system from chemotherapy." In other words, the chemotherapy agents compromised her immune system to the extent that her body could not fight off invasion by germs. In what would be her last words in the film, a bald and trembling Jennifer who tries to keep from crying says, "I guess I just want to say this all needs to change. This is just too much torture." Her words and presence serve as a reminder for the audience that current treatments do not suffice. To underscore this point, the film splices in earlier footage of a healthy-looking Jennifer with a full head of dark, curly hair, eating a piece of chocolate cake at the Women and Cancer walk in Golden Gate Park where she first met the film's directors. The movement between images from her past and present emphasize the tragedy of a thirty-two-year-old woman living through and dying from breast cancer that metastasized to her liver, brain, and bones.

Jennifer appears one more time in the documentary when her father takes her home to die. At that point the tragically short dates of her life—1964–1996—flash over a smiling photograph of a prepubescent, innocent child. The placement of her death—precisely halfway through the film—amplifies the sentimental tone as it becomes obvious that the funeral at the beginning of the documentary was hers. The film flashes back to scenes from the drive through central California and the funeral; this time we are placed in the perspective of a passenger in one of the cars driving toward the cemetery. Now when we see the funeral scene we are a part of it; we are more attuned to the fact that parents are burying their children. This is not merely a statistical fact. It's personal. And Jennifer's harrowing story and her death sensitize viewers to this by tugging at their emotions as she says goodbye to the directors and the other detectives from the back of her father's van. Something is out of order. This sentiment and fact guides and fragments the film's narrative time. It does so in part to remind the audience of the mystery these women try to unravel. But it also serves to tell a very different story about breast cancer. In this documentary, women are not "cured"; "survival" is as cunning as the cancer cells. Jennifer's life is cut short just as her death interrupts the film's narrative and charges it with an affective sentiment that has the potential to propel viewers into action.

The specter of DDT as a murder suspect—evidenced in the death of Jennifer—shows up in other interviews throughout the remainder of the film. Although the detectives explore a variety of suspicious toxins, DDT remains the one that turns up the most often. For instance, it comes up in discussions of cancer clusters in suburban Long Island, which is one of the places Carson followed while writing her manuscript; it also shows up in inner-city tenements inhabited primarily by African Americans (Lear 1997). But one aspect of pesticide use that was not explicitly on Carson's radar screen was the way that poor people and people of color were and are exposed to harmful chemicals at greater rates and for longer periods of time.

Perhaps because Jennifer's death leaves such an indelible mark on the other investigators, Essie adds to this mix an aspect of how environmental racism taints perceptions of breast cancer incidence and mortality. She wonders why epidemiologists study the farm owners rather than the migrant workers who live and work in and around the pesticides: "I read that some of the studies that were supposed to be done on farmworkers, that they did them on the farm owners." Complicating the issue of race and class is that of nation and language; Marion Moses's research reports that two-thirds of migrant workers are foreign born: "92 percent Mexican, 4 percent other Latinos, 3 percent Asian, and 1 percent Caribbean" (Moses 1993, 162). Moreover, this sometimes hidden distinction is significant, as Rachel, one of the film's investigators, concurs that scientists conduct less research on the workers even though they are the most exposed: "All the research that has been done on pesticide exposures has been done on growers, people who own the farms, and much less so on workers. And they don't speak English. But if we want to get at the answers those are the people we need to be studying." Nancy echoes Carson when she states, "Absolutely, and they are the most exposed. Really the pesticides are just creating bigger pests that become resistant to the chemicals." The detectives pose these questions to each other as they realize there are far more questions than answers.

The clues the investigators piece together may not yet reveal a unified, airtight case about the suspect pollutants. But the documentary offers some clear directions to guide research. For one function of the documentary, according to Paula Rabinowitz, is "to induce feeling, thought, and action" (Rabinowitz 1994, 8). It should be clear at this juncture that Light and Saraf infuse all of the above elements into their film. While certainly any breast cancer activist could easily be mobilized after viewing this film, scientists could also leave *Rachel's Daughters* with new hypotheses to investigate—the environmental question as it permeates categories of race, gender, and class. The scientific and personal narratives in the film underscore the direction science should follow: that is, in the footsteps of Rachel Carson. Midway through the film, Steingraber accentuates the powerful meaning of the documentary's title. "I consider myself a daughter of Rachel," she says in response to the criticism leveled against Carson by her critics, who could not understand why a woman without biological children would want to protect the environment for future generations. As she speaks, more black-and-white footage of Carson walking through the Maine woods and writing on her porch illuminates the screen. These silent images give way to one of Carson's only television interviews with *CBS Reports*. The camera remains close-up on her face as she says, "We have to remember the children born today are exposed to these chemicals from birth. Perhaps even before birth. Now what is going to happen then in adult life?" This segment supports Steingraber's awareness of the extent to which Carson worked hard to make her science useful to the public: "I often think of her while she was in radiation treatment trying to piece together scientific evidence, to try to make it a compelling narrative for the rest of us." Those words could be used to think about how this film and the scientists, survivors, and activists represented in it construct stories about breast cancer that are provocative enough to move viewers to action. For just as Carson intended *Silent Spring* to capture her audience's attention as concerned citizens— enough to motivate them to act—this film anticipates that viewers will become Rachel's daughters by taking on the role of detective and pushing scientists to be accountable to the public. That the film places the scene of Jennifer Mendoza's departure and death immediately following this interview with Steingraber and clip of Carson suggests that young women die when the children are not remembered. Moreover, the call to action followed by the film's most affective scene makes the case and film a compelling narrative for the audience.

Guilty Until Proven Innocent: The Precautionary Principle

In the documentary's final scene, the remaining detectives convene on a beach with a vibrant green, grassy hill in the background. They discuss how scary it feels to walk away from this investigation without solving the mystery. Their frustration and fear are understandable, but as a political tool this film can potentially help set the research agenda by changing the types of questions we ask about breast cancer. For instance, Rachel says, "part of the problem is that the field of science is such a competitive field that there is little incentive for scientists to actually try and work together. I mean we're told it's genetics or it's the environment. Well, the reality is it's probably both." Indeed. This film demonstrates how powerful multidisciplinary scientific collaboration can be by editing together a diversity of scientific voices. If all of the people studying cancer worked together as do the detectives in the documentary, it might be possible to achieve results that answer some of these lingering questions.

The investigation ends with another possibly lethal interruption, yet another sign that we remain far from a sure-fire treatment or "cure." Two investigators divulge that their breast cancer has recurred: Pamela, an African American woman in her forties, and Susan, a white woman in her fifties. Uttering the last words of the film, Susan says, "I'm alive now, but behind me there are four women who have died and behind each of them there are four more women." Susan's provocative remark is particularly striking because ten of the women featured in *Rachel's Daughters* are now dead.[6] Whether viewers know about these more recent deaths or not, her pronouncement sits indelibly in the audience's mind because these numbers become embodied as women wearing black dresses and veils draped over their heads cover the mountain behind the group. A statistic appears written over their image: "180,000 women are diagnosed each day. 44,000 of those women die." These women comprise a racially and ethnically diverse group. The juxtaposition of text and veiled women dressed in the color of mourning is a warning for what will happen if we do not tend to the environmental causes of cancer. But it is also a provocative form of protest. For although these women are not members of the international feminist peace network known as Women in Black, both groups practice a similar political strategy.[7] Women in Black renders visible the suffering of those who can no longer speak, oftentimes because they are dead. The presence of the women wearing black in this film, a group also called Women in Black, serves as an intervention: mothers can avoid burying their daughters if viewers become actively engaged in the push for environmental research about breast cancer. In other words, viewers must continue the work begun by Rachel Carson.

It should be remembered that Carson herself, while dying of breast cancer, worked through a daunting set of questions that seemed unanswerable at the time. To trace the complex history and science behind post–World War II chemicals, she also had to collaborate with activists and scientists from a variety of subspecialty fields. That collective effort grew into *Silent Spring*. And although there is no tangible solution to the mystery that Jennifer and her cohorts attempt to solve in the film, their labor produces some important outcomes. The detective process does not lead them to definitive answers, but it does show us a new way to look at cancer—or any public health issue, for that matter—and it leaves us with a new way of approaching research and activism. Therefore, the solution to the crime is not whodunit or whatdunit, but what can we collaboratively, collectively do about it? The film answers by asking the audience to take up where it left off. Concluding the film with Women in Black alerts us to the fact that Jennifer and the other women in the film who have since died are at risk of becoming a statistic if we do not act.

When activists, scientists, and policy makers gather together, the potential for new methodologies is remarkable. This was the case when Marion Moses worked with Cesar Chavez to create a union for farmworkers in Delano, California, she explains: "the signing of the table grape contracts was delayed by at least a year because the workers refused to compromise the issue of worker and consumer health and safety in regard to pesticide use" (Moses 1973, 848). Placing a set of social and economic concerns together on the table ultimately helped health care systemically—as opposed to sick care—for migrant farm laborers as well as those who would eat the food products they cultivated. More recently, one can witness a new attitude toward pesticide use in the statement that grew out of the 1998 Wingspread Conference in Racine, Wisconsin, which avows, "When an activity raises threats of harm to human health or the environment, precautionary measures should be taken even if some cause and effect relationships are not fully established scientifically. In this context the proponent of an activity, rather than the public, should bear the burden of proof" (Raffensperger 1998). This statement, otherwise known as the precautionary principle, asks that chemicals not be treated as innocent until proven guilty.[8] Rather, it implies, harm could be prevented if suspicious toxins or pollutants were studied *before* they were put on the market. Instead of asking people who are sick with illnesses like cancer to testify before Congress and actively work to hold industry accountable for their harm, the precautionary principle makes the corporate entity producing the substance take responsibility for showing their safety. One of the organizations that educates the public about the need for institutionalizing this practice is the Silent Spring Institute, which Light and Saraf feature towards the end of the documentary. This institute pays homage to Carson in name and practice by bringing together activists and scientists to study the cause of breast cancer on Cape Cod. By highlighting this collaborative organization, the film presents a model that could be reproduced in other contexts like farmworker communities to study the links between public health and pesticides.

Rachel's Daughters and the scientists presented in it all allude to the potential held in one of Carson's initial, bold proposals of testing a product's harm prior to placing it on the market for public consumption. As the film makes clear, however, such practices would not necessarily produce positive results unless every nation embraced it. For once harmful chemicals enter the atmosphere, they travel across national boundaries in the air, water, and soil. Zillah Eisenstein imagines what a world would look like if everyone agreed to place public health before profit:

> Agricultural pesticides would be largely eliminated. Foods would not be packaged in carcinogenic plastics. Cows would not be injected with hormones such as rBST to increase milk production. Instead, the stock market guides those in the seats of power. These types of choices are not part of a natural landscape but rather are specifically derivative of a corporate-consumer mentality set on efficiency, productivity, and profitability. This mental set draws the parameters for a particular kind of science. It makes it harder to get grant money for interdisciplinary research, which attempts to look at the multiple factors defining chemical risk. (Eisenstein 2001, 89)

While in some ways Eisenstein speaks of a U.S.-specific context, her concern is decidedly global. For she reminds readers that although DDT was outlawed in the U.S. in 1972, as a result of the work Carson initiated, "it remains in use as a cheap and effective control for malaria in most poor countries. As late as 1991, the U.S. exported at least 4.1 million pounds of pesticides banned or suspended from use here, including tons of DDT" (Eisenstein 2001, 89). Exporting DDT to the Third World while banning it in the United States does not reduce cancer incidence and mortality rates. What it does suggest is that corporations manufacturing toxic chemicals continue to operate with economic concerns overriding concerns about the ways in which exporting pesticides reproduces racism, classism, and sexism on a global scale. This confirms the need for activists to pressure companies to incorporate—not only in rhetoric but in practice—the precautionary principle.

Cognizant of the imperative for a world free from such carcinogenic substances, the United Nations included precautionary principle language in its treaty on persistent organic pollutants, signed by over 122 countries including the United States, at the 2001 Stockholm Convention. Steingraber alerts us to its significance: "The treaty is a strong one. It immediately abolishes from worldwide production and use eight toxic pesticides and severely restricts the use of two others. Beginning in 2025, it prohibits the use of PCBs in electrical transformers. . . . Dioxins and furans are to be reduced immediately and eventually eliminated "where feasible," and DDT is allowed only on a limited basis and strictly for malaria control" (Steingraber 2001, 286). *Rachel's Daughters* leads viewers along with its detectives to reach the conclusion that the precautionary principle is a logical preventative tool for cancer as well as for other public health concerns. The argument conveyed through the personal and scientific narratives in the documentary make it obvious that if such practices had been implemented soon after the publication of *Silent Spring* in 1962, many of these cancer stories either might not exist or they might have had less morbid endings. Through the union of affectively charged stories and scientific hypotheses and studies, *Rachel's Daughters* presents not only a paradigm shift that embeds the environment in every layer of cancer research, but it also asks us to think in dramatically different terms: that new chemical substances are guilty until proven innocent.

NOTES

I would like to thank Leslie Durham, Kate McCullough, Jacky O'Connor, Michelle Payne, and Tara Penry for their helpful comments on various drafts. I would also like to express my gratitude to Allie Light and Marion Moses who generously provided me with materials used in this article.

1. On Carson's breast cancer, see Linda Lear's *Rachel Carson* and Sandra Steingraber's *Living Downstream.*

2. Marion Moses's epidemiological work is importantly aimed at Spanish- and English-speaking audiences as she publishes her work in both languages. She has also created a bilingual video for training and education on the dangers of pesticides.

3. See Theo Colborn, Dianne Dumanoski, and John Peterson Myers' *Our Stolen Future* for a study of the myriad ways that endocrine disrupters affect (1) the immune system by making the body less resistant to disease, (2) human intelligence by increasing learning disabilities, (3) reproduction by lowering sperm counts, and (4) puberty by creating earlier menarche.

4. On pesticides that mimic female hormones, see Marion Moses's *Designer Poisons*.

5. For one of the most dangerous pronouncements of diet as a method of "preventing" breast cancer, see Bob Arnot's *The Breast Cancer Prevention Diet*.

6. The cover photograph of this book is from the film *Rachel's Daughters*.

7. Women in Black began in 1988 as a coalition of women who gathered in the West Bank to protest Israel's occupation. Since then this loosely organized group has convened in the United States, England, Italy, Spain, Azerbaijan, and the former Yugoslavia to stand in silent vigil on behalf of those who have been killed, tortured, or raped as a result of wartime atrocities. One of the film's directors, Allie Light, knew about this group and in fact participated in the initial vigils in Israel. However, those women are different from those who participate in the end of her film. See http://www.igc.org/balkans/wib/mission.html.

8. For an analysis of this corporate "presumed innocent until proven guilty" rhetoric, see Dan Fagin and Marianne Lavelle's *Toxic Deception*.

REFERENCES

Arnot, B. 1999. *The Breast Cancer Prevention Diet: The Powerful Food, Supplements, and Drugs That Can Combat Breast Cancer*. Boston: Little, Brown.
Carson, R. 1962. *Silent Spring*. Boston: Houghton Mifflin.
Colborn, T., D. Dumanoski, J. Peterson Myers. 1996. *Our Stolen Future: Are We Threatening Our Fertility, Intelligence, and Survival? A Scientific Detective Story*. New York: Dutton.
Eisenstein, Z. 2001. *Man-Made Breast Cancers*. Ithaca: Cornell University Press.
Fagin, D., and M. Lavelle. 1999. *Toxic Deception: How the Chemical Industry Manipulates Science, Bends the Law, and Endangers Your Health*. Monroe: Common Courage Press.
Lear, L. 1997. *Rachel Carson: Witness for Nature*. New York: Henry Holt.
Moses, M. 1973. "'Viva la Causa!'" *American Journal of Nursing* 73: 842–48.
———. 1992. *Harvest of Sorrow: Farm Workers and Pesticides*. San Francisco: Pesticide Education Center.
———. 1993. "Farmworkers and Pesticides." In *Confronting Environmental Racism: Voices from the Grassroots*, ed. R. D. Bullard. Boston: South End Press.
———. 1995. *Designer Poisons: How to Protect Your Health and Home from Toxic Pesticides*. San Francisco: Pesticide Education Center.
Pyrhönen, H. 1999. *Mayhem and Murder: Narrative and Moral Problems in the Detective Story*. Toronto: University of Toronto Press.
Rabinowitz, P. 1994. *They Must Be Represented: The Politics of Documentary*. New York: Verso.
Rachel's Daughters: Searching for the Causes of Breast Cancer. 1997. Directed by Allie Light and Irving Saraf. 107 minutes. New York: Women Make Movies.
Raffensperger, C. 1998. "Wingspread Conference on the Precautionary Principle." http://www.sehn.org/wing.html.
Sherman, J. D. 2000. *Life's Delicate Balance: Guide to Causes and Prevention of Breast Cancer*. New York: Taylor and Francis.
Steingraber, S. 1997. *Living Downstream: An Ecologist Looks at Cancer and the Environment*. Reading, Mass.: Addison-Wesley.
———. 2001. *Having Faith: An Ecologist's Journey to Motherhood*. Cambridge: Perseus.

10

Gender, Asthma Politics, and Urban Environmental Justice Activism

JULIE SZE

I've got asthma but asthma doesn't have me!

—New York City Department of Health's Childhood Asthma Initiative
Campaign

In the 1980s and 1990s, community concern over the problem of childhood asthma in minority communities in New York City reached a crescendo. At protests over controversial polluting facilities—incinerators, diesel bus depots, sewage and sludge treatment plants, solid waste transfer stations and power plants—in the South Bronx and West Harlem, groups of low-income African American and Latino children routinely protested with asthma pumps in hand. Many students attended rallies wearing gas and surgical masks, to dramatize how the air itself had become their enemy. "Fatigo," as asthma is known in Spanish, has became a way of life. A major advertisement campaign on bus shelters paid for by a community-based organization working to pressure the New York Metropolitan Transit Authority to convert its buses to natural gas read: "If you live Uptown breathe at your own risk. Diesel bus fumes can kill. Six out of seven of Manhattan's diesel bus depots are located Uptown. This puts the health of a half million mostly African-Americans and Latinos at risk. Don't just breathe this all in. Do something. Because clean air is a right, not a privilege, even if you live above 96th St." The text accompanied a dramatic photograph of a grandfather and two children of color wearing large gas masks.

This essay looks at urban environmental justice activism by low-income women around the problem of high rates of childhood and minority asthma. Issues of race, gender, and authority (moral and scientific) define the terrain of urban air pollution debates. In many urban neighborhoods in the United States, primarily low-income and comprised of blacks and Latinos, community concern (by parents, school administrators, and religious leaders) over high rates of childhood asthma and the disproportionate racial impact of asthma in low-income communities drives urban environmental justice activism.

Asthma is not a female health problem, nor is it a race disease in the sense that it only strikes a particular group of people. It is a disease that strikes a wide array of populations. However, diseases are racialized and gendered in how certain diseases are "defined, characterized, and dramatized," which provide a window on social relations and social values (Wailoo 2001). Asthma is a racialized and gendered disease in the sense that the environmental justice movement activism around asthma is fundamentally shaped by larger debates on disease causation, the role of gender, and asthma management. Asthma activism is gendered insofar as parents in general (themselves a gendered constituency) and mothers in particular occupy a dominant discursive authority in child asthma issues. Historically, mothers of asthmatics were thought to be ambivalent, overprotective, and rejecting toward their children, thereby contributing to the development of childhood asthma. (Gabbay 1982; Guyer 2000). Although this notion of maternal causation has been largely discarded, asthma management remains gendered. Because childhood asthma is a chronic condition, parents and other caretakers of children are heavily involved with its management. And although asthma has become a major public health problem affecting Americans of all ages, races, and ethnic groups, children have been particularly severely affected, and the epidemic is most severe among lower-income and minority children. Children of color in low-income neighborhoods have shown the highest increase in rates of asthma in recent years. The racial disparity has grown steadily since 1980. This essay is focused on asthma activism in New York City, specifically in the South Bronx and West Harlem. These two neighborhoods have the highest hospitalization rates for asthma in New York City as well as a long and vibrant history of environmental justice activism.

I address two main questions in what I call asthma politics: the question posed by environmental justice activists, particularly low-income urban women of color, which is why so many urban kids have asthma; and the clinical literature on management interested in how best to treat it. This is not a study of the clinical or medical literature on asthma but an analysis of how issues of racial and gender identity and power get played out in contemporary asthma politics. While the problem of high rates of childhood asthma in minority communities is understood in public health circles, the larger *social meanings* of this community-based activism in the context of the larger politics of asthma have been underexplored. The centrality of childhood asthma as a political issue is a response to increased incidences as well as an affirmation by environmental justice activists of the importance of the lives of poor children of color who have been historically marginalized. I will highlight the larger social meanings of this activism by closely examining how debates about the causes of asthma and solutions are gendered at the same time that they are related to race and poverty. In focusing on outdoor air pollution as a primary factor in why their communities face high asthma rates, environmental justice activists are involved in larger public health debates about the nature of disease causation. A central theme of this essay is how environmental justice asthma activists seek to make the problem of childhood asthma a political and structural issue and to emphasize precaution in public health in response to countervailing pressures to individualize and personalize the problem, an approach that is not unique to asthma but also central to debates about cancer and other diseases (Hubbard 1993; Steingraber 1997).

Childhood Asthma: The Growing Epidemic

For the past fifteen years, an epidemic of asthma has been occurring in the United States as defined by the Centers for Disease Control and Prevention (CDC), medical and public health communities, and health activists. In particular, it is a disease that has risen in spectacular numbers for children. The CDC reports that more than 4.8 million children under eighteen in the United States, or approximately 6.9 percent, have asthma, making it one of the most common chronic health conditions of childhood. Its prevalence increased by 52 percent for those ages five to thirty-four between 1982 and 1996 (ALA 2003; Wilson et al. 1998). The costs for asthma are numerous and multidimensional, negatively affecting children and their caretakers in work issues (school and housework); social life and recreation; and emotional well-being, personal, and financial relationships (Nocon and Booth 1989–1999). It is the leading cause of childhood hospitalizations and absenteeism (school and work). In 1998, in the United States, the National Heart, Lung, and Blood Institute (NHLBI) estimated that the annual costs of asthma were $11.3 billion (President's Task Force on Environmental Health Risks and Safety Risks to Children 1999). Asthma is receiving a great deal of attention and public funds.

Asthma and Environmental Justice Politics in New York City

Asthma is also a growing problem in New York City. The New York City Department of Health estimated recently that over 700,000 adults and 300,000 children in the city have been diagnosed with asthma at some time in their lives (2003). It is the leading cause of hospitalization for children. The overall asthma hospitalization rate increased by 22 percent from 1988 to 1997. Hospitalization rates are three times higher than the national average and low-income children have a rate 3.5 times greater than higher-income children (Stevenson 2000). One recent study estimated that one in four children in Central Harlem has asthma, double the expected rate and among the highest rates ever recorded (Pérez-Peña 2003).

Asthma is also a growing political issue, especially in environmental justice campaigns in New York City. Childhood asthma was an extremely important organizing issue in the South Bronx Clean Air Coalition (SBCAC) campaign against the Bronx-Lebanon Medical Waste Incinerator and the West Harlem Environmental Action (WEACT) campaign against the North River Sewage Treatment Plant. In 1986, community outrage erupted in response to beginning of operations of a $1.3 billion dollar North River Sewage Treatment plant located at 137th Street along the Hudson River in West Harlem. Residents persistently complained of rancid odors from hydrogen sulfide (which smells like rotten eggs) and grew increasingly concerned about air quality including higher-than-permitted levels of nitrogen oxide. In the 1980s, WEACT was founded to spearhead an organizing and legal campaign as well as to act as a community watchdog to monitor the operations of the plant, which was located near a densely populated housing development. The Bronx-Lebanon Medical Waste Incinerator opened in 1991, and immediately catalyzed a vibrant multiyear organizing campaign to shut it down. The incinerator was sited just blocks away from 2,300 units of public housing, three public schools, and several parochial schools in one of the poorest congressional districts in the nation. It was finally closed in 1998 at least in part due to the organizing against the facility. The smokestacks that released its fumes were torn down in 1999. The incinerator, which cost almost $20 million dollars to build, was built to burn forty-eight tons of medical waste per day from fifteen hospitals throughout the region. By the time the incinerator closed, the facility had been cited for over five hundred violations of toxic releases.

Both SBCAC and WEACT actively believed and organized around the belief that there was a direct relationship between the high asthma rates and the polluting infrastructure in their communities. The campaigns asserted that their neighborhoods were already exposed to disproportionate levels of outdoor air pollution, and that the addition of another polluting facility was unjust and potentially racially discriminatory, especially since the siting of the incinerator and plant have a long, convoluted and corrupt history (Miller 1994). Under circumstances of oversaturation of polluting facilities, campaigning against a new polluter was a natural mobilizing step. Significantly, these campaigns took place in the South Bronx and upper Manhattan, which have the highest hospitalization rates for asthma in New York City. One study reported that the overwhelmingly African American and Latino populations of east Harlem and South Bronx had the highest asthma hospitalization rates in the entire city. Overall, asthma hospitalization rates among African American and Latinos were five times greater than whites (De Palo et al. 1994).

Children's Urban Environmental Health Activism

Children with asthma are not generally activists, although they are the focal point of activist concern. Parents of asthmatics and administrators of schools with a large asthma problem tend to speak for the children of asthmatics out of serious concern for their health. The concern for health moves from an individualized focus on single children to a politicized asthma activism when a controversial noxious facility opens that exacerbates already poor environmental health conditions in a low-income neighborhood. The language and the discourse of the national environmental justice movement provide a politicized framework for childhood asthma. Consciousness of the role of outdoor air pollution in the disease tends to increase as a result of environmental justice asthma activism.

The centrality of childhood asthma as a political issue is simultaneously a response to increased incidences and an affirmation by environmental justice activists of the importance of the lives of poor urban children of color who have been historically marginalized. Asthma prevalence is higher in poorer populations and among urban as opposed to rural dwellers (Wilson et al. 1998). The racial disparity of rising asthma rates is a very real problem. According to the American Lung Association, asthma attack prevalence rates among African Americans are 32 percent higher than the rates in whites. Additionally, African Americans make up a disproportionate percentage of all asthma-related deaths. Black children are four times more likely to die from asthma than white children and three times as likely to be hospitalized for asthma. The prevalence of asthma among Hispanic children has also risen sharply (CDC 2000).

Suffering from poor health conditions as a result of substandard environmental conditions is an important part of the landscape of urban inequity—measurable and comparable to poor education, housing, income, and mobility. Additionally, this poor health is concentrated among people of color and the young and the old, who are already the most vulnerable to pollution exposures. Sociologists Cynthia Hamilton and Robert Bullard have suggested that the exposure of African Americans and other minorities in metropolitan areas to high levels of pollution is an outcome of racialized urban development. They argue that urban growth and development exist beside decay and blighted slums (Hamilton 1993). According to Bullard, "toxic time bombs" are not randomly scattered across the urban landscape, but in fact concentrated in communities that have a high percentage of poor, elderly, young, and minority residents (Bullard 1994). In addition to asthma rates, the communities of the South Bronx and West Harlem share racial and class demographics: they are primarily occupied by low-income people, racial minorities, and high numbers of young and old.[1] Along with demographics, the communities share a physical landscape of blight and despair. Both communities have an excess concentration of noxious facilities and a lack of environmental benefits, such as open space.[2] Harlem has six of the seven diesel bus depots in Manhattan. The South Bronx community is burdened with a punishing transportation and polluting infrastructure as a result of geography and a legacy of destructive urban planning. (As New York City's only borough linked to the mainland of the United States, it is bounded

by the city's most concentrated transportation infrastructure: Bruckner Expressway, Major Deegan Expressway, the Sheridan Expressway, Cross Bronx Expressway, the Willis Ave. Bridge, and Third Ave. Bridge. That infrastructure translates
into thousands of vehicles crossing through the community daily.) The South
Bronx is also where 70 percent of the city's sludge is treated, at the New York
Organic Fertilizer Company.

In both the SBCAC's campaign against the Bronx-Lebanon Medical Waste
Incinerator and the WEACT's campaign against the North River Sewage Treatment Plant, the issue of childhood asthma became a central organizing theme.
Environmental justice campaigns became largely movements for clean air and
children's health, in response to the increasing rates of childhood asthma and
as an organizing strategy. The South Bronx Clean Air Coalition, comprised of
sixty schools, churches, and community groups, successfully engaged large seg-
ments of the community, especially schools, through a culture of confrontation
combined with a language of morality/religion/righteousness. The coalition,
like the community overwhelmingly poor and nonwhite, relished its David versus corporate Goliath image. In naming the coalition the "Clean Air Coalition,"
the issues of air pollution, asthma, and health were pushed to the fore. The
emphasis on clean air seemed obvious from the beginning, as community residents grew concerned about air emissions from the incinerator stacks. The
campaign helped dramatize the human face behind alarming health statistics,
particularly around asthma. Carlos Padilla, a former chair of the coalition, has
a daughter who has asthma. According to Padilla, "[W]hat angers me is that
some want to get the better of life at the expense of others, including their
health. Profit at my children's expense makes me angry. These people from the
incinerator are not from the community. They don't employ the community.
But they take the resources and health of the community" (personal communication, April 15, 1999). Another community leader and member of the coalition,
Yolanda Garcia, executive director of a community-based organization called
Nos Quedamos (We Stay), had a son who died of an asthma attack. The princi-
pal of St. Luke's School connected the rising student absentee rate to the
asthma epidemic, estimating that 40 percent of children in pre-K to eighth
grade in her school have asthma (Nossiter 1995). Entire schools attended rallies
against the incinerator, and buses were chartered to press conferences at City
Hall to dramatize the human and social costs of the facility on the community,
costs that hit their children particularly hard.

The Politics of Asthma Causation and Treatment

Asthma politics encompasses debates on disease causation. Environmental justice activists are deeply involved in these debates. Asthma does not have a single
cause but results from a complex interaction of genetic and environmental fac-

tors. While there is no known biological reason for the greater prevalence of asthma among racial minorities, higher asthma rates may be a surrogate for lower quality of health care, limited health care access, lack of access to culturally appropriate medical care, and the higher number of minorities living in low-income neighborhoods with substandard housing, which exposes them to cockroaches, peeling paint and the resulting dust, and higher rates of exposure to smokers, all of which can trigger attacks among asthmatics.

Environmental justice activists in New York focus on the *outdoor air pollution* risks as exacerbating already poor health conditions in their communities. Children with asthma are sensitive to outdoor air pollution. Common air pollutants, such as ozone, sulfur dioxide, and particulate matter are respiratory irritants and can exacerbate asthma. Additionally, there is differential national exposure of racial groups to particulate air pollution. One study of air pollution in New York City found that nonwhites were more adversely affected by air pollution and that the nonwhite risk estimates were generally larger than those of whites, although not statistically significant (Gwynn and Thurston 2001).

In West Harlem and the South Bronx, supporters of each facility (either from the state or corporate sector) argued that there was no scientific proof that a particular facility contributed exacerbating asthma rates.[3] This point was countered with another narrative. Community activists, often women of color, testified at public hearings and public events, often citing their asthma or their child's asthma. They countered that the increase of childhood asthma rates must have something to do with outdoor air pollution, and the science of risk assessment was inadequate to deal with the cumulative exposure that their residents faced as a result of the multiple pollution exposures in their neighborhoods (as opposed to single sources in conventional risk assessment analysis). In essence, these activists argue that while it is difficult to scientifically prove the direct impact of a new facility (incinerator, solid waste transfer station, power plant, or sewage treatment plant) manifesting in increased asthma rates on the health of a community, the extra burden that these neighborhoods already face due to the higher rates of pollution exposure, and (therefore) more fragile health status to (particularly of young and old), special protective precautions should be taken. This concept draws from the "Wingspread Statement on the Precautionary Principle" that is being advanced by public health and cancer activists (Steingraber 1997). This "principle of precautionary action" or the "precautionary principle" calls for preventing harm to the environment and to human health. An international group of scientists, government officials, lawyers, and labor and grassroots environmental activists defined the principle as follows:

- The release and use of toxic substances, the exploitation of resources, and physical alterations of the environment have had substantial unintended consequences affecting human health and the environment. Some of these concerns are high rates of learning deficiencies, asthma, cancer, birth defects and species extinctions, along with global climate change, stratospheric ozone depletion and worldwide contamination with toxic substances and nuclear materials.

- We believe existing environmental regulations and other decisions, particularly those based on risk assessment, have failed to protect adequately human health and the environment—the larger system of which humans are but a part.

- We believe there is compelling evidence that damage to humans and the worldwide environment is of such magnitude and seriousness that new principles for conducting human activities are necessary.

- While we realize that human activities may involve hazards, people must proceed more carefully than has been the case in recent history. Corporations, government entities, organizations, communities, scientists and other individuals must adopt a precautionary approach to all human endeavors.

- Therefore, it is necessary to implement the Precautionary Principle: When an activity raises threats of harm to human health or the environment, precautionary measures should be taken even if some cause and effect relationships are not fully established scientifically. In this context the proponent of an activity, rather than the public, should bear the burden of proof. (Steingraber 1997, 284)

Significantly, asthma is identified as a key problem in the statement. The statements of New York City environmental justice advocates on the issue of causality, proof, and outdoor air pollution and its impact on asthma reflect the importance of the precautionary principle to their activism, although they did not phrase it as such.

Another major source of triggers for asthmatics is the indoor environment (Jones 1998). The home environment exposures include tobacco, mold, poor ventilation, water damage, heat irritants (electric, gas, oil, wood), chemical irritants (air fresheners, ammonia, and other chemicals), dust (carpet, cloth-covered furniture, drapes or curtains), pets, dust mites, and bed covers (comforters and wool, cotton, or acrylic blankets). The most controversial theory of indoor triggers involves cockroaches. The National Institute of Allergy and Infectious Diseases (NIAID) and the National Institute for Environmental Health Science (NIEHS) conducted the National Cooperative Inner City Asthma Study, a study of children with asthma in eight U.S. cities that tested the effects of interventions that reduce children's exposure to indoor allergens and that sought to improve communication with their primary care physicians. The study compared the effects of various allergens on asthmatic children living in poor urban areas. The results, published in 1997 in the *New England Journal of Medicine*, suggested that cockroaches may be the chief culprit in childhood asthma. Nearly 40 percent of the asthmatic children were found to be allergic to the insects' droppings and body parts.

However, community leaders in New York City questioned the emphasis on indoor air pollution, pointing out that dirt, dust mites, cockroaches, mice/rat urine, poor housing, or conditions of poverty are not new phenomena. The focus on indoor household triggers, particularly cockroaches, inspires particular ire by some environmental justice activists because of the racialized and gendered implications of dirty homes and substandard housekeeping as opposed to external outdoor pollution as the primary cause of high asthma rates. The focus on housekeeping rather than poor housing conditions (for example, mold in public housing, an endemic problem), represents this emphasis on individualized versus systemic approaches to the childhood asthma epidemic. As Marian Feinberg from the South Bronx Clean Air Coalition commented, "The problem with the National Inner City Asthma Study is how it was manipulated in the media. Two bad things happened: the emphasis on cockroaches implied that bad moms caused asthma, and it focused on cockroaches as the main factor" (personal communication, May 2002). She points out the ironic effects of this conclusion: after the media attention, pesticide companies started marketing their products on Spanish language and black radio stations in ads that portrayed a child gasping for air. These commercials ran despite the fact that pesticide sprays themselves can function as asthma triggers. Environmental justice activists, in contrast, have focused on a multidimensional approach to asthma causation and management, exemplified by the campaign slogan "Cleaner Air, Cleaner Housing, Cleaner Lungs."

The main aspects of asthma management are taking medication properly, taking care of the home, monitoring air flow, and reducing exposure to common indoor household triggers. Asthma medicines keep the air tubes in the lungs open. The main treatment regimen is the correct taking of preventative medication. This process has grown increasingly complex with the advent of more sophisticated medication, and some children take up to eight different medications a day. Taking care of the home environment means recognizing the indoor triggers for asthma and taking steps to remedy these conditions. Home inspection of household exposures is a common approach to asthma management programs. Typically in this approach, representatives of a "Healthy Homes" project inspect the home, measure the caregiver's knowledge about asthma triggers, and suggest steps to reduce exposures (Krieger et al. 2000). The homes chosen for inspection are usually poor households with asthmatic children. The question of how to choose what homes to visit is significant given that most homes in the developed world probably have at least one of the household exposures. An important question to consider, and a key area for further research, is how the "correction" of the household environment is done without implying that poor women or women of color have bad housekeeping practices and blaming mothers for their children's asthma.

Some environmental justice activists have an ambivalent view of the home visits approach to asthma for this very reason of where the burden of blame ends up. As one SBCAC leader, Mary Feinberg, explained, the emphasis on indoor allergens and housekeeping practices tends to privilege an individualistic versus a systematic approach to the problem: "I understand that it can help some individuals, and that if it helps even one household or child, then it's valuable. But aren't we then accepting the basic conditions of poor housing and outdoor air pollution by this approach, instead of systemically trying to improve housing and the external environment" (Feinberg, personal communication, May 2002).

The home visits can be a part of a balanced and fair asthma intervention approach. Also, community-based asthma education is increasingly being recognized as being an effective tool to deal with asthma in low-income and minority populations (Ford et al. 1996; Wilson et al. 1998). Another multidimensional approach to children's environmental health research is being advanced by WEACT, which is the community partner in a nationally recognized collaboration with Columbia University's School of Public Health through their Columbia Center for Children's Environmental Health (CCEH). WEACT has transformed its environmental justice activism into a vibrant and significant force in community-based public health research that is generating new knowledge about asthma. The CCEH was founded in 1998 as one of eight Centers for Children's Environmental Health and Disease Prevention established jointly by the National Institute of Environmental Health Sciences and the Environmental Protection Agency. The Columbia Research Project on Asthma is charting possible links between signs of asthma in very young children and exposure to allergens and pollutants in their homes and outdoor environment, the role of nutrition, as well as the impact of air pollution on birth weights. Preliminary findings from air quality tests in the homes of the first group of mothers suggest virtually universal exposure to two highly toxic pesticides during pregnancy, while biomarkers in maternal and cord blood show high rates of exposure to allergens, air pollutants, and secondhand tobacco smoke. (Miller 1999). The study also found air pollutants are linked to lower birth weights and skills in African American babies. This study suggests that the problems that low-income urban children face and the health effects of pollution exposure begin before birth, and one potential implication is an incentive to reduce pollution exposures that negatively affect children's environmental health.

Conclusion

By demonstrating that the environmental justice movement's concern with asthma politics encompasses environmental policy as well as health debates about causation and management, I hope to recognize the contribution that the environmental justice movement has made to explicating complex debates about asthma in particular, and the politics of race and urban environmental health more generally. Asthma rates in New York City are finally starting to fall, at least in part because the sense of community crisis catalyzed an action and research agenda that forced bureaucracy into action.[4] The politicization of asthma as an environmental justice issue contributed at least in part to the success in chipping away at the racial disparity of the disease. The larger political contribution the environmental justice movement makes is in re-envisioning environmental policy making, reintegrating the health aspects of environmental policy and in engaging questions of risk assessment.

Asthma is a complex disease and a fascinating one for this complexity. The high rates of asthma in minority communities are probably due to an intersection of genetics and environment and indoor and outdoor factors. The politics of asthma causation, the answer to the problem of racial disparities in asthma rates, and the gender politics of asthma management are tremendously complex, and much more research needs to be done on the various questions and issues I have raised, especially as tremendous federal resources pour into asthma research.

NOTES

1. According to the New York City Department of City Planning based on 2000 census data, West Harlem is primarily African American, low income, and over 90 percent are renters. Almost 50 percent of the South Bronx is on public assistance. Approximately 92 percent of the population is renters, and 96 percent of this community is Hispanic or African American. The South Bronx is one of the poorest congressional districts in the nation and houses the largest concentration of New York City Housing Authority Projects in the Bronx (http://www.nyc.goc/html/dcp/html/lucds/cdstart.html).

2. Harlem and the South Bronx are severely underserved by public space and parks because of a legacy of neglect in open-space planning. For example, in Robert Moses' capacity as commissioner of the New York City Department of Parks and Recreation, from 1934 to 1959, he built 255 parks, only one of which was in Harlem. Riverbank State Park in West Harlem was built on top of the North River Sewage Treatment Plant as a concession to the community.

3. A vast literature on risk discusses the politics of proof. For example, Tesh argues that the lack of scientific corroboration of environmental activists' claims may be an artifact of the slow incorporation of environmentalism into science rather than a statement about the actual effect of pollution on health (2000). See also Davis 2002.

4. At the city level, the New York City Department of Health (DOH) began a Community Asthma Program and a New York City Childhood Asthma Initiative that sponsored the asthma education campaigns on the New York City train and bus system. The DOH also coordinates the New York City Asthma Partnership (NYCAP), a coalition of individuals and organizations who share an interest in reversing the asthma epidemic in New York City.

REFERENCES

American Lung Association, Epidemiology and Statistics Unit. 2003. "Trends in Asthma Morbidity and Mortality." (Mar.).

Anderson, Nancy. 1994. "The Visible Spectrum." *Fordham Urban Law Journal* 21, no. 3: 723–38.

Becker, G., S. Jonson-Bjerklie, P. Benner, K. Slobin, and S. Ferketich. 1993. "The Dilemma of Seeking Urgent Care: Asthma Episode and Emergency Service Use." *Social Science and Medicine* 37, no. 3: 305–13.

Beckett, W.S., K. Belanger, J. F. Gent, T. R. Holford, and B. P. Leaderer. 1996. "Asthma among Puerto Rican Hispanics: A Multi-ethnic Comparison Study of Risk Factors." *American Journal of Respirator and Critical Care Medicine* 154: 894–99.

Berkman, L, and I. Kawachi, eds. 2000. *Social Epidemiology.* New York: Oxford University Press.

Bullard, Robert, ed. 1994. *Unequal Protection: Environmental Justice and Communities of Color.* San Francisco: Sierra Club.

Carr, W., L. Zeitel, and K. Weiss. 1992. "Variations in Asthma Hospitalizations and Deaths in New York City." *American Journal of Public Health* 82, no. 1: 59–65.

Centers for Disease Control, *Morbidity and Mortality Weekly Report*, Oct. 13, 2000. "Measuring Childhood Asthma Prevalence Before and After the 1997 Redesign of the National Health Interview Survey—United States." 49, no. 40: 908–11.

Claudio, L., L. Tulton, J. Doucette, and P. J. Landrigen. 1999. "Socioeconomic Factors and Asthma Hospitalization Rates in New York City." *Journal of Asthma* 36: 343–50.

Colp, C., J. Pappas, D. Moran, and J. Lieberman. 1993. "Variants of Alpha 1-Antitrypsin in Puerto Rican Children with Asthma." *Chest* 103: 812–15.

Crain, E. F., K. B. Weiss, P. E. Bijur, M. Hersh, L. Westbrook, and R. E. Stein. 1994. "An Estimate of the Prevalence of Asthma and Wheezing among Inner-City Children." *Pediatrics* 94: 356–62.

Davis, Devra. 2002. *When Smoke Ran Like Water.* New York: Basic Books.

De Palo, A., P. H. Mayo, P. Friedman, and M. J. Rosen. 1994. "Demographic Influences of Asthma Hospital Rates in New York." *Chest* 106: 447–51.

Dockery, D. W., et al. 1993. "An Association between Air Pollution and Mortality in Six U.S. Cities." *New England Journal of Medicine* 329, no. 24: 1753–59.

Drummond, N. 2000. "Quality of Life with Asthma: The Existential and the Aesthetic." *Sociology of Health and Illness* 22, no. 2: 235–53.

Ford, M., G. Edwards, J. Rodriguez, R. Gibson, and B. Tilley. 1996. "An Empowerment-Centered, Church-Based Asthma Education Program for African American Adults." *Health and Social Work* 21: 1, 70–75.

Freudenberg, N. 1998. "Community-Based Education for Urban Populations: An Overview." *Health Education and Behavior* 25: 1.

Gabbay, John. 1982. "Asthma Attacked? Tactics for the Reconstruction of a Disease Concept." In *The Problem of Medical Knowledge: Examining the Social Construction of Medicine*, ed. Peter Wright and Andrew Treacher. Edinburgh: Edinburgh University Press.

Guyer, Ruth. 2000. "Breath of Life: Stories of Asthma from an Exhibition at the National Library of Medicine." *American Journal of Public Health* 90, no. 6: 874–79.

Gwynn, R. Charon, and George Thurston. 2001. "The Burden of Air Pollution: Impacts among Racial Minorities. *Environmental Health Perspectives* 109, Suppl. 4: 501–6.

Hamilton, Cynthia. 1993. "Environmental Consequences on Urban Growth and Blight." In *Toxic Struggles: The Theory and Practice of Environmental Justice*, ed. Richard Hofrichter. Philadelphia: New Society.

Hubbard, Ruth, and Elijah Wald. 1993. *Exploding the Gene Myth: How Genetic Information is Produced and Manipulated by Scientists, Physicians, Employers, Insurance Companies, Educators, and Law Enforcers*. Boston: Beacon Press.

Jones, A. P. 1998. "Asthma and Domestic Air Quality." *Social Science and Medicine* 47, no. 6: 755–64.

Koren, S. H. 1995. "Associations between Criteria Air Pollutants and Asthma." *Environmental Health Perspectives* 103, Suppl 6: 235–42.

Kozyriskyj, A., and John O'Neil. 1999. "The Social Construction of Childhood Asthma: Changing Explanations of the Relationship between Socioeconomic Status and Asthma." *Critical Public Health* 9, no. 3: 197–210.

Krieger, J., L. Song, T. Takaro, and J. Stout. 2000. "Asthma and the Home Environment of Low-Income Urban Children: Preliminary Findings from the Seattle–King County Health Homes Project." *Journal of Urban Health: Bulletin of the New York Academy of Medicine* 77, no. 1: 50–67.

Ledogar, R., A. Penchaszadeh, C. Garden, and L. Acosta. 2000. "Asthma and Latino Cultures: Different Prevalence Reported among Groups Sharing the Same Environment." *American Journal of Public Health* 90, no. 6: 929–35.

Mailick, M., G. Holden, and V. Walther. 1994. "Coping with Childhood Asthma: Caretakers Views." *Health and Social Work* 19, no. 2: 103–11.

Marteau, T., and M. Johnston. 1986. "Determinants of Beliefs about Illness: A Study of Parents of Children with Diabetes, Asthma, Epilepsy, and No Chronic Illness." *Journal of Psychosomatic Research* 20, no. 6: 673–83.

Matte, T., and D. Jacobs. 2000. "Housing and Health: Current Issues and Implications for Research and Programs." *Journal of Urban Health: Bulletin of the New York Academy of Medicine* 77, no. 1: 7–25.

Mayo, D., and Rachelle Hollander, eds. 1991. *Acceptable Evidence: Science and Values in Risk Management*. New York: Oxford University Press.

Miller, R. L. 1999. "Breathing Freely: The Need for Asthma Research on Gene-Environment Interactions." *American Journal of Public Health* 89, no. 6: 819–22.

Miller, Vernice. 1994. "Planning, Power and Politics: A Case Study of the Land Use and Siting history of the North River Water Pollution Control Plant." *Fordham Urban Law Journal* 21, no. 3: 707–22.

Mitchell, E. A. 1991. "Racial Inequalities in Childhood Asthma." *Social Science and Medicine* 32, no. 7: 831–36.

New York City Department of Health. 2003. "NYC Vital Signs." *Community Health Survey* 2: 4.

Nocon, A., and Tim Booth. 1989–1990. "The Social Impact of Asthma: A Review of the Literature." *Social Work and Social Sciences Review* 1 no. 3: 177–200.

Nossiter, Adam. 1995. "Asthma Common and on the Rise in the Crowded South Bronx." *New York Times*, Sept. 5, p. A1.

Office of Lead Hazard Control, U.S. Department of Housing and Urban Development. 1999. "The Healthy Homes Initiative: A Preliminary Plan." (Apr.).

Pérez-Peña, Richard. 2003. "Study Finds Asthma in 25% of Children in Central Harlem." *New York Times*, Apr. 19, p. A1.

President's Task Force on Environmental Health Risks and Safety Risks to Children. 1999. "Asthma and the Environment: A Strategy to Protect Children." Revised May 2000.

Prout, A., L. Hayes, and L. Gelder. 1999. "Medicines and the Maintenance of Ordinariness in the Household Management of Childhood Asthma." *Sociology of Health and Illness* 21 no. 2: 137–62.

Ramirez-Valles, Jesus. 1998. "Promoting Health, Promoting Women: The Construction of

Female and Professional Identities in the Discourse of Community Health Workers." *Social Science and Medicine* 47 no. 11: 1749–64.

Shell, Ellen. 2000. "Does Civilization Cause Asthma?" *Atlantic Monthly* 285, no. 5: 90–100.

Snadden, David, and Judith Belle Brown. 1992. "The Experience of Asthma." *Social Science and Medicine* 34:12, 1351–61.

Steingraber, Sandra. 1997. *Living Downstream: An Ecologist Looks at Cancer and the Environment.* Reading, Mass: Addison-Wesley.

Stevenson, L., R. Garg, and J. Leighton. 2000. "Asthma Hospitalization in New York City 1988–1997." *Journal of Urban Health: Bulletin of the New York Academy of Medicine* 77: 1, 137–39.

Stevenson, L. A., P. J. Gergen, D. R. Hoover, et al. 2001. "Sociodemographic Correlates of Indoor Allergen Sensitivity among United States Children." *Journal of Allergy and Clinical Immunology* 108: 747–52.

Tesh, S. 2000. *Uncertain Hazards: Environmental Activists and Scientific Proof.* Ithaca: Cornell University Press.

Wailoo, Keith. 2001. *Dying in the City of the Blues : Sickle Cell Anemia and the Politics of Race and Health.* Chapel Hill: University of North Carolina Press.

Williams C. 2000. "Doing Health, Doing Gender: Teenagers, Diabetes, and Asthma." *Social Science and Medicine* 50, no. 3: 387–96.

Wilson, S., P. Scamagas, J. Grado, and L. Norgaard. 1998. "The Fresno Asthma Project: A Model Intervention to Control Asthma in Multi-Ethnic, Low-Income, Inner-City Communities." *Health Education and Behavior* 25, no. 1: 79–98.

11

No Remedy for the Inuit

Accountability for Environmental Harms under U.S. and International Law

ANNE E. LUCAS

> As we put our babies to our breasts, we feed them a noxious chemical cocktail that foreshadows neurological disorders, cancers, kidney failure, reproductive dysfunction. That Inuit mothers–far from areas where [persistent organic pollutants] are manufactured and used–have to think twice before breast feeding infants is surely a wake-up call to the world.
>
> –Sheila Watt-Cloutier, president of the Canadian branch of the Inuit Circumpolar Conference

In July 2000, the North American Commission on Environmental Cooperation (NACEC)[1] published a study finding that Inuit women living near the Arctic Circle in Nunavut, Canada, have dioxin concentrations in their breast milk at twice the levels observed in women living in southern Québec (Commoner et al. 2000, ix; Dewailly et al. 1992). According to the study, these elevated levels of dioxin can be attributed to the Inuit's relatively high consumption of animal foods, such as caribou and marine animals, which store dioxins efficiently in their fatty tissues (Commoner et al. 2000, 1). Once ingested, dioxins can alter the fundamental growth and development of cells, which can lead to reproduction and development problems, suppression of the immune system, and cancer (Commoner et al. 2000, 1; EPA 2003, G2). Using an air transport model that tracks dioxins through the atmosphere, the researchers determined the majority of the pollution in the Canadian Arctic originated at solid waste incinerators, copper smelters, and cement kilns located in the midwestern United States. Once emitted into the atmosphere, long-range atmospheric transport and ocean currents carry dioxin to the Arctic, where it settles into the food chain, air, and water where the Inuit live (Commoner et al. 2000, table 5.3).

Large-scale production of dioxins began in the 1920s in the U.S. (EPA 2003, G9). However, the U.S. Environmental Protection Agency (EPA) did not regulate dioxin emissions until the 1970s, when the EPA began to recognize their high toxicity.[2] Due to regulations, the EPA estimates that dioxin emissions in the U.S. decreased by about 75 percent between 1987 and 1995 (2003, F8). Despite the success of reducing emissions, however, the slow breakdown of dioxins in fatty tissues of humans and animals means emissions from the past and those that continue today will remain a significant health factor for years to come.

Recognizing the damaging effects of dioxin on human health, the EPA recommends the best way to minimize dioxin exposure is to reduce consumption of meat, especially meat containing high amounts of fat, and to follow the federal dietary guidelines to increase consumption of carbohydrates such as fruits, vegetables, and grain products (2003, G12). These guidelines do not take into consideration the traditional Inuit diet, which is composed primarily of proteins and fats from animal foods, including caribou, seal, beluga whales, salmon, and trout (Bell and Heller 1978). This traditional diet has been the means of survival for the Inuit for thousands of years in a harsh and cold land that provides little vegetation but a rich environment of animals for hunting. Sheila Watt-Cloutier, an Inuit woman, grandmother, and president of the Canadian branch of the Inuit Circumpolar Conference, which defends the rights of Inuit in Arctic countries, states, "we have few alternatives to the food we hunt as it is the same food through which we identify ourselves, binding us as family and community. We are the land and the land is us. When our land and animals are poisoned, so are we" (Brown 2001). Additionally, recent scientific studies have found that the Inuit's relatively low levels of heart disease and diabetes can be attributed to the long tradition of consumption of animal foods (Dewailly et al. 2001; Young 1996).

The harm inflicted upon the Inuit is poisoning their bodies and those of future generations. Given the efficient and long-lasting storage of dioxins in the human body, this threat will continue for many years to come. Inuit women should have the right to live in a healthy environment uncontaminated by waste products generated thousands of miles away, and a right to continue in their traditional culture, consuming a diet that has defined their communities and protected their health for centuries.

In this essay, I explore possible legal mechanisms in domestic and international law that could address this problem in order to expose the limitations of those legal mechanisms in remedying the harm committed against the Inuit women. Feminist and ecofeminist theories help articulate the reasons for such limitations. These theories offer critiques of the universality of international law—specifically unraveling the inherent racist, primitivist, sexist, and classist assumptions imbedded in a universal theory of international law, which currently fails to consider the needs of marginalized groups. Additionally, ecofeminist theories explore how the transnational capitalist regime elevates the importance of capitalist wealth and power over that of the rights of humans to a healthy environment. These theories offer powerful critiques, thereby revealing new perspectives on how the law might change so that human rights are elevated above the rights of First World polluters.

Possible Legal Claims by the Inuit

Inuit v. Polluter Companies: The Role of the Alien Tort Claims Act

If the Inuit had the economic means to consider a suit in U.S. courts against the companies responsible for the dioxin pollutants, the Alien Tort Claims Act (ATCA) might be a vehicle for pursuing a claim. This act enables non-U.S. citizens to sue for wrongs that violate customary international law in U.S. courts.[3] In order for a claim to be successful, the alleged wrong must rise to the level of customary international law, which means that nation-states generally feel obligated to adhere to a law prohibiting the action under scrutiny.[4] In order to determine what constitutes customary international law, one must examine international conventions, treaties, and opinions of experts and those of domestic and international judicial bodies (*Filartiga v. Pena-Irala* 883; *The Paquete Habana* 700). Additionally, in order for the defendant to be a proper defendant in an ATCA claim, the defendant must be a state actor, or one who engages in the alleged act in which the state is sufficiently involved (*Beanal v. Freeport-McMoRan* 371; *NCAA v. Tarkanian*).

In recent years, the ATCA has been invoked against transnational corporations in cases of environmental destruction. Many of these corporations allegedly engaged in human rights and environmental abuses while extracting natural resources on land inhabited by indigenous peoples.[5] While these cases have not been successful for a number of reasons, they provide a starting point from which to build the case of the Inuit women because they allege violations of indigenous rights and the right to a healthy environment, claims that could be useful to redress these harms.

During the past twenty-five years, there has been a growth of activity in the area of indigenous rights to cultural self-determination. In 1989, the International Labor Organization (ILO) adopted Convention No. 169 Concerning Indigenous and Tribal Peoples in Independent Countries, a binding document that protects indigenous people's right to cultural self-determination and their right to traditional lands and territories. In February 1997, the Inter-American Commission on Human Rights adopted the Proposed American Declaration on the Rights of Indigenous Peoples, which contains specific rights to a safe and healthy environment.

Although these international documents suggest that the indigenous right to cultural self-determination is growing stronger, it likely has not reached the level of the "law of nations" required under the ATCA. Several of these documents are merely proposed and are not binding to any states, while ILO No. 169 only binds four states. Therefore, it cannot be said that most states intend to protect indigenous rights to self-determination, and therefore it is unlikely that the Inuit women would put forth a successful claim under this rationale.

Because the Inuit women's environment has been rendered unhealthy from dioxin pollutants, a claim to a right to a healthy environment may be applicable. One-hundred and fourteen nations, including the United States and Canada, affirmed the Declaration of the United Nations Conference on the Human Environment in 1972, commonly known as the Stockholm Declaration, which states that each person has a fundamental right to a healthy environment. At the 1992 Conference on Environment and Development in Rio de Janeiro, 187 nations and 100 heads of state supported the Rio Declaration, which also includes a right to a healthy environment. The Stockholm Declaration Principle 21 and Rio Declaration Principle 2 hold that while states have sovereign rights over their natural resources, states must not cause damage to the environment of other states or of areas beyond the limits of national jurisdiction. Article 25 of the Universal Declaration of Human Rights recognizes the right of all people to a standard of living adequate for health.

Although the evidence supporting a right to a healthy environment is quite strong, no court in an ATCA case has recognized that the right rises to the level of customary international law. However, at least one commentator has suggested that a strong claim, showing great harm and severe environmental catastrophe, would enable a court to make such a finding (Herz 2000). In comparison to some of the egregious cases alleging environmental harms—the destruction resulting from twenty years of oil expeditions, or polluting rivers with mining by-products—the Inuit situation may not qualify as obviously and overtly egregious.[6]

Another major difficulty in previous ATCA claims alleging environmental harms has been establishing the appropriate nexus between the state and private actors.[7] As the history of the development of regulations on dioxin emissions shows, rather than acting with the government to perpetrate crimes, most likely these companies were operating under the Clean Air Act regulations established by the EPA. Under the Resource Conservation and Recovery Act (RCRA), the EPA regulates dioxin emissions from facilities that burn hazardous waste, including commercial hazardous waste incinerators and some cement kilns (EPA 2000b). Rather than contributing to the harm, as a state actor would need to do in order to find the private actor liable, the EPA has taken some steps to remedy the problem. Although some criticize that these steps have been insufficient, it is likely they are enough to sever any nexus between the public and private actor element of the ATCA.[8]

The probable lack of state nexus combined with the fact that the type of harm suffered by the Inuit women has not risen to the level of customary international law suggest that it is unlikely that an ATCA claim would be successful for the Inuit women.

Inuit v. the U.S. Government: Protection under the American Declaration of Human Rights

The Inuit may have a claim against the United States by alleging violations of U.S. obligations under the American Declaration of Human Rights. This Declaration came into existence in 1948 upon the formation of its sponsoring body, the Organization of American States (OAS), and incorporates the right to life, liberty, personal security, and preservation of health and well-being. In 1959, the Inter-American Commission on Human Rights (IACHR) was created with the function of monitoring the observance of human rights and promoting respect for these rights. In 1966, the role of the IACHR was expanded to examine individual petitions and make specific recommendations to member states relative to those petitions. The American Declaration of Human Rights is a source of international obligation for OAS member states, and therefore, as a member, the United States could be subject to the IACHR's review of a petition brought by the Inuit.

In 1980, the Yanomami Indians of Brazil filed a petition alleging that the government's construction of a major highway through their lands deprived them of several rights guaranteed to them under the Declaration of Human Rights. In its 1985 decision, the IACHR found that the building of the highway resulted in violations of the right to life, liberty and personal security, residence and movement, and preservation of health and well-being, despite the fact that many of the actual harms were committed by independent actors rather than the Brazilian government.

Despite these findings, the IACHR has not explicitly linked the right to life and the right to a healthy environment. Additionally, the type of harm suffered by the Inuit women may not be found severe enough to be considered a violation of right to life and that of a healthy environment cognizable under IACHR jurisprudence. In the case of the Yanomami, the IACHR's 1985 decision documented the increase of epidemics of malaria, tuberculosis, and smallpox introduced into the community by unvaccinated construction workers, which resulted in the death of one out of every four Indians (Report on the Situation of Human Rights in Brazil 1997, 64–66). The IACHR may not be willing to find dioxin poisoning, which has not caused death directly, as far as the scientific evidence shows, as a violation of the right to life, let alone link this right to that of a healthy environment.

Even if such a violation were found, it is questionable whether a decision by the IACHR would serve as useful redress to those who suffered harm by transboundary dioxin pollution. The IACHR cannot make enforceable rulings or award damages, but rather can only issue recommendations. Despite the IACHR's recommendation for preventative and curative measures to be taken in the Yanomami case, a recent report shows the Yanomami's cultural, physical, and political rights continue to be threatened (Report on the Situation of Human Rights in Brazil 1997, 67, 82[a] and [b]). Even if an Inuit claim to human rights violations were successful, while the IACHR recommendations may provide awareness of the problem, it would not likely make a great impact on the U.S. policy on dioxin control or transboundary pollution issues.

Canada v. United States: Assistance from the Agreement on Air Quality

While causes of action under the ATCA and petitions brought before the IACHR do not appear to be very effective means for redressing the harm done to the Inuit women, international law, on the level of nation-states, may provide some opportunity for remedying transboundary air pollution.

In 1992, the United States and Canada entered into a bilateral Agreement on Air Quality in efforts to control transboundary air pollution between the two countries. The agreement sets up a system for exchanging information on monitoring, emissions, technologies, atmospheric processes, and effects of air pollutants (article 7, 1–2). It requires state parties to assess the environmental impact of proposed projects, notify the other party of the proposed actions, and consult with the other party concerning activities that may be causing significant transboundary air pollution (article 5, 1–3). Additionally, each party must mitigate or avoid activities that may cause significant transboundary air pollution (article 5, 5).

Just as the ability of the Inuit to file a private claim would be severely restricted due to economic concerns, the success of a Canadian-U.S. redress to the problem is significantly limited by the Inuit's relative lack of political power. Convincing the Canadian government that it ought to seriously pursue the complaint and raise the issue with the U.S. government would be quite an undertaking for a group who is politically, as well as socially, economically, and geographically, marginalized. If the Canadian government could be moved to act, however, the scientific evidence of dioxin emissions linked to the U.S. might activate the agreement. However, the United States may object to the idea that dioxin is causing "significant" transboundary pollution as its effects are felt by a relatively small population, with the most dramatic effects, at least those that have been scientifically documented, on an even smaller population of pregnant and breast-feeding Inuit women. Even if this were recognized as significant, the U.S. would likely claim, consistent with the terms of the agreement, that it had met its obligation by significantly reducing dioxin emissions through regulations.

Inuit v. Canada: Protection Under the United Nations Human Rights Commission

If Canada refused or failed to use what legal mechanisms exist to attempt some redress from the U.S. government, it may be possible for the Inuit to seek redress from the Canadian government for failing to protect them as indigenous peoples.[9]

The U.N. Human Rights Committee (UNHRC) may be a useful forum for the type of complaint alleged by the Inuit women against Canada. The UNHRC has made significant findings in cases brought by indigenous groups, alleging violations of Article 27 of the International Covenant on Civil and Political Rights (ICCPR), which protects the rights of minorities to enjoy their culture. In 1994, the UNHRC stated in a general comment that Article 27 requires positive acts to protect the right to enjoy one's culture. Optional Protocol to Article 27 of the ICCPR allows individuals within states to complain directly to the UNHRC about alleged violations of the ICCPR. This protocol could be especially useful since Canada has ratified it. Therefore, in its failure to protect culture through ensuring environmental compliance, Canada could be the subject to a complaint at the UNHRC.

The UNHRC, as a U.N. body given the authority to implement U.N. human rights treaties and conventions, has considerable weight in the international realm. A favorable recommendation by the UNHRC may be beneficial in forcing Canada to rectify the situation. As one of only a few U.N. conventions ratified by the United States, a recommendation by the UNHCR may also force that government to act. Therefore, the UNHRC could also hold the U.S. responsible for sanctioning pollution that has caused harm to the Inuit and destroyed their enjoyment of cultural traditions. Even without a victory, bringing such a case would create more visibility around the issue of long-range contamination of the Inuit's traditional food source and may encourage assistance and remedy from both the United States and Canada.

U.S. pollution has caused significant global environmental degradation. Dioxin exposure will continue to cause health consequences for Inuit women and may restrict their ability to live their traditional lifestyles. However, the types of legal mechanisms available for redressing such harm appear to be quite limited.

The Role of Ecofeminist and Feminist Theory in Addressing the Harm to Inuit Women

Feminist and ecofeminist theories play a crucial role in questioning, critiquing, and re-creating the capabilities of the current international legal regime to hold accountable the U.S. polluters who have caused harm to Inuit women. These perspectives help move toward answering, in this situation of transnational environmental harm, how marginalized peoples can seek redress and justice. In a world where states and international bodies seem only to enable, rather than mitigate, environmental harm, how can feminist and ecofeminist theories shed light on the question of justice?

First, by rejecting universalizing knowledge, feminist and ecofeminist theories help point to the specific situation of the Inuit, rooted in history, culture, and experience, and present a new picture of the necessity of sustaining their rights to culture and a healthy environment. In its examination of hierarchies of oppressions, feminist and ecofeminist theories expose why Inuit concerns are not integrated into international law. By resisting dualisms, in particular the public/private dichotomy, feminists highlight the interaction between states and corporations in enabling continued environmental degradation.[10]

The Feminist Critique of the Notion of Universality

By its very definition, international law claims universality in doctrine and application (Anghie 1999). Despite this claim, feminist critics point out that international law is heavily rooted in Christian and European traditions, and that current practices of international law remain heavily Eurocentric (Otto 1997). Feminist critics question how international law "otherizes" those who are not centered in a white, male, First World tradition (Charlesworth 1999). Critical race theorists aim to deconstruct this claimed universality with special attention to how race- and ethnicity-based oppressions undermine and impede women's rights in the international realm (Andrews 2000). Third World approaches to international law also seek to "disavow white supremacy or any other racial hierarchies" with particular attention to the doctrines and practices of international law that "foster exploitation and the dehumanization of Third World cultures, communities and philosophies" (Mutua 2000, 852). These approaches offer powerful critiques of the notions of universality by exposing how oppressive structures impact and limit international law.

Feminist legal scholars point to the dichotomies inherent in traditional Western-dominated law as a conceptual tool to explore how such concerns are effectively disregarded as important issues under international law. The public/private divide is one conceptual tool that many scholars have identified as a way that international law serves to reinforce formal structures to oppress women (Romany 1994; Charlesworth 1999). One example of this is the Convention Against Torture's recognition of sexual violence against women as an abuse of human rights—only if such violence can be connected to the public realm, that is, committed by a state actor or for a state purpose. Since women are commonly victims of sexual crimes in their own homes by non-state actors, the public/private distinction disempowers their claims that such violations are human rights abuses under the Convention Against Torture.

In the context of the Inuit women's situation, the public/private divide is one of the reasons the nature of the dioxin contamination fails to be considered harmful enough to warrant protection. Because the harm takes place within bodies, causing cancer and reproductive problems, it does not create a public presence, unlike noxious gases in the air. If the public/private divide focuses attention on the need to address concerns affecting the body, it exposes the ways in which the laws are biased in failing to consider the harms committed in the "private" realm.

Another tangible example of feminist critique of the universality of environmental law is the examination of risk assessment. Risk assessments play an essential role when setting standards for environmental protection. As classically defined, risk is a product of "the severity of the threatened harm, and the probability of its occurrence" (Verchick 1996, 65). Federal agencies like the EPA use risk assessments to determine acceptable levels of toxins in setting environmental and occupational safety standards. However, risk assessments are often created on the basis of effects on the "average" person, who would have the average susceptibility to pollutant exposure. This "average" person does not reflect the higher sensitivity levels of certain minorities, young children, fetuses, or women in childbearing years; rather, as Robert Verchick notes, "this 'average' person is usually a white man" (1996, 65).

Inuit women's particular dietary needs and cultural traditions place them outside of the realm of the "average" person, and therefore their concerns have not been in the forefront of policy makers' goals either in the U.S. EPA or on a more global level. When the understanding comes that environmental risk assessment considerations must recognize the differences in race, class, cultures, and gender, and that in doing so the harm to Inuit women is clearly articulated, the claims raised by the Inuit women will have more merit.

If the specific impacts of dioxins on Inuit women are taken seriously, then the right to a healthy environment and the right to life will come closer to customary international law status. In particular, linking the severity of the harm in terms of health consequences of dioxin in the body, the long-term effects of passing on the contamination to children, and the understanding of the health benefits to the Inuit of maintaining their traditional diet show that this kind of harm approaches the realm of a violation of right to life. Focusing on the severity of the risk to Inuit women may also be helpful in a claim at the IACHR against the United States, because it may elevate the claim beyond the low-level risks that usually are not reprimanded by the IACHR. Under the Agreement on Air Quality between the United States and Canada, the severity of the harm should elevate the problem to be considered "significant" enough to warrant mitigation of some form by the U.S. government. This may also be true for a claim against Canada at the UNHRC.

Ecofeminist Exploration of Racist and Transnational Capitalist Oppression

At its core, ecofeminism begins with the premise that the oppression of women and the oppression of nature are inextricably linked. Ecofeminist theories explore how multiple human oppressions are interwoven with many forms of environmental degradation. The ecofeminist theories most useful for lending insight into the problem of Inuit pollution include antiprimitivist and anti-racist theories, an analysis of the transnational capitalist regime, and a critique of the global environmental movement.

One important ecofeminist critique stems from the work of Douglas Buege, who constructed an ecofeminist analysis of the Inuit. He argues that ecofeminism must explore the sexist, racist, and classist assumptions of European American perspectives of the Inuit and the way in which those assumptions disempower the Inuit people (Buege 1997, 103). One such assumption is based on "primitive ideologies," in which, as Marianna Torgovnick explains them, "Primitives are our untamed selves . . . libidinous, irrational, violent, dangerous . . . [p]rimitives exist at the 'lowest cultural levels'; we [nonindigenous, industrialized persons] occupy the 'highest'" (Buege 1997, 102). Such images do not come from an understanding or knowledge of Inuit culture but rather are created by European Americans, Buege argues, in order to "shape the Inuit and other groups into something we desire" (102). Another theme incorporated in these "primitive ideologies" is that the Inuit are childlike, a people who need to be taken care of by the modern world. This in turn creates a system that imposes religious, economic, educational, and economic determination upon the Inuit.

Another important aspect of ecofeminist theory is its effort to deconstruct racist essentialism. Essentialist notions hold that all women, regardless of their differences, are closer to nature than men.[11] The problem with this notion is that it erases the situation of particular women engaged in particular political, economic, or social struggles in dealing with the environment. The racist element is particularly prevalent with regard to indigenous women, since they are viewed as "closer to nature" because of the association with cultural traditions and practices. Theorist Noël Sturgeon states that, within this framework, indigenous women become "racialized Others to the white Self that is Western, modern, and industrialized" (1997, 113). This racialized othering takes place in the ecofeminist movement as well and becomes a tool for silencing and disregarding the voices of indigenous women.

The failure of international and national bodies in examining risk for environmental harm of groups like the Inuit is firmly rooted in oppressive structures the categorize women, indigenous peoples, people of color, and poor people as the "other," who clearly are not the "average" person regulations are enacted to protect. Inherent in this definition of average is a valuation of who deserves protection, but also the exclusion of voices of those considered invalid or unnecessary. These theories add insight as to why the indigenous right to cultural self-determination has not risen to the level of customary international law. A sentiment imposed by Western ideals that Inuit are childlike and must be taken care of stands in direct contrast to the rights articulated under the cultural self-determination doctrine. The childlike stereotype may also inhibit the Inuit's ability to get their concerns taken seriously on the scale of international negotiating between the United States and Canada.

Another crucial element of ecofeminist theories involves examining the transnational capitalist regime, which elevates pro-capitalist "development" above environmental protection. In *Ecofeminism as Politics: Nature, Marx, and the Postmodern*, Ariel Salleh argues that transnational corporate power has used nature and people defined as "Other" for profit, and in doing so has rendered nature and Others resources without intrinsic value (1997, chapter 12). Salleh argues that the resourcing of animals, women, native Others, and their habitats is an essential structural component of transnational capitalism. Destruction that is waged, either through the violation of the environment or human rights of the Others, is "legitimated by the global brotherhood of church and state, market and trade union, science and technology. The injury caused by this battery of capitalist patriarchal institutions remains comfortably invisible to those who benefit from them" (187). What this means in regard to the Inuit women is that the harm remains unrecognized because the dioxin poisoning of their bodies through their traditional food source is implicitly regarded as a costless consequence of economic development. International protections fail to recognize that harm because such recognition would be incongruent with the dominant understanding of "development."

Ecofeminism also points to nation-states' protection and enabling of the growth of First World capitalist domination in exchange for environmental harm. Under Salleh's theory, the nation-states, the primary actors on the international level, uphold organizations of transnational wealth, such as corporations, and privilege profit over the environment and human rights. Using the feminist critique of the public and private reaffirms this assessment by exposing how public entities such as nation-states work in collaboration with private-sphere corporations, and therefore should be held accountable for the acts of those private entities. Environmental violence presents a particularly clear example of this, which is illustrated in the state/private actor nexus requirement of the Alien Tort Claims Act. States often enable environmental harm by failing to impose limitations. Like the example of the Convention Against Torture that fails to consider sexual violence in the home as a form of torture, the nexus requirement, as it is now interpreted and understood, fails to understand that environmental harm, as it occurs on a transnational, transboundary level, is perpetuated by states' failure to adequately reign in the power of private entities who pollute.

Another facet of ecofeminism is its critique of global transnational

environmentalism, which, in cooperating with conservative transnational institutions, has failed to radically address the oppressions facing disempowered groups.
Sturgeon states that the problem with a globalizing environmental movement
is that it suggests a global answer is needed to address global environmental
problems (1997, 147). In failing to take into consideration the concerns of specific
groups in particular historical and political moments, the dominant environmental discourse makes claims about universal human conditions and reduces
the critique of the role of corporate agency in the maintenance of inequalities
or environmental problems (148).

Feminist and ecofeminist theorists provide valuable insight into decon-
structing the myths of universality prevalent in international law. International
law was not developed by a truly representative group of global citizens. By
upholding the structures that enable transnational corporations to seek profit
over human rights and healthy environments, international law fails to confront the growing ownership of such decisions not by nation-states or people
but by increasingly wealthy and powerful transnational corporations.

Ultimately, the project of ecofeminists and other feminists in the arena of
international law is to decenter the state and corporate entities while placing
Inuit women in the center of defining their struggles and creating a powerful
voice in articulating possible solutions, both within and outside of international organizations. One of the most important ways to ensure environmental
justice for the Inuit women is to ensure that their voices and concerns are
raised through Inuit women's definition and involvement in a movement. Inuit
women's voices must be heard at international, national, and local levels of
decision making.

Sheila Watt-Cloutier, president of the Canadian branch of the Inuit Circumpolar Conference, is a prominent leader and advocate for the voices of the
Inuit people and the protection of the environment for indigenous peoples. She
has fought for over ten years to protect Inuit from other people's pollution. Her
work, and that of many other advocates for the environment, resulted in a
United Nations treaty signed by 120 nations in May 2001 aimed at limiting persistent organic pollutants in the global environment. Watt-Cloutier states, "we
are only 150,000 people, but POPs [persistent organic pollutants] threaten our very
cultural existence. As a result, we insisted on a Convention that would address the
public health concerns of mothers in all parts of the globe. Our advocacy was
from the heart as well as the mind, but we avoided the often shrill politics of
blaming. The Inuit way is to engage in the politics of influence not the politics
of protest" (Wake-Up 2002).

Like the Inuit politics of influence, ecofeminist and feminist theoretical
tools envision a fuller remedy to the kind of harm suffered by the Inuit. These
theories begin by elevating the concerns of human health and the environment
above the rights of industrial countries to pollute in order to sustain a particu-

lar lifestyle of its inhabitants. If Inuit concerns were truly centered within the discussion of ending dioxin contamination, then their concerns would be part of the instigation of the need to consume less, burn less, and find alternative sources of energy—each ways of lessening dioxin creation in the environment. Indeed, if the lives of Inuit women were considered more important than the right of First World corporations to pollute, international and domestic laws would change shape and become responsive no longer to powerful wealth, but rather to human rights and the goal of a healthy environment.

NOTES

I would like to thank my classmates Kris Weller and Immeke Schmidt for their invaluable contributions to this work and support during its creation. I would also like to thank professors Bradford C. Mank, Catherine M. Raissiguier, and Ingrid Brunk Wuerth for their guidance and encouragement.

1. The NACEC was established by the United States, Canada, and Mexico under the North American Agreement on Environmental Cooperation (NAAEC). The NACEC was established to "address regional environmental concerns, help prevent potential trade and environmental conflicts, and to promote the effective enforcement of environmental law" (http://www.cec.org). The NAAEC is a side agreement to the North American Free Trade Agreement (NAFTA).

2. In 1991, the EPA Office of Research and Development undertook a major study on dioxins, which is not yet complete, documenting the pervasive health problems caused by dioxins. According to this research, the risk for dioxin-related cancers is 1 in 1,000 for the "general [U.S.] population." The 2000 report of the ongoing study characterizes dioxins as a "likely human carcinogen," and estimates a tenfold higher risk of cancer than estimated in a 1994 draft report. Fetuses, infants, and children fall into the category of those who "may be more sensitive" to problems because of their rapid growth and development. Breast milk appears to be a significant source of dioxin exposure for nursing infants (EPA Office of Research and Development 2000a).

3. Passed by the first Congress as part of the Judiciary Act of 1789, the ATCA states, "The district courts shall have original jurisdiction of any civil action by an alien for a tort only, committed in violation of the law of nations or a treaty of the United States."

4. Until recently, the ATCA has been used infrequently. However, in 1980, the family members of a Paraguayan man who was tortured to death in Paraguay by local police sued the officer in U.S. federal court under the ATCA in *Filartiga v. Pena-Irala*. The court held that torture violated customary international law, and based that finding on its examination of the U.N. Charter, U.N. declarations against torture, and international treaties and accords.

5. For example, see *Wiwa v. Royal Dutch Petroleum/Shell*, *Doe v. Unocal Corporation*, *Beanal v. Freeport-McMoRan*, and *Aquinda v. Texaco, Inc.*

6. During twenty years of oil exploration, Texaco opened over 300 wells, cut 18,000 miles of trail and built 300 miles of road in the rainforest. Additionally, Texaco dumped toxic by-products into streams and wetlands that local people used for fishing, bathing, and drinking and filled 600 pits with toxic waste that washed out during heavy rains. At least 30,000 people became ill from toxic chemical infiltration into their water supply (*Aguinda v. Texaco*, Aguinda U.S. Dist. LEXIS 4718). In *Beanal v.*

Freeport McMoran, Inc., it was shown that Freeport's mining operations resulted in huge amounts of untreated, toxic by-products in waterways, causing toxicity in the groundwater.

7. For example, in *Doe v. Unocal*, where plaintiffs alleged abuses during the construction of an oil pipeline in Indonesia, the court rejected the contention that only state actors can be held liable and found a corporation can be held liable as a state actor. Later the court found that Unocal did not operate in close enough connection with the Myanmar government of Burma to be considered a state actor.

8. In 1999, Earthjustice filed suit challenging the agency's national air rule for incinerators and cement kilns that burn hazardous waste ("Suit Filed to Require EPA to Protect Families from Airborne Toxics"). In July 2001, the District of Columbia Circuit Court held in favor of Earthjustice and struck down those rules as inadequate and unlawful EPA regulations ("Landmark Victory for Public Health and the Environment").

9. In addition to the UNHRC claim, the Inuit may have a claim for protection under the Canadian Constitutional Act of 1982, which includes protection for indigenous rights. Section 35(1) affirms and recognizes "[t]he existing aboriginal and treaty rights of the aboriginal peoples of Canada."

10. The phrases "rejecting universalizing knowledge," "refusing hierarchies," "resisting dualism," and "decentering the state" are from Dianne Otto's work. She identifies these concepts as modes for transforming human rights strategies (36–42).

11. Earlier ecofeminist theories were more prone to arguing from essentialist positions in part due to their foundation in the voices of white, Western, privileged women.

REFERENCES

Agreement on Air Quality, Canada-United States. 1991. Reprinted in *International Legal Materials* 30 (1991): 676.

Aguinda v. Texaco, Inc., No. 93 Civ 7527 (VLB) 1994 U.S. Dist. LEXIS 4718 (S.D.N.Y. Apr. 11, 1994).

Aquinda v. Texaco, Inc., 945 F. Supp. 625 (S.D.N.Y. 1996).

Alien Tort Claims Act of 2001. 28 U.S.C.S. §1350 (2001).

Andrews, Penelope E. 2000. "Making Room for Critical Race Theory in International Law: Some Practical Pointers." *Villanova Law Review* 45: 855.

Anghie, Antony. 1999. "Finding the Peripheries: Sovereignty and Colonialism in Nineteenth-Century International Law." *Harvard International Law Journal* 40: 1.

Archibald, Linda, and Mary Crnkovich. 1999. *If Gender Mattered: A Case Study of Inuit Women, Land Claims, and the Voisey's Bay Nickel Project.* Ottawa: Status of Women Canada; *http://www.swc-cfc.gc.ca/*.

Beanal v. Freeport-McMoRan, Inc., 197 F.3d 161 (5th Cir. 1999).

Bell, R. Raines, and Christine Heller. 1978. "Nutrition Studies: An Appraisal of the Modern North Alaskan Eskimo Diet." In *Eskimos of Northwestern Alaska: A Biological Study*, ed. Paul L. Jamison, Stephen L. Zegura, and Frederick A. Milan. Stroudsburg, Pa.: Dowden, Hutchinson and Ross.

Brown, DeNeen. 2001. "Native Peoples Pay the Price of a Poisoned Arctic." *Sydney Herald. http://www.commondreams.org/headlines01/0519–01.htm.*

Buege, Douglas. 1997. "Epistemic Responsibility and the Inuit of Canada's Eastern Arctic: An Ecofeminist Appraisal." In *Ecofeminism: Women, Culture, Nature*, ed. Karen J. Warren. Bloomington: Indiana University Press.

Canadian Constitution. 1982. Constitution Act of 1982, pt. I, Canadian Charter of Rights and

Freedom. Reprinted in *The Canadian Charter of Rights and Freedoms: Commentary 530*, eds. Walter S. Tarnopolsky and Gérald-A. Beaudoin. Toronto: Carswell.

Charlesworth, Hilary. 1999. "Feminist Methods in International Law." *American Journal of International Law* 93: 379.

Clean Air Act. 2003. 42 U.S.C.A. §7412(d)(3).

Commoner, Barry, et al. 2000. *Long-Range Transport of Dioxin from North American Sources to Ecologically Vulnerable Receptors in Nunavut, Arctic Canada: Final Report to the North American Commission for Environmental Cooperation.* Queens College, City University of New York: Center for Biology of Natural Systems; *http://www.cec.org/ pubs_docs/ documents/index.cfm?varlan=english&ID=73.*

Dewailly, É., et al. 1992. "Breast Milk Contamination by PCDDs, PCDFs and PCBs in Arctic Québec: A Preliminary Assessment." *Chemosphere* 25: 1245.

———. 2001. "N–3 Fatty acids and Cardiovascular Disease Risk Factors among the Inuit of Nunavik." *American Journal of Clinical Nutrition* 74: 464.

Doe v. Unocal, 110 F. Supp. 2d 1294 (C.D. Cal. 2000).

EPA. 2003. "Q & A about Dioxins." *http://www.epa.gov/ncea/dioxinqa.htm.*

EPA Office of Research and Development. 2000a. "Information Sheet 1: Dioxin: Summary of the Dioxins Reassessment of Science." *http://www.epa.gov/ncea/pdfs/dioxin/factsheets/ dioxin_short2.pdf.*

———. 2000b. "Information Sheet 4: Dioxin: Summary of Major EPA Control Efforts." *http://www.epa.gov/ncea/pdfs/dioxin/factsheets/dioxin_regs.pdf.*

Filartiga v. Pena-Irala, 630 F.2d 876 (2d. Cir. 1980).

Herz, Richard L. 2000. "Litigating Environmental Abuses under the Alien Tort Claims Act: Practical Assessment." *Virginia Journal of International Law* 40: 545.

International Labour Organisation. General Conference. 1991. Seventy-sixth Session. International Labour Organisation Convention No. 169. Geneva, June 27, 1989. Reprinted in *International Legal Materials* 28 (1989): 1384.

"Landmark Victory for Public Health and the Environment: Court Rules EPA Regulations for Hazardous Waste Burners Inadequate." 2001. *http://www.earthjustice.org/news/ print.html?ID=218* (July 24).

Mutua, Makau. 2000. "Critical Race Theory and International Law: The View of an Insider-Outsider." *Villanova Law Review* 45: 841.

NCAA v. Tarkanian, 488 U.S. 179, 192 (1988).

Organization of American States. 1975. Ninth International Conference of American States. *American Declaration of the Rights and Duties of Man.* Bogota, Colombia, May 2, 1948, at OEA/ser. L/V/II .71, at 17. *http://www.cidh.oas.org/basic.htm.*

Organization of American States. 1997. *Report on the Situation of Human Rights in Brazil.* OEA/Ser.L/V/II.97, Doc. 29 rev. 1, 64–66. *http://www.cidh.oas.org/countryreps/brazil-eng/index%20-%20brazil.htm.*

Organization of American States. Creation of Inter-American Commission on Human Rights, Declaration of the Fifth Meeting of Consultation of Ministers of Foreign Affairs, Santiago, Chile, Aug. 12–18, 1959, Final Act, Document OEA/Ser.C/II.5.

Organization of American States. Inter-American Commission on Human Rights. 1996. *Report on the Work Accomplished by the IACHR during its Thirteenth Period of Sessions.* OEA/Ser.L/V/II.14, doc. 35, June 30 1966.

———. 1997. Ninety-fifth Regular Session. *American Declaration on the Rights of Indigenous Peoples.* AEA/Ser/L/V/.11.95 Doc. 6.

Otto, Dianne. 1997. "Rethinking the 'Universality' of Human Rights Law." *Columbia Human Rights Law Review* 29: 1.

The Paquete Habana, 175 U.S. 677, 700 (1900).

Romany, Celina. 1994. "State Responsibility Goes Private: A Feminist Critique of the Public/Private Distinction in International Law." *Human Rights of Women: National and International Perspectives*, ed. Rebecca J. Cook. Philadelphia: University of Pennsylvania Press.

Salleh, Arial. 1997. *Ecofeminism as Politics: Nature, Marx, and the Postmodern.* New York: St. Martin's Press.

Sturgeon, Noël. 1997. *Ecofeminist Natures: Race, Gender, Feminist Theory, and Political Action.* New York: Routledge.

"Suit Filed to Require EPA to Protect Families From Airborne Toxics." 1999. *http://www.earthjustice.org/news/print.html?ID=122* (Nov. 30).

United Nations. 1972. Declaration of the United Nations Conference on the Human Environment. U.N. Doc. A/CONF.48/14. Reprinted in *International Legal Materials* 11 (1973): 1416.

———. 1992. *Rio Declaration on Environment and Development.* Preamble, Principle 1, U.N. Doc. A/CONF.151/5/Rev. 1, vol. 1. Reprinted in *International Legal Materials* 31 (1992): 874.

United Nations. General Assembly. 1948. Third Session. *Universal Declaration of Human Rights.* G.A. Res. 217A (III), U.N. GAOR, (Resolutions, pt. 1), at 71, art. 25, U.N. Doc. A/810(1948), reprinted in *American Journal of International Law* 43 (Supp. 1949): 127.

———. 1976. Twenty-first Session. Supplement 16. *International Covenant on Civil and Political Rights.* U.N. Doc. A/6316 (1966), 993 U.N.T.S. 3.

United Nations. Human Rights Committee. 1990. *Two Selected Decisions of the Human Rights Committee under the Optional Protocol.* Communication No. 67/1980, at 20, U.N. Doc. CCPR/C/OP/2.

———. 1994. *General Comment to Article 27 of the ICCPR.* General comment no. 23(50) (art.27), UN Doc. CCPR/C/21/Rev.1?Add.5.

Verchick, Robert R. M. 1996. "In a Greener Voice: Feminist Theory and Environmental Justice." *Harvard Women's Law Journal* 19: 23.

Watt-Cloutier, Sheila. 2002. "Wake-Up." *http://www.ourplanet.com/imgversn/124/watt.html.*

Wiwa v. Royal Dutch Petroleum/Shell, 226 F.3d 88 (2d Cir. 2000).

Yanomami case Res. 12/85, Case 7615, Inter-Am. C.H.R., OEA/ser.L./V./II.66, doc. 10 rev. 1 (Mar. 5, 1985), reprinted in 1985 *Inter-American Year Book on Human Rights*: 264.

Young, T. Kue. 1996. "Obesity, Central Fat Patterning, and Their Metabolic Correlates among the Inuit of the Central Canadian Arctic." *Human Biology* 68: 245.

PART FOUR

Gender, Sexuality, and Environmental Justice in Literature and Popular Culture

12

Bodily Invasions

Gene Trading and Organ Theft in Octavia Butler and Nalo Hopkinson's Speculative Fiction

RACHEL STEIN

Environmental justice calls for the strict enforcement of principles of informed consent and a halt to the testing of experimental reproductive and medical procedures and vaccinations on people of color.

–Principle 13 of the "Principles of Environmental Justice" adopted by the First National People of Color Environmental Leadership Summit, Washington, D.C., October 1991

Packaged in small tubes tucked in plastic foam containers, with careful instructions for feeding and handling, shipments of Henrietta's cells went out to Gey's colleagues around the world . . . to Minnesota, New York, Chile, Russia . . . the list goes on. Researchers welcomed the gifts, allowing HeLa to grow. They used the cells to search for a leukemia cure and the cause of cancer, to study viral growth, protein synthesis, genetic control mechanisms, and the unknown effects of drugs and radiation. And though Henrietta never traveled farther than from Virginia to Baltimore, her cells sat in nuclear sites from America to Japan and multiplied in a space shuttle far above the earth.

–Rebecca Skloot

Current environmental justice frameworks have demonstrated that poor and people of color communities often suffer unequal exposure to toxins, radiation, and other environmental risks at home, at work, and in the surrounding locale, endangering the health of their bodies. Speculative fiction writers Octavia Butler and Nalo Hopkinson expand our view of environmental justice health issues by articulating ways in which the bodies of women of color may also be directly manipulated and harvested as environmental resources for those in power. Butler's

Dawn presents the dilemma of forced gene trading and sexual/reproductive controls, and Hopkinson's *Brown Girl in the Ring* portrays a murderous case of organ theft. In both novels, black female protagonists must grapple with the moral issues created by the colonization and use of women's bodies as natural resource materials—extending the boundaries of our understanding of the inter-connections between environmental justice, gender, and sexuality.

The novels of Butler and Hopkinson warn us of the possibilities of biotech-nological colonization of vulnerable bodies, in particular the bodies of women of color. In *Biopiracy: The Plunder of Nature and Knowledge*, physicist and ecol-ogist Vandana Shiva makes it clear that biogenetic and medical manipulation of humans, plants, and animals are new forms of colonization that have now extended the ruinous exploitation of the planet *inward*. She writes:

> The land, the forests, the rivers, the oceans, and the atmosphere have all been colonized, eroded, and polluted. Capital now has to look for new colonies to invade and exploit for its further accumulation. These new colonies are, in my view, the interior spaces of the bodies of women, plants, and animals. Resistance to biopiracy is a resistance to the ultimate colonization of life itself—of the future of evolution as well as the futures of non-Western traditions of relating to and knowing nature. It is a struggle to protect the freedom of diverse species to evolve. It is a struggle to pro-tect the freedom of diverse cultures to evolve. It is a struggle to conserve both cultural and biological diversity. (Shiva 1997, 5)

Butler and Hopkinson's speculative fictions draw our attention to the shadowy possibility that new medical technologies such as biogenetic manipulation of DNA and organ harvesting might, in certain circumstances, be forms of literal objectification in which the body parts of women of color come to be deemed as usable, extractable, tradable, natural resources that the women will be coerced or violently forced into relinquishing for the purposes of those in power. In fact, the novels make clear the implicit violence of the perspective that the bodies of women of color have instrumental rather than intrinsic value, and that their body parts may be exploited as commodities that have more exchange value than the women themselves.

Furthermore, in both of these novels, such bodily invasions are presented within the context of unequal social/cultural relations and environmental/ social catastrophes, which underscores that these coerced bodily invasions are forms of environmental injustice. Frighteningly, in both novels, the coloniza-tion of women of color's bodies is justified as an aspect of environmental preservation, as a necessary response to environmental degradation. Thus both authors encourage us to examine how environmental struggles may be played out upon/within the bodies of women of color. Butler and Hopkinsons's novels feature black female protagonists who are subject to such biomedical incursions, and who must make practical/ethical choices about how to address these new forms of colonization given the imbalances of power and the environmental/social degradations within which they occur. If we examine these speculative fictions within the context of the historical colonization of women of color and current environmental justice health movement, they may be read as provocative cautionary tales about the potential for misusing biomedical processes to further exploit and objectify women's bodies, and to justify such expropriation in terms of environmental necessity.

In Octavia Butler's *Dawn*, the first novel in her "Xenogenesis Trilogy," environmental catastrophe becomes the justification for sexual/genetic manipulation of the surviving humans; the novel explores the premise that if human behavior is genetically determined, then genetic manipulation is the best means of shaping behavior, and forcible control of sexuality/reproduction is justified by the need for species evolution. In *Dawn*, an African American woman named Lilith is one of the humans who have been rescued from Earth by an alien species named the Oankali, following a nuclear war among the humans that has left the planet irradiated and uninhabitable. While the Oankali do not usually intervene in the death throes of suicidal species, they are fascinated with the biology of human cancers, which the Oankali believe might have the potential to teach them how to regenerate cells and organisms, and they are equally fascinated with the dangerously contradictory behaviors of human beings, who are, as her first Oankali acquaintance explains to Lilith, an incompatible genetic mixture of "hierarchical" and "intelligent" tendencies. In order to protect humans from these ill-matched genetic tendencies and to satisfy the Oankali's "acquisitive" need to incorporate new genetic materials for their own evolutionary purposes, the Oankali offer the captured humans a "trade": the Oankali will restore Earth to ecological balance and return the humans to the planet only if they agree to become genetic/reproductive partners with the Oankali, and to merge into a new species that blends human and Oankali genes and traits. Humans who do not agree to the trade will remain permanently sterilized in order to ensure that their genetic predisposition to intelligence and hierarchy will not be transmitted to offspring who might once again annihilate the species and the planet. Thus, according to the terms imposed by the Oankali, humankind as we know it will cease to exist, either through attrition or through genetic intermixing with the Oankali. Lilith, who has been awakened from suspended animation upon the Oankali space ship, is gradually acclimated to the Oankali and convinced to accept the terms of the trade. She is then trained for the role of "first parent," responsible for awakening a group of humans who will be prepared to return to Earth and partner with the Oankali.

While the Oankali believe that they are offering humans a fair form of salvation and the opportunity for new life, Lilith perceives the trade as a form of domination and exploitation, analogous to human domestication of and experimentation upon nonhuman species.[1] She often refers to the Oankali treatment of herself in terms of human treatment of other animals, such as pets, zoo animals, or biological experiments:

> In a very real sense, she was an experimental animal. . . . She was intended to live and reproduce. . . . Experimental animal, parent to domestic animals? Or . . . nearly extinct animal, part of a captive breeding program? Human biologists had done that before the war—used a few captive members of an endangered animal species to breed more for the wild population. Was that what she was headed for? Forced artificial insemination. Surrogate motherhood? Fertility drugs and forced "donations" of eggs? Implantation of unrelated fertilized eggs. Removal of children from mothers at birth . . . Humans had done these things to captive breeders—all for a higher good, of course. (Butler 1987, 58)

Lilith learns that, for such a "higher good," the Oankali have, in fact, created gene prints of the captive humans without their knowledge or consent, and have used human genetic materials to reproduce a larger stock of humans for experimental study and partnership.

While Lilith compares the Oankali treatment of humans to our behavior toward other animals, the notion of paternalistic control and genetic manipulation of captive populations for a "higher good" also echoes the historical and contemporary situations of women of color in the United States and around the globe who have been subjected to sexual and reproductive controls during centuries of colonization and neocolonial exploitation, and they too have often been justified in terms of environmental requirements or protections. A number of critics have pointed out how Lilith's situation invokes the treatment of enslaved African American women, who, after being stolen away from kin and country and imprisoned, were then subjected to sexual and reproductive atrocities including rape by their white owners and others in power, assignment to enslaved men as sexual partners, having their children deemed chattel property who could be sold away by their white masters, and being required to act as wet nurses and caretakers for white children while leaving their own children to uncertain care.[2] As I have written elsewhere, it has been well documented that these practices were justified in terms of environmental needs and requirements; free white landholders needed a labor force in order to cultivate the so-called virgin land, and because whites deemed Africans and Indians to be more animalistic than themselves, they could justify inhumane and genocidal practices as expedient in terms of achieving the "higher good" of conquest and colonization.[3] Even after slavery and other forms of colonization ended, women of color have continued to be treated exploitatively and paternalistically, and their sexuality/reproductivity has continued to be impinged upon in the name of environmental necessity. For example, in the United States and its protec-

torates, racist policies of sterilization, experimental and coercive use of potentially hazardous long-term birth control methods such as Depo-provera shots
and Norplant devices, and family size limits linked to economic support have
been imposed upon women of color even into the present day in the name of
wise use of environmental resources and creating proper home environments.[4]
The Committee on Women, Population, and the Environment, a contemporary
network of feminist scholars and activists, notes the disturbing trend of First
World environmental organizations (which are predominantly white and
middle- to upper-class) blaming environmental crises on overpopulation in the
Third World and urging the imposition of population controls upon women of
color instead of limiting the exorbitant consumption of natural resources in
developed nations. Jael Silliman explains that by this logic "population increases
are associated with faceless and undifferentiated poor women of color . . . those
'dark and irrational people' in those equally 'dark and primordial places'—who
are unaware and ignorant of the 'fuses' they are sparking. 'They' are the problem. 'We' are absolved of all responsibility" (Silliman 1999, viii). In light of this
pervasive attitude, some feminists and environmental justice activists fear that
the rapidly developing field of biogenetic research will provide new forms of
reproductive controls imposed by First World scientists, corporations, and governments upon Third World women: gene mapping, the patenting of DNA patterns, and prenatal gene testing could well lend themselves to the sorts of
colonialist scenarios that Butler foresees in *Dawn*.[5]

In this vein, although the Oankali in *Dawn* present themselves to Lilith as
an egalitarian society within which important decisions are reached through
group consensus, they impose such decisions upon their human "partners"
without their free consent and sometimes even without their knowledge, much
as earthly colonial powers did to those whom they conquered or enslaved. First
and foremost, the gene trade is presented to Lilith as a unilateral and non-
negotiable arrangement that the Oankali are determined to engage in with
their "partners." Jdahya tells Lilith, "We are as committed to the trade as your
body is to breathing. We were overdue for it when we found you. Now it will be
done—to the rebirth of your people and mine" (Butler 1987, 41). Lilith's initial
response to these terms is that she wishes that the Oankali had left her on Earth
to die, rather than to birth children who will be alien rather than fully human.
The Oankali's biotechnological superiority serves as their mandate to colonize
other species for their own needs, and to appropriate the genetic characteristics that will improve their own evolutionary survival, much as Vandana Shiva
warns against in her writings on biopiracy.[6]

Even within the parameters of the "trade," the Oankali grant Lilith very
little freedom, assuming that their superior understanding of sentient life
allows them to make the best decisions for her, much in the manner of historical and contemporary human groups that advocate external control of women

of color's sexuality and reproduction. For example, Lilith is simply assigned to a trio of Oankali who will become her family/mating partners, rather than being offered any choice of which aliens with whom to bond. She is offered a larger, but still limited choice of human partners, first being paired with a man who attempts to seduce and then rape her but then being allowed to "choose" Joseph. While Joseph and Lilith appear to freely choose each other as lovers, given the confines of their situation on the ship, Lilith later discovers that Nikanj, one of her Oankali partners, had selected Joseph as an appropriate mate for her and had made sure that he was among the candidates she would awaken. The paternalistic Oankali control of human sexuality and reproduction is expressed even more directly within the sexual encounters that Nikanj orchestrates with his human partners. As an ooloi, the Oankali third sex responsible for controlling sexual exchanges and genetic mixing of children, Nikanj imposes Oankali sexual/reproductive practices upon its human mates. During sex with Nikanj, Joseph and Lilith are physically separated by their Oankali intermediary, and the human lovers will no longer be permitted to touch each other directly; due to the chemical changes that Nikanj produces in their bodies, they will now find each other's touch physically repellant, and will only be able to share sexual experiences that Nikanj transmits neurologically between them. These are the terms of the trade: sexual pleasure and reproduction will occur only through the Oankali—no direct, unmediated human sexual contact will be permitted.

Furthermore, much like contemporary population control advocates, Nikanj makes sexual and reproductive choices on behalf of its human partners, sometimes without their knowledge or conscious consent, by rationalizing that it acts in their best interests or as the situation requires. For example, Nikanj engages in sexual activity with Joseph, even though he has verbally refused; Nikanj comments, "Your body said one thing. Your words said another." When Joseph again refuses permission, Nikanj insists, "Be grateful, Joe. I'm not going to let go of you" (190). Even though Joseph only struggles briefly, and then accepts the pleasure Nikanj offers him, the forced imposition of sexual activity after a verbal refusal could be legally defined as rape according to U.S. laws, and this scene presents the disturbingly familiar situation in which the colonizer overpowers the colonized, even if the colonized supposedly accedes to the situation once it is imposed. Even more disturbingly, after Joseph's murder, Nikanj biotechnologically impregnates Lilith without her informed consent, with genetic materials that it has preserved from Joseph and mixed with those of herself and her Oankali family partners, even though Lilith has continued to express resistance to the idea of the "trade" and Nikanj had formerly promised her that humans would not be forced into xenogenesis until they were ready and willing. Lilith reacts with horror to the news of her pregnancy, stating, "I'm not ready! I'll never be ready!" and exclaiming, "'It will be a thing—not human.' She stared down at her own body in horror. 'It's inside me and it isn't human'"

(246). Nikanj overrides her objections by explaining paternalistically that it believes this decision is for her own good. It tells her that "you are ready to have a daughter. . . . You never could have said so. Just as Joseph could never have invited me into his bed. . . . Nothing but your words reject this child" (246). It discounts Lilith's verbal objections and claims to know her better than she knows herself, even though Lilith's final statement about the pregnancy is to assert once again that "this will destroy us [humankind]" (247). In this final scene of *Dawn*, Lilith faces the reality that the Oankali have indeed expropriated her genetic/ reproductive materials without consent and have combined them into a mix that suits their needs for the "trade"; this coerced pregnancy is the first instance of xenogenesis, producing children who will be other than human, thus discontinuing the species. (In the two following novels, all decisions about reproduction and the fate of human/Oankali construct offspring will be decided by consensus of the Oankali. Lilith will not be able to protect her own children from such decisions—yet her children will continue to act as change agents who work to assure that the human perspective is understood and heard by the Oankali.)

Even though all surviving humans will be subject to the Oankali "trade" in the novel, Butler's use of a black female protagonist to act as the "first parent" is significant, focusing our attention on the position of actual women of color who must negotiate inescapable colonial forces that exert control over many aspects of their lives, particularly sexuality and reproduction. Throughout the novel, Lilith exhibits pragmatism, honesty, and directness in expressing dissent toward her captor/rescuers. Yet she also often accedes to their control since she believes she has no alternatives, since there is no escape from the ship and she wishes to preserve as many lives—of both species—as possible. She adopts a policy that she refers to as "learn and run" (248) that is reminiscent of the behavior of enslaved African Americans, who absorbed as much useful information from their masters as possible while they bided their time for flight or uprising. Lilith realizes the necessity of understanding her alien colonizers and of learning about the environmental changes that the Oankali have wrought in the vegetation and animals of the restored the earth, if she or any other humans are to have any hope of surviving independently upon the changed planet. While she is completely opposed to the trade that the Oankali demand, she also realizes that humans are now completely dependent upon their captors and cannot simply defy their control. Ironically, it is Lilith's very desire for environmental justice—for humans to return to earth, their home environment, and to reinhabit the restored planet, as well as her desire for humans to find some way to continue as a species, outside the terms of the trade—that leads her to assume the role of "first parent," responsible for convincing fellow captives to cooperate with each other and with the Oankali. Lilith is very conscious that the Oankali have placed her in the compromising position of "Judas goat" (an ambiguous term that implies that she is betraying others and/or that she is being betrayed, as well as acting as the scapegoat), and she realizes that other humans perceive her as a collaborator, even though she hopes that her actions will eventually lead to their freedom and reinhabitation of the earth. Lilith retains a long-range commitment to the survival of a human community on earth even while she remains entrapped, with no real freedom, only coerced, self-compromising choices.[7]

Lilith's compromised position and underground resistance illustrates the plight of actual women of color who face similar limits to their sexual and reproductive freedom, limits imposed in the name of environmental protection or environmental necessity. Butler's novel should put us on our guard against the insidiousness of racist theories of biological determinism and against state or transnational programs that control women's fertility and motherhood without their freely given consent. Through its plot of alien conquest and xenogenesis, *Dawn* emphasizes the painful loss of bodily integrity and informed consent, and illustrates the argument of Justine Smith, a member of the Committee on Women, Population, and the Environment, that we must include sexual/reproductive freedom and other health care concerns within the realm of sovereignty, that is, community self-determination over crucial aspects of life and environment that are fundamental aspects of environmental justice.[8]

Presenting another futuristic portrayal of women resisting bodily invasions, Nalo Hopkinson's *Brown Girl in a Ring* is set in the foreseeable future, within the decaying inner city of Toronto, Canada, which has been abandoned to the poor, the homeless, and the corrupt when the political, economic, and social collapse of the core city prompted those with means and mobility to flee to the suburbs. Through a series of newspaper headlines that outline the city's demise, Hopkinson suggests that colonialist and environmentally racist government policies underlie the collapse of Toronto. First and foremost, the refusal of the province of Ontario to settle an ongoing land-rights suit brought by First Nations Temagami peoples leads to an international trade embargo against wood taken from the disputed lands, which in turn leads the Canadian government to cut funding to the province. These events contribute to the demise of Toronto as one crisis sets off another: economic decline leads to unemployment, crime, failures of mass transit, deadly rioting, and finally flight from the city by all investors and public offices. Declared a "war zone," Toronto is abandoned by local and regional powers who set up roadblocks at the borders of the city to contain the problems; poor communities are left to grapple unaided with extreme urban decay and dislocation from the outer world. With no local government to provide public services such as schools, health care, or law enforcement and protection; no infrastructure or physical services such as utilities, sewage treatment, or transportation; and no commercial money economy, inner-city residents are thrown back upon their own resources. While the situation in this novel is extreme, it also outlines the inextricable connections between environmental and economic injustice, symbolizing the way that poor communities of color may be abandoned by the larger society, segregated into impoverished neighborhoods with problems no one else is willing to address.

The novel represents the struggle between two opposing responses to the vacuum left when commerce and government abandoned the community. As is typical of actual communities roused by environmental injustices, many of the characters in the novel band together to recreate new forms of interdependence and care that draw upon the indigenous practices of Toronto's varied immigrant cultures. Residents learn to plant gardens and hunt in erstwhile public parks, make squatter homes in hotels and other available spaces, and barter goods and services, creating subsistence modes of living within the limited resources of the city. Exemplifying this positive, resourceful response to the urban disaster is Mami Gros-Jeanne, a nurse/healer/spiritual leader who has made her home on a former model farm within the city where she grows herbs and plants for the traditional Afro-Caribbean remedies with which she tends her neighbors. She has also reclaimed the Toronto Crematorium Chapel, where she conducts traditional Afro-Caribbean ceremonies that nourish the souls of those who attend, as she explains to her granddaughter: "The African powers . . . The spirits. The loas. The orishas. The oldest ancestors . . . no matter what we call it, whether Shango or Santeria or Voudun or what, we all doing the same thing. Serving the spirits" (Hopkinson 1998, 126). As Mami serves the spirits, she also serves the community: offering healing to bodies and souls, preserving life, and modeling the ways that cultural heritage might be adapted to provide life-sustaining alternatives to Toronto's urban crisis.[9]

In contrast, Rudy, who was once Mami Gros-Jeanne's husband, along with his posse, takes full advantage of the lack of public governance systems to terrorize the helpless of the city through violent crime, drug distribution, and supernatural control. Rudy misuses the Afro-Caribbean spiritual traditions learned from Mami for his own foul purposes. He violently maintains control of the city drug trade and over his posse of young black men through use of the supernatural powers of duppy spirits whom he has enslaved, including that of his own daughter, Mi-Jeanne. Mami says of him, "Rudy is a shadow catcher. . . . Rudy does work the dead to control the living" (121). Rudy uses the duppy spirits to enforce his rule, ordering his duppies to torture and kill all those who stand in his way, and feeding the duppies a steady diet of human flesh and blood from Rudy's enemies and from the helpless street children of the city. Rudy has capitalized on the demise of the city, increasing his power by bringing suffering and death to those who remain, literally draining the life from their bodies and souls for his own ends. While Rudy may not be the typical perpetrator of environmental injustice, he does exemplify the disregard for others' lives and well-being that underlies many environmental ills, and he illustrates how the drug trade, and the crime and violence surrounding it, can destroy community environments, and is thus a part of the environmental justice struggle to restore common spaces.[10]

Interestingly, Hopkinson's novel presents organ harvesting/theft as the issue that exacerbates the conflict between Mami and Rudy and between the residents of Toronto and the provincial government. When the premier of Ontario's heart fails, she makes the politically expedient decision to seek a human heart donor instead of the accepted course of using a heart from the porcine organ farms, which have recently become controversial when the Epsilon Virus jumped from pigs to people due to the antigens used to suppress the pig immune systems on the organ farms. Premier Uttley's advisors suggest that she can regain the popularity she has lost through the debacle of Toronto by reviving the human organ donor program, thus satisfying the animal rights activists who are opposed to harvesting porcine organs and also allaying people's fears about the spread of the virus. However, Uttley's plea for a human donor sets the sinister plot of *Brown Girl* into motion when a hospital administrator bribes Rudy to find a viable heart, and Rudy orders his henchman, Tony, to murder Mami in order to steal her heart for transplantation into Premier Uttley.[11] The symbolism of this murderous heart theft is obvious: a weak-hearted, self-interested public leader in league with cold-hearted gang lord steals the still-beating heart of Mami, a poor woman of color who is at the heart of the urban Toronto community.

This plot illuminates the darker possibilities of cadaveric organ "harvesting" and frames organ theft as an environmental injustice in which certain people might be deemed natural resources, valuable only for their body parts, instead of as persons with intrinsic value and human rights, including the right to live.[12] Once human organs are viewed as harvestable resources, it then becomes possible to literally expropriate them, stripping them out of their original hosts for implantation into other bodies. This removal might be seen as an ultimate form of biopiracy and bodily colonization that literally dismembers the colonized person in order to incorporate their body parts into the colonizer's body.[13] Hopkinson emphasizes this point, when the hospital technicians completely disregard Mami's head injury and do nothing to see if her life might still be saved, focusing only on assuring the viability of her heart, which they refer to as "biomaterial" (152).[14] The novel makes visible some of the more ghastly aspects of current organ donation systems, such as the fact that most viable transplant organs are harvested from bodies that have undergone violent deaths, and that as violent deaths from car accidents, other accidents, and murders decrease, fewer donors are available to provide viable organs. As the novel illustrates, scarcity of voluntary organ donors has given rise to serious fears that the process of organ donation or organ sale might become corrupted, with vulnerable populations, such as poor people of color (particularly women and children), being targeted by those with money and power for purchase of "spare" parts such as kidneys, or, far worse, for the violent and deadly theft of their vital organs.[15]

In *Brown Girl*, Premier Uttley's desire for a human heart leads directly to Mami's murder, raising important questions about the race, class, gender, and geopolitics of organ "donors" and organ "recipients." This theft symbolizes the real inequities of the international organ trade, in which, for example, skin, corneas, and kidneys might be harvested for sale from executed Chinese prisoners, or desperately poor women in India might sell one kidney or a portion of a liver.[16] Furthermore, while the practice of organ transplantation clearly does save recipients' lives, it also raises ethical questions about our disparate health care system and inequitable funding of medical treatments. In the novel, as in much of the actual world, mainstream medical services are not available or affordable for the poor, and the exorbitantly expensive medical crews who visit the city on rare occasion have been dubbed "the Vultures": "The price for established medical care was so high that only the desperately ill would call for help. If you saw a Vulture making a house call, it meant that someone was near death" (8). Ironically, the only time the Vultures appear in the novel, they live up to their nickname of carrion eaters when they arrive to prey upon the dying by seeking Mami's viable heart. Not only does the medical establishment not serve the poor in Hopkinson's novel, but the poor now serve as a consumable medical resource, supplying the biomaterial for expensive organ transplant procedures for those in the wealthy suburbs. Clearly, as described in this novel, organ transplantation is an environmental justice health issue raising serious ethical, social, and environmental questions about the integrity of bodies and the power politics of health care.

Similar to *Dawn*, *Brown Girl in the Ring* also features a young black female protagonist who must strategically address the environmental injustices that threaten her family and community, and she illustrates the sorts of motivations that draw actual women into grass-roots environmental justice activism. Ti-Jeanne, who is Mami and Rudy's granddaughter, must seek recourse for Mami's murder and the theft of her heart, and muster the courage to challenge Rudy and end his exploitative and destructive reign. While Ti-Jeanne has lived with Mami and worked as her apprentice for as long as she can remember, she has also been fearful of Mami's spiritual powers and reluctant to learn about her own spiritual visions and visitations; she has been in love with Tony, a young man with medical training who is now a drug dealer and addict and who is the member of Rudy's posse assigned to secure Mami's heart. Mami's murder galvanizes Ti-Jeanne, pushing her to embrace her visionary powers, to call upon and imaginatively use the guidance of the loas, and to battle her grandfather in order to free the community from his bloody grasp. As a granddaughter and daughter, she must save her mother from enslavement as Rudy's duppy and avenge her foremothers' sufferings, and as a young mother, she must free her baby from the spirit who has taken refuge in his body and release Tony, the baby's father, from Rudy's influence. While Ti-Jeanne's battle with Rudy does not take the typical form of most environmental justice struggles, she resembles many of the women in these movements, who are radicalized through immediate family concerns that are enmeshed with larger social/environmental community issues driven by local and regional politics. In order to defeat Rudy's deadly powers, Ti-Jeanne assembles a force of supernatural allies. She calls the ancestors, or loas, down from the skies and the spirits of Rudy's many human victims, including numbers of street children sacrificed to feed his duppy, up from the earth. Together with Ti-Jeanne, these spirits release Rudy's supernatural powers, kill him, and set the spirits of his victims to rest. This cosmic battle overturns the praxis of Rudy and the provincial government that assumes urban people are mere resource objects for consumption—a view that endorses biopiracy, the theft of bodies, blood, souls—for someone else's advantage. Instead Ti-Jeanne and her forces represent a triumph of a holistic, affirmative, collective praxis that justly reclaims the urban environment of Toronto for its residents and signifies the way that indigenous and other spiritual practices may serve as a vital resource for environmental justice struggles, which have often originated in churches or other spaces of worship.

The novel also ends with a change of heart in the larger political realm. After Mami's heart is transplanted into Premier Uttley's body, an internal battle ensues in which the heart rejects the body and takes control of it, instituting a form of symbiosis whereby Mami's heart/values will be merged with Uttley's political strategies: while Premier Uttley had formerly been a self-serving politician, coldheartedly disinterested in the struggles of her urban constituents, she now announces her intentions to rejuvenate Toronto by offering assistance to the small businesses, squatters, and resourceful people of the city—a promising strategy for nurturing environmental justice for the city. She also announces her plan to create a "presumed consent" human organ donor program that would create a much larger pool of viable organs, and therefore, hopefully, put an end to any illicit traffic in human organs such as the murder that provided for her own transplant.[17] This novel ends optimistically, with a vision of environmental justice rising over the horizon, roused through the perseverance of women of color working with indigenous spiritual powers and other community members to defeat the corrupt and to infiltrate and transform the political establishment.

Nalo Hopkinson's and Octavia Butler's speculative visions of the future urge us to expand our understanding of environmental justice health issues to encompass the biomedical colonization of the bodies of women of color. When we read *Dawn* and *Brown Girl in the Ring* within an environmental justice context, both novels suggest that we must guard against possible misuse of new biotechnologies for purposes of exploitation and biopiracy, and that we must be especially wary of environmental justifications for biomedical incursions into the bodies of women of color. If, as Vandana Shiva argues, the next frontier for colonization is the internal worlds within Third World women, then our work for environmental justice must seek to protect these genetic and organic bodies from those who would prey upon them as natural resources, ripe for harvest. Butler and Hopkinson's speculative novels illuminate the complex and difficult position of black women who are currently negotiating such situations of environmental degradation, resisting bodily invasions, and working for the physical and cultural survival of their peoples and communities. By heeding these futuristic parables, we might better understand how gender and sexuality may function as sites of vulnerability but also as sources of subversion for women facing environmental injustices.

NOTES

I wish to thank Valerie Kaalund for telling me the remarkable, true story of Henrietta Lacks, a young African American woman who died of cervical cancer in 1951, but whose cervical cells had been "harvested," presumably with either coerced or no permission from her family, and then used by Dr. George Gay to create the first successful human cell lines for experimentation. As mentioned in the epigraph of this essay, the HeLa cells (that bear an abbreviated version of Henrietta Lacks' name, although few people know this) are incredibly resilient and have gone on to reproduce themselves around the globe and even in outer space, achieving a sort of immortality of their own. The idea that a black woman's cancerous cells would be harvested without her consent and become the essential basis for so much scientific research is a blood-chilling example of the sort of biopiracy that I discuss throughout this essay—and a fascinating parallel to what happens to Lilith in Butler's novel. In the case of Henrietta Lacks, truth is, unfortunately, every bit as strange and unsettling as fiction.

1. *Dawn* has received much critical attention, most of which focuses upon the interchanges and exchanges between the Oankali and the captive humans they have rescued. While critics agree that *Dawn* explores human fears of difference and alienness, and that the Oankali's social structure and ways of life offer some positive alternatives to terran social norms and human hierarchies and binaristic patterns of thought, critics are in disagreement as to whether or not the Oankali offer a utopian model of egalitarian exchange or institute another form of colonization and enslavement of the rescued humans. For example, Stacey Alaimo, in *Undomesticated Ground*, focuses upon the positive value of the Oankali employment of a "corporeally based empathic ethic" and the way that they "eschew hierarchies and affirm difference" (2000, 145–46). In contrast, Rebecca Holden argues in "The High Costs of Cyborg Survival" that despite such traits, the Oankali function as "imperialistic colonizers" whose "absorption of difference" is still a form of domination of their partner species (1998, 51).

2. See, for example, Holden 1998, Amanda Boulter 1996, Donna Haraway 1991, and Michelle Osherow 2000, among others.

3. See Rachel Stein, *Shifting the Ground: American Women Writers' Revisions of Nature, Gender, and Race.*

4. President George W. Bush has diverted funds into programs that will encourage poor

women to marry while at the same time cutting U.S. contributions to the United Nations programs that provide birth control counseling and materials to poor women. For more discussion of coercive controls of women of color's fertility, see Marsha J. Tyson Darling 1999 and April Taylor 1999.

5. See, for example, Vandana Shiva 1997, Taylor 1999, and Giovanna Di Chiro's chapter in this volume for discussion of the eugenics possibilities of biogenetic research.

6. Shiva writes that "the invasion and takeover of the life of organisms as the new colonies is being made possible through the technology of genetic engineering. Biotechnology . . . makes it possible to colonize and control that which is autonomous, free, and self-regenerative. . . . Technological development under capitalist patriarchy proceeds steadily from what it has already transformed and used up, driven by its predatory appetite, toward that which has still not been consumed" (1997, 45).

7. Rebecca Holden makes very strong points about Lilith's lack of free choice and the many forms of self-betrayal that her survival entails: "she must betray her gender, her race, and her species" (1998, 49). Holden notes that Lilith's lack of free choice is typical of that many African American women throughout history: "once they choose to survive, few other choices remain available" (52).

8. See Justine Smith 1999.

9. The "Principles of Environmental Justice" adopted by the First National People of Color Environmental Justice Leadership Summit in 1991 included respect for indigenous spiritual relationships between humans and the natural world. Devon Pena and Laura Pullido are two environmental justice theorists who describe how important cultural traditions and spiritual relationships to the natural world are to Hispano communities working to maintain themselves in the face of environmental injustices. Similarly, in her essay for this anthology, Valerie Kaalund describes the spiritual basis of many African American women's environmental justice work. Mami offers this sort of spiritual sustenance to the Toronto community.

10. For example, in Giovanna Di Chiro's interview with Baltimore activists Bryant Smith and Cinder Hypki, "Sustaining the 'Urban Forest' and Creating Landscapes of Hope," they discuss the process of community members reclaiming public spaces from drug activity in order to make parks and green spaces available to children and others. Peter Medoff and Holly Sklar's *Streets of Hope* describes a similar process of reclamation in Roxbury, Mass.

11. I am struck by the way that this instance of organ theft mirrors the way that Rudy already objectifies and consumes the bodies of those in his community when he feeds their blood and bodies to his duppy spirits.

12. Two other environmental justice novels that feature the theme of organ theft are Leslie Marmon Silko's *Almanac of the Dead* and Karen Tei Yamashita's *Tropic of Orange*.

13. Organ donation has been enabled by the legal/medical concept of "brain death" in which a person may be declared dead if brain functions cease, even though other bodily functions, such as heartbeat, continue. This has allowed surgeons to harvest organs in usable condition for transplantation. Countries such as the United States and Canada have adopted this definition of death, which allows for organ harvest, while many other countries of the world still do not accept this concept. Margaret Lock compares the different attitudes toward brain death and organ transplantation in the United States and Japan and writes about the ethical considerations raised by this changing definition of death in *Twice Dead: Organ Transplants and the Reinvention of Death*

(2002). One might argue that the concept of brain death allows us to colonize the bodies of the dying.

14. This gruesome fictional scene echoes descriptions of actual harvesting of organs from live Chinese prisoners, who have been shot in the head but also drugged and even respirated to keep their hearts beating until their organs can be removed for transplant to members of the Communist elite or foreigners who have purchased these body parts. No consideration is given to the pain and suffering of the prisoners. See Carl Becker 1999.

15. Several contributors to *The Ethics of Organ Transplants* (Caplan and Coelho 1998) express concerns about race and class inequities in the organ transplant system and raise fears about the real possibilities of present and future corruption of harvesting and distribution of organs. See Robert Gaston et al. 1998 and Renee Fox and Judith Swazey 1998.

16. Journalists and even medical practitioners have described such practices, which are driven by the scarcity of viable organs, the helplessness of certain populations such as prisoners, and the desperation of the poor. See Craig Smith 2001 and Fox and Swazey 1998.

17. There is currently debate about presumed consent systems, in which everyone is presumed to be a donor unless they have expressly forbidden the harvesting of their organs. While such systems create a greater supply of organs, they also essentially force all viable donors into the system without obtaining their assent.

REFERENCES

Alaimo, Stacy. 2000. *Undomesticated Ground: Recasting Nature as Feminist Space*. Ithaca: Cornell University Press.

Becker, Carl. 1999. "Money Talks, Money Kills: The Economics of Transplantation in Japan and China." *Bioethics* 13, no. 3 (July): 236–43.

Boulter, Amanda. 1996. "Polymorphous Future: Octavia Butler's *Xenogenesis* Trilogy." In *American Bodies: Cultural Histories of the Physique*, ed. Tim Armstrong. New York: New York University Press.

Butler, Octavia. 1987. *Dawn*. New York: Warner Books.

Caplan, Arthur. 1998. "Is Xenografting Morally Wrong?" In Caplan and Coelho 1998.

Caplan, Arthur L., and Daniel Coelho, eds. 1998. *The Ethics of Organ Transplants: The Current Debate*. Amherst, N.Y.: Prometheus Books.

Darling, Marsha J. Tyson. 1999. "The State: Friend or Foe? Distributive Justice Issues and African American Women." In Silliman and King 1999.

Di Chiro, Giovanna. 2002. "Sustaining the 'Urban Forest' and Creating Landscapes of Hope: An Interview with Cinder Hypki and Bryant 'Spoon' Smith." In *The Environmental Justice Reader: Politics, Poetics, and Pedagogy*, ed. Joni Adamson, Mei Mei Evans, and Rachel Stein. Tucson: University of Arizona Press.

Fox, Renee, and Judith Swazey. 1998. "Leaving the Field." In Caplan and Coelho 1998.

Gaston, Robert, Ian Ayres, Laura Dooley, and Arnold Diethelm. 1998. "Racial Equity in Renal Transplantation: The Disparate Impact of HLA-Based Allocation." In Caplan and Coelho 1998.

Haraway, Donna. 1991. *Simians, Cyborgs, and Women: The Reinvention of Nature*. New York: Routledge.

Holden, Rebecca. 1998. "The High Costs of Cyborg Survival: Octavia Butler's *Xenogenesis* Trilogy." *Foundation* 72 (spring): 49–57.

Hopkinson, Nalo. 1998. *Brown Girl in the Ring*. New York: Warner Books.

Lock, Margaret. 2002. *Twice Dead: Organ Transplants and the Reinvention of Death*. Berkeley: University of California Press.

Medoff, Peter, and Holly Sklar. 1994. *Streets of Hope: The Fall and Rise of an Urban Neighborhood*. Cambridge, Mass.: South End Press.

Osherow, Michelle. 2000. "The Dawn of a New Lilith: Mythmaking in Women's Science Fiction." *NWSA Journal* 12, no. 1 (spring): 68–83.

Shiva, Vandana. 1997. *Biopiracy: The Plunder of Nature and Knowledge*. Cambridge, Mass.: South End Press.

Silliman, Jael, and Ynestra King. 1999. *Dangerous Intersections: Feminist Perspectives on Population, Environment, and Development*. Cambridge, Mass.: South End Press.

Skloot, Rebecca. 2000. "Henrietta's Dance." *Johns Hopkins Magazine* (Apr.). http://jhu.edu/~jhumag/0400web/01.html.

Smith, Craig. 2001. "Doctor Says He Took Transplant Organs from Executed Chinese Prisoners." *New York Times*, June 29, A10.

Smith, Justine. 1999. "Native Sovereignty and Social Justice: Moving toward an Inclusive Social Justice Framework." In Silliman and King 1999.

Stein, Rachel. 1997. *Shifting the Ground: American Women Writers' Revisions of Nature, Gender, and Race*. Charlottesville: University Press of Virginia.

Taylor, April J. 1999. "High Tech, Pop-a-Pill Culture: 'New' Forms of Social Control for Black Women." In Silliman and King 1999.

13

Home Everywhere and the Injured Body of the World

The Subversive Humor of *Blue Vinyl*

ARLENE PLEVIN

Environmentalists talk about "sacrifice communities"–what the Citizens Awareness Network calls areas "generally poor and rural" chosen to house our toxic waste and nuclear power.

–Susanne Antonetta, *Body Toxic: An Environmental Memoir*

The comic way . . . is the path of reconciliation. When the usual patterns of life are disrupted, the comic spirit strives for a return to normalcy.

–Joseph Meeker, *The Comedy of Survival: Literary Ecology and a Play Ethic*

In "A Fable for Tomorrow," the first chapter of *Silent Spring*, a book many consider the harbinger of the modern environmental movement, Rachel Carson shows the snake in the Edenic suburban garden, the disrupter of innocence and surface beauty. For Carson, there is an "evil spell [that] had settled on the community," which threatens this once-upon-a-time "town in the heart of America where all life seemed to live in harmony with its surroundings" (Carson 1962, 13). The spoiler silences the birds and other animals: not only do trees wither but reproduction ceases. It is not, as Carson poignantly details, due to "enemy action" or "witchcraft" (14), but the deadly chemical DDT (dichlorodiphenyl-trichloroethane), part of the "chain of evil" that evokes Carson's apocalyptic narrative of this hypothetical town, one that could be Anywhere USA. "The most alarming," Carson writes, "of all man's assaults upon the environment is the contamination of air, earth, rivers, and sea with dangerous and even lethal materials" (16). Carson's seriousness could not be more clear; it is a problem of profound and pervasive depth, perhaps the more powerfully pronounced because it is in a lovely pastoral setting, a kind of domestic heaven in "the midst of a checkerboard of prosperous farms . . . where, in spring, white clouds of bloom drifted above the green fields" (13). As Carson continues to articulate her vision, its Shakespearean echoes of "Hamlet" are transparent: something is very, very rotten in the state.

Some forty years later, in the heart of East Coast suburbia, Florence Helfand opens her daughter Judith's latest documentary, *Blue Vinyl*, on a somewhat lighter note, disgustedly muttering "farkrokhn," her Yiddish for rotten.[1] For Florence and her husband Ted, rotten represents the softening, peeling wood on the outside of their Merrick, New York, home. Now falling apart at the touch and able to be excavated with just a fingernail, the wood must be replaced. This modest starter ranch of red clapboard was where daughter Judith and her brothers were raised; as is typical for many middle-class families, its sale will constitute most of Florence and Ted's retirement funds, and so the home must be maintained—its investment value preserved. As the disintegrating outside skin of the house is removed, Florence reacts to her daughter's pleas not to recover the house with blue vinyl, suggesting this change is small, one of many with which her daughter will have to deal. Florence ties the loss of the wood to the loss her daughter's own body underwent, a radical hysterectomy at age twenty-five due to cervical cancer caused by DES (diethylstilbestrol) exposure in utero. Florence speaks directly to the camera: "I think you're reacting to this like it's a loss in your life. You're gonna lose a lot of other precious things in your life as time goes on. And you already have, you've had one terrible loss. So I just feel you're overreacting a little bit" (2).[2]

With this opening, *Blue Vinyl*, produced and directed by Judith Helfand and Daniel B. Gold, aligns itself firmly with feminist concerns about treatment of the female body, raising issues of class and gender, while documenting an environmental activism that will prove to be both humorous and intergenerational. Over the course of the film, Ted and Florence's attitudes toward corporate and finally governmental responsibility, and toward their daughter's research, are reshaped. Their decision to replace their home's rotting clapboard with blue vinyl siding "embossed . . . with fake woodprint," Judith Helfand laughs almost disbelievingly, helps mobilize this stage of her environmental activism, a kind of muckraking, a step-by-step journey (complete with semicomedic heroine) into who is injured by the seemingly benign products with which the middle-class often naively surround themselves (2). For Ted and Florence Helfand, who had already learned harsh lessons when DES caused their daughter so much harm, *Blue Vinyl* pushes them into drawing from that experience to explore what is left of their unexamined consumer ideologies, which assume anything available for purchase must be beneficial—or at least benign—along with that perspective's corresponding neglect and sacrifice of economically powerless and usually invisible communities. Judith Helfand ironically transforms the last of her settlement money from a lawsuit against one of DES's manufacturers into seed money for exploring Lake Charles, Louisiana, a major site for the manufacture of polyvinyl chloride, and other sites of environmental injustice. She employs the film to document community activism and her own evolving relationship with her parents as their initial reluctance to question the status quo is ruptured. *Blue Vinyl* lays out the often unexamined story of the manufacturing side of the vinyl industry, all the while employing the subversive yet inviting tactic of humor to help create an approachable and vulnerable persona that bridges distance, generation, even class. Billed as a toxic comedy by directors Gold and Helfand, *Blue Vinyl* measures out its message of environmental coverup and industry collusion while setting up Helfand as a kind of quixotic hero. She is one that might be seen not as "overreacting a little bit," as her mother claims, but as employing humor to shape viewers' reactions to the environmental activism of *Blue Vinyl* while creating a space for anyone to join in, to see themselves as potential activists, part of the struggle.

The documentary's sense of humor is key to broadening its appeal, creating an unusual mix of comedy and tragedy, which helps reassert Helfand's own activism and power. In the face of loss of her own reproductive options, Helfand reaffirms her ability to be productive and, in the documentary's last scenes, build another kind of extended family, one predicated on environmental justice and one that is cognizant of the consequences of its actions. Whereas DES use and misuse disrupts the historical relationship between mothers and daughters, humor, environmental justice, and activism proffer another healing—that of the individual's efforts, the home, the community, and activist alliances. In many respects, producers Gold and Helfand create a primer for environmental activism, a blueprint for future endeavors. This blueprint may be seen as radical in its ability to connect the dots between workers, manufacturing communities at risk, and consumers—relationships that cross class, race, and geography. Connecting Helfand's own loss from the poisoning of her body to that of others' homes and communities, *Blue Vinyl* argues for a global concept of home. By its last reel, *Blue Vinyl* can be understood to suggest not only *why* one might explore the potentially harmful effects and origins of products in our daily lives but *how* to do so.

The film's initial exploration of the relationship between the individual female body and the world locates *Blue Vinyl* in the realm of a kind of ecological feminism. Helfand's apparent nostalgia for the former condition of her childhood home—the loss of which her mother encourages her to accept under the rubric of necessary change—suggests a standard marker of feminist concern, according to Carolyn Merchant. In *Earthcare* Merchant writes, "For ecologists and feminists the Earth's house and the human house are habitats to be cherished" (Merchant 1995, 146). This regard for both positions them as deserving attention and suggests such concern archetypally lodges with women. According to Merchant and others, aligning the earth's condition with that of the body and home is natural and an issue of equity: "The body, home, and community are sites of women's local experiences and local contestation. Women experience the results of toxic dumping on their own bodies (sites of reproduction of the species), in their own homes (sites of the reproduction of daily life), and in their communities and schools (sites of social reproduction)" (Merchant 1995, 161).

Female health is intrinsically linked with the community's health; to examine the ill health of one is to consider its repercussions on the other and to explore how genders are affected differently by corporate actions, which reify society's historical maltreatment of female bodies. Jim Tarter, in "Some Live More Downstream Than Others: Cancer, Gender, and Environmental Justice," investigates this, quoting feminist cancer activist and scientist Sandra Steingraber's response to "Why is cancer a feminist issue?" Steingraber explains, "It is a feminist issue because the parts of women's bodies that have been affected—our ovaries, our uterus, our breasts—are the parts of the body that have been despised, objectivified, fetishized" (Tarter 2002, 222).

Concerned in moving beyond an objectified and gendered treatment of her body, Judith Helfand offers her experience to show, among other things, her family and film viewers that we have been here before. However, with individual and community activism, there's a chance of moving beyond this point. While Helfand's mother evokes Judith's hysterectomy as a "tragic loss," for Judith it reinforces the realization that the corporate chemical and pharmaceutical world not only obfuscates the insidious nature of some of its products, harming female bodies and later the minority bodies of those without economic voices, but that the legal compensation for such doings (Judith wryly labels her settlement "uterus money") can deliciously enable the exposure of such practices. As workers strip the Helfand home of decaying wood in the first scene of the film, Judith narrates, "Back when she was pregnant with me, my mother was given a drug called DES, a synthetic estrogen that was supposed to prevent miscarriage. Turned out the pharmaceutical industry knew all along that it didn't. What it did do was give me a rare form of cervical cancer" (2). While the camera pans over the home being taken closer to its bones, Helfand adds, "Up to that point, the dangers of toxic chemical exposure hadn't really worried me. But then, I started questioning everything" (3).

For Helfand, the safety and sanity of the home is also to be questioned. While she never blames her mother for taking federally approved DES, she points out how the home and her mother's symbolic positioning as protector have been literally disrupted by a hormone-mimicking endocrine disrupter. By taking a drug whose overall effects on the developing fetus and the mother had not been adequately studied—DES was generally presented to prescribing gynecologists and obstetricians as a medication that would help prevent miscarriages—Florence Helfand unwittingly exposed her daughter in utero to what would later prompt removal of that child's own womb. The footnotes in the transcription of the HBO version of *Blue Vinyl* explain—and I offer just a sampling of the extensive research cited in a two-page, nine-point footnote on pages 2 and 3 of the documentary's transcript, which was actually from work done on "A Healthy Baby Girl," Helfand's first documentary. Emphasis is mine:

> *Pharmaceutical companies never did studies about the possible long term effects on pregnant women and the fetus* or controlled studies on the efficacy of the drug before or after the 1947 FDA approval for the use of DES during pregnancy, even in light of numerous early tests/studies on animals that indicated both carcinogenic and teratogenic effects of DES [C.F., Geschickter, "Mammary Carcinoma in the Rat with Metastasis Induced by Estrogen," *Science* 89 (1939), 35–37] . . . ; Specific questions were raised about the effect of DES on pregnant women and the fetus by the Rosenblum-Melinkoff Study (mentioned above) which was cited by pharmaceutical companies: ". . . although generally favorable to DES, *[the study] stated specifically that there were 'many questions which have not as yet been completely answered,' including 'Is diethylstilbestrol, in such large doses carcinogenic, and as such unsafe to give even to pregnant women?'* and 'Can diethylstilbestrol in any way affect the glandular balance of the child in utero, particularly the male child?'" Diana B. Dutton, Worse Than Disease (Cambridge: Cambridge University, 1988) 52–53. (2–3)

As the research in *Blue Vinyl* demonstrates, there was little reason that Florence Helfand—or the estimated five million other women encouraged to take the drug by their prescribing physicians—should have known that DES was not only not warranted but also not, as various researchers suggested, studied for dispensing to pregnant women and their unborn children.[3] Roberta J. Apfel's categorization of the broadening of the application of DES as "stunning," seen from the footnotes of *Blue Vinyl*, seems remarkably understated:

> In 1947, partly in response to studies by Olive Smith and George Smith, several drug companies filed a supplementary NDA [New Drug Application] to permit the use of DES during pregnancy and to allow the production of a 25mg pill in addition to the 1, 2 and 5 mg pills. This request was granted . . . *Stunningly the expansion of DES usage to pregnancy and the introduction of larger doses were done by simple administrative fiat.* No new research data or reviews were required and the use of DES was now exempted from official regulatory constraint." (emphasis added) Roberta J. Apfel PhD, *To Do No Harm* (New Haven: Yale University, 1984) 19–20. (3)

This focus on toxicity in the womb is also echoed in Susanne Antonetta's work in *Body Toxic: An Environmental Memoir*, where she shares what she suspects began her lifetime exposure to disruptive chemicals in New Jersey, underscoring

Rachel Carson's warnings: "DDT arrived commercially in 1942, making my mother at least twenty-two . . . I feel like those trucks powdered me in the womb. They came once a week or so, supplemented by planes: a spume, a round gray meteorological event of pesticide. The trucks stopped only when the United States banned DDT in the seventies" (Antonetta 2001, 17).[4] The womb, the first home of the child, often a symbol of sanctuary, and the familial home outside of that, is vulnerable, recast—and one might argue usurped—as the site of corporate earnings. Commenting on that reworking and highlighting this concern for feminism, Merchant cites Robert Bullard's work with the United Church of Christ's 1987 antitoxics campaign: in a report they titled "Toxic Wastes and Race in the United States," they noted, "Long term goals include the redistribution of wealth and environmental goods and services" (Merchant 1995, 161). Crucially, the need for such reform recognizes and reinforces what Merchant states earlier in *Earthcare*: "The home, where in fact women and children spend much of their time, is no longer a haven" (1995, 147).

For Susanne Antonetta and Judith Helfand, their time before birth affords little protection from what can be viewed as government-sanctioned heedlessness. Prompted in part by how their own bodies were affected by chemicals, they look outward, to their physical world and the community at large. Standing outside her parents' now vinyl-covered home, the vinyl provoking approval from Ted Helfand, Judith's own encounters with pharmaceutical companies' disingenuousness prompt her to wonder if the home is no longer a haven, what is the status of the community in which production of the vinyl siding was situated. Helfand narrates, "Everyone assured me vinyl siding was safe, and would only let off toxic gas in the rare event of a house fire. But, after my experience with DES I figured any material so loaded with synthetic chemicals had to pose some kind of risk" (4).

For Helfand, aware of her own body's transformation by chemicals whose effects were hidden from legions of mothers and doctors, out of sight cannot become out of mind. Reaching beyond orderly, tree-lined Bayview Avenue in Merrick, Long Island, Helfand begins her journey to understand just what her parents' purchase might represent. Uncertain of vinyl's toxicity but suspicious of synthetic chemicals, she cannot just let it go: she needs more information, the source of vinyl, its particular "home." And part of her search is also understanding the nature of what informed her parents' selection of vinyl, how consumers—and communities—are kept from information that would enable them not to poison their bodies and others. Foreshadowing what *Blue Vinyl* will uncover about vinyl and its by-products, Helfand asks at the film's beginning: "Later, I asked my dad, If 'SOMEONE HAD TOLD YOU THAT over the course of its lifecycle, from the factory to the incinerator, vinyl COULD PRODUCE a wide array of deadly pollutants that threaten our future with a global toxic crisis, would you still have put it on the house?'

'I hope not, honey,' he said. 'But they didn't write that on the box'" (4–5). With *Blue Vinyl*, however, filmmakers Judith Helfand and Daniel Gold will create a film that makes clear the writing on the "box," and with community activists, lawyers, epidemiologists, and scientists show just what a Pandora's box vinyl is. In this respect, it can be said that for *Blue Vinyl's* filmmakers, the world does not end with their bodies.

Crucially, the journey to uncover the truth about cradle-to-grave life cycle of vinyl mixes humor—and a dry sense of self-deprecation—with often tragic losses brought on by this pervasive product and its key ingredients. For producers Helfand and Gold, the consistently serious tone of Rachel Carson's warnings in her 1962 book *Silent Spring* is not the only way to go. As *Blue Vinyl* takes to the road, tracing vinyl's presence in Louisiana and Venice, Italy, it establishes the links between all communities and the provocative power of humor—that humor itself can indicate a personality undiminished by loss. Here *Blue Vinyl's* contradictory-sounding label of a "toxic comedy" aptly signals its approach to environmental activism, one that enables a fuller flavor of people's lives to emerge.

Carting with her a sheath of her parent's home siding approximately the size of an infant, Helfand travels first to Lake Charles, Louisiana, where one third of the manufacturing takes place of North America's PVC (polyvinyl chloride), an ingredient of all vinyl products. Contrasting tidy and seemingly benign Merrick, cinematographer Gold shoots an aerial view of the dramatic night skyline of industrial America, one and half hours from the part of the United States dubbed "Cancer Alley." Flares dot the horizon, and, pouring from industrial high rises, smoke and unidentified pollutants—the flora and fauna of chemical production—gray the night. It is both oddly beautiful and immediately daunting. Just what is being produced and who is breathing it? Following this footage, Helfand appears in a neighborhood grocery shop during Mardi Gras, wearing a brightly colored joker hat suitable for such exuberant celebrations. Standing at the counter, Helfand explains the reason for her visit to the amused clerk: "Oh. My parents put, um, vinyl siding on our house, and, um, I came to the vinyl capital of America to find out all about it" (6).

Outside, life continues as it would for Mardi Gras: people laugh and cavort, sometimes in skimpy clothes, and the film juxtaposes these images with shots of area chemical plants. Bringing her *Blue Vinyl* remnant from Merrick onto the scene, Judith invites two locals to decorate it with Mardi Gras beads. Laughing, they drape the brightly colored strings over the siding while Helfand exclaims, "All right! That's beautiful" (5). At once decorated and defused, the piece of blue vinyl bridges the two disparate worlds and helps the hat-clad Helfand create a persona that is both serious and accessible—she's just one of the folks just having fun, and she is not, despite the potential to characterize her as suffering from a loss, a victim. As the jaunty background music—"No It Ain't My Fault" by Joseph "Smokey" Johnson and Wardell Quezerque—invites one to tap feet, pick up another brass instrument, or join in the Mardi Gras rejoicing, the blue vinyl is present but not in one's face. We know it is there, lurking like some kind of chemical shark, but for now we have music and bodies happily moving to it, Mardi Gras juxtaposed with shots of smokestacks and plants. Plump cows graze in front of a barbed-wire protected plant and residents swim in water right next to manufacturing sites. The integration of the beginning of Helfand's quest to uncover vinyl's origins with this world-renowned Louisiana celebration demonstrates the tragic and comic elements of *Blue Vinyl* and invites viewer laughter and identification with the denial most live with in everyday life. Against the energetic, colorful backdrop of Mardi Gras, Helfand foregrounds another aspect of daily life for the people of Lake Charles—and reminds us of the unjust economy and the cost of doing toxic business operating here.

Building off her father's initial response to Helfand's query about vinyl's toxicity, *Blue Vinyl* unfolds the increasingly sorry story of vinyl and its by-products. As local industries hold what is billed as "the first ever community-wide risk management meeting," her voice-over intones, "Their goal was to reassure area residents that in the event of a worst-case scenario, everything is under control" (7). As Bob Hassler, a plant manager of the Conoco Refinery in Lake Charles, attempts to reassure, *Blue Vinyl* records the open fears of a woman, worried about the plant's emissions, her home, and her body. Her tone is both tentative and forceful: "I'd like to ask you a question please. During the summer we had one of the flares across the street from our house that let out some raw material. When I say raw material, it was falling on you as you were outside, you had to run in the house and—with your hands on your face to be able to breathe" (7). Mr. Hardy, an older African American, expresses more of the doubt and concern felt in the community: "You leave here and go up north of here and you look and see how green the trees is on both sides. Here, on the south side they brown. Do you, do you think that's a chemical that's killing 'em, or do you think that's natural?" (7).

With these observations, Hardy and the unidentified woman offer their firsthand experience, a knowledge that the plant manager attempts to devalue in a patronizing manner. Ignoring Hardy's experience in the community, even denying his grassroots understanding, Hassler's response is to cite corporate "safety" mechanisms. He addresses Hardy directly, saying, "Sometime we can give you a tour out there and let you see the control facilities on those tanks" (7). Hardy, however, is not persuaded by the offer to witness so-called control. Defiant and trusting his own judgment, he counters, "I worked out there for thirty-five years and five months, I don't need your tour. I know what goes on. I don't need your tour. I'm telling you what I know" (7–8). From querying about the possible contamination of trees "on the south side" near the plant to refusing to be quiet and relying on his own intuition and years of experience, Hardy demonstrates a beginning activism—speaking up for one's convictions and doing it in a public place. He resists what could be considered the canned response, the public relations spin: his is the neighborhood's knowledge and he will not be budged.

It is what Hardy, the community citizen, knows that Helfand seeks information about. New to Lake Charles, she is not content to stop with the industry's benign presentation of vinyl and vinyl products. Reminding us of vinyl's presence and her legitimate connection to her own seemingly distant New York home, Helfand narrates: "Maybe Mr. Hardy didn't need a tour, but I did. My father's answer to rotten wood was looking more and more like somebody else's toxic hazard. And I wanted a better idea of just what went on inside a vinyl plant" (7–8). Helfand's suspicions and recognition of her limitations prompts further investigation. Her home is also the home of the world; the film documents her growing need to move beyond Long Island into a familiarity with others' communities—and the consequences of vinyl production and incineration on them. Denied a tour of the plant, Helfand demonstrates another intrinsic characteristic of activism—tenacity, even creativity. She goes to the website of the Vinyl Institute, the industry's trade association, which carefully relates how pervasive vinyl is (http://*www.vinylinfo.org*). Through simply drawn animated images of pipes, cell phones, credit cards, skies, medical equipment, televisions, and even children's toys morphing into one another, *Blue Vinyl* animator Emily Hubley shows us that vinyl is everywhere. This theme is reiterated by the representatives of the Vinyl Institute Helfand meets next, conversations that illustrate, as well, a kind of logic that refuses analysis. Handling Helfand's piece of vinyl siding, by now a character in the film, vinyl industry representative Sandy enthusiastically notes: "I feel very comfortable touching it, I've hung it, I've put it on people's houses, I really like it. I think it's a really great product, it uses our, um, resources well. It's 56 percent chlorine. We have a lot of chlorine in the world. We've got a lot of salt in the ocean. We're not hurting the environment" (11). Helfand, as she confesses, may not be a scientist, but like her mother, she knows something is rotten. Like Mr. Hardy in Lake Charles, she will trust her instincts, noting, "Now I was really worried. The Vinyl Institute representatives wanted me to believe that vinyl and table salt were more or less the same thing. Even I knew they weren't. The problem was, my grasp of basic chemistry stopped there. I needed a science lesson, so I invited some experts to the house" (12).

In an echo of a door-to-door Avon sales call, *Blue Vinyl* segues to Charlie Cray and Rick Hind, two members of Greenpeace and experts in vinyl chloride and dioxin, ringing the Helfand doorbell. They are the first of many experts the film will employ to show the range of information available, for the most part, to the average person. Joined by Joe Thornton, a Ph.D. in biology who has written about dioxin, and either seated outside with the blue house as a backdrop or inside providing a slide show, all three look like the boys next door. In this most suburban of domestic settings, *Blue Vinyl* continues to link the domain of the home with that of the world, providing the first of many facts about vinyl. According to Thornton: "You look at a house like this and the vinyl seems perfectly harmless. It's just sitting there, in front of the house, nobody's falling down with any diseases. But that's if you are only looking at the product itself. If you look at its entire lifecycle, from the moment it's produced, through its use, to the way it's disposed of, vinyl turns out to be the most environmentally hazardous consumer product on Earth. Vinyl is the source of more persistent toxic pollutants, dioxin in particular, than any other single [consumer] product in the world" (12).

Narrated in front of the neat blue home, this message jars, and viewers can understand better why Helfand's father is skeptical. On a sunny day, in a place far from manufacturing's fumes and particulates, the vinyl house looks benign and serene, the danger exaggerated. In keeping with that disarming suburban show of innocence (an it-can't-happen-here ambiance), Rick and Charlie give a slide show, using as a screen a white sheet anchored with knickknacks. As a transparency with a skull and crossbones graphic depicting the vinyl chloride molecule floats onto the sheet, we see a small pitcher and some ceramics, the flora and fauna of the everyday living room, pressing the top part of the sheet against a shelf. Not only can the experts come to the house, but fancy technological equipment to discover and discuss the problems is not needed. Judith Helfand reads a statistic from the International Association of Firefighters, "[e]xposure to a single PVC fire can cause permanent respiratory disease," and quickly connects it to her home and others. "Let's just talk about this house. In its inert form on the house it's fine, unless of course there was a house fire, and then it would be harmful to and then it would be harmful to the neighbors" (12–13). Greenpeace staffer Charlie Cray adds to "yourselves," contextualizing the damage from vinyl and continuing Helfand's associations between the toxic potential of vinyl siding and the community in which it is sited.

If activism can be considered, in part, to be the act of making hidden connections *visible, Blue Vinyl* manifests this process. As Helfand asks about "dioxin—a toxic pollutant that's created at both ends at the PVC lifecycle, when it's manufactured and when it's thrown away and burnt," the film makes transparent the linkage between cancer and vinyl production in the home and community, all foregrounding Helfand's own poisoning. Cray's answer, that "[d]ioxin causes many types of cancer and a whole range of other effects, especially those that effect the unborn infant and the newly born child," leads Helfand to voice and translate this perspective. Turning to her father in the darkened living room, the temporarily rigged screen slightly askew, Judith says: "Um, and Dad, in this context, it's sort of, it could act on the fetus the way that DES acted on me" (14). Her father's restrained "Mm-hmm" suggests the disbelief Judith notes he has just two minutes later, prompting the quest for additional data. We follow her to the home of another expert, George Lucier, Ph.D., former director of the NIH Environmental Toxicology Program, described as "a scientist highly regarded by both environmentalists and industry" (14). With Lucier, *Blue Vinyl* furthers its exposé of the kind and range of information available about vinyl and its overall accessibility to the public. In part prompted by *Blue Vinyl* and Sandy's claim about table salt, we see that Helfand's science lesson is for all of us, even skeptics like her father.

From the Merrick, Long Island, house to the office of Lake Charles lawyer Billy Baggett, *Blue Vinyl*'s scope widens, building its case against the vinyl industry while making transparent how it is done, what motivates people. Introducing the film's first lawyer, we are presented with what many beginning activists might have thought went first, the law. In this case, *Blue Vinyl* offers a dedicated, somewhat rumpled, agreeable champion for the locals who is himself a local. Baggett, whose archive is described as "the most extensive collections of internal chemical industry documents anywhere," has been working on behalf of vinyl industry workers for ten years (24). Baggett's dedication to locals' struggles to prove the damage was caused to their loved ones knowingly is about their bodies and their lives as lawyer and clients share the emotional motivation behind their activism. One of Baggett's clients, Elaine Ross, the widow of Daniel Ross, a vinyl worker for twelve years, relates for the film her husband's long, drawn-out death from cancer. Focusing on Elaine Ross' face as she struggles with sorrow, the camera lets her words tell the story. Out of sight is Helfand's ubiquitous blue vinyl. There is no music. There is no Helfand: she interviews from behind the camera. Ross shares: "My husband worked with vinyl every day . . . . I would've liked to have the people responsible in my house and watch him die one piece at a time, because I remember all of it. When he couldn't use his right arm anymore, when he couldn't use his left arm anymore, when he couldn't use his legs, and when he couldn't speak to me anymore. [cries] And when I couldn't hear his voice anymore" (21). Midway through Elaine Ross' monologue, there's a snapshot of Dan Ross, his eyes swollen shut and head swathed in bandages, with what looks to be a thick pad over one ear. The caption in the lower third of the screen reads "Dan Ross/Conoco Employee, 1967–1990" (21).

Blue Vinyl pauses to let the image of Dan Ross and his wife's pain at his suffering linger, then it returns to Baggett's office stuffed with millions of documents and staffed by his own indefatigable energy to pursue the chemical companies. As epidemiologist Gerry Markowitz, Ph.D. at the City University of New York, explains, "If it had not been for Billy's persistence in getting these documents from industry, the story of vinyl would never have been told" (24).

Dan Ross' poisoned body and the papers Baggett has snagged send Helfand from Lake Charles to Venice, Italy, with *Blue Vinyl* reasserting the humor and irony of such a move while reminding viewers of the affirmative quality of this continuing search for information and environmental justice. Ruefully Helfand says, "Vinyl is not exactly the first thing that leaps to mind when most people think of Venice, but Billy's documents led me straight to one of the largest PVC manufacturers in Europe—the EniChem Corporation—and to a group of former workers and widows just like Dan and Elaine Ross in Louisiana" (25). The film juxtaposes Helfand and her constant companion, the scrap of blue vinyl siding, with one of Venice's trademark symbols, the gondola. The camera angles in on the vinyl under her arm, the lovely old and inviting buildings of Venice placed behind the unlikely global traveler. We learn of vinyl chloride's effect on the Italian men who worked in EniChem and the ongoing trial where members of upper management are being sued for manslaughter—as individuals—in the names of those who have lost their lives or have been stricken by cancer.

The blue vinyl's continual appearance throughout the film serves to gently add humor to Helfand's serious inquiry into vinyl, making it palatable, always connected to the consumer, to Helfand's house. Laughter serves as a kind of panacea for some of the film's grim encounters with vinyl's manufacturing legacy. Later, when Helfand interviews a representative from the Vinyl Institute, the Insititute demands ground rules that suggest understanding of the power of Helfand's blue vinyl totem to both introduce the consumer connection to vinyl and undermine their credibility. The interview, as Helfand describes it, is finally agreed to and held, at the Vinyl Institute's invitation, "in the heart of an area in Louisiana known as Cancer Alley, in a hotel at the intersection of Corporate and Trust" (52). At this intersection of perfectly named, actual streets, Louisiana and corporate America seem both impervious to responsibility for their actions (or inaction) and unconscious of the-in-your-face irony of such signage. Helfand, nervous about this particular encounter "with a Ph.D. in chemistry who'd been working for the vinyl industry for the last twenty-two years" (52), agrees to the vinyl industry's ground rules but undermines them by making them transparent. These rules include "no props. Which meant no sugar packets, no salt, and there went my question about sex toys. No surprise documents or videotapes. No questions outside the expertise of their expert, and no more than thirty minutes for the whole thing. I was told to leave my blue vinyl siding at home" (54).

Evidently, her piece of blue vinyl from Long Island is too dangerous, its comedic potential undesirable. (Helfand does not get to ask the poised Vinyl Industry representative her question about sex toys, either.) Functioning as a kind of comedic ventriloquist's dummy, silently "speaking" for the presence of suburbia and so-called benign vinyl, the piece of siding is disruptive. Indeed, as blue vinyl takes us from community meetings to vinyl industry settings, Helfand and her blue vinyl become a kind of Laurel and Hardy team. The unexpected joining of an inquisitive, assertive woman and a static, leftover scrap of housing material yoke the two together in humor as well as investigative efforts. This casting reaffirms the kind of gentle self-deprecating stance Helfand takes throughout the documentary, which opens up the film's message and positions Helfand as almost one of the folks. It is a shrewd move, suggesting the environmental justice work Helfand will do and support with the film is lively and among the living—that uncovering the linkage between her home and the homes of others sited in toxic locations will remind us of our humanity and our ability to laugh, suggesting it is possible to achieve important social change and live beyond the moment, to forge a life out of tragedy that embraces humor. The deadpan juxtaposition of images such as the Corporate and Trust street signs and the sight of Helfand carting her blue vinyl into the most unlikely places remind us of the pervasiveness of vinyl and of our own ability to protest, to create laughter, and to demand more healthy alternatives than vinyl.

In *Laughing Feminism: Subversive Comedy in Frances Burney, Maria Edgeworth, and Jane Austin*, Audrey Bilger writes, "Recent theories of feminist humor emphasize how humor can serve both as a psychological survival skill and an emancipatory strategy for women in a sexist society" (1998, 10). Quoting Regina Barreca, Bilger explains that Barreca "sees women's laughter as essentially feminist: 'anytime a woman breaks through a barrier set by society, she's making a feminist gesture of a sort, and every time a woman laughs, she's breaking through a barrier.'" Creating laughter both ruptures a boundary and offers a necessary space for viewers to enter; things are serious but not impossible. Bilger suggests, "Feminist humor demands that its audience share an awareness of women's oppression and a desire to reform an unjust system" (10, 11).

In many respects, blue vinyl introduces and explains this historical oppression, but while we may have begun with Helfand's own body, we have been witness to the damaged bodies of many, both male and female. In the film's last scene, we see another version of family. Having used her settlement money to re-side her parents' house with wood salvaged from the roof of an old mill and stained with as nontoxic a covering as possible, the Helfands now have some 2,000 square feet of used blue vinyl that they cannot recycle (it does not recycle). In keeping with its portrayal of everyday heroes, everyday activists, Helfand, driving a U-Haul full of the old siding, clips a utility pole while turning into a nearby machine shop, which is all set to chop the blue vinyl into much more manageable size. Emerging with boxes upon boxes of 2" x 2" squares of blue vinyl, Ted, Florence, and Judith Helfand gather around that standard marker of American suburbia, the picnic table. In a low aerial view of their backyard, we see them attach the vinyl squares one by one to Mardi Gras beads. Florence affixes labels that announce:

This is Vinyl.
Don't burn it!
And don't throw it away!
[skull and crossbones symbol] WARNING: [skull and crossbones symbol]
Manufacturing and burning vinyl creates
dioxin and other chemicals that can cause cancer and harm fetal development.
myhouseisyourhouse.org

In the spirit of making lemonade out of a very toxic lemon, the Helfands make a radical tchotchke (which in Yiddish means knickknack), a kind of throwaway that you are implored not to. Not only does the necklace yoke the lively appeal of Mardi Gras and the spirit of the people of Lake Charles to the deadly vinyl, but it reaffirms survival through humor as it spreads the word. Joined over the picnic table in front of the once-again wood-sided home, the Helfands—mother, father, and daughter—suggest another version of family. While Judith herself may not have a biological child, she has worked on behalf of all children, all families. With each necklace they create, her father and mother, no longer naive, suggest the promise of an aware consumer, one unwilling to turn a blind eye to the damage of certain choices. In *Blue Vinyl*'s vision, the potential for activism is present in all and all are connected. We see the various roles possible and the creative community it inspires. Less a collection of damaged parts than a whole working for long-term health and understanding of worldwide connections, *Blue Vinyl* suggests we are all one body, regardless of where we live—that each home is the home of the world.

Epilogue

A year after *Blue Vinyl* was produced, it appeared in numerous film festivals and was the documentary award winner for excellence in cinematography at the 2002 Sundance Film Festival. The buzz around the film has helped support a website and campaign described as "a consumer education and consumer organizing campaign" (*http://www.myhouseisyourhouse.org*).

NOTES

1. The final transcript of *Blue Vinyl*, dated April 2002, offers this footnote on page 1: "The Harkavy English-Yiddish-Hebrew dictionary has 'vern farkrokhn' as 'to get lousy.' Yiddishists at the YIVO Institute for Jewish Research concurred that 'farkrokhn' might not be the usual word used to describe a house, but they assumed that the intended meaning was 'falling down' or 'run down.'"

2. Page number citations from this and subsequent quotes from *Blue Vinyl* are from the HBO "Final Transcript Annotated v10 4–16–02."

3. This figure comes from Pat Cody, cofounder of DES Action USA and is corroborated by the firm of Aaron Levine in Washington, D.C., which successfully argued a class action settlement for DES daughters, of whom Judith Helfand was one.

4. Rachel Carson's *Silent Spring* was published in 1962. DDT was banned for use in the United States in 1973, although it is still in use in twelve countries.

REFERENCES

Antonetta, S. 2001. *Body Toxic: An Environmental Memoir*. Washington, D.C.: Counterpoint.
Bilger, A. 1998. *Laughing Feminism: Subversive Comedy in Frances Burney, Maria Edgeworth, and Jane Austen*. Detroit: Wayne State University Press.

Blue Vinyl. 2002. Produced and directed by Daniel Gold and Judith Helfand. Toxic Comedy Pictures.

Camacho, David E., ed. 1998. *Environmental Injustices, Political Struggles: Race, Class, and the Environment*. Durham: Duke University Press.

Carson, R. 1962. *Silent Spring*. New York: Fawcett Crest.

Merchant, C. 1995. *Earthcare: Women and the Environment*. New York: Routledge.

Tarter, Jim. 2002. "Some Live More Downstream than Others: Cancer, Gender, and Environmental Justice." *The Environmental Justice Reader: Politics, Poetics and Pedagogy*, ed. Joni Adamson, Mei Mei Evans, and Rachel Stein. Tucson: University of Arizona Press.

14

"Lo que quiero es tierra"

Longing and Belonging in Cherríe Moraga's Ecological Vision

PRISCILLA SOLIS YBARRA

In stark poetry and passionate essays, Cherríe Moraga has forged a brand of environmental justice in which sexuality and gender are as relevant as race and class. Surviving as a Chicana lesbian poet, playwright, and essayist, Moraga's work often narrates her pain and isolation, yet she unabashedly claims strength and courage from her life experiences. Her powerfully intimate stories about herself, her family, and her lovers line her path toward a radical politics. And it is a radical politics with a critical edge. As coeditor, with Gloria Anzaldúa, of the anthology *This Bridge Called My Back* (1981), she led the way in demanding that mainstream feminists listen to the voices of women of color. Her first collection of prose and poetry, *Loving in the War Years* (1983), challenged the Chicana and Chicano community to confront sexism, homophobia, and heteronormativity. In the same spirit of intracultural critique, she takes up environmental justice, with her more recent work especially condemning the parallel exploitation of the land and the oppressions endured by the queer, female, and dark-skinned body. In the process, she conjures an ecological vision of the homeland that she has longed for, a territory to which she can finally belong.

Foregrounding the way that her sexuality, her gender, and her Chicana identity have informed her understanding of the relationship between humans and nature, Moraga produces an expanded definition of nature, or "land": "Land remains the common ground for all radical action. But land is more than the rocks and trees, the animal and plant life that make up the territory of Aztlán or Navajo Nation or Maya Mesoamerica. For immigrant and native alike, land is also the factories where we work, the water our children drink, and the housing project where we live. For women, lesbians, and gay men, land is that physical mass called our bodies" (Moraga 1993, 173). She uses the word "land" to describe what might otherwise be called "nature" or "environment"—a choice that signals her concern with two of the historic shifts in the relationship between the peoples

and environment of North America. One of the most paradigmatically challenging shifts occurred as European forces began the takeover of Native American lands; she mentions the Aztec, Navajo, and Maya. Her use of the word "land"
also calls attention to the takeover of Mexican lands by the United States—an
appropriation that suddenly transformed a Mexican into a Mexican American
but not necessarily into a *citizen* with full legal rights to the ownership of his
rancho. By referring to the broadly defined "rocks and trees" and "animal and
plant life" as "land," Moraga infuses nature with the political history of possession and dispossession. This politicized context informs the way that she considers "land" to be a reason for radical action. The negotiations over borders for
respective "lands" are often matters that generate conflict, even wars. But Moraga
also notes that "land" is the physical location for those conflicts; "land" materi-
ally suffers the violence of exploitation, even as it is an extension of ourselves.
And "land" suffers these oppressions not only during times of war but every day.

Who would think of "land" as a factory, a glass of water, or even one's own
body? Someone who connects "land" to the quotidian notions of job, home, and
health is also someone who has likely been alienated from such basic elements
of life—whether because of gender, class, ethnicity, queer desire, or any other
marginalizing identifier found in the very body she or he also comes to consider
as "land." Moraga explains, "As a Chicana lesbian, I know that the struggle I share
with all Chicanos and Indigenous peoples is truly one of sovereignty, the sovereign right to wholly inhabit oneself (*cuerpo y alma*) and one's territory (*pan y
tierra*)" (Moraga 1993, 173–74). Land signifies not only the area associated with
a nation-state, but anything from which an individual can become alienated or
dispossessed on the mere basis of one's gendered or ethnic appearance to the
world, or even the self one has chosen to fashion. She puts physical territory in
the same context as elements that are vital to everyday life, such as job, home,
and health. Indeed, she puts the right to defining one's relationship to nature
in the hands of the individual rather than the state—a move that de-emphasizes
the significance of the nation-state as it enables an individual's interest in the
natural environment. One has the same right to one's body and soul as to bread
and soil (*cuerpo y alma* and *pan y tierra*). And it is the alienation of this right
that Moraga notes, especially in regard to sexuality, gender, and ethnicity. In short,
be your queer self and lose your job; be your female self and get paid less for
your work; be your brown self and get a low-paying and physically labor-intensive
job. Be your brown self and drink contaminated water, work and live with insecticide poisons; be your female self, drink contaminated water, and get breast cancer
or have a miscarriage. Be your brown queer female self and lose your home, your
family, your security. One's very sense of one's "sovereign right" stems from the
daily knowledge of how difficult it is to "wholly inhabit oneself (*cuerpo y alma*)."

Yet, in a characteristic move, Moraga does not simply lament the alienation
of the right to the body and the land. She recuperates the sense of an alienated

right by recognizing the connections it forges. Though the linking of oppressed bodies with the natural environment is the product of a parallel exploitation, Moraga's poetry testifies to an intuitive yearning for kinship that such an alignment awakens. Moraga's poetry evokes her sense of loss and her longing for sovereignty as they exist with her demand for a land and a community to which she can feel she belongs. Especially moving is her poem "War Cry," collected in *The Last Generation*:

WAR CRY

lo que quiero es
tierra
si no tierra, pueblo
si no pueblo, amante
si no amante, niño
soledad
tranquilidad
muerte
   tierra.[1]
(Moraga 1993, 42)

"Lo que quiero es / tierra," can be translated as both "what I want is territory" and "what I love is land." This line's double meaning thus demands social justice at the same time that it expresses environmental kinship. With its reference to territory, this poem sounds a political plea for the land that was taken from the indigenous peoples of North America and for the land that was subsequently taken in 1848 and 1853 with the Treaty of Guadalupe-Hidalgo and the Gadsen Purchase ("what I want is territory"), but its stark lines also give voice to the complex emotions that are internal to this claim for justice ("what I love is land"). The desire for kinship—the longing to belong—drives this poem through a series of intimacies. The first desire articulated is for the land. When the land is denied, the desire remains, though redirected: "if not land, community." The speaker longs for different kinds of relationships—to a community, to a lover, to a child—in succession, with one following when the other is withheld. The desire for kinship remains as consistent as the land—the land that eventually becomes the only companion along the inevitable trek toward *"soledad / tranquilidad / muerte"* ("solitude / tranquility / death"). The succession of relationships demonstrates not only the unwavering desire for connection, but also a firm commitment to resistance. Even when a people is denied territory, it will forge a community: *"si no tierra, pueblo"* ("if not territory, community"). Once the community is dispersed, one might still maintain a family of two: *"si no pueblo, amante"* ("if not community, lover"). And when the lover is also denied, one can at least raise the child with a memory of the community and the lover: *"si no amante, niño"* ("if not lover, child"). And always the land is the compan-

ion along this journey of resistance. Kinship with the land is never separated from the significance of a community, a lover, and a child. Indeed, *tierra* completes the circle—*tierra* frames and defines the terms of the poem; *tierra* remains a consistent comfort that initiates the longing and survives to the end.

In "Ni for El Salvador," a work of mixed genre—both poem and journal entry—also collected in *The Last Generation*, Moraga again contemplates the four elements (land, community, lover, child):

NI FOR EL SALVADOR

I am a woman nearing forty without children.
I am an artist nearing forty without community.
I am a lesbian nearing forty without partner.
I am a Chicana nearing forty without country.

And if it were safe, I'd spread open my thighs
and let the whole world in
and birth and birth and birth life.
The dissolution of self, the dissolution of borders.

But it is not safe.
Ni for me.
Ni for El Salvador.
(Moraga 1993, 41)

She goes on to state, in the paragraph immediately below these lines, her goals as an artist. Her ultimate vision is to reach the point at which it is "safe" as described in the lines—safe enough to "spread open my thighs" and to dissolve borders of all sorts. The act of spreading her thighs signals all at once an act of trust, love, motherhood, sexuality, and eroticism. It is a deeply intimate act. This comprehensive, and inspirational, ambition creates such a vision that she offers its analogue, as a cultural critic. She wants to be an artist "who can create a theatre, a poetry, a song that dares to expose that very human weakness where we betray ourselves, our loved ones, even our own revolution" (Moraga 1993, 41). Both statements reveal a very sensitive and deeply personal commitment to working toward a culture that will consistently examine its values and practices to eliminate exploitation of peoples and lands, even when that means possibly betraying the cohesion of a movement.

Indeed, in "Ni for El Salvador" Moraga, running the risk of denouncing her U.S.-based audience, broadens the scale of environmental justice from the domestic to a global level when she contemplates a Central American nation. This is a courageous act since she exposes her own complicity in the environmental injustice that sustains first-world consumption. Yet she still claims that "No sustainable development is possible in the Americas if the United States continues to demand hamburgers, Chrysler automobiles, and refrigerators from hungry, barefoot, and energy-starved nations" (Moraga 1993, 172). She suggests that Chicanas and Chicanos, who (after all) live in the U.S., realize the role our nation plays in the global sociopolitical arena. Indeed, "[g]lobal capitalism . . . has been dependent on the free labor of domestically confined women and of men and women who were slaves and indentured servants—to those outside their own families and usually their own races—but the global economic framework has also depended on much of that labor to be unacknowledged and economically unawarded" (Platt 1996, 74). In addition, U.S. (plus that of other First World nations) rates of consumption disregard the limits of nature in favor of convenience and comfort, and these privileges are often at the expense of peoples and environments in other nations,[2] particularly nations located in the global South.[3]

Moraga's frustrations with such exploitations fuel her demand for a Chicano homeland, often referred to as "Aztlán" by advocates of Chicano Nation.[4] Geographically, Aztlán would encompass the lands in the U.S. Southwest once owned by Mexico but acquired by the United States through various means— events described comprehensively by Moraga as "the theft of what was once our México and before that and still Tierra Tarahumara, Yaqui, Seri, Pima, O'odham" (Moraga 2000, 180). Bioregionally, Aztlán would include the Chihuahuan and Sonoran deserts as well as the fertile Rio Grande valley, the peaks of the Sierra Nevadas, the lower Gulf's wetlands, and the beaches along the Pacific. These claims for a Chicano homeland can be interpreted as a cry for a separate nation that would seem to conflict with her pursuit of social justice, especially for queer Chicanas who have hardly figured into the Chicano vision of Aztlán.[5] Yvonne Yarbro-Bejarano notes that Moraga's "emphasis on indigenous ecological concerns (Moraga 1993, 167 and 170) within Chicano nationalist discourse allows the textual conflation of Indian land and female brown bodies, a move that creates space for women within the ideal national subject" (Yarbro-Bejarano 2001, 108–9). However, even though Moraga attempts to make a place for women in Aztlán, history testifies to the oppression that women and queers suffer under any such "nationalist" regime.

Yet her demands persist, and what at first seems a contradiction actually demonstrates the way that Moraga longs for a homeland more than she actually claims to establish a new nation. Indeed, she revises the conventional understanding of "nation" to accommodate her vision of a homeland that would include justice for its peoples as well as its lands. Moraga's "project . . . of recuperating or revisiting nationalism from a queer perspective expands the notion of social or revolutionary change to include the politics of sexuality, a dimension of liberatory politics often lost in the search for nation" (Yarbro-Bejarano 2001, 108).[6] The conventional understanding of national identity relies on "a continuity of blood relations, a spatial continuity of territory, and linguistic commonality" (Hardt and Negri 2000, 95). Moraga alters all three. She shifts the terms of kinship from blood (descent) relations to not-necessarily-blood (consent) relations in a move that validates queer families and others who challenge traditional ties: "Coming to terms with [my lesbianism] meant the radical restructuring of everything I thought I held sacred. It meant acting on my woman-centered desire and against anything that stood in its way, including my Church, my family, and my 'country.' . . . [A]ct I did, because not acting would have meant my death by despair" (Moraga 1993, 146). She often encourages the creative invention of identity and relationships, not so much in the postmodern sense of "play" as much as a means for survival in a social context that sometimes tries to violently deny and suppress the existence of certain differences within the pursuit of a homogenous national identity—especially queerness and ethnicity. Her writings also work against any kind of linguistic purity in the way that her work blends at least two languages at a time (usually Spanish and English), and she repeatedly displays the inimitable ideas resulting from linguistic juxtapositions.

Most relevant to her ecological vision, Moraga challenges the aspect of national identity that pertains to the "spatial continuity of territory." She recognizes the "dangers of nationalism as a strategy for political change" and considers ways that it might undermine her effort to bring about environmental justice (Moraga 1993, 149). For example, concerning the physical territory of her proposed nation, she considers the changing political boundaries over the years and wonders: "Is our land the México of today or the México of a century and a half ago, covering thousands of miles of what is now the Southwestern United States?" (Moraga 1993, 152–53). Superficially, this line presents the conundrum of temporal scale—the question arises as to what time period this revolution speaks against. But this also offers a glimpse at the intriguing contradictions in Moraga's work regarding physical territory. She begins to question the validity of engaging with the concept of nation on the terms of the colonizers; "Aztlán at times seems more *meta*physical than physical territory" (Moraga 1993, 153). Conventionally, a citizen belongs to a nation and identifies with a politically and physically defined territory. In Moraga's projections, a citizen and a homeland belong *to one another* and maintain responsibilities to one another. Or, as Mary Pat Brady puts it in her outstanding study on the dynamics of space in Chicana literature, "Moraga actively suggests an anticartography—one that does not conceive of space as a thing to be possessed or a set of rationalized relations to be mapped. Moraga offers a different concept of spatiality, in which land and bodies blend in both metaphysical and real senses, in which perception and living cannot be distinguished so easily" (Brady 2002, 139). The ideal members of the imaginary homeland Aztlán refuse the appropriative attitude that nation historically engenders, and instead they enact a reciprocal relationship with nature in a way that sustains a broadly defined group: "Simply, we must give back to the earth what we take from it. We must submit to a higher 'natural' authority, as we invent new ways of making culture, making tribe, to survive and flourish as members of the world community in the next millennium" (Moraga 1993, 174).

Of course, Moraga's homeland includes a conventional notion of "land" as nature—the actual dirt and grass and hills and streams. But her "land" also includes one's body and the relations that go with it—social and environmental. And she recognizes the activists that already work within this environmental justice paradigm: "[T]here are examples of the Mothers of East Los Angeles and the women of Kettleman City who have organized against the toxic contamination proposed for their communities. In the process, the Mexicana becomes a Chicana . . . ; that is, she becomes a citizen of this country, not by virtue of green card, but by virtue of the collective voice she assumes in staking her claim to this land and its resources" (Moraga 1993, 156). Moraga remains significantly committed to emphasizing a necessary relationship with the actual, physical land. And she emphasizes a grassroots definition of citizenship, not as nation-state recognition, but as the responsibility that humans and nature maintain with one another.

Such is the challenge that Moraga keeps confronting and demanding her readers confront as well: only a developing relationship to identity; once a definition coheres it also begins to oppress. Moraga's work "brings 'difference' into the concept of nation" (Yarbro-Bejarano 2001, 125) and defies the "flip side of the structure that resists foreign powers [that] is itself a dominating power that exerts an equal and opposite internal oppression, repressing internal difference and opposition in the name of national identity, unity, and security" (Hardt and Negri 2000, 106). The simple, two-word title for the poem "War Cry" alone indicates the complexity and process-oriented nature of this writer's challenging reflections. She titles in English a poem that otherwise uses only Spanish to sound its lament, suggesting that only English can name the multiple valences that intermingle and emerge in her mother's tongue, Spanish. "War Cry" also points to the ironic way that Moraga proposes physical territory for Aztlán. To most contemporary citizens of the United States, such a demand for Chicano Nation doubtless sounds farfetched. However, Moraga simply follows the logic of colonizers, "call[ing] attention to the naturalizing work of the geopolitical narrative of the United States" (Brady 2002, 146). Moraga's cry is not so much to sound a call for military battle over physical territory as it is an epistemological challenge to move beyond paradigms of appropriation. And all along, some part of her longs for relief from the pain and losses suffered as the battle over her homeland continues, and she warns her sympathizers and fellow revolutionaries: we must not reproduce the same structures of power that we fight against.

NOTES

I am grateful to everyone who read and commented on drafts of this paper, including José Aranda, Ed Snow, and Ayşe Çelikkol. I take full responsibility for any errors. The poems "War Cry" and "Ni for El Salvador" by Cherríe Moraga originally appeared in *The Last Generation: Prose and Poetry*, published by South End Press and are used with permission. © 1993 Cherríe Moraga.

1. My translation:

    > what I want/love is
    >
    > territory/land
    >
    > if not territory/land, community
    >
    > if not community, lover
    >
    > if not lover, child
    >
    > solitude
    >
    > tranquility
    >
    > death
    >
    >> territory/land.

2. The concept of the "ecological footprint" quantifiably describes this inequity. An area's ecological footprint is calculated using several interdependent factors including consumption rates, biological carrying capacity, and population. These factors combine to estimate the area of natural resources that a nation or a region requires to maintain its current rates of consumption for its population. Some areas consume more than their local resources can provide, and no other nation is a larger culprit on this front than the United States—a nation whose ecological footprint exceeds that of Latin America alone by at least six times. Thus, a revolution in the material demands of the United States and other overprivileged nations must occur before anyone, North or South, can enjoy a genuinely sustainable way of life. For Moraga, this sustainability includes ethical human relations *on a global scale* along with ecologically sensitive uses of nature—a connection nurtured by developing a culture that intertwines the human and the natural.

3. For example, Chicano filmmaker Gregory Nava's film *El Norte* aptly demonstrates the dramatic differences between the negotiable environmental impact of Guatemala and the overwhelming environmental exploitation in the United States. *El Norte* shows the impact of these macrocosmic flows on a family level. Enrique and Rosa, as well as their murdered father and disappeared mother, suffer the consequences of the violent Guatemalan civil war. Many issues were in contention in this war, but the film specifically emphasizes the struggle over land-use rights, labor exploitation, and environmental degradation. These all work in combination to provide generous profit margins for owners or stockholders, often based in the First World, as well as agricultural resources for the far-reaching U.S. ecological footprint.

4. "A term Náhuatl in root, Aztlán was that historical/mythical land where one set of Indian forebears, the Aztecs, were said to have resided 1,000 years ago. Located in the U.S. Southwest, Aztlán fueled a nationalist struggle twenty years ago, which encompassed much of the pueblo Chicano from Chicago to the borders of Chihuahua" (Moraga 1993, 151).

5. To use Alicia Gaspar de Alba's paraphrase of *Animal Farm*, in the beginnings of the Chicano struggle for justice in the 1960s and 1970s, "some members of the Movement

were more equal than others" (1998, 126). Though women wanted to join the ranks of nonviolent and violent dissent alike, the role men often deemed appropriate for Chicanas was as domestic supporters and caretakers. If a woman chose a life outside this restricted definition, the men of the movement regarded her as a traitor and likened her to the Malinche stereotype. In the view of some militant Chicanos, "'real' Chicanas only lived for two things: for their men and families and for the struggle" (Gaspar de Alba 1998, 127). There was no room for queers in this formula.

6. Hardt and Negri also testify to the progressive, revolutionary potential for what they call "subaltern nationalism"—nationalism deployed by the colonized within an existing nation: "In some respects, in fact, one might even say that the function of the concept of nation is inverted when deployed among subordinated rather than dominant groups. Stated most boldly, it appears that *whereas the concept of nation promotes stasis and restoration in the hands of the dominant, it is a weapon for change and revolution in the hands of the subordinated*" (106).

REFERENCES

Brady, M. P. 2002. *Extinct Lands, Temporal Geographies: Chicana Literature and the Urgency of Space.* Durham, N.C.: Duke University Press.

El Norte. 1983. Directed by Gregory Nava, written by G. Nava and A. Thomas. 139 minutes. CBS/Fox Video.

Gaspar de Alba, A. 1998. *Chicano Art Inside/Outside the Master's House: Cultural Politics and the CARA Exhibition.* Austin: University of Texas Press.

Hardt, M., and A. Negri. 2000. "Sovereignty of the Nation-State." In *Empire.* Boston: Harvard University Press.

Moraga, C. 1993. *The Last Generation: Prose and Poetry.* Boston: South End Press.

———. 2000. *Loving in the War Years: Lo que nunca pasó por sus labios.* Boston: South End Press.

Moraga, C., and G. Anzaldúa, eds. 1983. *This Bridge Called My Back: Writings by Radical Women of Color.* New York: Kitchen Table Press.

Platt, K. 1996. "Ecocritical Chicana Literature: Ana Castillo's 'Virtual Realism.'" *ISLE: Interdisciplinary Studies in Literature and Environment* 3, no. 1: 67–96.

United Nations Population Fund. 2002. *State of the World Population 2001.* http://www.unfpa.org/swp/swpmain.htm.

Yarbro-Bejarano, Y. 2001. "Whiteness in *The Last Generation*: The Nation, the 'Half-breed,' and the Queer." *The Wounded Heart: Writing on Cherríe Moraga.* Austin: University of Texas Press.

15

Detecting Toxic Environments

Gay Mystery as Environmental Justice

KATIE HOGAN

The air is poisoned, ponds, rivers, lakes, whole oceans. The water under the land. The land itself. Farms, the animals on the farms. People. Whole towns have to be abandoned. Somebody has to stop it.

–Joseph Hansen, *Night Work: A Dave Brandstetter Mystery*

Homosexuality is the central reason [Joseph Hansen's] books were written.

–Robert A. Baker and Michael T. Nietzel, *Private Eyes: One Hundred and One Knights*

Striking similarities exist between recent developments in multicultural detective fiction and theories of environmental justice. Through a focus on racial, gender, class, ethnic, and sexual bias, multicultural detective fiction and criticism have shifted the idea of who or what is responsible for crime from a villainous figure or group to a toxic social structure bent on domination and neglect of people and their environments. In many multicultural detective narratives, the deadliest crime of all is a destructive and indifferent world outlook, one that disproportionately destroys the lives and homes of working-class people, people of color, women, and sexual minorities.

Lesbian and gay detective fiction writers also construct murder or crime as just one part of a greater crime; homophobia, and its interaction with other unjust social structures, is often the central crime of these narratives.[1] Heterosexism is another key element of the queer detective's investigation and of the narrative's overall plot.

Like multicultural detective narratives, the environmental justice framework is not only about the monitoring and identification of environmental hazards and those responsible for them; it also promotes the development of strategies for transforming ideologies of race, gender, and class as they relate to environments.

A basic tenet of environmental justice is that all people, regardless of their cultural heritage or background, deserve to live, work, and play in a safe, secure space; social structures that interfere with this are violations of human rights.

Sandra Steingraber unintentionally offers a profound rhetorical connection between multicultural detective fiction and environmental justice theory when she refers to environmentally caused cancer deaths in the United States as "a form of homicide" (in Tarter 2002, 218). Thus the multicultural detective writer and critic, and the environmental justice activist and theorist are all concerned with delineating how social and physical environments are inextricably linked. The overall purpose of both fields is to create social change.

One gay detective narrative that articulates an environmental justice paradigm is Joseph Hansen's 1984 novel, *Night Work: A Dave Brandstetter Mystery*. In addition to espousing an environmental justice theme—evident in Hansen's deliberate intertwining of seemingly unrelated issues such as exposure to workplace toxins, gang violence, police neglect, high unemployment among black teenagers, an inferior educational system, shoddy housing, illegal dumping of toxic waste in wilderness areas, and urban sprawl—Hanson's narrative also incorporates a critique of the destructiveness of white, male, heterosexual conceptions of nature and environment. *Night Work*'s gay detective is not an environmental activist; he is a gay insurance claims investigator who uncovers toxic dumping as well as toxic heterosexuality. In this way, Hansen's text makes explicit a queer perspective in environmental justice theory. It is Dave Brandstetter's sexuality that facilitates his understanding of the interconnections between social injustice and environment. It is his sexuality that also allows him to frame patriarchal, white, heterosexual conceptions of nature as the root cause of inequality.

Pastoral Politics

Environmental justice theory *implicitly* supports queer communities as expressed in some of the main beliefs stated in the "Seventeen Principles of Environmental Justice" (2001). This groundbreaking document demonstrates a commitment to protecting all people, regardless of race, gender, sexuality, and culture, from toxic exposure and from ideological control of land, bodies, and environments. Of particular interest to activists and theorists is the document's declaration of a bond between urban and rural environments. Principle twelve of the "Principles of Environmental Justice" states that environmental justice "affirms the need for urban and rural ecological policies to clean up and rebuild our cities and rural areas in balance with nature" ("Seventeen Principles" 2001, 499). This affirmation has far-reaching implications for environmental justice theory and activism and, by extension, for interpretations of environmental texts such as Hansen's. Linking the urban and the rural in terms of environmental injustice offers a bold challenge to Western pastoral ideology, a cultural construct of urban and rural environments that began with such classical writers as Theocritus and Virgil and that continues to influence environmental policies to this day. Hansen's text demonstrates how pastoral ideology still permeates our contemporary understandings of human interactions with environments and argues that the result of this pastoral legacy on contemporary life is disastrous.

In the Western pastoral literary tradition, the metropolis, or urban center, is positioned as the antithesis of the rural. The pastoral speaker—always male, white, educated, and either aristocratic or upper class—creates the rural as a refuge from the "artificial" and morally suspect city. The rural becomes, for the privileged pastoral speaker, a supposedly uncomplicated and untroubled landscape where he can find solace, simplicity, pleasure, and peace. But such a portrayal of rural environments depends upon the erasure of the histories and lived realities of rural communities as well as a suppression of the similarities between urban and rural environmental injustice. The pastoral literary tradition constructs the city as a place from which to flee, and nature becomes the property of the privileged. Hansen challenges this opposition by showing the interdependence of the rural and urban environments and focusing on the violence perpetuated by the privileged whose pastoral visions maintain this duality.

In writing against this pastoral tradition, Hansen neither adopts an anti-rural, pro-urban sentiment nor a pro-rural, anti-urban sentiment; rather, he uses the detective novel—and, I would argue, his entire Dave Brandstetter series—to articulate the consequences of the pastoral tradition for those communities and individuals, in urban as well as rural environments, who are erased and/or violently oppressed by it; he also rejects the idea that "rural folk" are only visible as quaint and innocent objects of the pastoral speaker's desire.[2] *Night Work* refutes the idea of the poor, women, and people of color as innately uncomplicated links to nature, an idea that frames their labor, pain, desires, feelings, and histories as unimportant. Hansen also challenges the idea of queers, who are presumed to be located in decadent cities, as having no place in rural landscapes.[3]

Queer people, construed for centuries as "crimes against nature," are, according to environmental justice theory, a part of "all peoples" who have "the fundamental right to political, economic, cultural and environmental self-determination" ("Seventeen Principles" 2001, 498). Because environmental justice theory rejects rural/urban divisions, it refuses to uphold this idea that any cultural group of people could exist outside of, or against, nature. Since the natural realm is inextricably linked to the cultural realm, the idea of one group as being "against nature" is not only ideological but also illogical. Thus environmental justice theory is implicitly "queer" as it broadens what counts as environment and exposes how the nature/culture binary is inhumane and unworkable.

The linkage of environmentalism, nature, and queers is directly and explicitly addressed in Hansen's *Night Work*. In this novel, Hansen's white (and wealthy) gay insurance claims investigator, Dave Brandstetter, lives and works with his lover, Cecil Harris, an African American television news reporter. With the help of a working-class African American boy, the two men discover connections between the murder of two truckers—one of whom was the boy's father who died from handling hazardous waste—and a plant east of Pasadena, California, called Tech-Rite. The three discover the behind-the-scenes machinations of Tech-Rite managers who, working with organized crime, hire outside truckers to perform "night work"—the illegal midnight dumping of toxic waste in wilderness areas. In pursuing the mystery of the two deaths, the narrative incorporates a critique of nature as both a refuge and profitable dumping ground for the able-bodied, white, heterosexual, and moneyed. In doing so, *Night Work* spells out the violence of both the pastoral and capitalist traditions. The senior vice president of Tech-Rite has built an expensive house in the woods for his young, beautiful wife, but he loses her to cancer caused by exposure to one of Tech-Rite's illegal toxic dumps. This character's actions not only perpetuate the idea of nature for the privileged but lead to the poisoning of nature and of working-class truckers; it also literally kills his wife. Hansen shows how this vice president destroys nature, people of color, women, and the working class by practicing corporate capitalism's plundering of resources and people for profit.

Through Brandstetter's ability to forge relationships across sexuality, age, race, class, gender, and neighborhood, *Night Work* challenges the traditional view of the hard-boiled, isolated, heterosexual male detective who, in solving crimes, routinely makes disparaging remarks about gays, women, and people of color. In contrast, Hansen's detective identifies with those positioned as marginal and never removes himself from intimate relationships or from society to solve a mystery.[4] Dave's marginality functions as a bridge to people whose racial, cultural, and class backgrounds also position them as outsiders. In a published interview, Hansen explains that his protagonist "understands any group or individual that stands outside the mainstream of society as we still erroneously think of it . . . Dave's wise: he sees that those things that can impede you in the world . . . are pretty much the same" (Gambone 1999, 35).

Dave moves in and out of various communities with a tenacious commitment to discovering the truth, including the consequences of unjust social structures and ideas. Like environmental justice theorists, writers, and activists, Hansen's Dave Brandstetter solves crimes of unequal power through affiliation in, rather than in isolation from, multiple communities. By presenting Dave as working on behalf of the environment, Hansen refuses to distance his gay detective from the historically problematic category of "nature"; instead, the narrative uses Dave's queer point of view to develop a link between capitalist heterosexuality and toxic conceptions of nature, thus undermining the association of queers as a threat to nature. The ultimate crime in this novel is the possessive idea of nature as the property of traditional, white heterosexuality.[5]

The Violence of Capitalism

While *Night Work* condemns the idea of nature as the entitlement of the powerful, it also vividly exposes the violence such an ideology creates, particularly when nature for the privileged merges with capitalist ideology. The novel opens with a significant description of the altering of nature in the construction of what eventually becomes a working-class neighborhood of Los Angeles called, ironically, Gifford Gardens: "Before the construction of these acres of shacky stucco houses in 1946, the creek bed was shallow, cluttered with boulders from the far-off mountains, shaded by live oaks, and clumpy with brush. He remembered it that way from the 1930s" (Hansen 1984, 1).

What makes this passage about a changing landscape different from the traditional pastoral lament over the loss of nature is Hansen's vision that the alteration of the land is a violation of nature and the people who will live there. Nature, people of color, and the working class will pay the price for this "development" with their lives, health, and families. In order to turn a profit, the developers had to build Gifford Gardens quickly; the trees were cut down and the creek bed was covered over with concrete slabs so that housing could be hastily erected. When the rains came, all of the houses flooded "until the County at last gouged out the creek bed and lined it with concrete slabs. Much too late" (2). This historical information—that Gifford Gardens residents live in shabby, unsound housing constructed because of greed—is thematically connected to Dave's investigation in present-day Gifford Gardens, where cracked sidewalks (or no sidewalks at all), roads with broken pavement, tacky homes with chain-link fences, visible gang activity, high unemployment, alcoholism, and shoddy services create a landscape of injustice.

Racially, Gifford Gardens is, as Dave puts it, a "mixed town," where African American, Latino American, and white working-class people are pitted against each other (16). A few white and Asian families are able to save enough money to send their children to a private academy, but the majority of the children attend unsafe, low-quality public schools. Gang violence between Chicano and African American youth is so severe that people stay in their homes, and the police are afraid to respond to the community's calls for help. Dave's lover, Cecil, characterizes Gifford Gardens as "a killing ground" and the community's black minister, Luther Prentice, says, "We are in the last days, it appears" (63, 31).

It is significant that Hansen presents Gifford Gardens' troubles as interlocking; the text refuses to compartmentalize the various social issues, a strategy that echoes a key strategy of environmental justice theory: "issues of toxic contamination fit within an agenda which can . . . include employment, education, housing, health care, and other issues of social, racial, and economic justice" (Austin and Schill 1994, 191). Toxic exposure on the job and poor quality education fall under the umbrella of environmental/social injustice in this text.

As H. Patricia Hynes explains, "environment is, foremost, the *lived* reality of a community," and Hansen's *Night Work* is deeply committed to delineating the inextricability of issues that comprise the "lived reality" of Gifford Gardens' residents (Hynes 1998, 172). Its repeated image of "summer-seared grass" and weeds poking through hot, bone-white concrete deliberately evokes the initial developers of Gifford Gardens who viewed this land, and the communities who would live here, as nothing more than a way to make money.

Despite the unrelenting economic injustice and racial strife afflicting this community, white trucker Paul Myers and African American trucker Ossie Bishop are close friends; it is Ossie who tells Paul about the high-paying "night work" that will allow these men a financial plan for their children's futures. Unfortunately, it is also the "night work" that leads to both men's exploitation and death. Like many members of working-class communities and communities of color, Ossie and Paul are being asked to choose between making a living and environmental health. Through what happens to these two characters, Hansen incorporates into his mystery the realities of toxic exposure on the job and illegal toxic dumping in wilderness areas as motives for murder.[6]

Building Alliances

Set against the history of the construction of Gifford Gardens and its subsequent racial and economic inequalities are several puzzles that Dave Brandstetter must solve: Who killed independent trucker Paul Myers, and why? Why did Ossie Bishop die suddenly and inexplicably? And what were both men hauling in their trucks late at night in remote areas outside of L.A.? What Dave and his team (his lover, Cecil, and Melvil, Ossie Bishop's fourteen-year-old son) uncover is that Ossie was poisoned by illegal toxic waste that he was hired to dump. The evidence they gather suggests that Paul Myers eventually realized that Ossie was dying because of toxic exposure. But Dave is not completely sure who planted the explosive that killed Myers in his truck. These two truckers' deaths seem to be linked to the powerful Tech-Rite, a corporate structure that has thwarted government waste regulations and state and local courts for years.

Dave, Cecil, and Melvil secretly visit the key sites associated with Tech-Rite's illegal disposal of toxic waste where they plan to take pictures with an infrared camera and later produce a report about those involved. They discover that Tech-Rite's manufacturing process includes separating out unauthorized chemical waste from authorized waste. Authorized waste is dumped at Foothill Springs, a legal dumping site about thirty minutes from Tech-Rite. However, Hansen includes a scene of local community members protesting Tech-Rite's legal dump, regardless of its "authorized" status: "All these men, women, adolescents, little kids, in jeans and parkas and slickers and stocking caps, carrying signs in the rain. Tech-Rite and the rest are poisoning the ground and water for miles around and dooming the people and their children for ages to come" (111). For the unauthorized toxic waste, the company uses a broker named the Duchess, who hires and manages independent truckers to pick up and dump unauthorized waste at various sites around the state in the middle of the night. One site is located in a remote wilderness area more than sixty miles away from Tech-Rite.

When Dave turns over his written report and the photos of the Duchess and her "goons" to Lieutenant Jaime Salazar, Salazar tells Brandstetter that the legal approach to environmental crime is useless: "the grand jury has been promising a report for months. It never comes" (156). Although Dave is aware that the illegal dumping of toxic waste has been going on for a long time and that the passing of local, state, and federal laws hasn't worked, he still feels compelled to do something: "Somebody has got to stop it" (156). Salazar warns Dave that organized crime is involved, and if Dave acts alone he will one day "turn on the ignition of [his] car, and blam! Instant cremation" (155). Salazar suggests that it is the grassroots activists—the men, women, and children who picket the government-authorized Foothill Springs dump and the numerous unauthorized illegal dumps around the state—who will stop the environmental poisoning. Even though Dave knows that Salazar is probably right, he still wants to expose Tech-Rite's environmental crimes and discover who killed Paul Myers.

Hansen uses this interaction between Lieutenant Salazar and Dave to convey a complex view of environmentalism. On the one hand, Salazar's argument that it will be the picketers who will stop the injustice may at first exhibit the dominant perspective that environmental injustice is the problem of those who suffer. But another interpretation is that Hansen is using Salazar's comments to bring to mind real-life examples of hazardous waste management being linked to organized crime and to corporate influence and greed—all of which impede legal action and social justice. In an effort to implicate such economic, legal, social, and cultural structures and standpoints in perpetrating environmental crimes, Hansen raises these issues in the context of the two men's conversation. Hansen's protagonist and his text are firmly committed to broad-based activism as perhaps the most potent response to environmental poisoning. Despite Salazar's warning, Dave pursues the case and the cause; he is taking action regardless of the danger involved in doing so. Both Salazar's warning and Dave's response to it suggest the complexity of environmental poisoning and the necessity of all citizens to engage in social justice movements.

This dialogue between Dave and Salazar also demonstrates another instance of Dave's ability to build cross-ethnic, cross-sexual, and cross-class alliances. Salazar is Latino, heterosexual, and from a working-class background while Dave is white, gay, and from a wealthy family.[7] Despite these differences, the two characters are friends and they help each other solve their cases; they clearly respect and admire one another. In this scene, Salazar is afraid for Dave, and he is trying to save Dave from the violence of organized crime when he tells his

friend to back off from the Tech-Rite case and from the Duchess. Hansen is linking illegal toxic dumping with organized crime in an attempt to relate his text
to lived experiences while also developing the theme of a mixed racial/ethnic/
class/and sexual alliance.[8]

Toxic Heterosexuality

Dave and Melvil return to Torcido Canyon, one of the illegal toxic dumpsites they
previously visited with Cecil, and the one Ossie Bishop frequented in his night
work. While there, the two find a protester's "No Dumping" sign, and beneath it
in "small print across the bottom of the sign were numerals from a County ordi-
nance book. And below that, TORCIDO CANYON HOMEOWNERS ASSN." Dave is surprised
to find evidence of homeowners, since the area seems so isolated and the smell
from the toxic dump permeates the air when there is a breeze. But Melvil discovers a beautiful house, "a picture for an architecture magazine," perched on
the side of the canyon. The house is very expensive but also "desolate"; it belongs
to Lorin Shields, the vice president of Tech-Rite (152). Ironically, in Shields's effort
to escape the ills of the world, he built a wondrous, peaceful house for himself
and for his wife near an illegal toxic dump his company helped create. In choosing this wilderness area, Shields inadvertently exposes his wife to the toxic dump
from which she contracts cancer on her daily walks; she dies shortly after their
marriage. Here Shields's relationship with his wife and with nature represents a
traditional, white, heterosexual male conception of the natural realm as "property"—beautiful house, beautiful wilderness, and beautiful wife. Such a pastoral
vision is merged with capitalism, and both are revealed as deadly to nature,
women, and people of color—all contaminated both by Shields's possessive view
of nature and of his view of people as profit-making commodities.

In this way, *Night Work* does more than develop Shields's complicity in his
wife's death from toxic poisoning; it shows how patriarchal, capitalistic, white,
heterosexual conceptions of nature, so often encased in the language of the pastoral, are toxic to everyone. Shields is responsible for the deaths of Ossie Bishop,
Paul Myers, and countless others who have been poisoned by Tech-Rite's toxic
dumps. Dave finds in Shields's house a tangle of wires used to bomb Myers's
truck. When Shields tries to murder Dave, he confronts Shields about his destructive and selfish framework. Dave correctly accuses Shields of not caring that his
company's illegal dump was poisoning people until it poisoned his wife (169).
But Shields refuses to take responsibility for the way he thinks or for what he
has done; instead he blames his wife's death on the least powerful. As explanation,
Shields admits to killing Paul Myers for "what he and his kind had done to Jennifer" (170). Shields even blames his company's toxic dumping on government
interference: "You don't understand how impossible all those government regulations make doing business" (169).

Lorin Shields's characterization of his dead wife's relationship to nature suggests a dominant ideology of nature as privileged men's escape: "Do you know what she wanted from life? Everything gentle and beautiful. A house in the woods. Quiet. Solitude. Nature. Away from the world" (168). Once again, *Night Work* identifies the rural/urban dichotomy undergirding this view as an ideology linked to those who "favor nature over society and the individual's experience of the natural realm over the collective" (Austin and Schill 1994, 58). In order to evaluate this prevalent view of the wilderness, Hansen deliberately departs from the typical case of a toxic dump in a poor urban or rural community of color because he wants to emphasize toxicity in the wilderness as a site of heterosexual men's conceptions of nature. Hansen is also implying that even those privileged few who construct nature as property and escape will have to face the consequences of this cultural fantasy.

The Pastoral Closet

Paradoxically, the critical literature on Joseph Hansen's *Night Work* characterizes the text both as being "anti-pastoral" and as downplaying homosexuality.[9] But by using the environmental justice framework as literary theory, it becomes clear that *Night Work* does neither. Rather than writing an anti-pastoral text, Hansen's narrative exposes the violence of the pastoral/anti-pastoral opposition. Furthermore, Hansen neither advocates a withdrawal of queers from nature nor promotes a closeted homosexuality; instead he shows the unfeasibility of dichotomous thinking about nature, and he challenges the domination of capitalist heterosexual male privilege.

Night Work presents white, pastoral heterosexuality as a flawed system implicated in the creation of serious social problems and prejudices. Its rejection of dominant conceptions of nature is merged with a critique of white male power. The romantic and transcendental idea of nature as the province of straight white men, a place for their reinvention of self, a refuge from the world, and the site of their property—including wife and children—is reframed here as brutality. *Night Work* uses a queer sensibility to illustrate how ideas about nature are neither innocent nor uncomplicated.

In this novel, as in all novels in Hansen's Dave Brandstetter series, the author openly and deliberately juxtaposes traditional heterosexual relationships with gay male relationships, a strategy that highlights homosexuality as a central theme. Throughout the series, Dave's father, who is in his mid-seventies, has nine unsuccessful marriages to increasingly younger women. At the center of many of the cases Dave investigates are bribery, greed, murder, substance abuse, and dishonesty in heterosexual relationships. Such unstable relationships are placed alongside the long-term, tender, loving, and caring relationships that Dave creates with men. In *Night Work*, Shields's traditional heterosexual relationship, a relationship based in greed and environmental poisoning, contrasts with the same-sex, interracial, cross-class relationship that Dave builds with his lover, Cecil, and with the couple's network of friends, family, and communities.

In addition, Hansen's *Night Work* constructs homosexuality as central to human society; he uses the mystery genre to show "homosexuality as an integral part of the fabric of contemporary life, rather than as something bizarre and alien" (Baker and Nietzel 1985, 222). But Hansen's idea of homosexuality as "integral" to society never translates into creating "straight acting" gay characters or in making all gay characters look and behave like Dave. Brandstetter wears Brooks Brothers suits, drives a Jaguar, and freelances as an insurance claims investigator.[10] Hansen's other queer characters include transvestites, porno stars, bankers, interior designers, hustlers, booksellers, and sometimes murderers. When the character DeWitt Gifford wears women's hats and makeup, Dave is neither unnerved nor disapproving. And after DeWitt is murdered by one of Gifford Gardens' gangs, Dave places a 1920s woman's hat on DeWitt as his body lies on a stretcher. "'You're kidding,'" says a member of the coroner's office, referring to Dave's action. Dave replies, as he looks at DeWitt's dead body, "He wasn't" (Hansen 1984, 162). In other instances, Hansen uses humor to stand gender on its head: "Men with cameras on their shoulders. Pretty girls of both sexes with microphones" (112). Showing homosexuality as "integral" means openly acknowledging the rich diversity of queer life. It also shows the impossibility of queer communities as being innately isolated or "against nature." In fact, Hansen rejects the idea of human isolation and explores the environment of the homosexual closet as "unnatural" in *Night Work* through the character of DeWitt Gifford.

Gifford Gardens was named after DeWitt Gifford's family, part of California's wealthy landed gentry that owned the enormous "Gifford Ranch" and sold most of it off to eager developers. Seventy-five-year-old DeWitt is the last living member of the Gifford family. Lonely, elderly, and in a wheelchair, Dewitt is a closeted white gay man who lives in a "white Victorian hulk, with cupolas, scalloped shingles, long porches bristly with jigsaw work." The house is located high upon a hill; DeWitt lives in the house's garret tower and looks down on the drab stucco community of Gifford Gardens. Matted honeysuckle, overgrown trees, dark ivy, and untrimmed bushes mask the house's fortress walls. With high-powered binoculars, DeWitt watches over the neighborhood and keeps track of all the comings and goings of the residents and of strangers; he records all activities in a ledger, which proves useful to Dave, but which also suggests DeWitt's disengagement from the community. DeWitt symbolizes a pre-Stonewall, upper-class white gay man whose best moment in life was a clandestine love affair with the early twentieth-century silent-screen idol Ramon Novarro. Through DeWitt's association with Dave, we also learn of the old man's secret assistance to, and sexual liaison with, Silencio Ruiz, a former Latino gang leader.

DeWitt is not an idealized gay character; he is selfish, self-absorbed, and totally isolated in the attic of his family's white Victorian house. He discusses his experiences with the environment in the past tense, when the ranch was free of housing developments and he, an isolated gay boy, spied on the hikers and lovers who visited the creek: "I saw some charming pastoral tableaux down among the oaks by the creek on warm summer days" (38). The reference to "charming pastoral tableaux," evokes a closeted gay pastoral tradition: as a white, privileged, property-owning man, nature and environment are vehicles for DeWitt's self-expression. He offers a gay/queer reading of the tradition in terms of homoeroticism but he does not question the racial, class, or gender ideology of the pastoral literary tradition.

Although DeWitt's pastoral ideology differs from Shields's, whose vision of the environment results in aggressive violence, both men are isolated from humanity and unfamiliar with the idea of nature and culture as intertwined. DeWitt's isolation is "the closet," represented by the attic of a house surrounded by uncared-for grounds. Shields's isolation derives from his investment in Western culture's idea that nature is for the self-discovery of privileged white men. In other words, Hansen's view of DeWitt is not the same as his view of Shields. Dewitt is destructive mostly towards himself; he is, as Dave puts it, a "silly old man," whereas Shields is destructive to all who come in contact with him. Through the inclusion of the similarities and differences between DeWitt and Shields, Hansen offers a view of environmental justice that includes the founding categories of race and class but one that also begins to suggest how sexuality is also a part of the framework.

Conclusion: Ecological Homophobia

Although Hansen's text was published in 1984, when the environmental justice movement was just beginning to form, the narrative foretells much of what has happened and is currently happening in environmental justice theory and activism today. Hansen understood environmental violations as a nexus of issues, and thus he refused the incoherent, fragmented approach to the environment that is so common in mainstream media and organizations. *Night Work* strategically and carefully weaves economic structures, race, work, and sexuality into its plot, characters, and themes. In addition, and related to this, is Hansen's interesting and powerful critique of the pastoral tradition as linked to capitalist violence and heterosexuality. The notion of people and nature as property and as expendable commodities for profit is a powerful theme in this text.

In terms of sexuality, Hansen incorporates a critique of toxic heterosexuality, but he also critiques closeted, privileged gay men such as DeWitt; he offers instead a vision of multiracial, cross-class, and cross-sexual alliance through his main character, Dave. As an out gay man, Dave encounters all of the real-life

challenges and difficulties facing environmental justice activists, including corrupt legal systems, repellant corporate greed, and organized crime, and he intuitively knows that activism and alliance across difference are the solutions. When
reading Hansen's text alongside the famous environmental justice principles, an
implicitly queer sensibility encoded in environmental justice emerges, in particular the principle that deconstructs the false urban/rural divide. Hansen's text
begins to raise the question of ecological homophobia as intertwined with more
traditional concepts such as ecological racism and classism. In doing so, he successfully aligns queers in and with nature instead of outside or against it.

NOTES

1. Adrienne Johnson Gosselin's *Multicultural Detective Fiction: Murder from the "Other"
   Side*, characterizes lesbian and gay detective fiction as multicultural: "Multiculturalism in this context views communities as cultures, and cultures in relation to social
   power; as such, so-called gay and lesbian 'subcultures' are here included as cultural
   communities along with communities based on race and ethnicity" (Johnson Gosselin
   1999, 12 n. 1). Johnson Gossellin's inclusion of lesbian and gay narratives within the
   rubric of multiculturalism suggests a model for incorporating more fully how ideas of
   environmentalism, nature, and wilderness are linked to ideas of queer sexuality.

2. While *Night Work* is, to my knowledge, the only Hansen mystery that directly incorporates a focus on toxics, Hansen's other novels also explore the implications and consequences of the legacy of the pastoral tradition for queers, women, people of color, and
   working-class communities from an environmental justice framework.

3. See M. Morgan Holmes's entry on the pastoral in *The Gay and Lesbian Literary Heritage:
   A Reader's Companion to the Writers and Their Works, from Antiquity to the Present.*

4. For an interesting discussion of the differences between Hansen's Dave Brandstetter
   and the traditional hardboiled detective, see Ernest Fontana's essay, "Joseph Hansen's
   Anti-Pastoral Crime Fiction."

5. Mei Mei Evans introduces and develops this idea in her essay "'Nature' and Environmental Justice" in *The Environmental Justice Reader.*

6. This theme of toxic exposure in the workplace is just one of the many remarkable overlaps between Hansen's text and environmental justice. Hansen's novel includes the
   theme of toxic exposure in the workplace through the reference to Ossie Bishop's symptoms: "Violent diarrhea, vomiting, coughing, lung congestion, paralysis," and then death
   (Hansen 1984, 109). Underscoring the fact that Ossie had no idea that he was being
   exposed to toxic chemicals, and that he felt compelled to engage in "night work" to save
   money for the purchase of another truck, Hansen's narrative evokes the nexus of work,
   race, class, and environmental health as an issue of environmental justice. David Naguib
   Pellow points out that the impact of toxins on the worker, and not just on the community or neighborhood, is a central issue in environmental justice theory and activism
   (in Glenn 2002, A 19).

7. Dave finds Salazar physically attractive, and while he never openly admits this,
   Hansen's third-person narrator reports on Dave's appreciation of his friend's beauty
   in several novels in the series, including *Night Work.*

8. See Alan A. Block and Frank R. Scarpitti, *Poisoning for Profit: The Mafia and Toxic Waste
   in America.*

9. For a summary of the analysis, see Ernest Fontana, "Joseph Hansen's Anti-Pastoral Crime Fiction" (1986).

10. Dave used to work full-time for Medallion, an insurance company founded by Dave's father. Once Dave's father dies, the company fires Dave because he's gay.

REFERENCES

Adamson, Joni, Mei Mei Evans, and Rachel Stein, eds. 2002. *The Environmental Justice Reader: Politics, Poetics, and Pedagogy.* Tucson: University of Arizona Press.

Austin, R., and Michael Schill. 1994. "Black, Brown, Red, and Poisoned." In *Unequal Protection: Environmental Justice and Communities of Color*, ed. Robert Bullard. San Francisco: Sierra Club Books.

Baker, R. A., and M. T. Nietzel. 1985. *Private Eyes: One Hundred and One Knights: A Survey of American Detective Fiction, 1922–1984.* Bowling Green: Bowling Green University Press.

Block, A. A., and Frank R. Scarpitti. 1982. *Poisoning for Profit: The Mafia and Toxic Waste in America.* New York: William Morrow.

Evans, M. 2002. "'Nature' and Environmental Justice." In Adamson et al. 2002.

Fontana, E. 1986. "Joseph Hansen's Anti-Pastoral Crime Fiction." *Clues: A Journal of Detection 7*: 89–97.

Gambone, P. 1999. "Joseph Hansen." *Something Inside: Conversations with Gay Fiction Writers.* Madison: University of Wisconsin Press.

Glenn, D. 2002. "Follow the Garbage." *Chronicle of Higher Education* (Sept. 13): A19.

Hansen, J. 1984. *Night Work: A Dave Brandstetter Mystery.* New York: Henry Holt.

Holmes, M. M. 1995. "Pastoral." In *The Gay and Lesbian Literary Heritage*, ed. Claude J. Summers. New York: Henry Holt.

Hynes, H. P. 1998. "Environmentalism." In *The Reader's Companion to U.S. Women's History*, ed. Wilma Mankiller, Gwendolyn Mink, Marysa Navarro, Barbara Smith, and Gloria Steinem. Boston: Houghton Mifflin.

Johnson Gosselin, A. 1999. *Multicultural Detective Fiction: Murder from the "Other" Side.* New York: Garland.

"Seventeen Principles of Environmental Justice." 2001. In *Women's Lives: Multicultural Perspectives*, ed. Gwyn Kirk and Margo Okazawa-Rey. 2nd ed. Boston: McGraw Hill.

Tarter, J. 2002. "Some Live More Downstream Than Others: Cancer, Gender, and Environmental Justice." In Adamson et al. 2002.

16

"The Power is Yours, Planeteers!"

Race, Gender, and Sexuality in Children's Environmentalist Popular Culture

NOËL STURGEON

Starting in the late 1990s, environmentalism has become a new moral framework for children's popular culture. But we should not rush to celebrate this because the messages contained in these environmentalist stories are often counter to what environmental justice activists are fighting for, and they contain problematic notions about what is "natural" that environmental justice practitioners need to think about. Instead of the recognition central to environmental justice that social equality and environmental sustainability are interconnected, these stories contain habits of thinking that naturalize social inequality and disconnect environmental problems from their corporate causes. I take a feminist environmental justice approach to analyze these children's cultural objects, an approach that fits into what T. V. Reed has called "environmental justice ecocriticism" (Reed 2002). While most environmental justice criticism, rightly, focuses directly on issues in and around the movement against environmental racism, we also need an approach that critiques the wider world of cultural values that reinforce environmental inequalities. Such an approach is useful in delegitimating stories—in literature, film, and popular culture—that directly and indirectly naturalize inequality, by paying attention to questions of gender and sexuality as well as race and class issues. In this essay, I point out the toxic effect of promoting ideas about what constitute "natural" men and women, "natural" families, "natural" racial/ethnic identities, and "natural" sexuality. These are mainstream environmentalist stories I am looking at, but because they are liberal stories that ostensibly want to promote racial and gender equality, those of us who support environmental justice issues want to be particularly wary of underlying messages that contradict their moderately progressive surface. We need to be aware of how these dominant cultural messages may undermine the understanding of environmental justice issues we want to promote.

The plots of the recent spate of environmentalist children's films, TV shows, and stories fit into a dominant Western cultural logic that "nature" is the foundation of truth and that only certain (patriarchal) gender relations and certain kinds of racial identities (such as presenting people of color as closer to nature) are "natural." For dominant U.S. culture, seeing something as "natural" (whether it is gendered characteristics, racialized identities, or corporate competition) is a way of rendering it to the realm of the unquestioned. Mainstream environmentalists, in their emphasis on wilderness, species extinction, and in general seeing the environment as excluding human beings, often fall into service to this dominant Western logic of seeing the natural as pure, unchanging, untainted by social influence and without history. This kind of mainstream environmentalism avoids environmental justice issues, which deal primarily with problems of human and community health using a broader, less reified definition of the environment and identifying power relations as central to the cause of environmental problems. Given the historical role these mainstream ideas about nature and what is natural have played in justifying unequal social relations, and given the close relationship between justifying social inequality and supporting a form of global capitalist economy that ruthlessly exploits the environment, environmental justice supporters must be very careful about accepting such arguments, in mainstream culture or in their own political and cultural contexts. Though it may sometimes go against our own unquestioned assumptions, we must be very careful of fostering cultural arguments or movement practices that accept the "naturalization" of gender and sexual relations or racial and ethnic identities. We may feel like we care more about one or the other of these aspects, but it is important to note that, in the children's stories discussed here as well as other dominant cultural products, these two aspects (sexism/heterosexism and racism) often reinforce one another.

In this essay, two aspects of these problematic environmentalist stories in children's culture are examined. One is the association continually created between homosexuality, evil, and environmental destruction, coupled with an anxiety about the successful reproduction of white, middle-class, nuclear families. In these stories, it is the white, middle-class, nuclear family form that is presented as "normal" and "natural" without any critique of its complicity in the overconsumption of corporate products in an environmentally destructive system in which the toxins, waste, pollution, and radiation produced are visited on the poor, the people of color, and the tribal peoples of the world. The patriarchal white, middle-class, nuclear family, organized in the 1950s specifically as a unit of increasing post–World War II consumption situated in environmentally problematic suburbs, was presented at the time as the antithesis to the extended family located in the immigrant communities of inner cities, rural close-knit communities, or tribal reservations (May 1999). The insistence that this family form is natural, normal, and the best for the planet that can be found in these children's stories goes against the argument of most environmental justice activists that healthy empowered communities, strong extended families, tribal sovereignty, participatory democratic politics, and interconnections with the land through sustainable practices are the social and economic forms we will need to create social justice and environmental health. Thus what I call in this essay the "heterosexist" family is meant to point to a particular emphasis of these stories on the "normal," "natural" status of a white, middle-class, nuclear family in which men have most of the power.

The second theme examined in this essay is the idea that environmentalism is best achieved through the work of gender-balanced, multicultural kids' teams like *The Animorphs* and the Planeteers of the cartoon *Captain Planet*. These stories work to "naturalize" racial/ethnic differences in a particular way. The multicultural kids' teams present all cultures as equally responsible for environmental problems, and their enemies are never corporations, or the military, or governments. Further, despite the evenhandedness of these racially balanced environmentalist kids' groups, white, male, and middle-class characters have the most power; people of color, especially women of color, are seen as closer to nature and less powerful. We may want to welcome environmentalism coupled with a certain promotion of liberal racial equality as a predominant theme in children's popular culture so that we could raise concerns about the role of inequality in creating environmental problems. Unfortunately, the logic of these stories ends up "naturalizing" white middle-class values and economic practices instead.

Bringing Up Baby to Reduce, Reuse, and Recycle

How and why did environmentalism become such a common framework for children's culture? As a new parent over a decade ago, I was exposed suddenly and rather overwhelmingly to U.S. kinderculture. One of the things I was struck by was the important of environmentalism as a theme in just about every aspect of my son's life. This environmental emphasis popped up everywhere: on unbreakable plastic plates and fast-food containers, on T-shirts and backpacks, in books and museum exhibits, in elementary science curricula and field trips—let alone in the movies and TV shows I will be concentrating on in this essay.

The appearance of this emphasis in my son's life, however, should not be accepted simply as the positive influence of environmentalism, but approached with a critical eye. Of course, as Susan Davis, among others, points out, there is a long-standing Western middle-class practice of using images from nature to educate children (Davis 1995).[1] But the thematic narratives U.S. children, especially from three to ten years of age, encountered in the 1990s were about saving nature, not just identifying with Moles who like to boat and Toads who like to drive automobiles. Something new was going on; what did it signify?

One of the pervasive qualities of this environmentalist material and popular kinderculture is the peculiarly American stories about nature that are being told.[2] The parochial status of these tropes about nature does not, however, make them incidental or marginal to processes of globalization. Rather, these U.S.-inflected children's cultural forms are sold and consumed around the world; further, they are frequently tales about a global world, a U.S. dream of a common planet and an undifferentiated childhood experience. This is particularly true of the movies and TV shows I will concentrate on here, which are objects that travel cross-culturally more easily than environmentalist museum exhibits or primary school practices. So in a strong but not totalizing way, I want to emphasize that these cultural objects reflect and reinforce a project of U.S. cultural hegemony that aims to assist the opening of global markets and the imposition on other cultures of the equation between liberal democracy, post-industrial economies, and free-market ideologies.[3] These are exactly the kinds of messages that environmental justice activists seek to counter.

Given the status of these objects as carriers of dominant raced, gendered, classed, sexed, and naturalized stories that are part of global contests for cultural, political, and economic hegemony, it is crucially important to examine what stories are being told, what values are being promoted, which actors get to have agency, and what solutions are being offered. What lessons are being learned, and what kind of environmentalism has become the medium of these messages? What connections are made for children between environmentalism and social justice, between nature and morality?

I will first discuss the theme of "naturalizing" the nuclear family, which is presented as a solution to environmental problems, and then I will look at the theme of multicultural kids' teams presented as examples of the best environmental activists.

Saving the Planet Is Saving the Family

One of my favorite examples of the theme of offering the nuclear family as the answer to environmental disruption is in *White Fang 2*. The ending of this 1994 movie neatly encapsulates several themes that I want to discuss. The main character, a young white man named Henry Casey, comes from a broken family, travels to the Alaskan wilderness, and ends up fighting against greedy miners (who are environmentally destructive) on behalf of what appear to be Northwest Coast Indians, along with his animal sidekick, the wolf White Fang. At the end, after the miners have been defeated, one of the young women of the tribe (who also happens to have, coincidentally, a female wolf sidekick) declares her love for the young white man, her willingness to form a family with him. The touching scene in which this happens shows her calling him as he walks away (supposedly leaving forever) and then, in classic Hollywood style, the two are shown running slowly towards each other for a heartfelt (but relatively chaste, given the PG rating) kiss. At the same time, intercut comically and ludicrously with the two human lovers, the two wolves also run together and kiss. The movie closes with a charming scene in which the female wolf has puppies, and White Fang is, in very unwolflike ways, behaving like a proud daddy.

Some of the themes found in this movie we could easily predict, given their long-standing involvement in the U.S. cultural imaginary, such as the figure of feminized nature and natural femininity, especially in its maternal form, or the naturally ecological noble savage. However, in the present historical inflection, these aspects are almost always combined, as represented in *White Fang 2* by the Northwest Coast Indian woman, or in *Pocahontas* by the title character. Earth Mothers are almost inevitably brown women, especially indigenous women, thus ensuring that nature and natural wisdom are feminized and raced simultaneously. These movies have been made after civil rights and women's movements have challenged many cultural stereotypes, and their makers, generally liberal-minded folks, clearly want to do the right thing. Postfeminist and civil rights–era inflections mean that these figures are also presented as tribally specific, independent, choosing beings, even if their choices are still narrowed to nice white guys such as Henry Casey in *White Fang 2* and Captain John Smith in *Pocahontas*.

This female noble savage trope does not, however, prevent the bad guys in these stories from sometimes being imagined as racial and sexual others. Sometimes the villain is orientalized, but more frequently the bad guy is a sexualized other, a nonreproductive, unnatural upper-class twit, the kind of campy, limp-wristed, unpatriotic male closet queen long seen as subversive to the naturalized patriarchal American nuclear family, the only legitimate reproductive unit in the Cold War era. Figures like Scar in *The Lion King* or Governor Ratcliff in *Pocahontas* represent the deeply problematic idea that gay men in particular are threatening to the "natural" family.

These days, the U.S. religious right wing anxiously and hysterically argues that civil rights, feminism, and gay liberation movements have destroyed the suburban Cold War family unit. Though the liberal makers of many of the environmentalist cultural items I am talking about here may reject this conservative position, a similar anxious message about the collapse of the "traditional" nuclear family (ignoring the limited historical, raced, and classed characteristics of this family form) is strongly promulgated throughout these children's stories. Those cultural, economic, and social factors that "threaten" nuclear families also involved challenges to masculinist power within the family and to images of white normality and superiority. The instability of the nuclear family is thus presented by these stories as a crisis, one that can only be solved by reinstating a "natural" order. Over and over, the plots of these movies involve nature in the task of saving young white boys (and sometimes white girls) from "broken" family circumstances. In particular, mothers are peculiarly absent; if an alien came down and watched kid's films in the 1990s, she would be convinced that there was a 95 percent chance of a kid's mother having met a fatal accident around the time the child was seven or eight. (An incomplete list of recent popular U.S. children's films in which the mother has died, or the child is completely orphaned, would include *Alaska, Free Willy, Finding Nemo, Fly Away Home, Beauty and the Beast, The Lion King, James and the Giant Peach, Anastasia, Once Upon a Forest, Harry Potter, Spider-Man, Jurassic Park 2, Star Wars, Batman, X-Men, Aladdin, The Black Stallion, Babe,* and *A Little Princess.*)

Responding to this postfeminist absence of the "good maternal woman," nature is deployed in many of these films to reconstitute the heterosexist patriarchal family, again and again, in movies like *Alaska* and *Free Willy,* in *Fly Away Home* and *Wild America,* in *White Fang 2* and *Homeward Bound,* in *The Emerald Forest* and *Jungle to Jungle.* Sometimes the nature that accomplishes this healing of the broken family is an animal character, such as the geese in *Fly Away Home* that teach the young girl who has lost her mother to accept a new family with her father and stepmother, or the orphaned bear cub in *Alaska* that helps bring two kids together with their missing dad. But as often, the nature that accomplishes this reconstitution of the nuclear family is a combination of an indigenous figure and an animal, as in *Free Willy's* Native American character Randolph, who along with the whale, Willy, helps the white boy Jesse accept his foster family, or in *Jungle to Jungle* in which the white boy has "gone native" and, with the help of a friendly tarantula, instructs his wayward father in how to get back together with his mother, or in *White Fang 2* mentioned above. A related figure to White Fang and Willy the Whale is the baboon/African-shaman character Rafiki in *The Lion King,* who reinscribes the boy/lion Hamlet/cub Simba properly into the patriarchal legacy he initially rejects, and thereby recovers the (environmentally sound) circle of life from its dangerous and deadly nonreproductive state.

In equating the restoration of natural harmony with the restoration of the two-parent, suburban family, then, this kind of environmentalism naturalizes the nuclear family. In perfect symmetry to this dominant message of mainstream environmentalist popular culture that protected and valued nature equals white heterosexist reproduction (meant on both biological and social levels), the figure of the evil male homosexual often inhabits the ecovillains of these films. One of the best illustrations of this figure is the character Scar, the evil uncle in *The Lion King,* voiced by Jeremy Irons, who depends on his past history of playing sexually perverse, socially dangerous male characters to animate his depiction of Scar. This is clearly evidenced in a famous interchange with the lion cub Simba, in which, when Simba says, "You're so weird, Uncle Scar," Irons replies, "You have no idea," the exact same line he spoke in the exact same plummy overtones as the sexually ambivalent Claus Van Bulow in the film *Reversal of Fortune* (with enough style to win an Oscar nomination).

There is a segment from *The Lion King* that chillingly demonstrates the way in which racialized and sexualized identities inhabit the depiction of environmental villainy. This is the scene where the nasty hyenas, voiced by Whoopi Goldberg and Cheech Marin to lend them the proper "ghetto" feel, are given a demonstration of Scar's desire to become king in Simba's father's place. Scar's musical number begins with a thoroughly campy intro, in which he prances about in classic drag queen style, and ends disturbingly with a scene of goose-stepping hyenas borrowed almost image by image from Leni Reifenstahl's film promoting Hitler, *Triumph of the Will*. Scar is figured here first as an evil homosexual, and then as a Hitler worshiped by hyenas with "ghetto" voices. My narrative description of this scene does nothing to convey the emotional power of these images and sounds for kids and their accompanying parents, carried by the high production values of these movies. The audacity of the use of the Reifenstahl images to depict a campy gay male figure as a Hitler in league with untrustworthy and moronic people of color is appalling. Here, Hitler as the embodiment of evil is equated with Scar's "unnatural" sexuality and his anti-nature power politics—quite contrary to the history of the Nazis' deadly combination of racism, the slaughter of Jewish, gay, and disabled peoples, their celebration of heterosexist reproductive family forms, and their deep love of nature.[4]

In case it seems that the importance of this evil gay male figure is exaggerated in my argument, I can point to other examples. For instance, in the film *Ferngully*, subtitled *The Last Rainforest*, and a specifically pro-environmentalist film, there is the evil character Hexxus, voiced by another sexually ambivalent actor, Tim Curry (best known and most well-loved as the actor who played the "sweet transvestite from Transylvania," Dr. Frankenfurter, in *The Rocky Horror Picture Show*). Hexxus is not only campy and creepy; he is very, very black, both in color and in his mutable features. In his signature musical number, "Toxic Love" (the title alone gives away the sensibility), Hexxus oozes dangerous and nasty dark sexuality tied to a stomping rock beat. (Once again, the high quality of the music and images makes this movie, like *The Lion King*, a product that is intensely pleasurable. Try to watch the two scenes I have just referenced from a critical perspective without tapping your feet.) There's another one of these evil gay male figures in *Pocahontas*, the nasty imperialist Governor Ratcliffe, who is more concerned about the state of his hair than the people he callously orders to kill as "savages." He carries a little dog around with him on a velvet pillow, and his valet is always close behind with a mirror.

That people of color, particularly indigenous people, should be exploited as natural resources for white environmentalism is an old story in U.S. environmentalist history, a story the environmental justice and Third World environmentalist movements are determined to disrupt. But the persistence of combining this story with the notion that part of restoring natural balance involves promoting heterosexist patriarchal family forms as the only means to healthy reproduction (of white people in particular) points to our dominant culture's constant confusion between "nature" and the naturalization of social inequality. In fact, successful environmental strategies may require us to rethink entire modes of production and reproduction built on this nuclear family form. But our children, particularly the U.S. white male children like my son who will grow up privileged in multiple ways, will not learn to think through these connections between environmental destruction, middle-class consumerism, and racism if all they have are these particular environmentalist stories to go on. We need instead stories of other kinds of reproduction, that don't depend on these heterosexist, racist, and naturalized tropes.[5]

In these films, not only is the white nuclear family naturalized, but kids are given the responsibility to fight environmental problems on their own without adults. Often they do this work in racially balanced, gender equal kids' teams. What kind of environmental and social messages are contained in promoting multicultural kids' teams as the ultimate ecowarriors?

Combining Powers: Liberal Multiculturalism or Environmental Justice?

Of course, and ironically, my criticisms would come as a shock to the producers of much this environmental children's culture, who clearly want to create liberal messages about racial and gender equality (they don't yet care much about equality for those that challenge sexual norms). Everywhere in this material, there is an insistence on a certain notion of easily achievable multiculturalism and gender equality, a diversity just as naturally achieved as biodiversity is imagined to be. Yet, as environmental justice activists know, achieving collaboration across racial differences in U.S. society is no easy task for coalition politics.

In popular culture texts, this diversity is often represented by groups of five or six teenagers with particular patterns that unfortunately ensure the reinstantiation of white middle-class men in the position of leadership. Thus the Animorphs (characters in popular books as well as a less popular TV show) are teenagers who are given the power to acquire animal DNA and morph into animals in order to fight against the invasion of mind-controlling sluglike communards called "Yeerks." Like the Power Rangers, the Animorphs are a group of five kids: two white boys, one white girl, one boy of color, and one girl of color. This is a liberal form of multiculturalism, of course, in which racial differences are seen as naturally necessary to an effective team, like certain notions of ecosystems in stasis, in which differences never have competing interests or signal histories of genocide, slavery, rape, or exploitation but instead are examples of good managerial theory.[6] Just as static notions of biodiversity (sometimes found in mainstream environmentalism) only make sense within depictions of ecosystems as closed, circular, in balance, and without history, the easy necessity of racial and gender diversity of these kids' teams exist within a homogenous middle-class existence in which the favorite place for the kids to meet is the suburban mall (a kind of closed ecosystem in itself!).

These discourses of mainstream biocentric environmentalism and liberal multiculturalism effectively combine in these children's stories to eviscerate power-laden histories of socially constructed difference. For example, in the *Animorphs* books, Cassie, the African American girl in the team, is figured as closer to nature by her ability to befriend animals (both of her parents are vets), and by her comfort with her body (she is the most controlled and graceful morpher, given her natural affinity with animals). When faced with the Animorphs' risky attempt to free two members of the enslaved alien species Hork-Bajir, who are almost always defined in the books by the adjective "enslaved," Cassie responds not by referencing abolitionist discourses one would assume to be easily deployed by a fourteen-year-old African American girl. Instead, Cassie passionately wants to save them because they are a breeding pair of an endangered species (Applegate 1997, 72).

This liberal multiculturalism serves a more distinctively post–Cold War purpose in the service of a globalizing environmentalism in the *Captain Planet* TV series. Here our group of five teenagers hew pretty much to the pattern mentioned above (one white U.S. guy, one black African guy, one brown South American guy, one white Russian girl, and one "Asian" (in other words, generically Asian) girl), but this pattern of biodiversity is very much about globally significant cultural diversity, a quasi-U.N. version of multiculturalism. When we learn that *Captain Planet* is a product of Turner Enterprises, we aren't surprised by the program's support of the idea of an international strike force against global environmental problems.

Despite, or rather through this cultural diversity, the Planeteers are a United Nations clearly led by the United States while dependent on the work, body, and knowledge of a brown woman. Gaia, voiced in the first Captain Planet by the distinctive tones of Whoopi Goldberg, is a brown woman who is the spirit of Earth and the source of the Planeteers' abilities. Once again, the Mother Earth figure is a woman of color. But for the animating life force of Earth personified, Gaia is curiously powerless, dependent on the work of the five teenagers she gives rings to so they can call up the powers of fire, water, earth, wind, and the fifth element, heart. (Of course the U.S. alpha male, the white Wheeler, has the power of fire; the African male, Kwame, naturally has the power of earth; and the geopolitically marginal brown male, the South American Ma-Ti, is given the feminized power of heart.)

When the Planeteers are in deep trouble, however, they combine their powers and call up a real superhero, Captain Planet, who, despite his blue skin and green hair, is a typical wisecracking suburban white guy straight out of sitcom land. For example, when faced with a mutant giant octopus created by toxic dumping off Japanese coastal waters, Captain Planet says, "I've got to stop that super-squid before it turns the city into sushi!" And, zipping into the sky, he calls out, "Calamari, dudes!" The character Captain Planet, to quote from the "Mission to Save Planet Earth" section of the show's Web page, is meant to be "a metaphor for that which can be accomplished by teamwork," and thus he "symbolizes that the whole is indeed greater than the sum of its parts." But it seems that this particular whole created by the unification of the "world's cultures and ethnic diversity" is—far from being anything like the "sum of its parts"—a good old American white male adolescent superhero. The notion of the world's cultures "combining powers" may seem like a nice metaphor for political coalition, but not if its purpose is creating a unity that looks and acts like a southern California surfer dude with body paint.

In some ways, it may seem supercritical to pick on *Captain Planet*, which is a thoroughly self-conscious environmental cultural product, and a very successful one (especially according to its own promotional material), having garnered several media and educational awards, and reaching over 7 million people a week in the United States alone while being distributed in over sixty countries during its heyday in the mid–1990s.[7] Further, *Captain Planet* is unusual and commendable as a media product in its effort to provide action-oriented information, political inspiration, and organizational linkages. At the end of every episode is a thirty-second bit called "Planeteer Alert," which focuses on a specific problem, for instance, the safe disposal of household wastes, and gives kids tips on how they can be environmentally conscious consumers and citizens.

Captain Planet has also set up a number of links with other institutions in a position to influence kids and their parents, a process that the producers call "combining powers" (which is what the Planeteers do when they summon Captain Planet). The Captain Planet Foundation makes the shows available to teachers for classroom use, and has collaborated with such organizations as the American Public Transit Association, the EPA, and the U.S. Fish and Wildlife Service. (With the latter, it has held a program called "Earth Day with the Braves," neatly combing Turner's environmentalism with his love of baseball while ignoring the Atlanta Braves' use of Native American stereotypes.) The Captain Planet Foundation also funds numerous children's grassroots environmental efforts.[8]

So why pick on *Captain Planet*? After all, wouldn't we rather have environmentalist messages than nonenvironmentalist ones? Messages of multiculturalism rather than messages of bigotry? Messages in which women play important roles rather than ones in which they are powerless or invisible? Messages that allow agency to non-Western peoples rather than ones that assume the only teenagers with power are middle-class U.S. suburbanites?

But its very status as the most radical example of children's environmentalist popular culture shows the deep dependence of these stories on problematic tropes of powerless (but proto-feminist) brown indigenous women, exoticized pure nature like Gaia's Hope Island, and naturalized differences operating in conflict-free teams.

Captain Planet's attempt to produce a liberal message is also beholden to certain assumptions about the necessity to preserve corporate America's good reputation. As the producers explain:

> The use of villains to delineate good and evil is common in action-adventure series. However, given that we deal with real life issues, we were concerned children might come to the conclusion that if their parents worked in a pollluting industry they were somehow villians. Although our show is basically realistic, our eco-villains are intentionally exaggerated so that they are clearly operating outside of the law. They are symbolic of the environmental problems rather than representative of the actions of individuals. We are careful not to be critical of business/industry, but to encourage responsible business practices and a balance between the needs of people, environment/wildlife, and industry.[9]

Like every one of the environmentalist objects of children's popular and material culture I have encountered, then, Captain Planet presents solutions that are almost entirely restricted to individual lifestyle changes, to legitimating the rule of law rather than challenging business as usual. Environmental catastrophes always happen "outside the law" rather than the reality in which legal parameters often protect polluting corporations or governments. Ecovillains are nasty male queens, dark spirits, mustachioed men with accents, brittle and demented white female scientists, or mutant human/animal paranoids with delusions of grandeur. Though children get the notion that trees are cut down and animals killed because of greedy behavior, it is almost always the greedy behavior of a single ecovillain. Never are the ecovillains corporations, or militaries, or governments, or white patriarchal science—the real ecovillains on our planet, the ones the environmental justice movement is presently confronting. Gaia lives on a pure tropical island far away from urban sites of environmental struggle. Solutions that romanticize ecological noble savages lock both nature and people of color in an imagined preindustrial past, but they are almost the only solutions offered, along with the idea that recycling and disposing of toxic waste "properly" (rather than identifying the source of the waste and preventing it from being made) are important tasks for children acting alone without responsible adults.

Conclusion

In a story like *Captain Planet*, which, like other examples of children's environmentalist popular culture, wants to equate environmentalism with social equality, how do we evaluate the notion that "The Power Is Yours"? There are a number of ways to read the show's slogan, and to speculate about its likely results as an internalized message. We might start by thinking about who gets to be Planeteers, who most easily can imagine themselves as global citizens, empowered to combine powers with others on a planetwide scale. That this story might be most invested in interpellating privileged Western children comes as no surprise. And it may be an appropriate strategy, given the inordinate amount of the world's resources these children will consume over their lifetime. So perhaps this message will have unforeseen radical results. After all, one of the important demographic actors in the 1960s movements were privileged children like myself, who, having been brought up on the notion that we were empowered to promote Truth, Justice, and the American Way, realized with shock that it was up to us to follow the lead of those less privileged and to force our country and our parents to correct deeply held hypocrisies. Perhaps the Planeteers of tomorrow will someday rebel against the corporate forces that are destroying the planet and causing suffering for so many of the world's peoples. Perhaps the megamedia empires, like Turner Enterprises, will take responsibility for the misleading stories they are promoting, in which environmental damage can be cured by constructing a suburban nuclear middle-class family or by promoting superficial multiculturalism. A utopian hope, but maybe one day the multinationals will wish they never told these kids that "The Power Is Yours," allowing the liberal, superficial, and individualistic solutions presently offered to be rejected for collective, social, and revolutionary action.

But another, more pessimistic reading of this message is possible. It is clear that the dominance of the environmentalist theme is not centrally about environmentalism at all, but about producing morally uplifting and privilege-maintaining stories that legitimate the notion that especially for white middle-class children, the Power Is Theirs to do what they will with the world. Like the idea of easy multicultural kids' teams, the "environment" is a safe issue when freed from questions of power. Given the Planeteers' superpowers, their incapacity for wrongdoing, and the overwhelming priority for saving an otherwise doomed nature, the privileged kids that identify with them might feel fully justified in imposing putatively environmentalist solutions undemocratically on less powerful non-Planeteers.

And what about the kids who don't so easily identify as Planeteers? Certainly the kids being poisoned by lead in the cities, the kids who are malnourished by corporately produced salinification and erosion, the kids who are drinking pesticide-laced water at migrant farmworkers camps, the kids who are living on uranium tailings on Navajo land—are Captain Planet's producers worried about whether *they* will start holding *their* parents responsible for "polluting industries"? Will these kids be satisfied with the idea that nature will be restored if they all form happy, consuming nuclear families? It is less likely that these kids, in a post-feminist, post–civil rights environmental justice era, will not know the shape and character of the real ecovillains. These kids can't wait, and in fact aren't waiting, for an awakened force of white middle-class Planeteers to take on the combined problems of environmental destruction and social inequalities.

Looking critically at environmentalist children's popular culture underscores the difficulty of telling stories about saving nature from the point of view of dominant U.S. culture without engaging in problematic stories about social difference, which depend upon the naturalization of social inequalities via the invocation of the "natural order," nature as truth, foundation, all that is right and valuable. And these themes are particular to our present historical and political context, showing the traces of recent social movement critiques while transposing them onto justifications of white, male, straight, liberal capitalist hegemony—that is, they tend to be post-feminist, post–civil rights stories about environmentalist new world orders. But even when apparently promoting the kind of environmentalist values shared by environmental justice activists, for instance, struggling against toxic waste or mining on Native American lands, these stories often portray people of color either stereotypically or as the villains. Even more disturbingly, they combine homophobic and racist portrayals in ways that distract audiences from remembering that the ecovillains of the real world are corporations, militaries, and governments (Seager 1993).

Rather than thinking the Power Is Yours, or Ours, or Theirs, or the planet's, we must think about powers that arise out of struggle and contest, which are justified on the basis of participatory democratic practices rather than what is natural. Rather than look to superpowered teams that naturalize U.S. white male middle-class leadership, we need to think about combining powers in political coalitions that go against the present "natural" order. And this is what the environmental justice movement, in its refusal to depend only on biocentric environmentalist arguments about saving a "pure" nature, has the potential to do.

NOTES

1. Some listeners have asked me whether I would include in this criticism nature-based spiritual and cultural practices such as those found in many indigenous cultures, which use animals and natural entities as significant characters in educational stories and spiritual practices. But I think there is a fundamental difference between stories from cultures that do not display a Western culture-nature dualism and the way in which animals are used as characters in moral stories for young children in Eurocentric cultures.

2. These conclusions are tentative. There is no research, as far as I am aware, of the frequency of environmentalist themes in children's education and culture worldwide and cross-culturally. There is some work done in the United States, mostly prompted by conservative concerns that kids were being "brainwashed" by environmentalists in the public schools. This research does not cover popular culture. I am therefore forced to make tentative statements here, backed up by my attention to this phenomenon in the United States and Europe over a period of ten years of personal observation and,

it should be said, with the assistance of my son, who parried my constant questions and critical observations with his own as well as bringing me numerous examples of this material as he came to understand my interest in it. So I thank Hart Sturgeon-Reed for his research assistance. Thanks are also due to T. V. Reed for many useful editing suggestions. I would also like to thank the Center for Cultural Studies at UCSC, Patsy Hallen and Peter Newman of the Institute for the Study of Technology and Policy at Murdoch University, and the many audiences whose comments contributed to this final version. This essay is dedicated to Zoë Sofoulis, who taught me a lot about the problems with Planeteer tendencies, especially my own.

3. One of the things I would do if I were to pursue this project is to explore the reception of these children's products in different cultural contexts, in which I would expect to find them the subject of surprising and different narrative reconstructions and oppositional practices. And this should be true not only in international contexts, but in subjugated cultural contexts internal to the United States.

4. Audiences to this essay as a talk have disputed my characterization of *The Lion King* as homophobic by pointing out that *The Lion King*, whose famous musical team included the openly gay Sir Elton John, portrays a happy and helpful gay male couple in the loving and committed relationship of Timon, the meerkat, and Pumba, the warthog. Though I think this is an accurate reading of a relationship that should have been far scarier to Jerry Falwell than the proclivities of the purple Teletubby, Tinky Winky, it remains true that the central resolution of the plot requires the restoration of Simba to the throne and to a heterosexual, nuclear family form quite unlike that of real lions.

5. One could see the movie *Babe*, for instance, as a counterexample to most of these other films. In *Babe*, the story of a pig who wants to be a sheepdog, an argument against naturalizing social orders, "racial" identities, or social roles is clearly, charmingly, and humorously presented. Containing strong statements against the exploitation of animals as workers or as meat as well as the importance of certain participatory democratic practices, the film deserves a more complex treatment in light of the framework of my arguments than I can give here, but it can serve as one example of a different way of imagining the connection between environmentalism and social equality that doesn't naturalize the dominant order. Though I strongly believe in this positive reading of *Babe*, the movie is alarmingly sexist in its portrayal of the farm wife. For another analysis of the nonnaturalizing effect of *Babe*, as well as other interesting insights into the message of the movie, see Plumwood 2002, esp. 600–606.

6. I've written elsewhere about the dangers of assuming that racial balance in numbers is the solution to creating effective antiracist coalition politics (Sturgeon 1997).

7. From "Mission to Save Planet Earth," Captain Planet Web page, *http://www.turner.com/planet/static/mission.html (1998, 2002).*

8. Captain Planet Foundation Web page, *http://www.captainplanetfdn.org (2002).*

9. From "Mission to Save Planet Earth," Captain Planet Web page, *http://www.turner.com/planet/static/mission.html (1998, 2002).* The last sentence I quote here was on the page in 1998, but was removed in the 2002 page.

REFERENCES

Applegate, K. A. 1997. *The Change.* Vol. 13 of *The Animorphs.* New York: Scholastic.
Davis, S. 1995. "Touch the Magic." In *Uncommon Ground*, ed. William Cronon. New York: Norton.

May, E. 1999. *Homeward Bound: American Families in the Cold War Era*. 2nd ed. New York: Basic Books.

Plumwood, V. 2002. *Environmental Culture: The Ecological Crisis of Reason*. London: Routledge.

Reed, T. V. 2002. "Toward An Environmental Justice Ecocriticism." In *The Environmental Justice Reader*, ed. Joni Adamson, Mei Mei Evans, and Rachel Stein. Tucson: University of Arizona Press.

Seager, J. 1993. *Earth Follies: Coming to Feminist Terms with the Global Environmental Crisis*. New York: Routledge.

Sturgeon, N. 1997. *Ecofeminist Natures: Race, Gender, Feminist Theory, and Political Action*. New York: Routledge.

NOTES ON CONTRIBUTORS

BETH BERILA is assistant professor of women's studies at St. Cloud State University, where she teaches classes that analyze intersections of race, class, gender, and sexuality in feminist studies, American studies, and twentieth-century U.S. multiethnic literatures. Her most recent project examines the artistic practices of feminist experimental writing and cultural activism that disrupt habits of making meaning in order to work toward feminist social transformation.

GIOVANNA DI CHIRO teaches environmental studies and women's studies at Mount Holyoke College. She has published widely on the topics of community-based knowledge production and environmental justice. She is a coeditor of the forthcoming collection *Appropriating Technology*.

GRETA GAARD has worked as associate professor of composition and women's studies at the University of Minnesota–Duluth and as associate professor of humanities at Fairhaven College, Western Washington University. She is the author of *Ecological Politics: Ecofeminists, and the Greens*, and the editor of *Ecofeminism: Women, Animals, Nature*. She is at work on a volume of creative non-fiction essays, titled *Home Is Where You Are*.

KATIE HOGAN is director of women's studies and associate professor of English at Carlow College. She is the author of *Women Take Care: Gender, Race, and the Culture of AIDS* (Cornell 2001) and coeditor of *Gendered Epidemic: Representations of Women in the Age of AIDS* (Routledge 1998). Her current project is called "Crimes against Nature: Detecting Queer Environmental Justice."

VALERIE ANN KAALUND is currently an assistant professor in the African and Afro-American studies department at the University of North Carolina–Chapel Hill. She also serves as a faculty consultant for the Meharry Clinical Research Education and Career Development Program. Valerie lives in Durham, North Carolina, with her loving husband Barry and marvelous five-year-old daughter, Kamaria.

ANNE E. LUCAS received her masters in women's studies and her law degree from the University of Cincinnati in 2002. She is currently an attorney at

Connecticut Legal Services. She is interested in environmental justice and helping poor people assert their legal rights.

MARCY J. KNOPF-NEWMAN is assistant professor of English at Boise State University. She is the author of the forthcoming *The Transformation of Breast Cancer into Language and Action* (Rutgers University Press) and the editor of *The Sleeper Wakes: Harlem Renaissance Stories by Women* and Jessie Redmon Fauset's *The Chinaberry Tree and Selected Writings*.

ARLENE PLEVIN has been involved with environmental issues as a writer/editor for the National Wildlife Federation. Her work has appeared in *The Literature of Nature: An International Sourcebook, Ecocomposition:Theoretical and Pedagogical Approaches*, and *Wild Things: Ecological Criticism, Ecological Literacy, and Children's Literature*, among others. She received an MFA in poetry from the University of Iowa Writer's Workshop and completed a Ph.D. in English at the University of Washington. Recently she was a Fulbright lecturer in Taiwan, doing research and teaching at Tamkang University.

DIANE-MICHELE PRINDEVILLE is assistant professor of government at New Mexico State University. Her teaching and research interests include women's leadership, environmental policy, and race/ethnic politics. Her work appears in *Women and Politics, The Social Science Journal*, and in *Frontiers: A Journal of Women's Studies*. Dr. Prindeville recently received an award for her research from the American Political Science Association.

CATRIONA (CATE) SANDILANDS is associate professor in the faculty of environmental studies, York University, Toronto. Her writing sits at the intersections of sexuality, gender, and ecology, including her book *The Good Natured Feminist: Ecofeminism and the Quest for Democracy* (1999). She has published articles on queer ecological philosophy and politics in *Environmental Ethics, NWSA Journal*, and *Alternatives*, and is currently working on two manuscripts, *E(c)co Homo? Writings Toward a Queer Ecology* and *From Pastoral Sex to Queer Landscapes: Lesbian Histories of Nature Writing*.

RACHEL STEIN is professor of English and director of women's and multicultural studies at Siena College. She is the author of *Shifting the Ground: American Women Writers' Revision of Nature, Gender and Race* (1997) and coeditor of *The Environmental Justice Reader: Politics, Poetics, and Pedagogy* (2003).

NOËL STURGEON is chair of women's studies and graduate faculty in American studies at Washington State University. Her research centers on environmental, antiracist, women's, antimilitarist, and direct action movements, especially the interrelations between them, and her publications include *Ecofeminist Natures: Race, Gender, Feminist Theory and Political Action*.

JULIE SZE is a University of California President's Postdoctoral Fellow in ethnic studies at the University of California at San Diego. She is also an assistant professor in American studies at University of California at Davis. Sze has worked on urban and environmental justice issues for the past ten years.

NANCY C. UNGER is assistant professor of history, women and gender studies, and environmental studies at Santa Clara University. Her publications include the award-winning *Fighting Bob La Follette: The Righteous Reformer* (University of North Carolina, 2000). Her book in progress is *Beyond Nature's Housekeepers: American Women and Gender in Environmental History.*

ROBERT R. M. VERCHICK is the Ruby M. Hulen Professor of Law and Urban Affairs at the University of Missouri at Kansas City. He is also coeditor of the *Urban Lawyer* and a research scholar with the Center for Progressive Regulation. Professor Verchick holds an A.B. degree from Stanford University and a J.D. degree from the Harvard Law School.

PRISCILLA SOLIS YBARRA is a doctoral candidate in Chicana/o literature at Rice University. She earned her B.A. in English at the University of North Texas where she also participated in the Ronald E. McNair Post Baccalaureate Achievement Program. She is writing her dissertation on the intersection between environmental issues and Chicana/o cultural productions from 1848 to the present.

INDEX

activists: community based organizing, 95; as family and community caretakers, 64, 100–101; and asthma prevention, 177–185; motivations, 98–101; and racial and class identities 98–100; in New Mexico, 93–107; using gendered and sexual modes of resistance, 45–58. *See also* spirituality

African American women, 78–89; and asthma activism, 177–185; and ethical/spiritual sensibility and activism, 79–80; and black feminist activism, 82–84; resisting enslavement, 49–52; and environmental justice issues in North Carolina, 84–88; in speculative fiction, 209–221. *See also* asthma; spirituality

agropastoral cultures, 98–99

Ahmed, Sara, 130

AIDS Coalition to Unleash Power (ACT UP), 127–135; challenging stereotypes, 133; cultural activism, 132–133; demonstrations, 131, 133–135; history of, 129; graphics by Gran Fury, 129, 13; parallels to environmental justice tactics 127–135

Alaimo, Stacy, 111

Alien Tort Claims Act, 193–195

Allen, Paula Gunn, 104

Alston, Dana, 84

Animorphs, 269–270

Antonetta, Susan, 229–230

Apfel, Roberta: *To Do No Harm*, 229

asthma, 177–187; activism, 172–187; as childhood illness in NYC minority communities, 179–182; and cockroaches, 184–185; community based education on, 182–184; and gender, 178–179, 184–187;

and "Healthy Homes," 185–186; and National Inner City Asthma Study, 184–185; and outdoor air pollution, 183–184

Augustine, Rose, 150–151, 153, 156

Aztlan, 244–246. *See also* Cherríe Moraga; homelands; sovereignty

Baggett, Billy, 235–236

Berlant, Lauren, 131

berylliosis, 149–151

beryllium, 145, 149–151; at Brown Wellman factory, 150–151; and nuclear weapons production, 150

Bilger, Audrey: *Laughing Feminism*, 237

Billings, Paul, 148–149

biotechnological research, 139–156; and colonization of bodies in *Dawn* and *Brown Girl in the Ring*, 209–221; and gender, 209–221; and new reproductive technologies, 212–213; activist responses to, 150–156; and race, 151–156. *See also* Environmental Genome Project; and biopiracy

biopiracy, 210; and women of color, 209–221. *See also* gene trading; organ harvesting; and organ theft

Bloom, Lisa, 36–37

Blue Vinyl: A Toxic Comedy, 225–238

bodies mirroring Mother Earth, xii

Bolton, Reverend Carrie, 80–81

Brady, Mary Pat, 245

breast cancer, 161–175; and endocrine disruptors, 167; environmental causes of, 161–175; as homicide, 163–164, 170–175; and pesticides, 166–168; and race and class, 166–168, 170–171; in *Rachel's Daughters*, 161–175